Securing the Digital Frontier

Scrivener Publishing
100 Cummings Center, Suite 541J
Beverly, MA 01915-6106

Advances in Cyber Security

Series Editors: Rashmi Agrawal and D. Ganesh Gopal

Scope: The purpose of this book series is to present books that are specifically designed to address the critical security challenges in today's computing world including cloud and mobile environments and to discuss mechanisms for defending against those attacks by using classical and modern approaches of cryptography, blockchain and other defense mechanisms. The book series presents some of the state-of-the-art research work in the field of blockchain, cryptography and security in computing and communications. It is a valuable source of knowledge for researchers, engineers, practitioners, graduates, and doctoral students who are working in the field of blockchain, cryptography, network security, and security and privacy issues in the Internet of Things (IoT). It will also be useful for faculty members of graduate schools and universities. The book series provides a comprehensive look at the various facets of cloud security: infrastructure, network, services, compliance and users. It will provide real-world case studies to articulate the real and perceived risks and challenges in deploying and managing services in a cloud infrastructure from a security perspective. The book series will serve as a platform for books dealing with security concerns of decentralized applications (DApps) and smart contracts that operate on an open blockchain. The book series will be a comprehensive and up-to-date reference on information security and assurance. Bringing together the knowledge, skills, techniques, and tools required of IT security professionals, it facilitates the up-to-date understanding required to stay one step ahead of evolving threats, standards, and regulations.

Publishers at Scrivener
Martin Scrivener (martin@scrivenerpublishing.com)
Phillip Carmical (pcarmical@scrivenerpublishing.com)

Securing the Digital Frontier

Threats and Advanced Techniques in Security and Forensics

Edited by

Kavita Sharma

Vishnu Sharma

Parma Nand

Anil Kumar Sagar

and

Gulshan Shrivastava

Scrivener Publishing

WILEY

This edition first published 2025 by John Wiley & Sons, Inc., 111 River Street, Hoboken, NJ 07030, USA and Scrivener Publishing LLC, 100 Cummings Center, Suite 541J, Beverly, MA 01915, USA

For more information about Scrivener publications please visit www.scrivenerpublishing.com.

Wiley Global Headquarters
111 River Street, Hoboken, NJ 07030, USA

For details of our global editorial offices, customer services, and more information about Wiley products visit us at www.wiley.com.

Library of Congress Cataloging-in-Publication Data

ISBN 978-1-394-26888-7

Front cover images supplied by Adobe Firefly
Cover design by Russell Richardson

Set in size of 11pt and Minion Pro by Manila Typesetting Company, Makati, Philippines

Printed in the USA

10 9 8 7 6 5 4 3 2 1

Contents

Preface

Welcome to *Securing the Digital Frontier: Threats and Advanced Techniques in Security and Forensics*. In today's interconnected world, where our lives are increasingly intertwined with technology, safeguarding our digital information cannot be overstated. This book is a comprehensive exploration of the evolving landscape of cybersecurity, offering insights into the latest threats, innovative techniques, and proactive measures employed to protect our digital assets.

Chapter 1, "Pegasus - A Menace to Privacy and Security," sheds light on the Pegasus spyware developed by the Israeli-based cyber group NSO. Authors Raunaq Khurana and Shilpa Mahajan examine the workings of this advanced spyware, which exploits zero-day vulnerabilities to access and collect data from target systems without user consent. Through detailed analysis and case studies, the chapter highlights Pegasus's challenges. It encourages using advanced technologies such as AI and ML/DL to develop effective countermeasures.

In Chapter 2, "Data Privacy and Compliance in Information Security," authors Rakesh Nayak, Umashankar Ghugar, Praveen Gupta, Satyabrata Dash, and Nishu Gupta explore the sophisticated relationship between data privacy and compliance in information security. They discuss the challenges, regulations, and best practices in protecting sensitive data in today's digital age, emphasizing the importance of implementing robust security measures and fostering privacy awareness within organizations.

Chapter 3, "Unveiling Cyber Threats: Exploring Crime, Security Techniques, and Digital Forensics," authored by Nidhi Gupta, Arpita Trivedi, Parveen P Terang, and Hasmat Malik, delves into the escalating landscape of cybercrimes and the various advanced techniques used to protect devices from cyberattacks. The chapter also highlights the importance of digital forensics in investigating cybercrimes and identifying perpetrators.

In Chapter 4, "A Customised Privacy Preservation Mechanism for Cyber-Physical Systems," authors Manas Kumar Yogi and A.S.N. Chakravarthy advocate for a novel privacy approach for cyber-physical systems, allowing users to customize their privacy settings based on their usage. The chapter explores the trade-off between privacy and utility in CPS entities and presents a provisional privacy-preserving method designed to enhance data utility while maintaining user privacy.

Chapter 5, "Securing the Future: Emerging Threats and Countermeasures in Cryptography," authored by Debosree Ghosh, Kishore Ghosh, Chandrima Chakraborty, Atanu Datta, and Somsubhra Gupta, focuses on emerging threats to cryptographic systems and innovative countermeasures. The chapter highlights the importance of post-quantum cryptography and secure implementation practices in safeguarding data security in an evolving digital landscape.

In Chapter 6, "Cyber Threats and its Impact on Electronic Transactions," authors Ramalingam Dharmalingam and Vaishnavi Dharmalingam explore the impact of cyber threats on electronic transactions, particularly during the COVID-19 pandemic. The chapter discusses the growth of digital transformation, current cyberattacks, and frameworks for combating cyber threats, emphasizing the need for collaborative efforts to secure future transactions.

Chapter 7, "A Robust Model for Enabling Insider Threat Detection and Prevention: Techniques, Tools, and Applications," authored by A Sheik Abdullah, Shivansh Dhiman, and Arif Ansari, addresses the growing threat of insider threats in organizations. The chapter explores techniques and tools for accurately detecting and mitigating insider threats, leveraging machine learning, artificial intelligence, and behavioral analytics.

In Chapter 8, "Digital Vulnerabilities Unveiled: A Multidisciplinary Exploration of Emerging Threats to Security and Privacy in the Age of Networked Communication," authors Priya Sachdeva and Archan Mitra offer a multidisciplinary analysis of digital vulnerabilities, highlighting the interplay between socio-technical factors underlying security issues. The chapter emphasizes the value of interdisciplinary approaches in comprehending and solving complex security challenges.

Chapter 9, "Tools of Emancipation as Global Web and its Digital Ecosystem: Steering IoT Landscape, Cloud Computing Unravel Safe Spaces Lensing New Cyber Risks and Emerging Threats," authored by Bhupinder Singh and Christian Kaunert, explores the symbiosis of tools of emancipation, the global web, and the digital ecosystem in navigating cybersecurity challenges. The chapter discusses the role of IoT and cloud computing in mitigating cyber risks and proposes strategies for fortifying safe spaces in the digital realm.

Chapter 10, "IoT and Smart Device Security: Emerging Threats and Countermeasures," authored by Geo Francis E, S. Sheeja, Anotony Johen E.F., and Jismy Joseph, delves into the security challenges posed by IoT devices and explores emerging threats and countermeasures. The chapter emphasizes the importance of addressing IoT vulnerabilities and implementing robust security measures to safeguard data privacy and integrity.

In Chapter 11, "Secured IoT with LWC and Blockchain," authors Srishti Priya Chaturvedi, Ajay Yadav, Santosh Kumar, and Rahul Mukherjee discuss lightweight encryption and blockchain solutions for securing the Internet of Things. The chapter explores using lightweight cryptographic algorithms and decentralized blockchain structures to protect IoT ecosystems from cyber threats.

Chapter 12, "Social Engineering Attacks: Detection and Prevention," authored by Rajat Singh, Priyanka Soni, and Animaw Kerie, focuses on social engineering attacks and proposes detection and prevention techniques. The chapter discusses various social engineering attack models and preventive measures, including security information and event management (SIEM) systems and human-as-a-security-sensor frameworks.

In Chapter 13, "Multilayer Perceptron of Occlusion and Pose-Sensitive Ear Attributes for Social Engineering Attack Mitigation," authors O. Taiwo Olaleye, Oluwasefunmi Arogundade, Adebayo Abayomi-Alli, Wilson Ahiara, Temitope Ogunbiyi, Segun Akintunde, Segun Dada, and Olalekan Okewale explore the use of multilayer perceptron for detecting social engineering attacks. The chapter investigates the effectiveness of MLP in handling occlusion and pose variations, offering insights into its potential applications in digital forensics.

Chapter 14, "Study and Analysis of Cyberbullying Message Detection and Prevention Using Machine Learning Techniques," authored by Dr. S. Gunasekaran, Dr. S. Shanmugam, and Dr. N. Anusha, focuses on detecting and preventing cyberbullying using machine learning techniques. The chapter compares different machine-learning approaches for cyberbullying detection and proposes future research directions for improving detection accuracy.

Chapter 15, "Future Directions in Digital Forensics and Cybersecurity," authored by Elipe Arjun and Priyanka Singh, offers insights into the future trends and challenges in digital forensics and cybersecurity. The chapter explores the potential impact of emerging technologies like quantum computing and AI on cybersecurity practices, emphasizing the need for interdisciplinary collaboration and ethical considerations.

In Chapter 16, "Tomorrow's Shields: Exploring Future Trends in Cyber Security and Forensics," authors M. Sharma, R.K. Kohli, and K. Sharma provide a holistic perspective on future trends in security and forensics. The chapter discusses emerging technologies, regulatory frameworks, and industry trends shaping the future of cybersecurity, highlighting the importance of proactive measures and continuous learning in combating evolving threats.

We extend our sincere gratitude to all the authors who contributed their expertise & insights to this book. Their dedication and passion for advancing cybersecurity knowledge have made this book a valuable resource for researchers, practitioners, and students alike.

We hope that *Securing the Digital Frontier: Threats and Advanced Techniques in Security and Forensics* catalyzes ongoing discussions & collaborative efforts to fortify our digital defenses and navigate the ever-changing cybersecurity landscape.

Dr. Kavita Sharma
Galgotias College of Engineering & Technology, Greater Noida, India
Dr. Vishnu Sharma
ITS Engineering College, Greater Noida, India
Dr. Parma Nand
Sharda University, Greater Noida, India
Dr. Anil Kumar Sagar
Sharda University, Greater Noida, India
Dr. Gulshan Shrivastava
Bennett University, Greater Noida, India

1

Pegasus—A Menace to Privacy and Security

Raunaq Khurana* **and Shilpa Mahajan**

Department of Computer Science, The NorthCap University, Gurugram, Haryana, India

Abstract

The Israeli-based cyber group NSO developed Pegasus, a spyware that can access and collect data from a target system without the user's consent. Pegasus commonly exploits zero-day vulnerabilities, which are system weaknesses that the manufacturer has not addressed or is unaware of. This chapter thoroughly examines the Pegasus spyware, highlighting its unique features that pose significant challenges in its detection as compared to other malicious software. It presents an extensive analysis of Pegasus on both iOS and Android operating systems, with the intention of educating readers about its capabilities and advocating for the use of advanced technologies such as AI, ML/DL to develop effective countermeasures against spyware, malware, and adware. The chapter also includes various case studies that illustrate the transformation of Pegasus over time and the measures taken to prevent its infiltration into user devices. To facilitate reader's understanding, the chapter provides essential security checklists that help identify Pegasus's monitoring mechanisms.

Keywords: Malware/spyware, encryption, vulnerability, vishing

1.1 Introduction

Spyware is harmful software made with the intention of stealing data from a system and sharing it with unidentified outside third parties. Pegasus is a sophisticated programme that can break into mobile devices like smartphones and tablets and eventually go over security precautions like internal

**Corresponding author*: raunaq.khurana18@gmail.com

Kavita Sharma, Vishnu Sharma, Parma Nand, Anil Kumar Sagar and Gulshan Shrivastava (eds.) Securing the Digital Frontier: Threats and Advanced Techniques in Security and Forensics, (1–16)

encryption and two-factor authentication to allow hackers complete access to the targeted device once it is plugged in. If that is the case, Pegasus can control all communication between devices, including calls, messages, emails, microphone and camera providers, location data, contacts and calendars [1]. The memory consumption can be discovered using covert methods, CPU cycles, and network traffic monitoring, despite the fact that the Pegasus file store was initially intended to target officials, politicians, journalists, and influencers.

Pegasus tool is produced by the Israeli company NSO Group. This surveillance tool is designed purposely to monitor specific individuals for national security. Although this tool is developed to be used by the government agencies but it has been a subject of significant controversies. These controversies arises as they are considered to be threat to human privacy, an abuse to human rights and potential misuse of surveillance technologies.

The allegation involves that government is spying on its officials and political opponents and even individuals or not even legitimate targets for surveillance. NSO group gave his assurance that their tool is used for legitimate purposes like for frightening crimes and terrorism. However, number of evidences and investigations have suggested that Pegasus has been used for questionable purposes by some people.

The way that this tool operates is by taking advantage of flaws in mobile devices, especially smartphones, to access personal data, including calls, texts, emails, and other communications. It may also be used to activate the camera and microphone, monitor the device's position, and do a variety of other things, thereby transforming it into a robust surveillance tool.

The properties of Pegasus are thoroughly covered in this chapter, with special emphasis placed on those aspects that set it isolated from different spyware and malware in terms of difficulty in detection [2]. It also explains how Pegasus operates on both iOS and Android operating systems and suggests using advanced technologies like machine learning and AI to develop systems that can identify and prevent Pegasus, safeguarding devices from adware, malware, or spyware. Additionally, the chapter presents case studies demonstrating Pegasus's evolution over time and proposes methods to prevent spyware from infiltrating and spreading on user devices. By following the practical safety guidelines outlined in this chapter, readers can learn how to protect themselves from Pegasus's surveillance tool.

- Investigating the market origins and distribution of Pegasus.
- Examining how Pegasus operates and its ability to turn smartphones into listening devices by exploiting multiple vulnerabilities.

- Proposing various techniques to detect potential Pegasus attacks.
- Sharing advice on how to recognize the presence of Pegasus spyware on a device.
- Suggesting the utilization of command-line or terminal utilities to lower the likelihood of being affected by the Pegasus spyware.
- Providing practical recommendations to enhance awareness and protect devices from Pegasus spyware.

Spyware attacks have become increasingly sophisticated in recent years. In the past, malicious software could be installed by opening a suspicious email as early as a decade ago [3]. However, Pegasus spyware has now adopted a "mobile first" strategy, whereby it impersonates its users by sending links in text messages that appear to be from trusted sources. Clicking on these links gives Pegasus access to sensitive information, such as location data and financial information. From 2016 to 2021, Pegasus has become even more advanced and now uses "zero-click" technology, which relies on zero-day threats that are unknown to the user and remain unpatched [4]. To limit the success of Pegasus on user devices, the research paper titled "Pegasus: A Privacy Killer" recommends adopting basic precautions, like avoid unknown links, categorization of devices, and using reliable VPNs for all devices [5, 6]. Pegasus uses complex zero-day infection vectors to infiltrate devices. Once installed, try different ways to get access to victim's data and transmits it to the server [7]. The way how Pegasus can attack and exploit your phone can be seen in Figure 1.1.

1) It uses GPS information to identify and differentiate targets and obtain precise information
2) The Pegasus spyware does not require coordination with local Mobile Network Operators (MNOs), making it independent of service providers.
3) It control both the content and devices it infects by utilizing proprietary protocols and SSL, commonly used in complex communications, which allows it to surpass encrypted information.
4) The surveillance includes monitoring various applications, such as Instagram, Twitter, WhatsApp, Skype, Viber etc.
5) Monitor VoIP and voice calls in real time (call interception).
6) Pegasus can recognize operational identities without the need for regularly switching virtual identities or while continuously surveilling/observing the device.

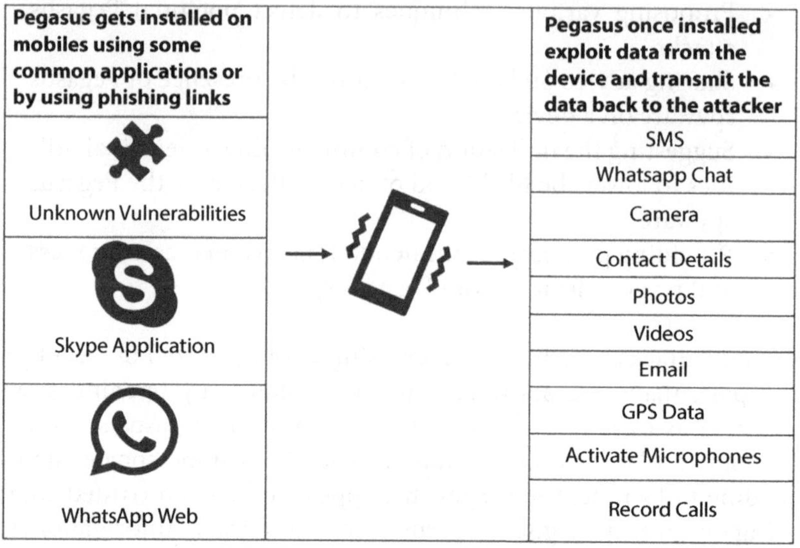

Figure 1.1 Pegasus impact.

1.2 Working of Pegasus

This spyware name Pegasus is a highly advance and dangerous tool that exploits "Zero-day Vulnerability," a security weakness for which no patch or update is available or known by the manufacturer. Pegasus can silently infiltrate various Android and iOS devices and covertly monitor all device activities. By exploiting vulnerabilities in third-party spyware, Pegasus can take complete control of the device, allowing the attacker to perform various actions. To protect against such attacks, users must take proactive measures, such as installing antivirus software, regularly updating device firmware, and being vigilant when clicking on links from unknown sources.

Pegasus can access data like access your messages, location tracking, content surfing, can make calls from compromised phones, call logs can be accessed, access to photo, camera and Microphone can be accessed and an delete data and even retrieve the deleted files from the mobiles. Pegasus spyware directly transmit the data obtained from target's phone straight to the data server of NSO group [8].

Pegasus spyware is a highly advanced malware that can be installed easily through physical contact, text or email and through calls and messages. It exploits vulnerabilities that have not been updated with a patch or are not known to the relevant parties. It can infiltrate a device through a missed call on WhatsApp or an iMessage on iPhones [9]. The Pegasus spyware utilizes a zero-click method that does not require any user interaction, making it challenging to detect. Even if a user tries to delete a suspicious message, the spyware can persist on the device and infect it [10].

Pegasus spyware is a highly sophisticated tool that can decrypt end-to-end encrypted messages and files, making it a potent weapon in espionage [11, 12]. Recent findings indicate that the latest versions of Pegasus can infiltrate devices through missed calls and delete the call logs to cover up the attack, making it harder to detect and track its actions. This poses a significant challenge for users who may not even be aware that their devices have been compromised [13].

A diagram depicting the general workflow of Pegasus can be seen in Figure 1.2.

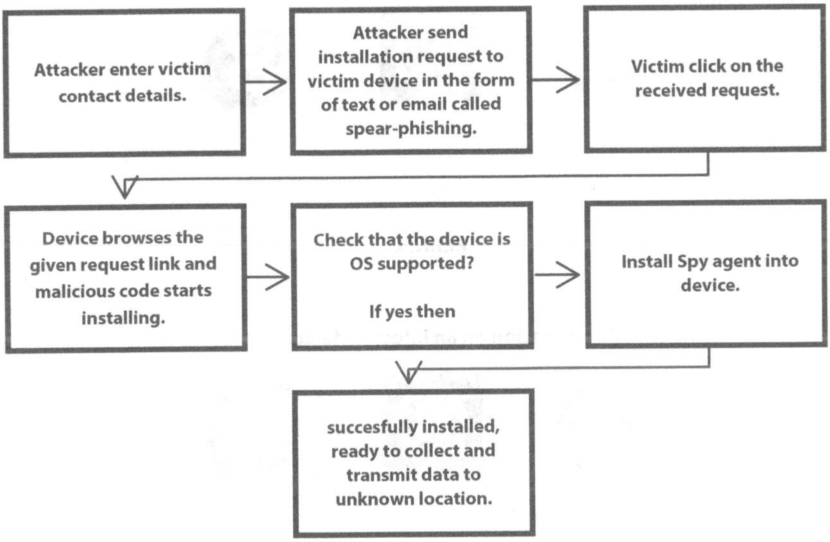

Figure 1.2 Pegasus workflow.

The workflow of Pegasus on a normal device vs. an infected device can be seen in Figure 1.3. It is interesting to find how an infected device behave differently from the normal device. In normal device, the common phasis include

Device Setup	*The user purchases a new mobile device and goes through the initial setup process, which typically includes connecting to Wi-Fi, signing in with their Apple ID or Google Account, and configuring settings.*
App Installation	*Users can install applications from authorized application marketplaces such as the Apple App Store or Google Play Store. These apps undergo a vetting process to ensure they do not contain malicious code.*
Regular Usage	*The individual utilizes the device for a multitude of functions, including placing calls, sending messages, surfing the web, and accessing applications. The device operates normally without any unexpected behavior.*

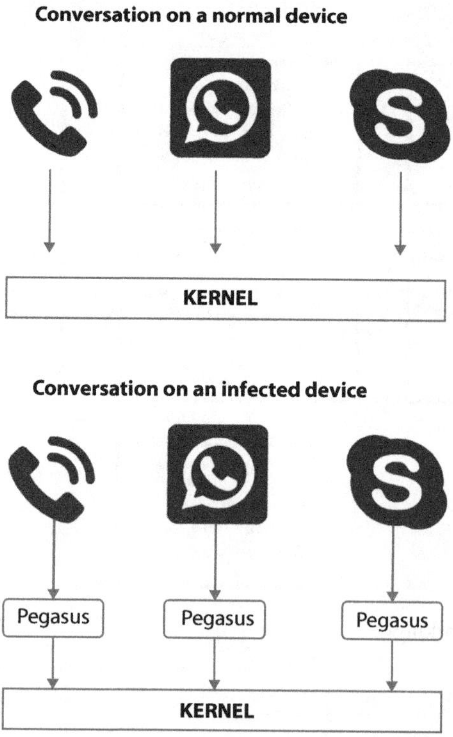

Figure 1.3 Work-flow of normal device vs infected device.

For a device infected with Pegasus, the phasis includes

Initial Infection	*Pegasus spyware typically infects a device through a variety of means, such as a malicious link in a text message, a spear-phishing email, or exploiting vulnerabilities in the device's operating system or apps.*
Silent Installation	*Once the device is infected, Pegasus silently installs itself without the user's consciousness or approval. It often hides its presence to avoid detection.*
Monitoring and Surveillance	*Pegasus begins its surveillance activities, collecting various forms of data from the infected device. This can include call records, messages, emails, photos, videos, GPS location, and more.*
Communication with Command and Control Server	*Pegasus communicates through a command and control (C&C) server operated by the attacker. It sends collected data to the server and receives instructions or updates from the server.*
Persistent Operation	*Pegasus is designed to be persistent, meaning it survives device reboots and software updates. It continues to operate in the background, constantly monitoring and exfiltrating data.*
Remote Control	*Attackers can remotely control Pegasus-infected devices, enabling them to execute commands, steal data, or even activate the device's microphone and camera for real-time monitoring.*
Exploiting Vulnerabilitie	*Pegasus may use undisclosed or zero-day vulnerabilities in the device's operating system or apps to gain access and evade security measures.*
Advanced Evasion Techniques	*Pegasus employs advanced evasion techniques to avoid detection by antivirus software and security scans.*
Regular Device Usage	*From the user's perspective, the device may appear to function normally, but their activities and data are being monitored and recorded by the spyware.*

1.2.1 Pegasus Attacking iOS

Pegasus took advantage of a vulnerability (zero-day) in the Safari browser on iOS devices. It downloaded a zipped file and performed the following steps [14].

- Installed a program called daemon to share files with an attacker who could remotely monitor the device.
- Turned off the device's deep sleep mechanism.
- Injected its code into running processes to remain hidden in the memory used by other applications and software.
- Removed any other jailbreak programs and installed a suicide feature to erase all evidences of Pegasus.
- Installed a root TLS certificate to create a fake CA that allowed the attacker to encrypt data that the device would trust.
- Installed an unsigned JavaScript (JS) file that executed a script at reboot time to jailbreak the device, as iOS typically only allows signed code verified by third parties.
- Installed a sniffer tool to listen and record the device's running program traffic.

CVE's used in Pegasus CVE-2016-4657, CVE-2016-4655, CVE-2016-4656 etc.

An iOS device running an earlier version of the operating system than 9.3.5 was vulnerable to the CVE-2016-4657 security issue. The flaw allows attackers to use a modified picture file to run any arbitrary code on the targeted device. Without needing user involvement, Pegasus, a spyware programme, used this flaw to access the victim's device. Since neither Apple nor the cybersecurity community were aware of this security hole until it was discovered and revealed by researchers, it was referred to as a zero-day vulnerability. In order to protect customers against future threats, Apple advised consumers to update their iOS devices to the most recent version in August 2016.

CVE-2016-4655 security vulnerability affected iOS devices before version 9.3.3. By exploiting this flaw, attackers were able to intercept and decode encrypted traffic sent over SSL/TLS protocols to obtain sensitive data such as login credentials, financial information, personal data, and etc. Pegasus spyware exploited this vulnerability to secretly extract data from the device without the owner's knowledge or consent. In July 2016, Apple released CVE-2016-4655, a patch to address a zero-day vulnerability previously unknown to the company and the cybersecurity community.

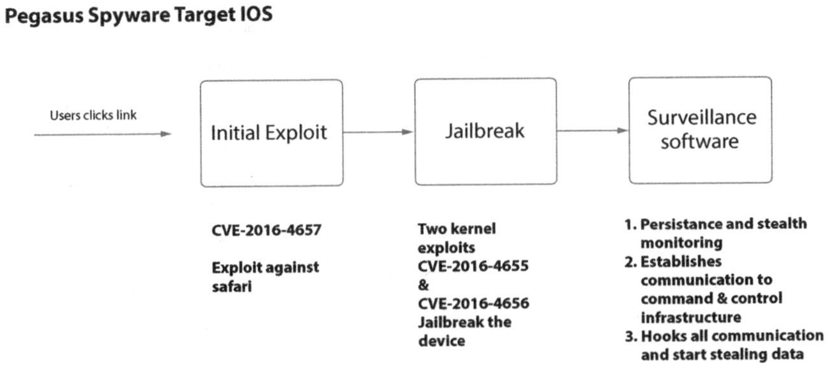

Figure 1.4 Pegasus attacking iOS using zero-day vulnerability.

When researchers made their discovery and dream followed, Apple recommended that users update their iOS devices to the latest version to reduce the risk of possible attacks.

CVE-2016-4656 is a security vulnerability that affected IOS devices before version 9.3.3. The vulnerability allowed attackers to exploit a flaw in the handling of IOKit calls in the iOS kernel to gain control of the target machine. Pegasus spyware exploited this vulnerability to monitor device activities without the user's consent or knowledge as shown in Figure 1.4. CVE-2016-4656 was classified as a zero-day vulnerability because it was unknown to Apple and the cybersecurity community until it was discovered by researchers To protect against potential attacks, Apple issued a patch on the vulnerability in July 2016, advising all users to do so update their iOS devices to the latest version.

1.2.2 Pegasus Impacting Android

Chrysaor, a variant of Pegasus spyware, was tailored for Android devices and had comparable capabilities. However, it differed from Pegasus as it utilized the widely known Android rooting method, frame root, to infect devices instead of exploiting zero-day vulnerabilities in iOS [15]. If this method failed, Chrysaor would deceive users by pretending to be legitimate software and ask for their permission, enabling the spyware to acquire and transmit data from the device [16]. Once installed, Chrysaor would disable system updates by deleting the app responsible for system update and also deactivates auto-update functions. Moreover, it would eliminate WAP push messages and modify WAP message settings to complicate forensic analysis [17]. The general workflow of the Chrysaor spyware on Android devices is depicted in Figure 1.5.

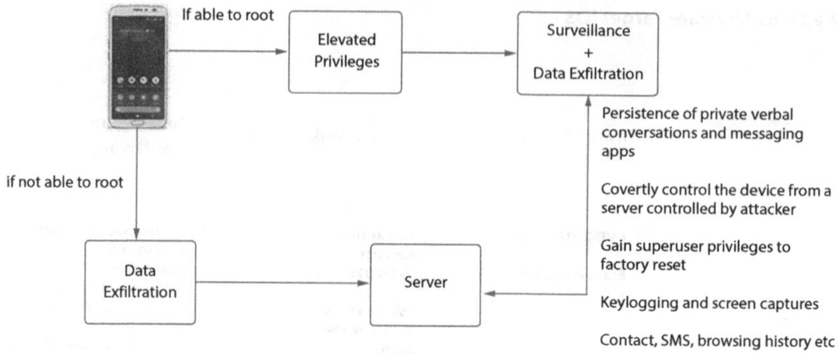

Figure 1.5 Chrysaor working.

1.2.3 Differentiating Android and iOS Pegasus

Lookout lab, a cybersecurity company conducted a study on the samples provided by Google and identified significant findings about the spyware, revealing similarities between Pegasus's capabilities on both iOS and Android. Lookout lab researchers analysed exploit samples and created a table comparing the similarities and differences between the Pegasus spyware on iOS and Android platforms [18]. They found that Pegasus targeted Android devices using known exploits, including the Framaroot root strategy [19]. While other Android attacks may use zero-day exploits, in the samples examined by the researchers, the exploits were already known to them [20].

Table 1.1 represents Different features of Pegasus in android and iOS devices.

1.3 Literature Review

According to Timberg Pegasus [9], which was once seen as the state-of-the-art mobile spyware in the world, is capable of infecting both iOS and Android devices. Since its disclosure, Pegasus has consistently transformed and become more sophisticated in terms of the level of control it gives to malicious actors over their victims' devices, the information it can pull out, and its ability to perform zero-click attack. Pegasus can pull out a variety of data types, including extremely precise geolocation coordinates, pictures, mail attachments, and encoded messages from popular applications like WhatsApp and Snapchat. Additionally, Pegasus can activate the microphone to listen in on personal conversations or phone calls and turn on the camera to capture videos.

Table 1.1 Effect of Pegasus in android vs iOS devices.

	iOS	Android
Zero-Day Exploits	✓	×
Process Hooking	✓	✓
SMS Command and Control	✓	✓
Code Obfuscation	✓	✓
Screenshot Capture	×	✓
Disabling System Updates	✓	✓
Suicide Functionality	✓	✓
Extracting Personal Data	✓	✓
Compromising Functionality	×	✓
Audio Surveillance	✓	✓
Messaging Protocol MQTT	✓	✓
Standalone App	×	✓
Method Of Infection	Phishing	Unknown*

Zero-click vulnerabilities are particularly challenging to defend against since they do not require user interaction. While there are standard operational security steps that users can follow to secure their devices, even following all security best practices does not provide a complete guarantee of protection against new attacks. To reinforce device security, two fundamental security principles can be employed attack surface reduction and device compartmentalization. These principles can significantly reduce the probability of a security breach occurring on a device.

The forensic examination of the phones belonging to Pegasus victims indicates that NSO's hunt for loopholes may have expanded to other commonly used applications. In some of the instances analysed by Guarnieri and his team, unusual network traffic related to Apple's Music and Photos apps was detected in different patterns of infections, suggesting that NSO may have begun utilizing new loopholes. Pegasus can alternatively be deployed through a wireless transceiver proximate to the target in instances where neither social engineering nor zero-click attacks yield success. Furthermore, an NSO catalogue mentions that the spyware can be manually installed if an agent steals the target's phone.

This Spyware, which is considered a Potentially Unwanted Program (PUP), can monitor users' online activities and cause significant privacy concerns and security risks to computer systems. Although various measures have been implemented to counteract spyware, anti-spyware software is still the main defence against it. However, current spyware tools are stateless, meaning that new systems added to a network must have their own anti-spyware software to protect themselves. To address this issue, Dwoskin proposes a new technique that uses the basics of the network and application layers instead of anti-spyware software to eliminate spyware. By scanning outgoing HTTP requests at the browser and introducing a new add ons both the Domain Name Server and network layer, this method can identify spyware and filter out certain unused programs.

1.4 Methodologies

In 2016, earlier version of Pegasus relied on spear phishing attack make users to click on a malicious link. As per NSO employees, the USA varient of Pegasus had a single click capability for all mobiles except blackberry devices which could pervade zero click exploits.

In 2019, Whatsapp discovered a flaw that allows Pegasus to attack cellphones via adware. This adware may be loaded into a goal's target smartphone by phoning the goal's target phone; the adware can be mounted even if the call is no longer returned.

In the year 2020, Pegasus began to focus more on network-based assaults and zero-click vulnerabilities. These methods allowed users to call target phones without having to interact with anyone and without leaving any traces that might be traced.

1.5 Pegasus Implantation Techniques

Spyware can enter any system without the owner's consciuosness through an application installation , a file attachment, or a malicious website. Spyware may be a script that executes when the system boot up and operates consistently in the background, which is how it manifests itself in its least harmful form. The web browser will practically become useless due to the intrusion's ability to consume random access memory, processing resources, and produce endless pop-up advertising.

Modular malware makes up Pegasus. Following a device scan, it downloads the required scrips/modules to read the user's personel information(messages and mails), record calls, take screenshots, record keystrokes, exfiltrate browsing history, contacts, and so on and so forth. In essence, it is able to monitor all aspects of target system.

Without the user's consciousness or consent, the malware is capable of turning on cameras and microphones to record brand-new photos and audio. It can gather location information from the past and present, including whether he's stationary or moving, and listen to calls and voicemails. Since Pegasus grabs the data even before it is encrypted, it can read encrypted messages from WhatsApp and Signal as well as listen to encrypted audio streams.

To install malware on phones, the original iteration of Pegasus employed a spear-phishing assault. A user must first get a website URL by SMS, email, social media, etc. The surveillance software packages are installed after remotely jailbreaking the smartphone with a single click on the link. A certain amount of knowledge can aid in the prevention of such attacks, but since NSO's attack capabilities have evolved through time, they are now more effective and nearly difficult to detect or stop.

Pegasus malware can also infect devices through so-called zero-click attacks, which do not need the device's owner to do anything. It implies that even if you take care not to click on those malicious links, your phone might still be compromised. The majority of these assaults take use of operating system flaws that the phone's maker may not yet be aware of and hence has not been able to address.

Despite Apple iPhones' claims to provide greater privacy and security than competitors, "zero-click" assaults are still possible, according to a research by Amnesty International. As Apple repaired each security flaw, the Israeli company NSO Group infected several iPhone models over time, according to the research. The gang used an iMessage zero-click in 2019, an Apple Photos vulnerability in 2020, and finally an Apple Music vulnerability in 2021.

1.6 Mitigation Measures

There are number of ways to minimize the outspread of Pegasus spyware include the following measures [21, 22].

- Avoid clicking on links from untrusted sources, as Pegasus was able to exploit an iMessage link to infect iPhones. Fraudsters commonly use this technique to compromise devices.

- Ensure that your device is regularly updated with official patches from trusted organizations, as vulnerable devices are often targeted by attackers.
- If you use an Android device, do not solely rely on the manufacturer for OS updates. Regularly check for updates yourself, as some smaller manufacturers may not notify you about them.
- Mostly try to avoid providing physical access of your device and enhance your device security by using Biometric lock, PIN lock, etc.
- Avoid accessing public or unencrypted networks that make your data available over the internet. It is advisable to use Virtual Private Networks or proxy servers when someone uses these kinds of Access Points [23].
- Encrypt the data saved/stored on your devices to protect your information leakage in the event of loss or theft.

1.7 Conclusion

This chapter provides an in-depth examination of how Pegasus spyware operates by exploiting zero-day vulnerabilities in order to gain unauthorized access to devices. While malware and spyware often rely on system vulnerabilities to remotely monitor devices, Pegasus can infect devices through its zero-click feature, which does not require any user interaction. Amnesty International's Mobile Verification Tool is currently the most effective means of detecting whether a device has been compromised by Pegasus. The chapter provides a comprehensive comparison of Pegasus on iOS and Android operating systems, as well as suggesting several preventative measures that can be implemented to safeguard against Pegasus and other forms of malicious code.

References

1. Kirchgaessner, S., Lewis, P., Pegg, D., Cutler, S., Lakhani, N., Safi, M., Revealed: leak uncovers global abuse of cyber-surveillance weapon. The Guardian, https://www.theguardian.com/world/2021/jul/18/revealed-leak-uncovers-global-abuse-of-cyber-surveillance-weapon-nso-group-pegasus.
2. Johnson, D.B., The threat of Pegasus-style spyware could creep toward the business community. SC Media, 2021, https://www.scmagazine.com/analysis/the-threat-of-pegasus-style-spyware-could-creep-toward-the-business-community.

3. Avery, D., Apple no match for Pegasus as Israeli spyware found on journalists and activists iPhones. Mail Online, 2021, July 28, https://www.dailymail.co.uk/sciencetech/article-9802839/iPhones-belonging-journalists-hacked-proving-Apples-security-no-match-NSO-spyware.html.
4. Mvt-Project, GitHub - mvt-project/mvt: https://github.com/mvt-project/mvt, 2021.
5. Pegg, D. and Cutler, S., What is Pegasus spyware and how does it hack phones? The Guardian, 2021, July 20, https://www.theguardian.com/news/2021/jul/18/what-is-pegasus-spyware-and-how-does-it-hack-phones.
6. Amnesty International, Forensic Methodology Report: How to catch NSO Group's Pegasus. Amnesty International, 2023, https://www.amnesty.org/en/latest/research/2021/07/forensic-methodology-report-how-to-catch-nso-groups-pegasus/.
7. Dwoskin, E. and Rubin, S., 'Somebody has to do the dirty work': NSO founders defend the spyware they built. Washington. Post, 2021, July 22, https://www.washingtonpost.com/world/2021/07/21/shalev-hulio-nso-surveillance/.
8. Ortolani, S., Giuffrida, C., Crispo, B., Unprivileged Black-Box detection of User-Space keyloggers. *IEEE Trans. Dependable Secure Comput.*, 10, 1, 40–52, 2013, https://doi.org/10.1109/tdsc.2012.76.
9. Timberg, C., Birnbaum, M., Harwell, D., Sabbagh, D., On the list: Ten prime ministers, three presidents and a king. Washington Post, 2021, July 20, https://www.washingtonpost.com/world/2021/07/20/heads-of-state-pegasus-spyware/.
10. Everything You Need to Know about the Pegasus Spyware. CloudSEK, 2021, https://www.cloudsek.com/blog/everything-you-need-to-know-about-the-pegasus-spyware.
11. Mahajan, S., Phishing uniform resource locator detection using machine learning: A step towards secure system. *Secur. Privacy*, 6, 6, e311, 2023.
12. Chawla, A., Pegasus Spyware – 'A Privacy Killer', July 21, 2021, Available at SSRN: https://ssrn.com/abstract=3890657 or http://dx.doi.org/10.2139/ssrn.3890657.
13. Pegasus Spyware, What You Need To Know, 2020, https://www.eurasian-research.org/publication/pegasus-spyware-what-you-need-to-know/.
14. Tyagi, G., Ahmad, K., Doja, M.N., A novel framework for password securing system from key-logger spyware. *2014 International Conference on Issues and Challenges in Intelligent Computing Techniques (ICICT)*, Ghaziabad, India, pp. 70–74, 2014, doi: 10.1109/ICICICT.2014.6781255.
15. Wang, X. and Chen, J., Interests-Based Spyware Detection. *2009 International Forum on Computer Science-Technology and Applications*, Chongqing, China, pp. 175–178, 2009, doi: 10.1109/IFCSTA.2009.164.
16. Javaheri, D., Hosseinzadeh, M., Rahmani, A.M., Detection and Elimination of Spyware and Ransomware by Intercepting Kernel-Level System Routines. *IEEE Access*, 6, 78321–78332, 2018, doi: 10.1109/ACCESS.2018.2884964.

17. Mittal, A., Resolving the menace of spyware through implementations in application layer and network layer. *2012 Students Conference on Engineering and Systems*, Allahabad, India, pp. 1–4, 2012, doi: 10.1109/SCES.2012.6199053.
18. Mallikarajunan, K.M.E.N., Preethi, S.R., Selvalakshmi, S., Nithish, N., Detection of Spyware in Software Using Virtual Environment. *3rd International Conference on Trends in Electronics and Informatics (ICOEI)*, Tirunelveli, India, pp. 1138–1142, 2019, doi: 10.1109/ICOEI.2019.8862547.
19. Shahzad, R.K., Hyder, S.I., Lavesson, N., Detection of spyware by mining executable files. *International Conference on Availability Reliability and Security*, Poland, pp. 295–302, 2010.
20. Wazid, M. *et al.*, A framework for detection and prevention of novel keylogger spyware attacks. *2013 7th International Conference on Intelligent Systems and Control (ISCO)*, Coimbatore, India, pp. 433–438, 2013, doi: 10.1109/ISCO.2013.6481194.
21. Bansal, Y. and Mahajan, S., Network Security Breaches: Comprehension and Its Implications, in: *Perspectives on Ethical Hacking and Penetration Testing*, pp. 239–254, IGI Global, University of Petroleum and Energy Studies, Dehradun, India, 2023.
22. Saroiu, S., Gribble, S.D., Levy, H.M., Measurement and analysis of spyware in a university environment. *Proceedings of the First Symposium on Networked Systems Design and Implementation*, San Francisco, pp. 141–153, 2014.
23. Arora, K. and Mahajan, S., Detecting denial-of-service attack using dendritic cell approach, in: *Proceedings of the Second International Conference on Information Management and Machine Intelligence: ICIMMI 2020*, Springer Singapore, pp. 509–516, 2021.

2

Data Privacy and Compliance in Information Security

Rakesh Nayak[1]*, Umashankar Ghugar[1], Praveen Gupta[2], Satyabrata Dash[2] and Nishu Gupta[3]

[1]Department of CSE, OP Jindal University, Raigarh, India
[2]Department of CSE, GITAM School of Technology (Deemed to be University), Visakhapatnam, India
[3]Future Communication Networks, VTT Technical Research Centre of Finland Ltd, Kaitoväylä 1, Oulu, Finland

Abstract
In today's digital age, protecting sensitive data is a paramount concern. This chapter explores the intricate relationship between data privacy and compliance in information security, discussing the challenges, regulations, and best practices involved. Data privacy is crucial in a world where personal information is constantly collected, stored, and shared. The chapter highlights the potential risks and consequences of data breaches and unauthorized access, emphasizing the importance of implementing robust security measures. Compliance in information security is a complex landscape. The chapter examines legal frameworks like the GDPR and CCPA, which aim to safeguard privacy rights. It discusses the challenges that organizations face in achieving compliance and the potential repercussions of non-compliance. To ensure data privacy and compliance, the chapter outlines best practices. It emphasizes a comprehensive approach, including encryption techniques, access controls, security audits, and fostering privacy awareness within organizations. The chapter concludes by emphasizing the evolving nature of data privacy and compliance. It highlights the need for continuous learning and adaptation to keep pace with emerging technologies, changing regulations, and ever-changing threats. Overall, this chapter provides a comprehensive overview of the critical issues surrounding data privacy and compliance in information security. It serves as a valuable resource for individuals, organizations, and

**Corresponding author*: nayakrakesh8@gmail.com

Kavita Sharma, Vishnu Sharma, Parma Nand, Anil Kumar Sagar and Gulshan Shrivastava (eds.) Securing the Digital Frontier: Threats and Advanced Techniques in Security and Forensics, (17–34)

policymakers navigating the complex landscape of data protection and ensuring the privacy and security of sensitive information.

***Keywords*:** Data privacy, information security, GDPR, CCPA

2.1 Introduction

Data are becoming the new money in the digital era. Every click and contact creates massive data, ranging from transactional records to personal information. Although there are benefits to having a lot of data, privacy issues and compliance requirements are also discussed. This chapter will examine data privacy and compliance's rising significance, causes, and effects on people and businesses [2].

- The Evolution of Data Privacy: Although the idea of data privacy is not new, its importance has increased dramatically due to the quick development of technology. Digital technology has revolutionized our lifestyle, employment, and social interactions, resulting in private data being continuously vulnerable to theft or unauthorized use. Strong data protection measures are therefore becoming more and more necessary.
- The Rise of Data Breaches: A concern in recent years has been the disturbing frequency of data breaches that impact both people and corporations. Cybercriminals persistently target databases holding private data, including social security numbers, bank account information, and medical records. In addition to jeopardizing individual privacy, these breaches may result in identity theft, monetary losses, and harm to one's reputation. Consequently, governments, corporations, and people worldwide have begun to pay close attention to data privacy.
- Frameworks for Regulations: Acknowledging the pressing necessity of data privacy and compliance, governments have implemented strict restrictions. Two prominent examples are the California Consumer Privacy Act (CCPA) [4] and the General Data Protection Regulation (GDPR) [1, 3] of the European Union. The purpose of these laws is to uphold the rights of individuals and make companies responsible for

how they handle personal information. Adherence to these principles has become a prerequisite for businesses functioning inside the digital realm.

- Trust and Customer Expectations: Data privacy directly impacts customer trust [13]. People expect companies to manage their data properly as they grow more conscious of the dangers of disclosing personal information. Businesses that put a high priority on data privacy gain the trust of their clients, which promotes enduring partnerships and brand loyalty. On the other hand, companies that disregard data privacy run the danger of losing clients and tarnishing their brand.
- The Role of Technology: Technology has two roles in data privacy. Technology advancements have, on the one hand, made data breaches and privacy violations easier. However, technological advancements have also offered ways to improve data privacy and compliance. A few examples of how technology can protect personal information include encryption, anonymization methods, and secure data storage.

This chapter contains five sections. In the first section, we describe the introduction. The second section describes the discussion on risks, consequences, and security measures for data privacy. The third section describes data privacy and compliance in information security: the changing nature. The four sections describe the emerging technology and its regulations. Finally, the last section describes the concluding remarks and future scope.

2.2 Discussion on Risks, Consequences, and Security Measures for Data Privacy

Data privacy has become crucial for individuals and organizations in our increasingly connected world. The widespread use of the internet and the quick pace of technological advancement have made personal data more vulnerable than ever. This chapter aims to clarify the dangers and repercussions of data privacy breaches and offer crucial security precautions to protect sensitive data as shown in Figure 2.1 [4].

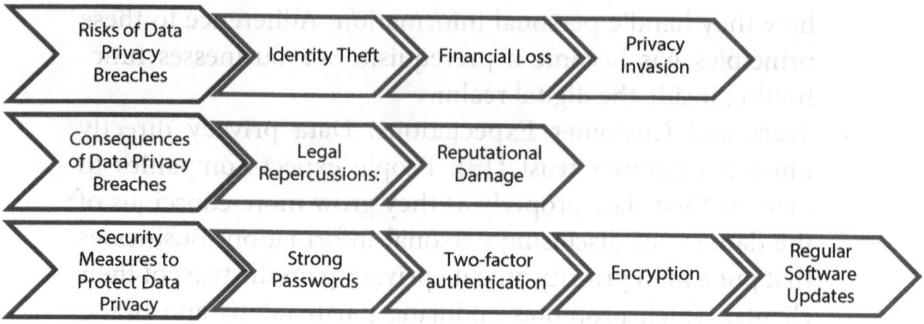

Figure 2.1 Risks, consequences, and security measures for data privacy.

Risks of Data Privacy Breaches:

- Identity Theft: Identity theft is one of the most severe risks associated with data privacy violations. Cybercriminals can assume someone's identity for fraudulent activities when personal information like social security numbers, addresses, or financial details end up in the wrong hands, causing the victims great financial and emotional distress.
- Financial Loss: Both individuals and organizations may suffer financial losses due to data breaches. Unauthorized transactions can be made using stolen bank accounts or credit card information, resulting in economic losses and harm to a person's credit score. The financial consequences for businesses, including legal liabilities, a loss of client confidence, and reputational damage, can be severe.
- Privacy Invasion: Breach of data privacy can lead to a severe invasion of privacy. Personal emails, messages, or images could be made public, resulting in humiliation, harassment, or even blackmail. Individuals may experience emotional distress and lose faith in online platforms as a result of this invasion of privacy, which can have long-lasting effects.

Consequences of Data Privacy Breaches:

- Legal Repercussions: Organizations may face serious legal repercussions due to data privacy violations. Numerous nations have put data protection laws into effect, such as the General Data Protection Regulation (GDPR) in the

European Union, which calls for businesses to adopt stringent security measures and alert individuals during a data breach. Heavy fines and other legal repercussions may result from breaking these regulations.

- Reputational Damage: Data privacy violations can harm a company's standing. Customers lose faith and confidence in a company's ability to protect sensitive data when their personal information is compromised. It may take years to recover from this breach of trust, leading to a decline in customer loyalty, lower sales, and unfavorable publicity.

Security Measures to Protect Data Privacy:

- Strong Passwords: Each online account should have a different, complex password, which should be updated regularly. Combining uppercase and lowercase letters, numbers, and special characters can significantly increase password security.
- Two-factor authentication (2FA): Adding 2FA to online accounts gives them an additional layer of security. Before accessing their account, users must provide a second verification form, like a fingerprint scan or a unique code sent to their mobile device.
- Encryption: To safeguard sensitive data, organizations should use encryption methods. Information is encrypted into an unintelligible format that can only be unlocked with the correct key. This makes sure that data are secure even if it is intercepted.
- Regular Software Updates: Keeping software and devices current with the most recent security patches is essential. Software updates frequently include security patches that address flaws that hackers could exploit.

Data privacy breaches carry severe risks and repercussions for both individuals and organizations. It is crucial to be aware of these risks and implement the necessary security measures to protect sensitive information. Individuals and organizations can reduce their chances of becoming victims of data privacy breaches by using strong passwords, two-factor authentication, encryption techniques, and updating software. Data privacy can help us make the digital world safer for everyone.

2.2.1 Getting Around the Compliance Landscape in Information Security

Regarding information security, compliance refers to following pertinent rules, frameworks, and standards to secure sensitive data. It entails putting security controls, policies, and procedures in place and keeping them up to date to safeguard data from unauthorized access, use, disclosure, alteration, or destruction. The type of data being handled, the location, and the industry all have different compliance standards. The General Data Protection Regulation (GDPR), the Payment Card Industry Data Security Standard (PCI DSS), and the Health Insurance Portability and Accountability Act (HIPAA) are a few of the well-known laws and standards [2].

Navigating the Compliance Landscape:

- Conducting a Compliance Assessment: A thorough evaluation of the organization's security controls, policies, and procedures is the first step in navigating the compliance landscape. This evaluation aids in locating any vulnerabilities or gaps that must be closed to comply with regulatory requirements. Organizations need to have a thorough understanding of the laws and standards that are relevant to their sector.
- Understanding Applicable Regulations. This is part of knowing the precise requirements, deadlines, and consequences of non-compliance. Maintaining compliance necessitates staying informed about any modifications or updates to these regulations.
- Creating a Compliance Framework: A compliance framework offers a methodical means of observing various regulations. It facilitates organizations' efforts to harmonize their security procedures with industry standards and guarantees a uniform approach to compliance. The National Institute of Standards and Technology (NIST) Cybersecurity Framework and the ISO 27001 standard are two examples of compliance frameworks.
- Implementing Security Controls: To reduce risks and safeguard sensitive data, organizations must implement the proper security controls. These safeguards may consist of administrative safeguards like training programs, incident response plans, routine security audits, and technical safeguards like intrusion detection systems, access controls, and encryption.

- Monitoring and Reporting: Compliance is a continuous process that calls for ongoing observation and documentation of security activities. Regular audits, vulnerability analyses, and penetration tests aid in finding any vulnerabilities or non-compliance problems. Organizations should also maintain appropriate documentation and reporting systems to prove their compliance efforts.

Organizations today need help navigating the compliance landscape for information security. Organizations can create efficient plans to safeguard sensitive information and uphold compliance by comprehending the rules, frameworks, and best practices. It is crucial to continuously evaluate and enhance security controls and stay current on any updates or changes to the compliance landscape. Information security compliance is not just a legal requirement but also essential to establishing trust with clients, business partners, and other stakeholders.

2.2.2 Legal Frameworks: Protecting Privacy Rights, CCPA, and GDPR

Privacy has become a top priority for individuals and businesses in the digital age. It is essential to have robust legal frameworks to protect privacy rights, given the enormous amount of personal data being gathered and shared. The California Consumer Privacy Act (CCPA) in the United States and the General Data Protection Regulation (GDPR) in Europe are two well-known laws that have significantly impacted how personal data are handled. This chapter will discuss the main components of GDPR and CCPA and how they protect privacy rights [5].

2.2.2.1 General Data Protection Regulation (GDPR)

This comprehensive privacy law, which took effect in May 2018, applies to all EU member states. The goal of the regulation is to give people more control over their data and ensure that businesses handle it responsibly. Essential features of the GDPR include:

- Data Protection Principles: The GDPR places a strong emphasis on concepts like accurate data collection, purpose limitation, data minimization, accuracy, storage capacity restriction, integrity, and confidentiality.

- Consent: Organizations must get that person's explicit and informed consent before collecting and using a person's personal information, according to the regulation.
- Rights of Data Subjects: Under GDPR, people have the right to obtain a copy of their data and access, correct, erase, and restrict the processing of that data. The "right to be forgotten" and the "right to data portability" are also introduced.

2.2.2.2 California Consumer Privacy Act (CCPA)

The CCPA is a state-level privacy law in California, USA, and will go into effect in January 2020. It gives Californians more transparency and control over their personal information. The CGPA's key components are as follows:

- Consumer Rights: The CCPA gives consumers the right to request the deletion of their personal information, the right to know what personal information is being collected, and the right to refuse the sale of their data.
- Business Obligations: The CCPA places obligations on businesses, such as disclosing how they collect and use customer data, keeping a "Do Not Sell My Personal Information" link on their websites, and treating customers who assert their privacy rights reasonably.
- Enforcement and Penalties: The California Consumer Privacy Act (CCPA) gives the California Attorney General the authority to enforce compliance and imposes severe penalties on companies that violate the law.

2.2.3 Challenges in Achieving Compliance and the Repercussions of Noncompliance

Compliance with various laws and regulations has become a significant challenge for organizations across industries where business is increasingly regulated. Serious repercussions can result from non-compliance, including financial penalties and reputational harm. This chapter examines businesses' difficulties in achieving compliance and the possible consequences of disregarding legal requirements [6].

Evolving Regulatory Landscape: The constantly shifting regulatory environment is one of the main obstacles to achieving compliance. It is challenging for organizations to stay current with the most recent requirements because laws and regulations are constantly updated and revised. This difficulty is more evident in sectors with global operations where companies must simultaneously navigate multiple jurisdictions and adhere to various regulatory frameworks.

- Complexity and Ambiguity of Regulations: Many regulations are challenging to understand and implement correctly because they are ambiguous and complex. Regulations' ambiguity can result in different interpretations and inconsistent compliance practices. Legal jargon can be complicated for businesses, leading to unintentional non-compliance.
- Resource Constraints: Resources, including financial, human, and technological, are needed to achieve compliance. Small and medium-sized businesses (SMEs) frequently experience resource shortages, making it challenging to allocate the money and people required to ensure compliance. Additionally, keeping up with technological developments and spending money on systems that support compliance can be very expensive.
- Data Privacy and Security: Organizations must establish strong privacy and security measures due to the growing relevance of data protection to comply with laws like the GDPR and CCPA. Significant obstacles are posed by the difficulties of managing and safeguarding enormous volumes of data, especially in fields that deal with sensitive personal data. Personal data protection violations can incur severe fines and harm an organization's image.

Consequences of Non-Compliance: Businesses may suffer severe repercussions if regulatory obligations are not met, including [7]:

- Financial Penalties: Organizations that disregard rules may receive hefty fines from regulatory agencies. These fines can be financially catastrophic, particularly for smaller enterprises with constrained financial resources.
- Legal Repercussions: Failure to comply may result in expensive and time-consuming legal proceedings, such as lawsuits and legal disputes. Legal liability, reputational harm, and significant economic opportunity loss are all possible outcomes for organizations.

- Reputational harm: Non-compliance can cause severe reputational damage, resulting in declining consumer loyalty and confidence. A company's brand image may be harmed by bad press, leading to a decrease in market share and earnings.

2.2.4 Principles to Follow to Ensure Data Privacy and Compliance

In the digital world, protecting data privacy and adhering to relevant standards have become a significant priority for enterprises. Errors in sensitive data handling can have substantial consequences, including financial penalties and reputational loss. This chapter discusses a few suggested strategies organizations may employ to secure consumer information while complying with requirements.

- Establish a Robust Data Governance Program: A strong data governance program is critical for protecting data privacy and compliance. Clear rules and processes for data collection, storage, access, and destruction should be included in this program. It should also define accountability and responsibility for data protection, with authorized persons monitoring compliance activities.
- Conduct DPIAs (Data Privacy Impact Assessments): Regular Data Privacy Impact Assessments assist firms in identifying and mitigating any privacy issues related to their data processing operations. This technique entails selecting suitable methods to resolve any detected risks and examining the impact of data processing on persons' privacy rights.
- Maintain honest data-collecting processes: Organizations should be transparent about their data-collecting processes and provide clear information to individuals about the goal, scope, and techniques of data processing. Implementing robust consent processes, such as gaining explicit agreement and making it easy for users to opt-out, helps ensure compliance with rules such as the GDPR.
- Put in Place Strong Data Security Measures: Data security is essential to data privacy and compliance. Organizations should use robust security measures such as encryption, access restrictions, and frequent security audits to safeguard data from unauthorized access, breaches, and cyber threats. Regular staff training on data security best practices is also

required to foster a data-protection culture throughout the firm.

- Review and Update Privacy Policies regularly: Privacy policies should be reviewed and updated regularly to reflect changes in legislation and the organization's data processing activities. These policies should clearly explain how personal data are collected, utilized, kept, and shared and provide individuals with information about their data rights.
- Conduct Regular Compliance Audits: Conducting regular compliance audits assists firms in identifying gaps or flaws in their data privacy processes. These audits should evaluate compliance with applicable rules, corporate policies, and industry standards. Any discovered flaws should be corrected as soon as possible to assure compliance and reduce any hazards.

For businesses to keep customers' confidence, stay out of legal trouble, and protect their brand, data privacy protection and ensuring they align with current rules are essential. Organizations can build a solid foundation for data privacy and compliance by implementing comprehensive data governance programs, carrying out routine data privacy impact assessments, maintaining open data collection practices, putting strong data security measures in place, updating privacy policies, and conducting regular compliance audits. These best practices assist in safeguarding people's right to privacy while demonstrating a dedication to ethical data processing and fostering consumer and stakeholder confidence [8].

2.2.5 Integrated Approach: Audits, Access Controls, Encryption, and Privacy Awareness

The need to adopt a holistic data privacy and security strategy has increased in today's linked world. Organizations need to use various tactics to secure sensitive information and people's privacy. To develop a complete data privacy and security strategy, this chapter examines the significance of encryption, access restrictions, audits, and privacy awareness.

- Encryption: An essential method for protecting data and preventing unwanted access is encryption [12]. Organizations may ensure that even if data are intercepted, it will stay worthless without the decryption key by turning it into an unreadable format using encryption techniques. Sensitive data must be protected from potential breaches and unauthorized access using robust encryption techniques at rest and in transit.

- Access restrictions: Strong access restrictions are essential for protecting data privacy. Organizations should follow the concept of least privilege, allowing access to sensitive information only to those who need it to fulfill their assigned responsibilities. Robust authentication techniques, like multi-factor authentication, may be used to make sure that only authorized workers have access to sensitive data. Other crucial procedures include routinely checking access records and promptly revoking access for those who no longer need it.
- Regular Audits: Regular audits are crucial to evaluate the efficiency of data privacy and security safeguards inside a company. Internal and external audits make finding possible weaknesses and holes in security procedures easier. Audits should cover various topics, including checking access records, examining encryption techniques, determining compliance with applicable laws, and pinpointing problem areas. The results of audits can help firms improve the security and privacy of their data.
- Privacy Awareness: A thorough data privacy and security strategy must include privacy awareness. Organizations should invest in privacy awareness training programs to inform their staff on the value of data protection, privacy laws, and best practices. It is important to remind staff members of their data privacy duties, the potential repercussions of non-compliance, and the value of managing sensitive information with care. A culture of privacy awareness may be cultivated inside the organization through regular training sessions and communication activities [9].

2.3 Data Privacy and Compliance in Information Security: The Changing Nature

Data privacy and compliance are becoming significant issues for individuals and enterprises in the digital era. Understanding the changing nature of data privacy and compliance in information security is crucial, given the rising dependence on technology and the quantity of sensitive and personal data being gathered, kept, and shared. This chapter examines the difficulties and developments in data privacy laws, the effects of new technological developments, and the significance of adhering to compliance standards as shown in Figure 2.2.

- Data Privacy rules: Data privacy rules are essential for safeguarding individual privacy rights and ensuring the safe management of personal data. Several laws have been passed to regulate data privacy, including the California Consumer Privacy Act (CCPA) in the United States and the General Data Protection Regulation (GDPR) in the European Union. These laws outline people's rights, place demands on organizations, and inflict harsh punishments for breaking them. Organizations must stay up-to-date on the constantly changing world of data privacy laws to avoid legal repercussions and keep customers' confidence.

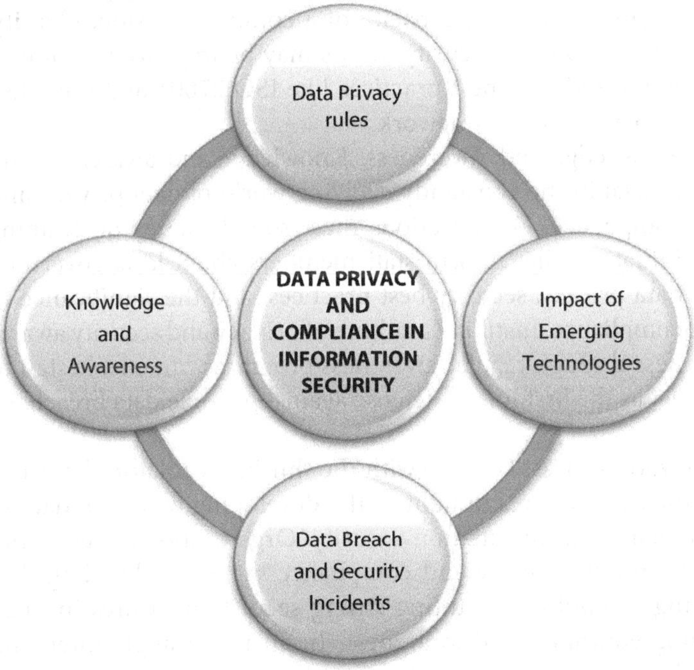

Figure 2.2 Data privacy and compliance in information security.

- Impact of Emerging Technologies: Emerging technologies' effects include possibilities and difficulties for data privacy and compliance. Technology is advancing quickly. New technologies, including artificial intelligence (AI), the Internet of Things (IoT), and big data analytics, have transformed data gathering and processing. Although these technologies have significant advantages, they also raise questions about how personal data are gathered, utilized, and safeguarded. Organizations must overcome these obstacles by applying privacy-by-design principles, performing privacy effect analyses, and guaranteeing openness in data handling procedures.
- Data Breach and Security Incidents: In recent years, data breaches and security incidents have increased frequently, revealing sensitive data and jeopardizing people's privacy. Threats and strategies used by cybercriminals change along with technology. Proactive security measures, such as solid cybersecurity frameworks, attentive monitoring, and incident response plans, must be given top priority by organizations. The capacity of a company to stop, identify, and respond to security events may be improved by adhering to industry best practices like ISO 27001 and the NIST Cybersecurity Framework.
- Knowledge and Awareness: Knowledge and awareness Are crucial in the constantly evolving world of data privacy and compliance. Organizations must spend money on training initiatives that inform staff members about laws governing data privacy, security best practices, and the significance of compliance. Instilling a culture of privacy and security awareness through regular awareness programs can enable staff to act as the first line of defense against possible data breaches.

Organizations must keep up with the shifting regulatory landscape and modify their procedures in light of the developing nature of data privacy and compliance in information security. Organizations may manage the intricacies of data privacy and compliance by comprehending the effect of evolving technologies, putting strong security measures in place, and prioritizing education and awareness. In an increasingly interconnected world, adopting a proactive and comprehensive approach to information security is crucial for securing personal data, upholding regulatory compliance, and retaining consumer confidence [10].

2.4 Continuous Learning and Adaptation: Keeping Pace with Emerging Technologies and Regulations

The environment of data privacy and compliance in information security is continually changing in the current digital era. Organizations must employ a continual learning and adaptation approach to stay ahead of the curve when new technology and laws arise. This essay examines the value of ongoing education, its difficulties, and the tactics businesses may use to navigate this dynamic environment successfully.

The Value of Constant Learning: Data privacy and compliance laws protect personal information about persons, including the General Data Protection Regulation (GDPR) and the California Consumer Privacy Act (CCPA). However, new dangers and weaknesses appear as technology develops, calling for constant knowledge and vigilance. Organizations can keep up with these developments, modify their procedures, and guarantee compliance using continuous learning.

Continuous learning challenges: Data privacy and compliance require ongoing education, which has its share of difficulties. The quick evolution of technology is one of the main challenges. Organizations find it challenging to keep up with the constant introduction of new platforms, apps, and devices. The complicated and dynamic regulatory environment adds a further degree of complexity, which requires firms to negotiate several frameworks and comprehend their ramifications [11].

Techniques for Adaptation and Continuous Learning:

- Stay Informed: Businesses should designate a team or individual who keeps abreast of new technology, market trends, and legislative changes. This group can monitor pertinent sources such as trade journals, government agencies, and security discussion boards.
- Participate in Training and Certification Programs: Encourage staff members to participate in Data Privacy and Compliance-related Training Programs and get relevant Certifications. These classes offer insightful information about ethical standards, governing policies, and new dangers.
- Promote a Culture of Privacy Awareness: Establish a culture that promotes privacy and compliance across the organization. Inform staff members regularly about the value of

privacy and data security, stressing their part in upholding compliance. Launch initiatives to raise privacy awareness and offer tools for continued learning.\Collaborate with Experts: Consult outside specialists in data privacy and compliance, including consultants and lawyers. These professionals may offer advice and help implement the necessary safeguards to guarantee compliance.

- Conduct Regular Audits: Conduct internal or external audits regularly to evaluate data privacy and compliance processes. These audits aid in pinpointing areas that require improvement and ensure the firm complies with ever-changing rules.

For enterprises to negotiate the constantly changing requirements for data privacy and compliance in information security, ongoing learning and adaptation are crucial. Organizations may successfully handle the issues and make sure they remain compliant with changing technology and laws by remaining educated, participating in training, establishing a culture of privacy awareness, working with specialists, and carrying out frequent audits. Accepting ongoing learning is essential to safeguarding people's data and upholding trust in a society that is ever more interconnected [1].

2.5 Conclusion

Protecting sensitive information is essential in the digital era for both businesses and people. To reduce threats, it is crucial to implement strong security measures, including encryption, access limits, audits, and privacy awareness. Access restrictions limit access to authorized persons, but encryption technologies can make data unreadable to unauthorized people. Regular audits find weaknesses and verify that rules are followed. Promoting privacy awareness encourages careful information management. Organizations must implement a continual learning strategy, following market trends, and working with specialists. Cutting-edge technologies like AI, machine learning, and blockchain are completely reimagining data privacy and compliance. Establishing best practices and creating thorough rules need cooperation between companies, business associations, and regulatory agencies. By implementing best practices, staying informed, and embracing collaboration, organizations can ensure the integrity, confidentiality, and availability of sensitive information in the digital era.

References

1. Xadjayev, S., Information Security: Strategies, Challenges, and Emerging Trends. *J. Tech. Res. Dev.*, 1, 2, 253–257, 2023.
2. Kuan Hon, W. *et al.*, Cloud accountability: The likely impact of the proposed EU data protection regulation. *Queen Mary Sch. Law Legal Stud. Res. Pap.*, 172, 18, 2014.
3. Chua, H.N. *et al.*, Impact of employees' demographic characteristics on the awareness and compliance of information security policy in organizations. *Telemat. Inf.*, 35, 6, 1770–1780, 2018.
4. Regulation, General Data Protection, General Data Protection Regulation (GDPR), Intersoft Consulting, Accessed on October 24.1, 2018.
5. Edemekong, P.F., Annamaraju, P., Haydel, M.J., Health insurance portability and accountability act, 2018.
6. Gunningham, N., Negotiated non-compliance: a case study of regulatory failure. *Law Pol'y*, 9, 69, 1987.
7. Mendrinou, M., Non-compliance and the European Commission's role in integration. *J. Eur. Public Policy*, 3, 1, 1–22, 1996.
8. Calopereanu, M.F., Şuică, M., Calopereanu, A.N., Considerations regarding compliance with the Regulation (EU) 2016/679 (GDPR) in Human Resources Departments. *Proceedings of the International Conference on Business Excellence*, vol. 13, no. 1, 2019.
9. Killmeyer, J., *Information security architecture: an integrated approach to security in the organization*, CRC Press, Taylor & Francis, New York, 2006.
10. Kshetri, N., Privacy and security issues in cloud computing: The role of institutions and institutional evolution. *Telecommun. Policy*, 37, 4-5, 372–386, 2013.
11. Nguyen, T., An Empirical Evaluation of the Implementation of the California Consumer Privacy Act (CCPA), arXiv preprint arXiv:2205.09897, 2022.
12. Nayak, R., Sastry, C.V., Pradhan, J., Algorithmic Comparison between polynomial base and Matrix based NTRU cryptosystem. *Int. J. Comput. Network Secur. (IJCNS)*, 2, 7, 27, July 2010. (ISSN Print:2076-2739, ISSN Online: 2076-9199).
13. Sharma, D.K., Chawla, N., Anand, R.K., Online Trust Evaluation, in: *New Age Analytics: Transforming the Internet through Machine Learning, IoT, and Trust Modeling, Cyber Crime and Forensic Computing: Modern Principles, Practices, and Algorithms,* Role of Cyber Security in Today's Scenario, Role of Cyber Security and Cyber Forensics in India, pp. 103–134, Apple Academic Press, USA, 2020, 978-1-77188-857-2.

3

Unveiling Cyber Threats and Digital Forensics

Nidhi Gupta[1*], Arpita Trivedi[1], Parveen P. Terang[2] and Hasmat Malik[3]

[1]*Department of EEE, Maharaja Surajmal Institute of Technology, Delhi, India*
[2]*Department of EE, JSS Academy of Technical Education, Noida, India*
[3]*Department of Electrical Power Engineering, Faculty of Electrical Engineering, Universiti Teknologi Malaysia (UTM), Johor, Malaysia*

Abstract
Cybercrime has become sophisticated with the advancement in technology. In this era of digitalization, from getting valuable insights into the world to making large transactions online, people are doing everything digitally at their convenience, leading to cyber threats. This chapter examines the escalating landscape of cybercrimes, from the insidious tactics of phishing and man-in-the-middle attacks to the disruptive power of denial-of-service assaults, all designed to exploit user information in the interconnected web. It also focuses on the various advanced techniques organizations use to protect devices from these cyberattacks. These include threat modeling, penetration testing, access control, and many more techniques. It talks about the significant issues and challenges faced in this field. Furthermore, this chapter discusses cyberattacks related to Internet of Things (IOT) devices in the healthcare sector. It also highlights the digital forensics, its branches, and techniques.

Keywords: Information security, phishing, encryption, access control, denial of service

**Corresponding author*: nidhi@msit.in

Kavita Sharma, Vishnu Sharma, Parma Nand, Anil Kumar Sagar and Gulshan Shrivastava (eds.) Securing the Digital Frontier: Threats and Advanced Techniques in Security and Forensics, (35–58)

3.1 Information Security

Information security means preventing and protecting information on the network and computer systems from unauthorized access [1]. Everyone should focus on understanding information before learning about cyber-attacks and the techniques used to avoid them. Information is any data on the network of systems that can be used to exploit an individual or organization. It can be in the form of text, audio, image, or video. For example, we integrate digitally and provide valuable data to websites and devices. At an individual level, cyber attackers can easily use saved passwords or card information to hack into people's accounts. With the development of techniques to prevent cyberattacks, attackers are also increasing their levels. They find ways or paths to breach the security frameworks of different organizations. Information security is a very complex and ever-evolving field. With the advent of new threats, new measures for security must be developed and implemented [2].

There are three pillars of information security. First is Confidentiality, which means that the information provided on the network can only be accessed by authorized users. Second is Integrity, which means available information is accurate and complete. Any malicious attack has not corrupted it. Third is Availability, which means that whenever authorized individuals need the information, they should be able to access it. Information security is essential for all, whether an organization is big or small.

3.1.1 Issues and Challenges

This vast field of information security faces several challenges. Day by day, the sophistication of cyberattacks is increasing. Attackers are constantly developing new and more advanced methods of attack. Organizations or societies require support from these three pillars of cyber security, as shown in Figure 3.1 [1].

These are just some of the critical issues and challenges in information security. Organizations need to be aware of these challenges and take steps to mitigate them. By implementing appropriate security measures, organizations can protect their information and reduce the risk of security incidents. Careful assessment of their suppliers' security must ensure they are not introducing new risks to their organizations.

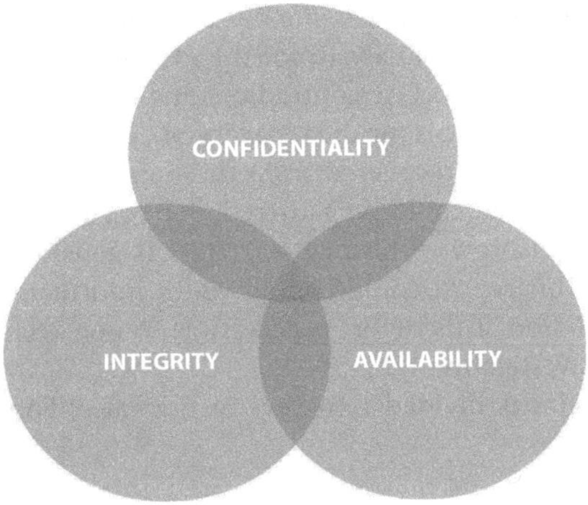

Figure 3.1 Three pillars of cyber security.

3.1.2 Digital Forensics

Cybercrime is Digital Forensics, which identifies, analyses, and presents the digital evidence in digital crimes [20]. 1978, the first computer crimes were recognized in the Florida Computers Act; the digital forensics field proliferated in the 1980s to 1990s. This covers analyzing storage media, hardware, operating systems, networks, and applications. In this digital era where cybercrimes are rising rapidly, all criminal activities consist of electronic evidence, and digital forensics assistance has become necessary for investigations. This evidence can be collected from various sources like computers, smart devices, remote systems, storage devices, and many more [21]. Thus, digital forensics aims to extract and process evidence from various sources using sound forensic techniques to be admissible in court.

Digital forensics uses a variety of strategies that guide forensic examiners on how to gather, process, analyze, and extract data. It generally consists of four stages, which are explained further. The first step is to seize the digital media. That is why seizure is the first stage of the investigation. The law enforcement personnel perform this step to preserve the chain of custody in criminal cases. The second stage is Acquisition. The data is duplicated for forensic use after seizing assets using a hard drive duplication or software imaging tool. After data duplication, original evidence is returned to a secure storage to prevent tampering. MD5 or SHA-1 hash functions are used for the verification. Throughout the analysis, this image will be verified at several stages to check whether the evidence is still in its original state. The third stage is analysis; for the identification of the evidence, files are analyzed to support or contradict a hypothesis. Forensic analysts use several methods or tools for the recovery of evidence material. Deleted information can also be recovered from these methods. Various types of data are analyzed. Data could be gathered from chat logs, emails, images or documents, and browser history. A report is generated after analysis of all the data. This report could contain audit information or any other meta-documentation. This report is accessible to non-technical individuals for further investigation [22].

Digital forensics is divided into several branches. Some of those are described below.

Computer forensics is the branch of digital forensics related to computers and digital storage evidence. Examination of digital data for identification, preservation, recovery, and analysis is involved in this branch. Along with the principles and techniques similar to data recovery methods, this branch also uses additional practices and guidelines. These guidelines create a legal audit trail with a transparent chain of custody [23].

Mobile device forensics primarily focuses on recovering digital evidence from mobile phones. This branch involves investigating any device with internal memory and communication functionality. Mobile phones, tablets, and GPS devices could be devices [24].

Network forensics is the branch that is related to network activities. Capturing, recording, and analysis of events is done. The nature of network data is dynamic. It is a proactive investigation process [25].

Forensic Data Analysis (FDA) is the branch that focuses on examining structured data found in application systems and databases. This branch mainly plays a role in financial crimes. The main objective of the FDA is to detect and analyze patterns of fraudulent activity.

Database forensics is the branch in which database access is investigated and changes made to the data are reported. This branch can be helpful for various purposes. It can be used to identify database transactions that are indicative of fraud. It can also be used to validate and verify the actions of a particular database user by inspecting and testing the database.

3.2 Cyberattacks

Cyberattacks are actions or efforts done by hackers or cyber criminals intentionally to get unauthorized access to a computer system, a digital device, or a network. Data or information is stolen, exposed, altered, disabled, or destroyed. These attacks can be done on a single system or a group of systems and devices connected to a network by single or multiple devices. Through these attacks, one can restrict authorized users' access to their devices. Several methods are available to execute a cyberattack, including ransomware, phishing, denial of service, and many more [1]. A hacker or attacker can launch the attack from any location. It can be done individually also. Sometimes, a group of hackers come together to breach a more extensive organization or hack many devices. These hackers are known as cybercriminals. Firstly, they try to identify the vulnerabilities and loopholes of a system. They analyze the problems or weaknesses present in a device and then use these to accomplish their goals. Cyberattacks can be of an active or passive nature. Active cyberattacks focus on modifying or altering the data, which destroys data integrity. These attacks are generally used to damage the systems and are not hidden from the victim. In passive cyberattacks, attackers monitor and analyze the information and plan a suitable time for attack. Information can get copied or exposed in these types of attacks. Data does not remain confidential. As in these attacks, attackers silently observe, so victims remain unaware of the attack [4]. The reasons behind cyberattacks could be personal or political. Some attacking techniques are described below.

3.2.1 System Exploitation

In this technique, cybercriminals find vulnerabilities or security flaws in a computer system or an application and use this to install malware [1]. An exploit is a program or piece of code designed for this technique. A sequence of suspicious operations is initiated by an attacker to take advantage of vulnerabilities effectively and to set up an exploit successfully. Bugs in software or system architecture are the primary reasons for the vulnerabilities. Several types of malware are injected into the system by attackers. Some techniques of security exploits are used more by the attackers. These are SQL injection attacks, cross-site request forgery, and cross-site scripting. Abuse of broken authentication codes or security misconfigurations is also one of the common vulnerabilities related to the web.

Zero-day exploit is a type of computer exploit that takes advantage of the vulnerability in the part of the software or operating system. The user remains unaware of this flaw until a hacker exploits it after detection of the vulnerability. That is why this is known as a zero-day exploit [5]. When this type of exploit occurs, affected systems or applications running the software become vulnerable to more attacks. Security can be achieved again after the vulnerability has been corrected.

Some common attacks are denial of service, remote code execution, and privilege escalation. Buffer overflow exploits, code injection, or other types of input validation vulnerabilities, as well as side-channel attacks, are some of the vulnerabilities.

These exploits could occur in several ways. In local exploits, attackers require prior access to the vulnerable system. It increases the attacker's privilege past those granted by the security administrator. An attacker cannot access the system in remote exploits before exploiting the vulnerability. In client exploits, attackers require an interaction from the user to exploit client applications. This is achieved with the help of social engineering techniques like phishing. Modified servers are constructed to send an exploit.

Exploits damage all three pillars of information security: confidentiality, integrity, and availability.

3.2.2 Phishing

The most common social engineering technique is phishing, in which attackers pretend to be a trusted person or entity. Generally, fraud emails and websites are constructed to manipulate or trick computer users into clicking a malicious link, installing a malicious file, or providing sensitive and confidential information such as access credentials. This type of cyber security attack is usually combined with other attacking techniques such as code malware injection and network attacks [1, 6]. Phishing techniques could be categorized into the following types:

Bulk email phishing is the most used method. An attacker or scammer takes advantage of the fact that a large, renowned, authentic business or organization, such as a global or national bank, online retailer, popular software applications, or app makers, could send messages to millions of users. An email message that looks like it came from an authentic source is created. Users needed help differentiating between the original and fraudulent emails and fell into the trap of scammers. Bulk email phishing is dependent on the number. Attackers pretend to be the more popular sender with more customers, members, or subscribers.

Unlike bulk email phishing, in which bulk emails are delivered to random individuals, the spear phishing method focuses on specific individuals or groups within an organization. It is a malicious technique executed using emails, social media, and other popular platforms. The main target of an attacker is to get personal information or to trick users into performing actions that could lead to data loss, network compromise, or financial loss. This method required prior research as it is target-specific. In this type of email, specific target information, such as name and job profile, is mentioned, and an attachment is also included. This increases the chances of users getting manipulated and performing actions such as opening the email and including attachments, which is necessary for malware infection.

Business Email Compromise (BEC) is used to defraud the company. It is a phishing technique in which an attacker targets a particular business after research. It is independent of whether the organization is big or small; these scams are found to be growing and becoming a serious threat as they cause losses of billions of dollars.

Email Account Compromise (EAC), or Email Account Takeover, is a cyberattack technique. Hackers use several social engineering methods and password-cracking tools to compromise a legitimate email account. EAC and BEC could be used in combination. Both methods are difficult to detect and prevent.

3.2.3 Man in the Middle Attack

Man-in-the-middle attacks are a type of cybersecurity attack in which the communication between two targets is not confidential. Attackers use illegitimate ways to eavesdrop on the communication link and collect sensitive information from the conversation they should not be listening to [1]. This collected data will be used for malicious purposes against the victims. These attacks are accomplished using rogue access points, address resolution protocol, and DNS spoofing.

A rogue access point provides unauthorized wireless access to the network's wired infrastructure without the permission or consent of the network's administrator or owner. It is a wireless access point generally set up by employees who want wireless access. Multiple risks are associated with rogue access points. With these attacks, theft and destruction of data could happen, which means essential corporate data may be compromised or completely erased. Network services could also be disabled, and victims could be restricted from accessing their data. Portals formed using this technique could be used to upload viruses or malicious files. One of the most significant risks of this attack is that the attacked company's wired network may be used for third-party attacks against other networks available on the internet.

An attacker could take advantage of the Address Resolution Protocol. ARP is used in LAN to translate IP addresses into MAC addresses. Whenever a host needs to communicate with another host identified by a specific IP address, it consults the ARP cache to map the address to its corresponding MAC address. If this address is unknown, a request is initiated to ask for the device's MAC address with that IP address. An attacker with malicious intent takes this as an opportunity and responds to these requests with its own MAC address. They sniff the private traffic between the hosts by placing some packets precisely, and essential information can be extracted from this traffic. Credential information could give hackers access to accounts, which could be used dangerously [7].

Domain Name Server (DNS) spoofing, also called DNS cache poisoning, is a type of cybersecurity attack that involves the manipulation of DNS records to redirect the users toward an unauthentic malicious or fraudulent website that resembles the actual authentic website. After redirecting, users try to log in to their accounts with the correct credentials. This lets the attacker steal the credentials and other confidential and sensitive information. Such sites could also secretly install viruses or worms on the user's system or device. It gives the attacker long-term access to the user's device and data.

3.2.4 Denial of Service

As the name suggests, a denial-of-service (DoS) attack is a cybersecurity attack that denies the service to the users. These attacks shut down a machine or a network. This is achieved by sending the data that triggers a crash in the system or network or by flooding the target with many service requests [1]. Both situations lead to the authorized users' denial of service or resources. The information or content becomes unavailable to legitimate users. Generally, web servers are the primary targets for DoS attackers in banking, media companies, commerce, government, trade organizations, or other significant and high-profile organizations. These attacks do not result in data loss or stealing, but they waste much of the victim's time.

DoS attacks are mainly of three types. First is application-layer flood; in this type of attack, an attacker floods the web server or system with a few thousand or millions of requests per second from a spoofed IP address. This slows down the service and sometimes crashes the system. Many requests eat up the resources. Prevention of application-layer DoS attacks can be very tricky.

The second is Distributed Denial of Service (DDoS) attacks. It is similar to DoS attacks. In DoS, requests are sent from just one client, whereas in DDoS, requests are sent from many clients. Many "zombie" machines are involved in these types of attacks. Zombie machines were previously compromised and are now being controlled by attackers. These machines send enormous requests to a service to deactivate it [3].

Third is Unintended Denial of Service; these attacks are not heinous. The Slashdot effect is an example of these types of attacks. This effect refers to a situation in which a website experiences a temporary surge in traffic. This happens because a high-traffic website posts a link to a smaller site. This directs a significant amount of traffic to a smaller site. This makes the site slow or unreachable.

3.2.5 Ransomware

Ransomware is a type of malware that restricts the user's access by locking or encrypting information, data, files, systems, or devices. Information becomes inaccessible and unusable [9]. Attackers give back access to the encryption key after receiving a ransom payment. Earlier, only data encryption was done to make the data inaccessible to the victim. Victims could restore the data with regular backups and were not required to pay a ransom. So, attackers started incorporating cyber extortion tactics such as phishing emails or infected sites to produce additional threats to the victims. They used sensitive data to blackmail the victims for ransom payments. Attackers also started attacking victim's backups to prevent them from restoring data [10]. Ransomware causes damage to various organizations, either big or small.

The basic approach of the attackers is to lead the users to click a link, install a file, application, or program, or visit a web page that contains malicious code. This code is designed to automatically download and install the ransomware in the system. This can be achieved in several ways. Phishing email is the most common way. Victims click a link in the email that redirects them to a malicious website. Opening a random email attachment could also enable malicious macros or download a document embedded with a Remote Access Trojan. Social media also provides a platform for these attackers to provide malicious links. Sometimes, clicking a legitimate advertisement could also lead to the installation of malware because the attacker seeds these advertisements with code.

Ransomware remains inactive on a device and waits for the device to become most vulnerable to the attack. The attack consists of seven stages. First is the infection stage, which we discussed earlier. The second stage is execution. Scanning and mapping locations for the targeted file types is done in this. File types also include locally stored files. In some attacks, backup file folders are encrypted or deleted. After this, in the third stage, encryption is performed by exchanging keys with the Command-and-Control Server. This locks access to the data. In the fourth stage, instruction files with the details of payment for the decryption process are added by ransomware. These files are used to display a ransom note to the victim. The fifth stage is the cleaning process. Ransomware gets terminated and deleted itself. Only the payment instruction files are left. Payment is asked in the sixth stage. The victim clicks the link in the payment instructions; it leads to a web page with hidden TOR services to avoid detection by network traffic monitoring. This webpage consists of additional information for required ransom payments. The last stage is decryption. When the victim pays the ransom, the decryption key is received. There is no guarantee about the authenticity of the decryption key. This is how ransomware is performed [11].

3.3 Protection Techniques

Nowadays, when everyone is connected digitally worldwide, much information or data is available in the network. A network, in simple words, is any interconnection between two or more computer systems or devices. The sensitive information can be misused, altered, or destroyed by attackers. Cyberattacks [12] are becoming more and more common. The results of these persistent attacks could be very disastrous. Network breaches are severe threats to both people and organizations as they could lead to identity theft and financial losses. That is why cyber security is of utmost importance. Cybersecurity means protecting data or information from hackers or attackers with malicious intent. It means keeping the three pillars of cybersecurity—confidentiality, integrity, and availability—intact. Several protection techniques can be applied to ensure proper security.

Data are a vital asset of an organization. Securing data at every stage of its life cycle is crucial for effectively protecting data. Various cyber protection techniques exist to ensure proper data storage, processing, or transmission. People often confuse themselves between cyber protection and cybersecurity. These two concepts are related but distinct. Cybersecurity [2] is focused on protection from cyber threats, such as phishing, ransomware, etc., of an organization's systems and networks, whereas cyber protection is mainly for data security. Cyber protection combines cybersecurity and data protection. The same tools and techniques are used for these, but data protection from unauthorized access is the primary concern of cyber protection [35, 36].

3.3.1 Firewalls

A firewall is a hardware or software-based device designed for network security. Its primary function is to monitor all incoming and outgoing traffic by agreeing or rejecting them. Accepting means allowing the traffic, rejecting means blocking the traffic and replying with an "unreachable error," and dropping means blocking the traffic but with no reply. A firewall acts as a wall between secure internal and outside networks, such as the Internet, that cannot be trusted. Firewalls are classified into several types. Some of them are described below [2].

Packet filtering works in the network layer of the OSI model. It is done at Open Systems Interconnection (OSI) data link, network, and transport layers. It applies a set of rules on each packet based on the contents of IP and transport header fields. Based on the outcome, it decides whether a packet will be forwarded or discarded. Packet filter firewalls give control access to packets. This depends on the packet source and specific transport protocol or destination address. Only the essential attributes of each packet are considered. As each packet is examined in isolation, there is no need to remember any information about the traffic. This is why packet flow is decided very quickly [13].

The most secure form of firewall is the proxy firewall. It is also known as a gateway or application firewall; it protects network resources by filtering all the messages at the application layer. This firewall limits applications supported by a network. This increases the security levels but at the cost of functionality and speed. Generally, firewalls are not designed to decrypt or inspect application protocol traffic. For protection against threats, these firewalls use an intrusion prevention system (IPS). These firewalls provide an intermediary link or a gateway between computers and servers connected to the internet for securing the incoming and outgoing data in a network.

Stateful inspection is also called dynamic packet filtering. It uses the information collected from monitoring the state of active connections to determine which network packets should be allowed to pass through the firewall. This firewall is used for Transmission Control Protocol and other similar protocols. It is generally used in place of stateless inspection or static packet filtering. It can also support some other protocols, such as User Datagram Protocol. Like packet filtering, this firewall also works in the transport and network layers of the OSI model to examine how applications communicate over a network. Application layer traffic can also be discussed, but only to a certain extent. Data packets are filtered based on state and context. This information is derived from a session's packets. The state of the connection is reflected in specific flags; it depends on the protocol. For example, in TCP, state information can be taken from flags such as SYN, FIN, and ACK. All this information is stored in a table by a firewall and updated regularly. Context encompasses details such as source and destination IP addresses, ports, sequence numbers, and various types of metadata. The firewall also stores and updates this information. These firewalls can provide a greater degree of security by monitoring and tracking both state and context information. Inbound and outbound packets are also compared against the stored session data to assess communication attempts.

A next-generation firewall (NGFW) is a device designed for network security with more capabilities and features than a traditional stateful firewall [14]. Based on administrator-defined rules, a traditional stateful inspection firewall allows or blocks the traffic. This is done based on state, port, and protocols. However, a next-generation firewall comprises features like cloud-delivered threat intelligence, application awareness and control, and integrated intrusion prevention. A vital feature of these firewalls, i.e., application awareness, is to block traffic from specific applications and maintain greater control over individual applications. Intrusion Prevention System (IPS) checks the network for malicious activity and blocks it wherever it occurs. This monitoring could be signature-based, policy-based, or anomaly-based. These firewalls can monitor large amounts of network efficiently without slowdown.

3.3.2 Threat Modeling

Threat modeling is a structured process of identifying, communicating, and understanding threats and mitigations while protecting computer systems or devices [15]. Its main objectives are identifying security requirements, pinpointing security threats and vulnerabilities, critically quantifying them, and prioritizing remediation methods. Threat modeling methods create an abstraction of the system. It considers profiles of potential attackers, including their goals and strategies. In this method, a catalog of threats that could arise is made.

The simplest threat model includes a description of the subject to be modeled and all the potential threats to the system or device [16]. It also consists of the actions that should be taken to mitigate each threat. Ways for validation of the model and threat and verification of success of actions are also mentioned in a threat model. Threat modeling is a simple process that captures, organizes, and analyses all the information related to the system for protection from threats.

Threat modeling can be divided into five steps, as stated in Figure 3.2. The first step is to identify the assets. It is a very crucial step. An asset could be any intellectual property, account data, or an entire system or device. The second step is to diagram the system because it provides an asset-centric view of systems and shows how the data flows. It becomes easy to find the possible origins or paths of attacks. These form an attack tree or graphic representation of the attack path.

The third step is to analyze the threats. Specific threat types are further examined using different methods. This step also involves the identification of potential threats, mapping data flows, and quantizing risks. Risk management and prioritization are performed in the fourth step. With the help of several threat modeling tools, threat scores and data are produced to calculate risk. Stakeholder input is essential for this step. The final step is to find mitigation strategies. It could include changing firewalls, encrypting data, or adding multi-factor authentication.

Organizations must constantly tweak and fine-tune threat models to keep the system, network, or device safe and secure from attackers and data breaches. The threat landscape is continually evolving.

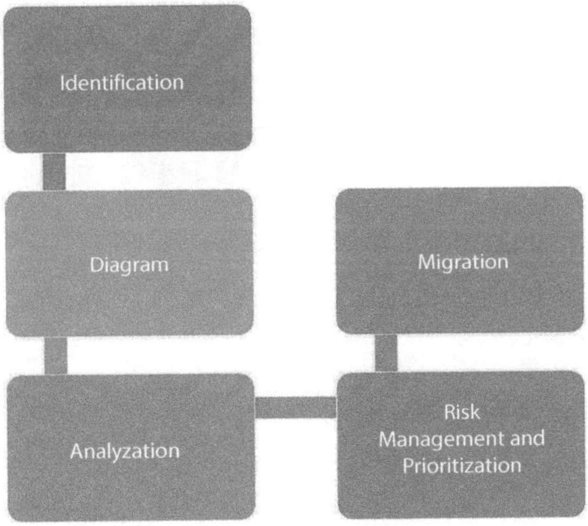

Figure 3.2 Threat modeling stages.

3.3.3 Penetration Testing

For the evaluation of the security of a system, an authorized simulated attack is performed on a computer system. This test is called a penetration test or pen test. The business impacts of weaknesses in a system are found and demonstrated by penetration testers with the help of the same tools, techniques, and processes that attackers use. In penetration tests [18], various attacks are simulated, which could be possible threats to a business. These tests examine whether a system can withstand attack from unauthenticated and authenticated positions. It checks the robustness of the system by considering various scenarios. A penetration test dives into every aspect of a system.

Penetration testing [17] is divided into five stages, as in Figure 3.3. The first stage comprises Planning and Reconnaissance. In this, systems to be addressed are identified. The testing scope and goals are defined, and testing methods are selected. Information like network and domain names is gathered to understand how a target works and potential vulnerabilities. The second stage is scanning. In this step, responses of target applications to various intrusion attempts are analyzed. This can be done using Static Analysis or Dynamic analysis. Static analysis inspects an application's

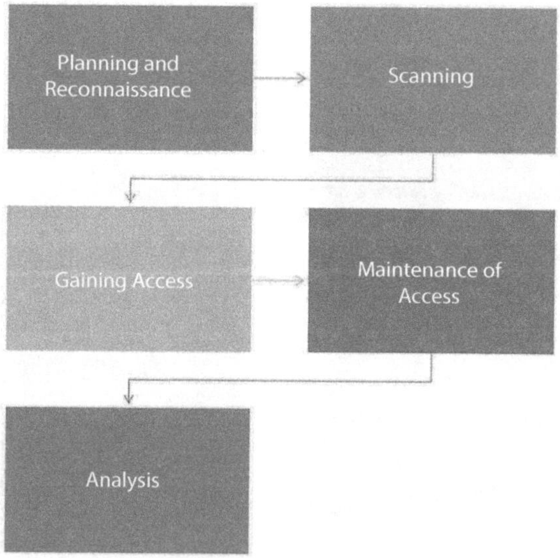

Figure 3.3 Penetration testing procedure.

code to estimate the system's behavior while running. In a single pass, the entirety of the code is scanned. Dynamic analysis involves the inspection of an application's code in a running state. This method provides a real-time view of the performance of an application. It is a more practical way to scan. The third stage is Gaining Access. Several web application attacks are used in this stage, such as SQL injection, cross-site scripting, back-doors, etc. Target's vulnerabilities are uncovered. After this, testers deliberately try to exploit these vulnerabilities for a better understanding of the damage these can cause. This can be done by escalating privileges, stealing data, intercepting traffic, etc. Maintenance of access is the fourth stage. Testers try to keep the access to check if attackers can use the vulnerability to maintain a persistent presence in the system they exploited. Testers try to imitate advanced persistent threats because these attacks remain in the exploited system for months, which helps attackers steal the most sensitive data of an organization. The fifth and last stage is analysis. A compiled report containing the results of the penetration test is formed. This report includes exploited vulnerabilities, information about the sensitive data accessed, and the time the tester can access the system undetected.

Security personnel analyze this detailed report to help configure an enterprise's WAF settings and other application security solutions. This is done to patch vulnerabilities and protect against future attacks. Penetration testing is classified into several types [19], such as external, internal, blind, double-blind, and targeted.

External penetration testing, also known as external network penetration testing. It is a security assessment of an organization's perimeter systems, including all the systems directly accessible from the Internet. These are highly exposed systems. This is why these systems are the easiest and most regular targets of attackers. The objective behind these tests is to determine how attackers will exploit the accessible systems and services and the methods they could use to attack the clients or users of an organization.

Internal penetration testing is done by simulating the actions of an actual attack. It is done to protect the systems from an attack by an insider or someone with initial access to the network. These attacks are called Advanced Persistent Threat (APT) attacks. An internal penetration test is performed to find the loopholes in the network that attackers can exploit. This gives time for the organization to fix the problem before the attack. Several companies adopt the approach of creating two teams, red and blue, internally. Software developers and security specialists are the members of these teams. The red team attempts to find the flaws present in the security and weaknesses in the system, whereas the blue team will make protection strategies and guard the system from attacks. System security is improved considerably when these two teams work together.

Blind penetration testing severely limits the information given to the tester or team performing the test. This test analyzes the system by simulating the actions and procedures followed by an actual attacker. Information such as only the company's name could be given to the team. This test can be expensive as it requires considerable time for reconnaissance.

Double-blind penetration testing is similar to blind testing. It tries to make tests more accurate and practical. A test is being conducted and is known by only one or two people in that organization. These penetration tests test the organization's security monitoring, incident identification, and response procedures.

Another type of penetration testing is targeted testing. In this type of testing, corporate IT teams and external professionals work together to determine the flaws and vulnerabilities of the company's systems or devices. Several tasks are conducted on an open network. The team can compare their analysis and results. This helps find better solutions to strengthen an organization's systems to prevent potential attacks.

3.3.4 Encryption

Encryption is an information security technique. Nowadays, a lot of data or information sharing occurs on the internet. Data goes through multiple networks and devices which form part of the public network. This traveling through the public network makes it vulnerable. The possibility of data being compromised and stolen increases. To prevent these, users install specific software or hardware to secure data. Information or data is converted into cipher text, which can only be deciphered by people with a decryption key. Only authorized people can access the original plaintext information [26]. Simply put, it is a way of encoding information that makes data unreadable to unauthorized people. This is done to protect data from cybercriminals trying to gain access to a complete network by using sophisticated means. Encryption makes their efforts futile as encrypted data remains unreadable to them. The confidentiality of information or data is ensured with the help of Encryption. Due to this technique, the available data or messages in the network could not be altered from their original state. This proves that Encryption provides authentication and integrity.

A cryptographic key [27] is involved in the encryption process. The cryptographic key is a set of mathematical values to which both the sender and receiver agree. The recipient uses this key to decrypt the data and turn it back to readable plaintext sent by the sender. The complexity of cryptographic keys needs to be increased to secure encryption. This is done because several third parties try decryption using brute force attacks. A brute force attack is when a hacker tries random numbers until they find the correct combination of the password. Passwords are also protected using encryption. Scrambling passwords is done using password encryption methods to make it unreadable by hackers. Data that is in transit or at rest is protected through encryption techniques. Whenever someone buys something through online websites with a mobile phone or laptop or uses an ATM, the information relayed is protected through encryption. More and more businesses rely on encryption to protect applications and sensitive information from alteration or damage during data breaches. The three major components of an encryption system are data, encryption engine, and key management. Usually, the three components run or are stored in separate places. This is done in application architectures to decrease the possibility of compromising the entire system due to compromising any single component. While in laptop encryption, all three components are run or stored in the same place, i.e., on the laptop. Data encryption can be done through different approaches. Most internet security professionals break encryption down into three distinct methods. These methods are symmetric and asymmetric. These are further classified into various types.

Symmetric encryption method, also called private-key cryptography or a secret key algorithm, is a method by which the sender and the receiver access the same key. For the decryption of the message, the recipient must have the key. This method is best suited for closed systems with fewer third-party inclusion risks. Symmetric encryption is faster than asymmetric encryption, but in this technique, the key needs to be stored securely by both parties. It should be available only to the software that needs it for encryption or decryption.

Asymmetric encryption is also referred to as public-key cryptography. Two keys, a public and a private key, are used for the encryption process. These two keys are mathematically linked. One key is employed for the user's encryption, and the other is used for decryption. It does not matter which is selected first. As per the name, only intended recipients who need the key to decipher the messages can access the private key, whereas the public key is available to anyone. Both keys constitute large numbers that are not identical, as the name suggests, "asymmetric." But these keys are paired with each other.

3.3.5 Access Control

This is a technique in which system access or virtual or physical resources are restricted [28]. It protects the business or organizations from cyberattacks. Electronic access control systems are used to establish a secure system. These depend on user credentials, access card readers, auditing, and reports for tracking employee access to restricted business locations and areas. In this, users are identified by verification of various login credentials. These include usernames, passwords, PINs, security tokens, and biometric scans. Multifactor authentication is included in many access control systems. This method uses multiple authentication methods to verify the user's identity. After the user authenticates, the appropriate level of access is then authorized by access control. The system allows actions associated with that user's credentials and IP address.

Access control methods are classified into four types as per Figure 3.4: Mandatory access control (MAC), Role-based access control (RBAC), Discretionary access control (DAC) [29], and Rule-based access control (RB-RBAC). A method is chosen based on each user's access level, security requirement, infrastructure, etc.

Mandatory access control restricts access to resources based on how sensitive the information they hold is. It also checks if the user is authorized to access that sensitive data. A security label is used to define the sensitivity of the resource. The security level of zero or more categories is composed of security labels. The security labels, such as restricted, confidential, or internal, indicate a level or hierarchical classification of the information. The security category defines the group or project to which the information belongs. Users can only access information from a resource based on

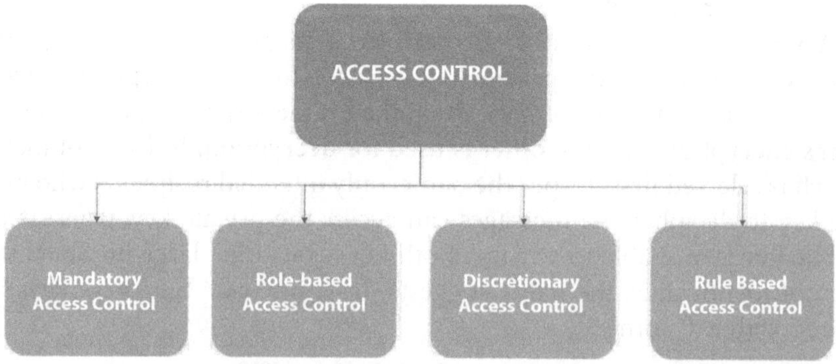

Figure 3.4 Access control classification.

their security labels. The user will be unable to access the information in the resource with a security label having less authority.

Role-based access control is a method that restricts network access based on the roles and positions of the individual users within an organization or enterprise. It grants users access based on their roles and responsibilities. This access control method is most suitable for organizations with many workers, contractors, or companies that allow network access to third parties, such as vendors and customers. Limiting network access in these enterprises is crucial, as monitoring network access effectively can be very challenging. Sensitive data and critical applications are more secure with this method. This method gives users access only to the information they need for their task's completion or job responsibilities. It prevents them from accessing the information which they do not even require.

Discretionary Access Control is a method of access control in which access is granted or restricted based on the access policy. This access policy is formed by an object's owner group or the subjects. In this method, the owner has the supreme power and determines the object access privileges. They can transfer or give other users access to authenticated objects or information. During the authentication process, these mechanism controls are defined by user identification with login credentials. In this method, each system object, file, or data has an owner that determines the access policy.

Rule-based access control is a method in which system owners can personalize the type of access a user can have based on their role in an organization or company. In this method, based on preset criteria, an administrator sets the security system to allow users to enter. Access hours for regular business days can be set. An employee will only be able to enter the building during these hours. Firstly, the system administrator creates access rules. After this, these rules are integrated throughout the access control system. The control mechanism grants or denies access to the user after verification of access credentials. This method reduces IT support and administrative work. It improves safety, security, and compliance [30].

3.4 Internet of Medical Things

Internet of Medical Things (IoMT) is the extension of IOT in the medical sector [8]. It is gaining popularity as it helps decrease healthcare expenses. It provides fast response, and the quality of medical treatment is also improved. IoMT devices establish communication between medical devices and networks [31–33]. Patient data is collected through medical devices and sensors to monitor patients' pathological aspects. These sensors could be small wearable devices or implantable sensors. These collected data are automatically transmitted to healthcare professionals via networks. This data is vast and must be protected from information security threats. Sensitive information and patient data such as vital signs, blood sugar levels, and heart rate are collected and transmitted by IoMT devices. This makes them targets for cyber attackers. There are several security and privacy challenges associated with IoMT devices. These devices often have weak authentication and authorization mechanisms, making them easy for attackers to compromise. These challenges can be overcome by using artificial intelligence and machine learning with IoMT [33–36]. New technologies will be developed to protect the privacy of MIoT data, such as differential privacy and secure multi-party computation [4].

3.5 Conclusion

The ever-expanding digitization has undeniably changed the way we live and communicate. However, this convenience comes at a price because digitization causes a rise in cybercrime, posing severe threats to individuals and organizations. Robust cyber security measures are required against the techniques used by hackers, such as phishing, MITM attacks, and DoS attacks. Threat modeling, penetration testing, and access control are some advanced security techniques organizations adopt to combat these threats by identifying vulnerabilities. However, there is a constant need for skilled cybersecurity professionals to face ongoing challenges, such as the dynamic nature of cyber threats. The healthcare industry, which consists of Internet of Things (IoT) devices, has emerged as a prime target for cybercriminals. Sensitive health data needs to be protected by securing IoT devices. Nowadays, digital forensics plays a crucial role in investigating and mitigating cybercrimes. It is imperative to remain alert and adaptable to evolving cyber threats. With the help of information security techniques, a secure digital environment can be created that allows everyone to benefit from technological advances without compromising data and privacy.

References

1. Perwej, Y., Abbas, S.Q., Dixit, J.P., Akhtar, N., Jaiswal, A.K., A systematic literature review on the cyber security. *Int. J. Sci. Res. Manage.*, 9, 12, 669–710, 2021.

2. Debnath, S., Das, A., Sarkar, B., Securing Cloud-Based Enterprise Applications and Its Data, in: *Cyber Security and Network Security*, Chapter 1, vol. 1, pp. 1–26, Wiley Online Library, 2022.
3. Garg, A., Singh, A., Sharma, K., Sharma, V., A Taxonomy for Internet of Things in Security Distributed Denial of Service Attacks, in: *2022 4th International Conference on Advances in Computing, Communication Control and Networking (ICAC3N)*, 2022, December, IEEE, pp. 1274–1281.
4. Perwej, Y., Akhtar, N., Kulshrestha, N., Mishra, P., A methodical analysis of medical Internet of Things (MIoT) security and privacy in current and future trends. *J. Emerg. Technol. Innov. Res.*, *9*, 1, d346–d371, 2022.
5. Vaisla, K.S. and Saini, R., Analyzing of zero day attack and its identification techniques, in: *Proceedings of First International Conference on Advances in Computing & Communication Engineering (ICACCE-2014)*, p. 3, 2014.
6. Sharma, K. and Gupta, B.B., Attack in smartphone Wi-Fi access channel: State of the art, current issues, and challenges, in: *Next-Generation Networks: Proceedings of CSI-2015*, pp. 555–561, 2018.
7. Javeed, D., MohammedBadamasi, U., Ndubuisi, C.O., Soomro, F., Asif, M., Man in the middle attacks: Analysis, motivation and prevention. *Int. J. Comput. Netw. Commun. Secur.*, *8*, 7, 52–58, 2020.
8. Lu, Y. and Da Xu, L., Internet of Things (IoT) cybersecurity research: A review of current research topics. *IEEE Internet Things J.*, *6*, 2, 2103–2115, 2018.
9. O'Kane, P., Sezer, S., Carlin, D., Evolution of ransomware. *IET Networks*, *7*, 5, 321–327, 2018.
10. Beaman, C., Barkworth, A., Akande, T.D., Hakak, S., Khan, M.K., Ransomware: Recent advances, analysis, challenges and future research directions. *Comput. Secur.*, *111*, 102490, 2021.
11. Kharraz, A., Robertson, W., Balzarotti, D., Bilge, L., Kirda, E., Cutting the gordian knot: A look under the hood of ransomware attacks, in: *Detection of Intrusions and Malware, and Vulnerability Assessment: 12th International Conference, DIMVA 2015, Proceedings 12*, Milan, Italy, July 9-10, 2015, Springer International Publishing, pp. 3–24, 2015.
12. Zheng, Y., Li, Z., Xu, X., Zhao, Q., Dynamic defenses in cyber security: Techniques, methods and challenges. *Digital Commun. Netw.*, *8*, 4, 422–435, 2022.
13. Bellovin, S.M. and Cheswick, W.R., Network firewalls. *IEEE Commun. Mag.*, *32*, 9, 50–57, 1994.
14. Neupane, K., Haddad, R., Chen, L., Next generation firewall for network security: A survey, in: *SoutheastCon 2018*, 2018, April, IEEE, pp. 1–6.
15. Crothers, E., Japkowicz, N., Viktor, H.L., Machine-generated text: A comprehensive survey of threat models and detection methods. *IEEE Access*, 11, 70977–71002, 2023.
16. Marback, A., Do, H., He, K., Kondamarri, S., Xu, D., A threat model-based approach to security testing. *Softw.: Pract. Exper.*, *43*, 2, 241–258, 2013.

17. Shah, S. and Mehtre, B.M., An overview of vulnerability assessment and penetration testing techniques. *J. Comput. Virol Hacking Tech.*, *11*, 27–49, 2015.
18. Al Shebli, H.M.Z. and Beheshti, B.D., A study on penetration testing process and tools, in: *2018 IEEE Long Island Systems, Applications and Technology Conference (LISAT)*, 2018, May, IEEE, pp. 1–7.
19. Bacudio, A.G., Yuan, X., Chu, B.T.B., Jones, M., An overview of penetration testing. *Int. J. Netw. Secur. Appl.*, *3*, 6, 19, 2011.
20. Årnes, A. (Ed.), *Digital forensics*, John Wiley & Sons, New Jersey, U.S., 2017.
21. Soltani, S. and Seno, S.A.H., A survey on digital evidence collection and analysis, in: *2017 7th International Conference on Computer and Knowledge Engineering (ICCKE)*, 2017, October, IEEE, pp. 247–253.
22. Jafari, F. and Satti, R.S., Comparative analysis of digital forensic models. *J. Adv. Comput. Netw.*, *3*, 1, 82–86, 2015.
23. Maras, M.H., *Computer forensics*, Jones and Bartlett Learning, Boston, MA, 2015.
24. Barmpatsalou, K., Damopoulos, D., Kambourakis, G., Katos, V., A critical review of 7 years of Mobile Device Forensics. *Digital Invest.*, *10*, 4, 323–349, 2013.
25. Corey, V., Peterman, C., Shearin, S., Greenberg, M.S., Van Bokkelen, J., Network forensics analysis. *IEEE Internet Comput.*, *6*, 6, 60–66, 2002.
26. Prabha, C., Sharma, N., Singh, J., Sharma, A., Mittal, A., A review of cyber security in cryptography: Services, attacks, and key approach, in: *2023 Third International Conference on Artificial Intelligence and Smart Energy (ICAIS)*, 2023, February, IEEE, pp. 1300–1306.
27. Begovic, K., Al-Ali, A., Malluhi, Q., Cryptographic ransomware encryption detection: Survey. *Comput. Secur.*, *132*, 103349, 2023.
28. Sandhu, R.S. and Samarati, P., Access control: principle and practice. *IEEE Commun. Mag.*, *32*, 9, 40–48, 1994.
29. Samarati, P. and De Vimercati, S.C., Access control: Policies, models, and mechanisms, in: *International school on foundations of security analysis and design*, pp. 137–196, Springer Berlin Heidelberg, Berlin, Heidelberg, 2000.
30. Carminati, B., Ferrari, E., Heatherly, R., Kantarcioglu, M., Thuraisingham, B., A semantic web based framework for social network access control, in: *Proceedings of the 14th ACM Symposium on Access Control Models and Technologies*, 2009, June, pp. 177–186.
31. Jain, V., Chatterjee, J.M., Kumar, P., Kose, U. (Eds.), *Healthcare Monitoring and Data Analysis Using IoT: Technologies and Applications*, vol. 38, IET, India, 2022.
32. Sharma, K., Gigras, Y., Sharma, V., Hemanth, D.J., Poonia, R.C. (Eds.), *Internet of Healthcare Things: Machine Learning for Security and Privacy*, John Wiley & Sons, New Jersey, U.S., 2022.
33. Sharma, K., Internet of healthcare things security vulnerabilities and jamming attack analysis. *Expert Syst.*, 39, 3, e12853, 2022.

34. Shrivastava, G., Peng, S.L., Bansal, H., Sharma, K., Sharma, M. (Eds.), *New age analytics: Transforming the internet through machine learning, IoT, and trust modeling*, CRC Press, Florida, US, 2020.
35. Shrivastava, G., Gupta, D., Sharma, K. (Eds.), *Cyber Crime and Forensic Computing: Modern Principles, Practices, and Algorithms*, De Gruyter, Berlin, Germany, 2021.
36. Shrivastava, G., Sharma, K., Khari, M., Zohora, S.E., Role of cyber security and cyber forensics in India, in: *Handbook of Research on Network Forensics and Analysis Techniques*, pp. 143–161, IGI Global, US, 2018.

4

A Customised Privacy Preservation Mechanism for Cyber-Physical Systems

Manas Kumar Yogi[1]* and A.S.N. Chakravarthy[2]

[1]CSE Department, Pragati Engineering College (A), Surampalem, India
[2]CSE Department, JNTUK, Kakinada, India

Abstract
As modern-day cyber-physical systems (CPS) play a crucial role in enhancing the daily dependence on them in a smart ecosystem, the security and privacy aspects cannot be ignored. This research advocates a novel privacy approach for CPS, where the user can select the level of privacy based on their usage. It attempts to increase the degree of data utility at the user's customized usage level. As observed by all the stakeholders of a CPS, the degree of privacy and utility has a significant trade-off in determining the effectiveness of a CPS. Hence, this approach brings about a fair amount of flexibility for the users of a CPS entity. This need has motivated the design and development of a provisional privacy-preserving method, which shows appreciable results compared to current popular privacy-preservation methods in a cyber-physical system.

***Keywords*:** Cyber-physical systems, privacy, customized, security, utility

4.1 Introduction

The paradigm of cyber-physical systems came into existence in the early 20th century when the interconnection of cyber and physical components helped achieve a significant amount of functionality in terms of communication and computation [1]. Below discussed is the brief history of CPS:

**Corresponding author*: manas.yogi@gmail.com

Kavita Sharma, Vishnu Sharma, Parma Nand, Anil Kumar Sagar and Gulshan Shrivastava (eds.) Securing the Digital Frontier: Threats and Advanced Techniques in Security and Forensics, (59–90)

1. Primitive Concepts:
   The feedback-based control systems used in mechanical engineering domains required cyber and physical systems interoperability, laying the basis for CPS concepts' development.

2. Rise of Embedded Systems:
   In such systems, computer processors were combined with hardware devices to control the applications used in automation control and other electronic devices [2]. This propelled the role of CPS towards communication technologies.

3. Emergence of the era of Internet of Things (IoT) and Industry 4.0:
   In the early 21st century, the Internet of Things (IoT) aspects helped combine numerous heterogeneous components for passing information and realizing intelligent functionalities in a controlled environment [3]. Now, the CPS is also involved in decision-making.

4. Cross-Disciplinary Research and Development:
   CPS development has involved collaboration between various disciplines, including computer science, electrical engineering, mechanical engineering, control systems, and data analytics. Interdisciplinary research has accelerated the progress in CPS and enabled the realization of complex cyber-physical systems with far-reaching applications.

4.1.1 Role of CPS

Cyber-physical systems (CPS) play a crucial role in modern-day society and are increasingly becoming essential components of various industries and everyday life. CPS represents integrating computational elements (cyber) with physical components (physical) to create intelligent, interconnected systems that can monitor, control, and adapt to the real world. In below we discuss are some key reasons why CPS is of significant importance in the modern era [4]:

1. Industrial Automation Advancement: CPS leverages efficiency, reduces errors related to human negligence and improves productivity by automating industrial-related manufacturing processes.

2. Smart Infrastructure: Smart cities and smart grids enhance the overall public services and utilities by optimizing the available resources and facilitating extensive data analysis from the data collected from the sensors.
3. Development of e-healthcare systems: Personalised healthcare systems are being deployed in hospitals and other medical institutions due to the facilities provided by medical CPS, which provide smart wearables for remote health monitoring.
4. Smart transportation systems: CPS provides facilities for autonomous vehicles with enhanced road safety, traffic management, and traffic congestion reduction by applying optimal routing algorithms for smart vehicles.
5. Disaster Management: Prediction of natural disasters and enabling quick responses to handle a disaster has been a research challenge to the design of CPS. In this regard, real-time sensor data collection and analysis have succeeded in disaster management.
6. Precision Agriculture: Rural agriculture has been given a boost by enabling the precision agriculture paradigm and helping the farmers to optimize crop yield by reducing the inherent wastage related to agriculture and resulting in better outcomes due to data-driven decisions, which are being made possible by CPS entities [5].

4.1.2 Privacy Preservation in CPS

The importance of privacy preservation during involvement with the CPS ecosystem is necessary due to the below-mentioned reasons [6, 7]:

1. Protection of Private Data: In a CPS environment, sensitive and private data of users may be accessed by unauthorized or malicious users, thereby putting their personal lives at risk. So, to avoid such cases, privacy methods must be incorporated into the design of CPS components.
2. Protection of individual identity: The risk related to identity theft and impersonation cannot be ruled out during CPS application design and development. These risks result in loss either in the user's reputation or the stakeholder's trust.
3. Preventing Data Breaches: Mitigating data breaches and preventing unauthorized access to private data are essential in a CPS as they are prone to such attacks with malicious intent.

4. Resistance against bias: AI algorithms, when used in CPS applications, may suffer from unintentional bias, due to which the CPS application's decision-making ability may suffer adversely. In such instances, the privacy-preserving measures will protect the users from discrimination by inducing fairness in the decision-making process.
5. National Security and Critical Infrastructure Protection: In specific CPS applications, such as those used in defense, transportation, or energy sectors, privacy preservation is essential for safeguarding national security and protecting critical infrastructure from potential cyber threats.
6. Long-term Sustainability: Ensuring privacy in CPS can contribute to the long-term sustainability of these systems. As privacy concerns increase among consumers and regulatory bodies, organizations prioritizing privacy will be better positioned for success and continued growth.

Overall, privacy preservation in cyber-physical systems is necessary to protect personal data, prevent unauthorized access, maintain user trust, comply with regulations, and ensure fair and ethical use of data. By addressing privacy concerns proactively, organizations can build secure and reliable CPS applications that benefit individuals and society.

Privacy in cyber-physical systems is crucial for ensuring long-term sustainability on multiple fronts. Cyber-physical systems (CPS) are integrated systems that bridge the gap between the digital and physical worlds. These systems encompass various domains, including smart cities, industrial automation, healthcare, transportation, etc.

4.1.3 Motivation for CPS Privacy

Maintaining privacy in CPS is of paramount importance for the following reasons [8, 9]:

1. Data Protection: CPS generates and collects vast amounts of data from sensors, actuators, and various interconnected devices. This data often includes personal and sensitive information about individuals and organizations. Preserving privacy ensures that this data is protected from unauthorized access, misuse, or exposure, thus preventing potential data breaches and cyber-attacks.

2. Trust and Adoption: The long-term sustainability of CPS relies heavily on public trust and widespread adoption. Individuals and organizations who don't trust CPS systems to protect their privacy may be reluctant to adopt these technologies or share critical information. With user acceptance and adoption, the full potential of CPS can be realized, hindering its sustainability and growth.
3. Regulatory Compliance: Many countries have strict data protection and privacy regulations, such as the General Data Protection Regulation (GDPR) in the European Union. Noncompliance with these regulations can result in hefty fines and legal repercussions for the organizations responsible for the CPS implementation. Ensuring privacy in CPS helps meet these compliance requirements and avoids potential legal challenges.
4. Preventing Discrimination and Bias: CPS often uses data-driven algorithms to make decisions and automate processes. Without proper privacy measures, there is a risk of unintended discrimination and bias in decision-making based on sensitive attributes of individuals. These biases can negatively affect certain groups in the long term, eroding trust in CPS and leading to sustainability concerns.
5. Intellectual Property Protection: In industrial CPS applications, protecting sensitive information related to designs, manufacturing processes, and intellectual property is critical. A breach in privacy could expose trade secrets and proprietary information, jeopardizing a company's competitive advantage and long-term viability.
6. Resilience and Security: Privacy and security are interconnected. A robust privacy framework enhances the overall security of CPS by reducing attack surfaces and limiting the amount of exploitable information available to potential attackers. This improved resilience is essential for the long-term sustainability of CPS, as it helps prevent and mitigate potential cyber threats.
7. Ethical Considerations: Privacy is inherently linked to ethics and human rights. Respecting individuals' right to privacy is essential in upholding ethical standards in CPS development and deployment [10]. Ethical considerations are vital in ensuring CPS's acceptance and social sustainability over the long term.

In conclusion, privacy is a fundamental aspect of cyber-physical systems that directly impacts long-term sustainability. By protecting sensitive data, fostering trust, complying with regulations, preventing biases, and upholding ethical standards, CPS can flourish and deliver long-term benefits to society while minimizing potential risks and drawbacks.

4.2 Background

Differential Privacy is a privacy-preserving data analysis technique that aims to provide strong privacy guarantees for individuals whose data is used in aggregate analysis. It ensures that the results of a computation or analysis do not reveal sensitive information about any specific individual in the dataset [11].

It is well known that Differential Privacy is a cutting-edge and rapidly evolving field of research that focuses on preserving the privacy of individuals in datasets while still allowing valuable analysis and data-driven insights. It addresses the privacy concerns arising from the increasing collection and analysis of vast amounts of sensitive data in various domains, including healthcare, finance, and social sciences.

The core idea behind Differential Privacy is to add controlled noise or randomization to the data before releasing or performing computations. This noise ensures that the individual contributions of any specific data point cannot be distinguished, thereby protecting the privacy of individuals in the dataset while maintaining statistical accuracy for aggregate analyses.

4.2.1 Current Trends in CPS Privacy

Below are few of the critical aspects of the state-of-the-art in Differential Privacy [12–14]:

1. Formal Definitions: Researchers have developed rigorous mathematical frameworks to define Differential Privacy and quantify the privacy guarantees provided by different privacy mechanisms. The primary metric to assess privacy protection is the budget, typically denoted by ε (epsilon). Smaller ε values indicate more robust privacy protection, but they may come at reduced data utility costs.
2. Advanced Mechanisms: Various Differential Privacy mechanisms have been proposed to achieve privacy-preserving data analysis. Some popular techniques include Laplace

Mechanism, Exponential Mechanism, and Randomized Response. Researchers continually explore and design novel mechanisms to improve utility and reduce privacy loss.
3. Scalability: Initially, many Differential Privacy algorithms were computationally expensive, making them impractical for large-scale datasets and real-time applications. Recent advancements have focused on developing more efficient algorithms for big data and high-dimensional datasets.
4. Deep Learning and Differential Privacy: Integrating Differential Privacy with deep learning models has been an active area of research. Privacy-preserving deep learning techniques aim to safeguard the privacy of individuals' data used to train machine learning models while maintaining high accuracy in the learned model.
5. Federated Learning: Differential Privacy is employed in federated learning, where models are trained across multiple devices or servers without centralizing the data. Applying Differential Privacy in federated learning ensures that individual data contributions remain private while enabling model training and updates across decentralized devices.
6. Privacy Regulation and Adoption: With increasing privacy concerns and regulations like the General Data Protection Regulation (GDPR) and the California Consumer Privacy Act (CCPA), organizations and researchers are showing greater interest in adopting Differential Privacy as a means to comply with these regulations and protect sensitive data.
7. Robustness and Adversarial Attacks: There is ongoing research to understand the robustness of Differential Privacy mechanisms against potential adversarial attacks. Adversarial analysis helps ensure that even sophisticated attackers cannot infer private information through advanced inference techniques.

4.2.2 Trade-Off Between Privacy and Data Utility

Over time, as the field of Differential Privacy continues to evolve, researchers are exploring new techniques, refining existing ones, and addressing various challenges. The goal is to strike the right balance between privacy protection and data utility, making Differential Privacy a powerful tool for responsible and privacy-conscious data analysis in the age of big data and advanced analytics [15].

Variable Privacy Budgets are an extension of the traditional Differential Privacy scheme that allows for adaptive and dynamic privacy levels depending on the data sensitivity and the privacy requirements of different queries or computations [16]. In the traditional Differential Privacy scheme, a fixed privacy budget is allocated to a dataset, and all queries must abide by this fixed budget, which ensures a uniform level of privacy protection for all computations.

In contrast, Variable Privacy Budgets enable more flexibility by allowing different queries or computations to use varying levels of privacy budget based on their specific needs. Some queries might be less sensitive and require less privacy protection, while others might involve more sensitive data and need more privacy preservation [17].

The idea behind Variable Privacy Budgets is to allocate the privacy budget dynamically depending on the nature of the queries or the data being accessed. Some potential advantages of Variable Privacy Budgets are:

Enhanced utility: By allowing some queries to use a more private budget, the overall utility of the differentially private analysis can be improved. This is because less noise needs to be added to the results of less sensitive queries, leading to more accurate outcomes.
Customized privacy protection: Different data points in a dataset may have varying degrees of sensitivity. With variable privacy budgets, data points with high sensitivity can be protected more, while data points with lower sensitivity may have looser privacy constraints.
Resource optimization: Since some queries require less privacy protection, allocating more budgets to high-privacy-impact queries allows for efficient utilization of the overall privacy budget.

4.2.3 Challenges in Variable Differential Privacy Implementation

However, implementing Variable Privacy Budgets can be challenging and requires careful consideration of various factors, such as [18, 19]:

The nature of queries: Determining the sensitivity of each query accurately is crucial for allocating variable budgets effectively.
Differential Privacy Composition: Ensuring that the overall privacy budget remains within acceptable limits when combining multiple queries with different budgets.
Robustness: Variable Privacy Budget mechanisms should be designed to be robust against potential attacks and privacy breaches.

Researchers continually explore techniques and mechanisms to effectively and efficiently implement Variable Privacy Budgets. As with any privacy-preserving approach, trade-offs between privacy and utility must be carefully considered to strike the right balance for a given application.

Variable privacy budgets in Differential Privacy offer several advantages in hiding sensitive data in a dataset. The concept of privacy budget refers to the amount of privacy protection allocated for a given data analysis task. A variable privacy budget allows adjusting the level of privacy protection based on the specific requirements of the data analysis, striking a balance between privacy and data utility [9, 20].

Here are the advantages of using variable privacy budgets:

1. Flexibility in Privacy Guarantees: Different data analysis tasks may have varying degrees of sensitivity and requirements for privacy protection. By using a variable privacy budget, it becomes possible to customize the level of privacy guarantees based on the specific needs of each task. Some analyses might require stronger privacy guarantees with a smaller privacy budget, while others can tolerate a slightly larger budget for better data utility.
2. Improved Data Utility: A larger privacy budget typically implies more noise added to the data, which can adversely impact the utility of the analysis. Allowing variable privacy budgets lets data analysts or system administrators make informed trade-offs between privacy and data utility. A larger budget can be allocated for less sensitive tasks, improving data accuracy and analysis quality.
3. Differential Privacy for Diverse Data: Different individuals in a dataset may have varying sensitivity to privacy concerns. Variable privacy budgets enable personalized privacy protection, ensuring susceptible individuals receive stronger privacy guarantees while allowing more data exposure for less sensitive individuals. This way, the privacy protection can be customized to each individual's privacy needs.
4. Dynamic Data Sharing: The data sensitivity level may change over time in specific scenarios. With variable privacy budgets, data-sharing policies can adapt to these changes. For example, during heightened privacy concerns or in response to new regulations, the budget can be adjusted to provide stronger privacy guarantees.

5. Economical Privacy: Resources like computation power or privacy-preserving mechanisms may be limited in some applications. By using variable privacy budgets, organizations can optimize the usage of these resources, allocating more privacy protection to critical tasks and less to less critical ones, thus achieving better overall privacy efficiency.
6. Privacy-Accuracy Trade-off: Variable privacy budgets allow data analysts to explore the trade-off between privacy and data accuracy. By adjusting the budget, they can determine the level of privacy protection that balances between maintaining reasonable data utility and achieving acceptable privacy guarantees [21].
7. Scalable Privacy: Applying a fixed privacy budget across the entire dataset might be impractical or too restrictive for large-scale data analysis. Variable privacy budgets allow for scalable privacy protection, providing an efficient and effective privacy solution for big data scenarios.

It is important to note that while variable privacy budgets offer advantages in certain situations, setting appropriate budgets requires careful consideration. Balancing privacy and data utility is a complex task, and it is crucial to use rigorous methodologies to determine the optimal budget for each data analysis task, considering the specific privacy requirements and the nature of the data.

Personalized Differential Privacy is a relatively new research area that aims to enhance the privacy protection of individuals in data-sharing scenarios. Traditional Differential Privacy (DP) techniques focus on providing a fixed privacy guarantee for the entire dataset, but in real-world applications, individuals may have varying privacy needs and risk preferences. Personalized DP seeks to address this limitation by tailoring the privacy guarantees for each user based on their specific requirements [22].

The research work in personalized differential privacy can be broadly categorized into the following areas [23, 24]:

1. Privacy Budget Allocation: One key aspect of personalized DP is the allocation of privacy budgets to individual users. Instead of allocating a uniform privacy budget for all users, researchers have explored techniques to adaptively allocate privacy budgets based on user attributes, data sensitivity, and utility requirements. This approach allows for more flexible and efficient privacy protection.

2. Risk Analysis and Individual Privacy Level: Researchers have worked on developing methodologies to assess the privacy risks individual users face in a dataset. This involves considering user-specific attributes, data contribution patterns, and potential inference attacks to accurately quantify the personal privacy level. By understanding the risk faced by each user, personalized privacy mechanisms can be better customized to meet their specific needs.
3. Personalized Data Perturbation: Personalized DP techniques often involve customizing the perturbation applied to individual data points to align with the user's privacy requirements. This consists of devising personalized noise addition strategies, data aggregation techniques, and data transformation methods that optimize privacy and utility trade-offs for each user.
4. Contextual Privacy Preservation: Contextual information, such as location, time, and user behavior, defines individual privacy needs. Researchers have explored incorporating contextual factors into personalized DP models to adapt privacy protection measures to different situations better.
5. Machine Learning and Personalized DP: Machine learning algorithms are often used to learn individual user preferences and privacy risk profiles. Researchers have investigated machine learning techniques to dynamically adjust privacy parameters and improve the overall utility of personalized DP mechanisms.
6. Privacy Preference Elicitation: Understanding individual privacy preferences is vital for effective personalized DP. Research has focused on developing methods to elicit privacy preferences from users directly or indirectly through their data contribution behavior.
7. User-Centric Privacy Dashboards: To enhance transparency and control, some work has been done on designing user-centric dashboards, allowing users to monitor their privacy levels, assess potential risks, and manage their data-sharing preferences.

Personalized Differential Privacy is an active area of research, and various challenges remain to be addressed, including scalability, privacy-utility trade-offs, and integration with real-world data-sharing systems. Nonetheless, this emerging field holds promise in providing a more granular and user-centric approach to privacy protection in data-driven applications and services [11].

Personalized Differential Privacy (PDP) aims to tailor privacy protection to individual users' specific requirements, considering their privacy preferences and utility needs. Handling privacy-utility trade-offs is a crucial aspect of PDP to strike a balance between maximizing privacy protection and maintaining the usefulness of the data for intended purposes. Here are some ways PDP handles privacy-utility trade-offs [11]:

1. Adaptive Privacy Budget Allocation: Traditional Differential Privacy allocates a fixed privacy budget to the entire dataset, which can lead to a conservative level of noise addition, reducing data utility. PDP dynamically allocates privacy budgets based on individual users' privacy requirements. Users with higher privacy needs receive a larger budget, allowing for less noise addition and better utility.
2. User-Specific Noise Addition: In PDP, the noise added to each user's data can be personalized based on their sensitivity levels and privacy preferences. Users with more sensitive data or higher privacy concerns may receive additional privacy protections, while others with less sensitive data may experience less distortion for improved utility.
3. Contextual Privacy Preservation: PDP considers contextual information when applying privacy mechanisms. Certain situations may require stronger privacy protections; in others, the trade-off can be adjusted to favour higher utility. Contextual factors, such as location, time, and user behavior, influence the privacy-utility trade-off and can be considered in the personalization process.
4. Machine Learning for Utility Optimization: PDP may leverage machine learning algorithms to understand users' utility preferences and learn the optimal level of noise that maximizes utility while adhering to privacy requirements. The system can dynamically adjust privacy parameters to optimize the trade-off by learning from user interactions and feedback.
5. User-Centric Privacy Preferences: PDP aims to elicit individual users' privacy preferences and provide them with control over their data-sharing settings. Users can express their privacy-utility trade-off preferences through privacy preference elicitation mechanisms or user-centric privacy

dashboards. This way, users have more control over the privacy protection and utility level they receive.

6. Privacy-Utility Optimization Algorithms: Researchers are exploring novel optimization techniques explicitly designed for personalized differential privacy scenarios. These algorithms attempt to find the best trade-off between privacy and utility while considering individual user preferences and constraints.
7. Feedback and Iteration: PDP systems can incorporate feedback loops, allowing users to assess the impact of privacy protections on data utility and adjust their privacy preferences accordingly. This iterative process enables users to fine-tune their privacy-utility trade-off as needed.

It's important to note that the privacy-utility trade-off in PDP is not a one-size-fits-all approach. Different users may have diverse needs and expectations, and PDP aims to accommodate these variations. Striking an optimal balance between privacy and utility is an ongoing challenge, and researchers are continually developing new techniques to improve the effectiveness of personalized differential privacy mechanisms.

Adaptive, personalized differential privacy (APDP) is an advanced privacy mechanism that aims to provide customized privacy guarantees to individuals in data-sharing scenarios [25]. Unlike traditional differential privacy, which offers uniform privacy protection for all data subjects, APDP considers an individual's privacy needs and preferences. This approach is particularly relevant in scenarios where different users have varying sensitivity levels toward data disclosure.

The main components and mechanisms of Adaptive Personalized Differential Privacy are as follows:

1. Personalized Sensitivity Calibration: APDP starts by estimating the individual privacy sensitivity of each user. Sensitivity refers to the influence an individual's data can have on the outcome of a data analysis or machine learning model. By customizing the sensitivity for each user based on their data contributions and characteristics, APDP adapts to the privacy requirements of different individuals.
2. Personalized Privacy Budget Allocation: In traditional differential privacy, a global privacy budget is allocated for a dataset, and all individuals' data contributions are combined to adhere to this budget. In APDP, each user's privacy budget

is personalized, reflecting their privacy preferences. Users with higher privacy concerns may receive a stricter privacy budget, resulting in stronger privacy guarantees for their data.

3. Privacy-Utility Trade-off Management: APDP involves a trade-off between privacy and utility. More robust privacy protection often reduces utility in data analysis or machine learning. By allowing users to personalize their privacy preferences, APDP enables them to make informed decisions about the level of privacy they want while balancing it with the utility they expect from data analysis.
4. Adaptive Noise Injection: In differential privacy, random noise is added to the data to ensure privacy protection. In APDP, the amount of noise injected for each user is customized to their personalized privacy budget and sensitivity level. Users with stricter privacy budgets may receive more noise, while users with more relaxed privacy preferences may experience less noise injection.
5. User Interaction and Feedback: APDP involves interaction and feedback to improve personalized privacy guarantees. Users may provide feedback on the privacy-utility trade-off, helping refine the mechanism and strike an optimal balance that meets their needs.

Benefits of Adaptive Personalized Differential Privacy [26]:

1. Customized Privacy: APDP ensures that privacy protection is not a one-size-fits-all approach. Instead, it considers individual preferences and requirements, enhancing the overall user experience and acceptance of data-sharing initiatives.
2. Enhanced Utility: By allowing users to customize their privacy budget, APDP can provide higher utility than traditional differential privacy, where a strict global budget may hinder data analysis and machine learning performance.
3. Better User Engagement: Involving users in privacy decision-making fosters trust and transparency. APDP empowers users to participate actively in the privacy protection process, leading to increased engagement and cooperation in data-sharing initiatives.
4. Scalability and Flexibility: APDP can be implemented in various data-sharing scenarios, making it scalable and

adaptable to different application domains, such as healthcare, finance, and smart cities.

However, it's essential to balance personalized privacy guarantees and data utility. Excessive noise injection to protect privacy may adversely impact the usefulness of the data for analysis and modeling purposes. Proper user education and clear communication about privacy-utility trade-offs are crucial to successful APDP implementations. Additionally, ongoing research and collaboration between privacy experts, data scientists, and end-users are essential to refining and optimizing the mechanism for diverse use cases.

4.3 Motivation

In this research work, we are motivated to extend the design of customized differential privacy. Customized Differential Privacy is an approach to implementing the concept of differential privacy in a more customizable and adaptive manner. Differential privacy is a rigorous privacy framework that provides a mathematical guarantee of privacy protection for individuals whose data is used for analysis or computation. It ensures that the inclusion or exclusion of any individual's data does not significantly impact the computation results, thus protecting individual privacy.

Traditional differential privacy mechanisms, such as Laplace noise addition or exponential mechanisms, offer a one-size-fits-all approach to privacy protection. However, in many real-world scenarios, data sensitivity, the nature of the queries, and the privacy requirements can vary significantly. Customized Differential Privacy addresses these variations by customizing the privacy mechanisms to suit specific situations.

The primary motivation for introducing the approach of customized differential privacy is to tune the privacy parameters (e.g., noise scale or privacy budget) and the choice of privacy mechanism depending on the specific data and query characteristics. This method can be developed only after careful analysis of the data, the type of queries to be performed, and the necessary level of privacy guarantees [27].

4.3.1 Variants of Differential Privacy

Some examples of tailoring differential privacy mechanisms include:

Query-Specific Privacy Budgets: Allowing different queries to have distinct privacy budgets based on their sensitivity and impact on privacy.

Data-Dependent Noise Scaling: Adjusting the amount of noise added to query results based on the characteristics of the data being analyzed.
Context-Aware Privacy Mechanisms: Using different privacy mechanisms depending on the data context or the specific application domain.
Adaptive Privacy Control: Dynamically adjusting privacy parameters during the data analysis to optimize utility and privacy trade-offs.

Customized Differential Privacy is still an active area of research, and various techniques are being explored to develop more efficient and effective privacy mechanisms that can be customized to specific use cases. The goal is to strike the right balance between privacy protection and data utility, ensuring privacy is preserved while enabling helpful analysis and insights derived from the data.

4.3.2 Impact of Noise Addition in Variants of Differential Privacy

Adding noise in varying privacy budget queries in customized differential privacy has several impacts on privacy protection and data utility. Customized differential privacy refers to adapting privacy protection to individual data points or specific groups within a dataset, allowing personalized privacy guarantees.

Here are the key impacts of adding noise in varying privacy budget queries [12, 28]:

1. Enhanced Privacy Protection: By applying customized differential privacy with varying privacy budgets, sensitive data points or individuals with high privacy concerns can receive stronger privacy guarantees. The noise added to their data will be more significant, making it harder for attackers to isolate and identify their specific contributions to the analysis.
2. Personalized Privacy Levels: Different data points or individuals may have diverse sensitivity to privacy concerns. Customized differential privacy allows tailoring the noise level and privacy budget for each data point based on their specific privacy requirements. This approach ensures that privacy protection aligns with individual preferences and privacy needs.
3. Improved Data Utility for Less Sensitive Data: Customized differential privacy enables allocating larger privacy budgets to less sensitive data points or individuals. Consequently, these data points experience less perturbation due to noise,

resulting in improved data accuracy and utility for analysis tasks that do not involve sensitive information.

4. Complex Privacy-Utility Trade-offs: Customized differential privacy introduces more complex trade-offs between privacy protection and data utility. Data analysts must carefully assess the privacy-utility trade-offs for different data points and queries, finding the optimal balance to achieve the desired level of privacy while maintaining sufficient data accuracy.
5. Computational Challenges: Implementing customized differential privacy with varying privacy budgets can be computationally demanding, especially when dealing with large datasets and complex queries. Noise generation and application must be efficiently managed to achieve timely and scalable privacy protection.
6. Data Aggregation and Inference: Customized differential privacy might impact the aggregation and inference of results from different queries. When combining results from queries with varying privacy budgets, it is essential to consider the noise characteristics and how they affect the overall analysis accuracy and privacy guarantees.
7. User Acceptance and Transparency: Users may have concerns about the noise addition and how it affects the quality and privacy of their data. Transparency in the privacy mechanisms and clear communication about the privacy-utility trade-offs are essential to gain user acceptance and trust in the data analysis.
8. Differential Privacy Compliance: Customized differential privacy introduces additional complexity in ensuring compliance with privacy regulations and standards. Data controllers must demonstrate that privacy protection aligns with the specific privacy budgets and that the overall data analysis adheres to privacy guidelines.

Adding noise in varying privacy budget queries in customized differential privacy allows for personalized privacy guarantees customized to individual data points or groups. It enhances privacy protection for sensitive data while improving utility for less sensitive information. However, it also introduces complex trade-offs and computational challenges that must be carefully managed to achieve effective and efficient privacy-preserving data analysis. Transparency and user acceptance are critical for successful implementation and compliance with privacy regulations.

4.4 Proposed Mechanism

Query-Specific Privacy Budgets are a concept in customized differential privacy that allows for a more fine-grained and efficient privacy protection mechanism when dealing with multiple queries or computations on a dataset. In traditional differential privacy, a global privacy budget is set, and all queries share this budget, which can lead to excessive noise addition or diminished privacy guarantees for specific queries. Customized differential privacy addresses this issue by allocating individual privacy budgets for each query, considering their particular characteristics and requirements.

Let us illustrate this with an example:

Suppose we have a dataset of medical records containing information about patients' ages. We want to allow researchers to perform two types of queries on this dataset:

1. Count the number of patients whose age is above 70.
2. Calculate the average age of the patients.

To ensure privacy, we apply differential privacy to both queries. In the traditional approach, we would allocate a global privacy budget (epsilon) for both queries, say $\varepsilon = 1.0$. Each query would use a fraction of this budget to add random noise to its result, which ensures privacy but might lead to inaccurate results, especially for the average age calculation.

With customized differential privacy and Query-Specific Privacy Budgets, we can independently optimize the privacy guarantees for each query. For instance, we might set ε_1 = 0.5 for the count query and ε_2 = 0.3 for the average age query.

For the count query:

- A lower privacy budget (ε_1 = 0.5) means less noise addition.
- The count query will provide a more accurate result with stronger privacy guarantees than the traditional approach.

For the average age query:

- A slightly higher privacy budget (ε_2 = 0.3) can be allocated to allow more noise, which helps preserve privacy while providing a better approximation of the actual average.

By tailoring the privacy budgets, we balance privacy and data utility for each query. Queries with less sensitive or more straightforward computations might require a lower privacy budget, while more complex or sensitive queries may require a higher one.

Customized differential privacy allows for more flexible and adequate privacy protection, ensuring that the privacy budget is wisely distributed across queries to achieve better data accuracy and privacy guarantees, thus improving the overall utility of the dataset.

Balancing query sensitivity in customized differential privacy involves carefully assessing the level of privacy protection required for each query based on its sensitivity and impact on individual privacy. Here are some steps to achieve this balance:

1. Analyse Query Sensitivity: Understand each query's sensitivity in the dataset's context. Queries that reveal more detailed or specific information about individuals are considered more sensitive. For example, counting the number of individuals in a specific age range might be less sensitive than revealing the exact age of a particular individual.
2. Consider Data Granularity: The granularity of the data used in a query can affect its sensitivity. Aggregated queries that involve a large number of individuals are generally less sensitive than queries on individual-level data. Assess the granularity of each query to determine its impact on privacy.
3. Evaluate Query Impact: Consider the potential consequences if the query's results were to be exposed or leaked. Some queries might lead to more significant privacy risks or implications if their results were disclosed. Evaluate the impact of each query on privacy to inform the privacy budget allocation.
4. Assign Individual Privacy Budgets: Tailor a privacy budget (e.g., epsilon, denoted as ε) for each query based on sensitivity. More sensitive queries should be assigned a lower privacy budget, whereas less sensitive queries can be allocated a higher one. This ensures that queries with higher privacy risk are protected with stricter privacy guarantees.
5. Privacy Budget Trade-offs: Consider the trade-offs between privacy and data utility when assigning individual privacy budgets. Stricter privacy budgets (lower ε) provide more robust privacy protection but might introduce more noise,

reducing data utility. Conversely, higher privacy budgets (higher ε) can offer better data utility but with less stringent privacy guarantees. Balance these trade-offs based on the requirements of each query and the overall analysis goals.

6. Consult Domain Experts: Involve domain experts familiar with the specific queries and data to assist in accurately assessing query sensitivity. Domain knowledge can help understand each query's context and implications, leading to better decisions about privacy budget allocation.
7. Iterative Approach: Customized differential privacy might require an iterative approach. Start with initial privacy budget allocations, analyze the utility and privacy trade-offs, and adjust the budgets to strike a better balance. Repeat this process until the desired privacy and data utility level is achieved.
8. Monitor and Refine: Continuously monitor the data analysis process to evaluate the impact of the privacy budgets on the results. If the privacy protection is inadequate or data utility is compromised, consider refining the privacy budget allocation strategy.

By following these steps, data custodians can effectively balance query sensitivity in customized differential privacy, providing stronger privacy guarantees for more sensitive queries while preserving data utility for less sensitive ones. This approach enhances the data's usability for analysis while appropriately safeguarding individual privacy. Customized differential privacy involves allocating individual privacy budgets for each query based on their sensitivity. The privacy guarantees are achieved by adding noise to the query results proportional to their allocated budgets. Below is an algorithm for customized differential privacy, along with the mathematical equations involved:

4.4.1 Algorithm: Customized Differential Privacy

1. Input:

   - Dataset D: The original dataset contains sensitive information about users.
   - List of queries Q: A set of queries to be performed on the dataset.

2. Initialize:

- Set a variable `global budget` to ε, representing the global privacy budget available for the entire analysis.

3. For each query q in Q:

   3.1 Calculate the sensitivity of the query (sensitivity_q) based on the specific characteristics of the query and the dataset. The sensitivity_q represents the maximum change in the query result caused by removing or adding a single individual's data.

   3.2 Query-Specific Budget Allocation:

- Allocate a privacy budget (ε_q) for the query q based on its sensitivity and the remaining global privacy budget (`global_budget`).

  The allocation can be based on various techniques, but a simple approach can be:

  ε_q = min(sensitivity_q, global_budget)

  Here, we ensure that the privacy budget allocated to the query does not exceed its sensitivity or the remaining global budget.
- Deduct ε_q from `global_budget` to keep track of the remaining privacy budget.

4. Noisy Data Analysis:

- For each query q in Q, perform the data analysis on the dataset D with the allocated privacy budget (ε_q) for that query.
- Apply a differential privacy mechanism to the query result to ensure privacy. Common mechanisms include adding Laplace noise for count queries and Gaussian noise for aggregate queries.
- For a count query, the noisy result (N_q) can be obtained using the following equation:

$$N\_q = q(D) + \text{Laplace}(0, \text{sensitivity\_q}/\varepsilon\_q) \tag{4.1}$$

Where Laplace(0, b) represents adding Laplace noise with mean 0 and scale b.

- For an aggregate query (e.g., average), the noisy result (N_q) can be obtained using the below equation:

$$N\_q = q(D) + \text{Laplace}(0, \text{sensitivity\_q}/\varepsilon\_q) \tag{4.2}$$

Where Gaussian (0, σ^2) represents adding Gaussian noise with mean 0 and variance σ^2.

5. **Output:** The differentially private query results (N_q) for each query in Q.

Note: This algorithm provides a basic framework for customized differential privacy and noisy data analysis. The implementation might involve advanced techniques like privacy amplification or accounting to ensure that the overall privacy guarantees meet the desired level of privacy protection. Additionally, the choice of specific noise distributions (e.g., Laplace or Gaussian) might vary depending on the nature of the queries and the level of privacy required.

Balancing privacy and utility in differential privacy is a challenging task that involves carefully managing the trade-off between adding noise to protect privacy and preserving accurate data utility for analysis. Below is a simple algorithm outline that aims to achieve this balance:

4.4.2 Algorithm: Privacy-Utility Balancing in Differential Privacy

Input:

- Dataset D: The original dataset containing sensitive information.
- List of queries Q: A set of queries to be performed on the dataset.
- Global privacy budget ε: The total privacy budget available for the entire analysis.

Step 1: Input Dataset D, List of queries Q, Global privacy budget ε;
Step 2: Set ε=remaining_budget;
Step 3: For each query q in Q:

{
querysensitivity(qsi)=value of sensitivity;
}

Step 4: Sort the queries in descending order of sensitivity scores;
Qs={qs1,qs2,...qsi}

Step 5: For each query q in the sorted list of queries:
While (qsi<ε) do
{
maximum privacy budget =qi;
}

Step 6: If remaining_budget > 0
then distribute remaining_budget among q1,q2,...qn.

Step 7: For each query q in Q:
{
Perform the data analysis on dataset D with the allocated privacy budget for that query qi;
}

Step 8: Output the differentially private query results values for each query in Q.

Note: This algorithm provides a basic framework for balancing privacy and utility in differential privacy. The implementation might involve more sophisticated techniques, such as advanced privacy accounting mechanisms or adaptive budget allocation based on query sensitivity and data characteristics. Additionally, it's essential to evaluate the trade-offs and assess the allocated privacy budgets' impact on privacy protection and data utility to ensure an appropriate balance.

4.5 Experimental Results

Considering the scenario where we have two queries on a dataset of individuals' ages:

1. Count the number of individuals whose age is above 70.
2. Calculate the average age of the individuals.

We will use a simple privacy mechanism of Laplace noise addition for both queries. The sensitivity of the count query is 1 (since adding or removing an individual can change the count by at most 1), and the sensitivity of the average query is the maximum absolute difference between any two ages in the dataset.

Let's assume the global privacy budget ε is set to 1.0.

1. Privacy Budget Allocation:

   For the count query (ε_1):
   Since the sensitivity is 1, we can allocate the entire global budget ε (1.0) to the count query: ε_1 = 1.0.

   For the average query (ε_2):
   Assume the sensitivity of the average query is 10 (this value may vary based on the dataset).
   We allocate a portion of the remaining budget (ε - ε_1 = 1.0 - 1.0 = 0.0) to the average query: ε_2 = 0.0.

2. Noisy Data Analysis:

   For the count query:
   Let's say the true count of individuals above 60 is 75.
   We add Laplace noise to the true count using ε_1:

   Noisy count (N_1) = 75 + Laplace(0, 1/ε_1) = 75 + Laplace(0, 1) (assuming ε_1 = 1.0).

   For the average query:
   Let's say the true average age is 50.
   We add Laplace noise to the true average using ε_2:

   Noisy average (N_2) = 50 + Laplace(0, 10/ε_2) = 50 + Laplace(0, ∞) (assuming ε_2 = 0.0).

4.5.1 Interpretations of the Results

1. The count query provides a noisy count of individuals above 60 (N_1) centered around the true count of 75.

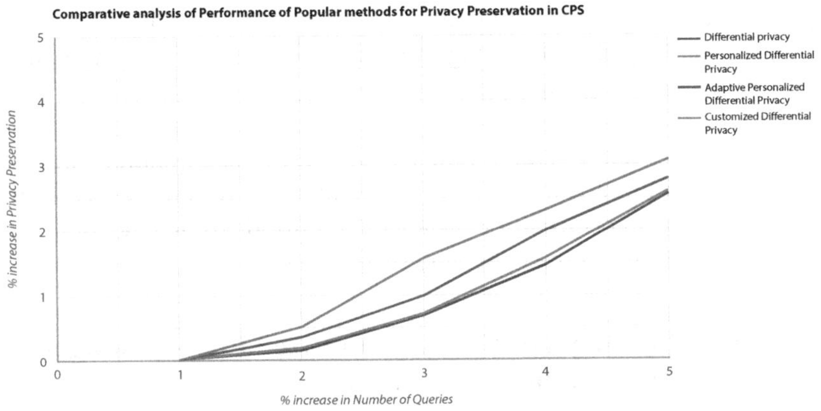

Figure 4.1 Comparative analysis of performance of current popular methods.

2. The average query provides a noisy average age (N_2), essentially the same as the true average age of 50, since no privacy budget was allocated to this query.

It may be noted that the above is a simplified representation, and in practice, the privacy budget allocation and noise addition can be more complex. The noise values will depend on the specific mechanism used and the values of ε_1 and ε_2 in the customized differential privacy setting.

Figure 4.1 shows that the proposed method of customized differential privacy outperforms the currently popular methods when the percentage

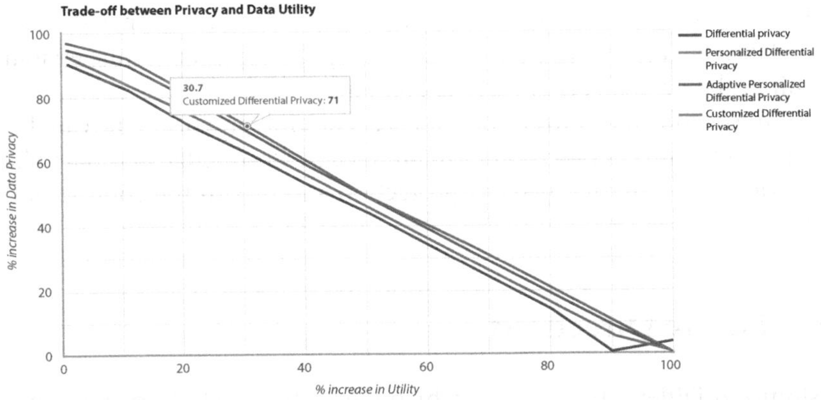

Figure 4.2 Plot showing trade-off between privacy and data utility of popular mechanisms for privacy preservation.

of queries increases to four times and maintains the highest degree of privacy preservation. The percentage improvement when compared to its nearest competitor is about 0.40%.

Figure 4.2 shows that the proposed method maintains an optimal balance between privacy and data utility by maintaining a balance point at a 30% increase in privacy and a nearly 71% increase in data utility so that the cyber-physical entities' functionality does not degrade over time. This impacts the usability of the cyber-physical system.

4.5.2 The Advantages of Using Customized Privacy Budgets are Evident in the Following Ways

Enhanced Privacy Protection: Tailoring privacy budgets allows us to allocate stronger privacy guarantees to more sensitive queries, ensuring that susceptible information remains well-protected. This granular approach prevents over- or under-provisioning of privacy, which can occur with a global privacy budget in traditional differential privacy.
Improved Data Utility: By allocating appropriate privacy budgets to each query, customized differential privacy preserves data utility better than a one-size-fits-all approach. Less sensitive queries can receive higher budgets, reducing the noise added to their results and improving the accuracy of the analysis.
Flexible Trade-offs: Customized privacy budgets enable data custodians to make flexible trade-offs between privacy and data utility, allowing them to adapt the level of privacy protection to the specific needs of each query and application.
Real-World Applicability: Customized differential privacy is highly applicable in real-world scenarios where multiple queries are performed on sensitive datasets. It provides a practical way to protect privacy while enabling meaningful data analysis in various domains.
Domain-Specific Optimization: Researchers and practitioners can fine-tune privacy budgets based on domain-specific knowledge and data characteristics, ensuring that privacy protection aligns with the context of the analysis.

4.6 Future Directions

Customized Differential Privacy, which tailors the level of privacy protection to individual data points or specific groups within a dataset, offers personalized privacy guarantees. However, it also comes with certain limitations that must be carefully considered.

Some of the main limitations of customized differential privacy are as follows:

1. Complexity: Implementing customized differential privacy can be complex and computationally demanding. Customizing privacy budgets for individual data points or groups requires additional computational overhead, especially for large datasets and complex queries [29]. This complexity can impact the scalability and efficiency of privacy-preserving data analysis.
2. Privacy-Utility Trade-offs: Customized differential privacy introduces more complex trade-offs between privacy protection and data utility. The noise level added to each data point depends on its sensitivity, affecting the overall data analysis accuracy. Striking the right balance between privacy and data utility for each data point becomes challenging and requires careful optimization [30].
3. Data Aggregation Challenges: Combining results from queries with varying privacy budgets can pose challenges in data aggregation and analysis. The noise characteristics introduced during privacy protection may influence the aggregation process and the accuracy of the final analysis results.
4. Interpretability: Customized differential privacy can produce less interpretable results than a uniform privacy approach. When privacy budgets vary across data points or groups, it becomes harder to understand the impact of privacy protection on individual data contributions.
5. Communication Overhead: In systems where customized differential privacy is employed, there might be a need for additional communication overhead to negotiate and manage privacy budgets for each data point [31]. This overhead can become significant, particularly in distributed or decentralized systems.
6. User Acceptance and Trust: Users may have concerns or reservations about the differential privacy mechanism and the varying levels of privacy protection applied to their data. Ensuring user acceptance and building trust in the privacy-preserving process may require clear communication and transparency about the privacy-utility trade-offs.

7. Regulatory Compliance: Compliance with privacy regulations can be more challenging in customized differential privacy setups. Demonstrating adherence to privacy guidelines and ensuring that individual data protections align with specific privacy budgets may require additional effort.
8. Robustness against Inference Attacks: Customized differential privacy might be more susceptible to inference attacks that extract sensitive information from multiple queries or responses with varying privacy budgets [32]. Robustness against such attacks needs to be carefully evaluated and addressed.
9. Data Sparsity: In datasets with sparse or limited data points, customizing privacy budgets for each data point can lead to noise dominance, reducing the data utility significantly.

Customized differential privacy offers personalized privacy guarantees, but it introduces complexities, challenges in data aggregation, and a need for careful optimization of privacy-utility trade-offs. Addressing these limitations requires a thoughtful design, efficient implementation, and transparency in the privacy mechanisms to ensure adequate privacy protection while maintaining data utility and user trust.

While the field was relatively new then, there were several potential future directions of research that researchers could explore to advance customized differential privacy further. Some of these directions include [29]:

1. Advanced Privacy Accounting: Develop more sophisticated privacy accounting methods to accurately measure and quantify the privacy guarantees provided by customized differential privacy. This involves understanding the interplay between privacy budgets, sensitivity, and noise addition for various queries and data distributions.
2. Privacy Budget Optimization: Investigate methods to optimize the allocation of privacy budgets for different queries to maximize data utility while ensuring strong privacy protection. This could involve dynamic budget allocation based on the data characteristics, query workload, or the privacy requirements of different users.
3. Privacy-Accuracy Trade-offs: Study the trade-offs between privacy protection and data accuracy in customized differential privacy. Explore techniques for fine-tuning these trade-offs to strike an optimal balance based on specific application requirements.

4. Query Complexity and Sensitivity Analysis: Investigate how the complexity of queries affects their sensitivity and privacy budget allocation. Explore ways to handle complex queries more efficiently while maintaining privacy guarantees.
5. Differential Privacy for Machine Learning: Extend customized differential privacy to machine learning, where multiple queries and computations are involved in training models on sensitive data. Research on customized privacy mechanisms for machine learning can enable privacy-preserving model training without sacrificing utility.
6. Privacy for Time-Series Data: Explore customized differential privacy techniques for time-series data, where the sensitivity of queries might vary over time. This includes developing privacy mechanisms that account for temporal dependencies in the data.
7. Integration with Other Privacy Techniques: Investigate how customized differential privacy can be integrated with other privacy-enhancing technologies, such as federated learning, secure multi-party computation, and homomorphic encryption, to achieve stronger privacy guarantees in complex scenarios.
8. Real-World Case Studies: Conduct case studies and practical implementations of customized differential privacy in real-world applications to evaluate its effectiveness, scalability, and usability in various domains, such as healthcare, finance, and social sciences.
9. Privacy for Graph Data: Explore customized differential privacy for graph data, addressing challenges related to graph structure and preserving privacy while allowing for meaningful analysis of the underlying network.
10. Theoretical Foundations: Develop a deeper theoretical understanding of customized differential privacy, including formal proofs of its properties, composition theorems, and privacy amplification techniques.

These future research directions have the potential to enrich the field of customized differential privacy, making it more practical, robust, and applicable to a wide range of data analysis scenarios while ensuring individuals' privacy protection. Remember that progress in this area might have occurred beyond my last update, so it's essential to consult the latest research literature for the most recent advancements in customized differential privacy.

4.7 Conclusion

The research work presented to customize the privacy budgets for a CPS stakeholder motivates us to work further in the direction of the impact of privacy factors on the type of queries and types of datasets maintained. In the future, we plan to extend the work to distributed databases where the query results are obtained after optimizing the query in terms of local and global queries. Nevertheless, the proposed approach outperformed its nearest competitors regarding accuracy and data utility by an appreciable amount. The proposed approach also has a few inherent challenges like accurate sensitivity analysis, optimization of privacy budget allocation, and privacy amplification techniques. Further research will address such issues. By adjusting the privacy guarantees to the specific needs of each query, the proposed mechanism unleashes new aspects for meaningful data analysis while safeguarding individuals' sensitive information. Given the evolving nature of the modern data-driven world, where privacy is essential in CPS applications, the proposed mechanism will continue to grow to more significant bounds.

References

1. Hassan, M.U., Rehmani, M.H., Chen, J., Differential privacy techniques for cyber-physical systems: a survey. *IEEE Commun. Surv. Tutorials*, 22, 1, 746–789, 2019.
2. Ruggles, S. *et al.*, Differential privacy and census data: Implications for social and economic research. *AEA Papers Proc.*, 109, pp. 403–08, 2019, American Economic Association, 2014 Broadway, Suite 305, Nashville, TN 37203.
3. Yang, M. *et al.*, Local differential privacy and its applications: A comprehensive survey, arXiv preprint arXiv:2008.03686, 2020.
4. Bhattacharjee, A., Badsha, S., Sengupta, S., Personalized privacy preservation for smart grid. *2021 IEEE International Smart Cities Conference (ISC2)*, IEEE, 2021.
5. Chen, X., Miao, S., Wang, Y., Differential privacy in personalized pricing with nonparametric demand models, arXiv preprint arXiv:2109.04615, 2021.
6. Xu, C., Ding, A.S., Liao, S.S., A privacy-preserving recommendation method based on multi-objective optimisation for mobile users. *Int. J. Bio-Inspired Comput.*, 16, 1, 23–32, 2020.
7. Papernot, N. and Steinke, T., Hyperparameter tuning with renyi differential privacy, arXiv preprint arXiv:2110.03620, 2021.
8. Kartal, H.B., Liu, X., Li, X.-B., Differential privacy for the vast majority. *ACM Trans. Manage. Inf. Syst. (TMIS)*, 10, 2, 1–15, 2019.

9. Cui, L. *et al.*, Improving data utility through game theory in personalized differential privacy. *J. Comput. Sci. Technol.*, 34, 272–286, 2019.
10. Bebensee, B., Local differential privacy: a tutorial, arXiv preprint arXiv:1907.11908, 2019.
11. Jiang, B. *et al.*, Differential privacy for industrial internet of things: Opportunities, applications, and challenges. *IEEE Internet Things J.*, 8, 13, 10430–10451, 2021.
12. Zhao, Y. and Chen, J., A survey on differential privacy for unstructured data content. *ACM Comput. Surv. (CSUR)*, 54, 10s, 1–28, 2022.
13. Ji, T. and Li, P., Less is More: Revisiting Gaussian Mechanism for Differential Privacy, arXiv preprint arXiv:2306.02256, 2023.
14. Zhang, M., Liu, X., Yin, L., Sensitivity estimation for differentially private query processing, arXiv preprint arXiv:2304.09546, 2023.
15. Ebadi, H., Sands, D., Schneider, G., Differential privacy: Now it's getting personal. *ACM Sigplan Not.*, 50, 1, 69–81, 2015.
16. Dankar, F.K. and El Emam, K., Practicing differential privacy in health care: A review. *Trans. Data Priv.*, 6, 1, 35–67, 2013.
17. Tang, J. *et al.*, Privacy loss in apple's implementation of differential privacy on macos 10.12, arXiv preprint arXiv:1709.02753, 2017.
18. Dandekar, A., Basu, D., Bressan, S., Differential privacy at risk: Bridging randomness and privacy budget, arXiv preprint arXiv:2003.00973, 2020.
19. Jorgensen, Z., Yu, T., Cormode, G., Conservative or liberal? Personalized differential privacy. *2015 IEEE 31St international conference on data engineering*, IEEE, 2015.
20. Niu, B. *et al.*, AdaPDP: Adaptive personalized differential privacy. *IEEE INFOCOM 2021-IEEE Conference on Computer Communications*, IEEE, 2021.
21. Tian, F. *et al.*, A novel personalized differential privacy mechanism for trajectory data publication. *2017 International Conference on Networking and Network Applications (NaNA)*, IEEE, 2017.
22. Zhang, Y. *et al.*, APDP: Attack-proof personalized differential privacy model for a smart home. *IEEE Access*, 7, 166593–166605, 2019.
23. Tang, P. *et al.*, Marginal Release Under Multi-party Personalized Differential Privacy. *Joint European Conference on Machine Learning and Knowledge Discovery in Databases*, Springer Nature Switzerland, Cham, 2022.
24. Li, S., Ji, X., You, W., A personalized differential privacy protection method for repeated queries. *2019 IEEE 4th International Conference on Big Data Analytics (ICBDA)*, IEEE, 2019.
25. Machanavajjhala, A., He, X., Hay, M., Differential privacy in the wild: A tutorial on current practices & open challenges. *Proceedings of the 2017 ACM International Conference on Management of Data*, 2017.
26. Lee, J. and Clifton, C., How much is enough? choosing ε for differential privacy. *Information Security: 14th International Conference, ISC 2011, Proceedings 14*, Xi'an, China, October 26-29, 2011, Springer, Berlin Heidelberg, 2011.

27. Ye, Q. and Hu, H., Local differential privacy: Tools, challenges, and opportunities. *International conference on web information systems engineering*, Springer Singapore, Singapore, 2020.
28. Hassan, M.U., Rehmani, M.H., Chen, J., Differential privacy techniques for cyber physical systems: a survey. *IEEE Commun. Surv. Tutorials*, 22, 1, 746–789, 2019.
29. Shrivastava, G., *et al.* (Eds.), *New age analytics: Transforming the internet through machine learning, IoT, and trust modeling*, CRC Press, Nashville, TN, 2020.
30. Shrivastava, G., Gupta, D., Sharma, K. (Eds.), *Cyber Crime and Forensic Computing: Modern Principles, Practices, and Algorithms*, De Gruyter, Berlin, Germany, 2021.
31. Khari, M. *et al.*, Role of cyber security in today's scenario, in: *Detecting and mitigating robotic cyber security risks*, pp. 177–191, IGI Global, Hershey, PA, 2017.
32. Shrivastava, G. *et al.*, Role of cyber security and cyber forensics in India, in: *Handbook of Research on Network Forensics and Analysis Techniques*, pp. 143–161, IGI Global, Hershey, PA, 2018.

5

Securing the Future: Emerging Threats and Countermeasures in Cryptography

Debosree Ghosh[1]*, Kishore Ghosh[1], Chandrima Chakraborty[2], Atanu Datta[3] and Somsubhra Gupta[3]

[1]Department of CSE, Shree Ramkrishna Institute of Science and Technology, West Bengal, India
[2]Department of Electrical and Computer Engineering, The Ohio State University, Columbus, OH, USA
[3]School of Computer Science, Swami Vivekananda University, Barrackpore, West Bengal, India

Abstract
The emergence of quantum computing, cryptanalysis, and the Internet of Things (IoT) have presented new hurdles for cryptographic systems. These threats seriously threaten the security of cryptographic systems. Researchers are developing novel countermeasures, such as post-quantum cryptography, which aims to design encryption algorithms resistant to quantum computing attacks. Efficient hardware security modules and secure implementation practices are also crucial. Rigorous testing and validation processes are also being implemented to ensure the robustness and reliability of cryptographic systems. A comprehensive approach, including critical management practices, secure protocols, and development methodologies, is essential for building resilient cryptographic systems. By adopting these advancements, organizations can improve data security and maintain information confidentiality in an ever-changing digital world.

***Keywords*:** Quantum threat, post-quantum algorithms, cryptanalysis techniques, side-channel vulnerabilities, fault-tolerant implementations, hardware security modules (HSMs), key management practices, quantum key distribution (QKD)

**Corresponding author*: debosree_ghosh@yahoo.co.in

Kavita Sharma, Vishnu Sharma, Parma Nand, Anil Kumar Sagar and Gulshan Shrivastava (eds.) Securing the Digital Frontier: Threats and Advanced Techniques in Security and Forensics, (91–108)

5.1 Introduction

Data and communication security are vital in the information era and the shift to digital media. Cryptography is the foundation of secure communication because it shields personal information from tampering and unauthorized access. However, as technology advances, cryptographic systems become more vulnerable. The emerging threats to cryptography are discussed in this chapter, along with the precautions being developed to preserve secure communication in the future. Knowing the weaknesses and implementing the most recent advancements will help us protect sensitive data and communications against ever-evolving attackers. We can protect the future by integrating state-of-the-art cryptographic techniques, secure implementations, and an all-encompassing security strategy and pave the way for a more robust and safer digital environment.

Data security has been seriously threatened by the advent of quantum computing, which has caused significant worries for traditional encryption techniques in recent years. Post-quantum cryptography is a dynamic area of research that endeavors to offset the threat posed by quantum computing by developing cryptographic techniques resistant to quantum attacks. Apart from the dangers of quantum computing, cryptanalysis keeps developing and regularly looks for weaknesses in cryptographic algorithms. Safe hardware and software techniques must be implemented to strengthen cryptographic systems. Side-channel attacks and fault attacks take advantage of implementation flaws.

5.2 Quantum Computing and Post-Quantum Cryptography

Quantum computing and post-quantum cryptography are two linked fields that have the power to change the field of data security drastically. Quantum computing is a new paradigm in computing that processes information using the ideas of quantum physics. Unlike classical computers, quantum computers employ quantum bits, or qubits, which can exist in several states simultaneously because of superposition and entanglement. Bits (0s and 1s) are the basic unit of information used in classical computers. The likelihood of defeating popular cryptographic algorithms like RSA and ECC (Elliptic Curve Cryptography) increases as quantum computer technology develops. As quantum computing technology evolves, it will be possible to tackle issues like discrete logarithms and integer factorization efficiently, making standard encryption techniques susceptible.

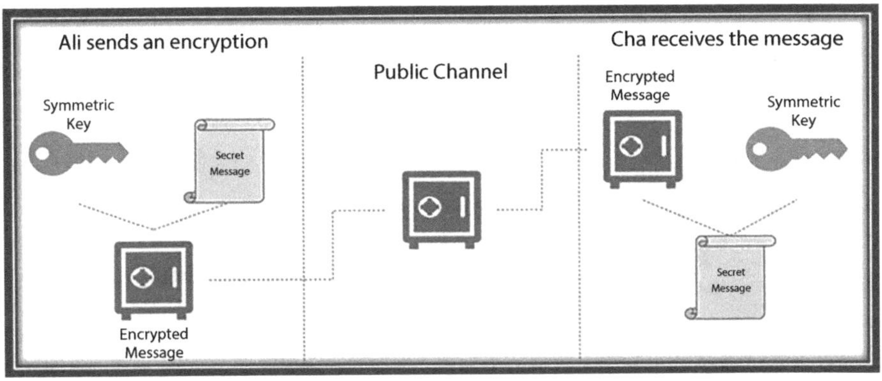

Figure 5.1 Post-quantum cryptography.

Figure 5.1 shows the various cryptographic algorithms developed to withstand the threats posed by quantum computing. It highlights the key characteristics and comparative advantages of post-quantum cryptography techniques over traditional cryptographic methods. This figure provides visual evidence of how these advanced algorithms are designed to secure data against the computational power of quantum machines, which could potentially compromise existing encryption schemes.

Post-quantum cryptography, also known as quantum-resistant cryptography, aims to develop cryptographic techniques impervious to attacks from both traditional and quantum computers in response to the threat presented by quantum computing. It provides a practical foundation for safe interaction in the quantum era by employing mathematical riddles that challenge attackers with quantum skills. Many post-quantum encryption techniques have been proposed, including multivariate quadratic equations (MQ) cryptography, code-based, hash-based, and lattice-based techniques. Compatibility with previous generations and interoperability must be adequately considered when converting to post-quantum cryptography. In the digital age, sensitive information security and communication primarily depend on the rapidly developing fields of post-quantum encryption and quantum computing.

5.3 Cryptanalysis: Cracking the Code

Cryptanalysis, or "cracking the code," is the art and science of dissecting cryptographic systems to find flaws and vulnerabilities that allow outsiders to get encrypted data. Information security is ensured by cryptography, but cryptanalysis is a countermeasure that tests and enhances the security of cryptographic algorithms, protocols, or implementations to allow illegal access to plaintext.

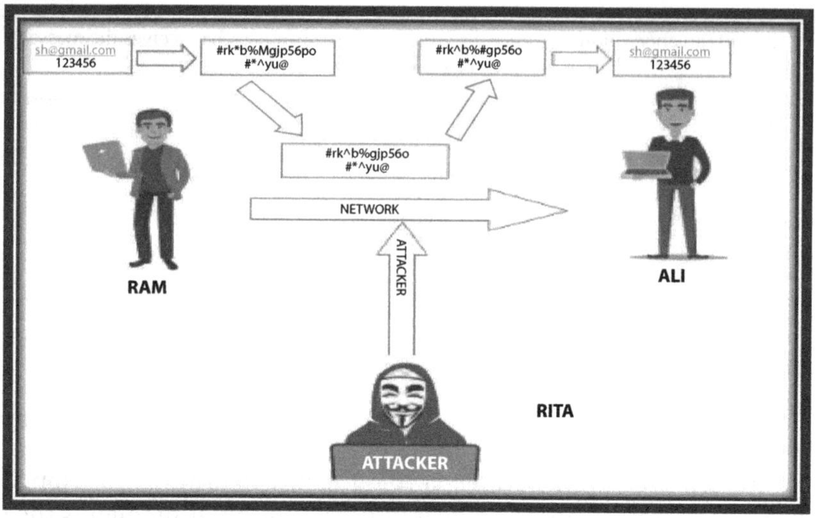

Figure 5.2 Cryptanalysis.

Figure 5.2 illustrates the different techniques used in cryptanalysis to break various encryption schemes. The figure provides a detailed view of the methods employed to exploit vulnerabilities in cryptographic algorithms, including both classical and modern approaches. This visual representation helps to understand the challenges faced in securing cryptographic systems and underscores the importance of ongoing advancements in cryptographic research.

Substitution ciphers were used to hide messages, which is where the history of cryptanalysis began. Cryptanalysts have been essential to the development of cryptographic techniques because they have been involved in espionage, military tactics, and intelligence operations throughout history. Famous examples include breaking the German Enigma code during World War II and cracking the Lorenz cipher by British code breakers at Bletchley Park.

Moderncryptanalysis:

- ***Brute Force Attack*:**
  Attempting all possible combinations of keys until the correct one is found. While effective against weak keys, it becomes impractical for vital cryptographic keys with large key spaces.
- ***Mathematical Analysis*:**
  Leveraging mathematical principles to find weaknesses in cryptographic algorithms or exploit implementation flaws.

- ***Known Plaintext Attack:***
  Using plaintext-cipher text combinations can infer details about the encryption procedure and possibly even uncover the key.
- ***Chosen Plaintext Attack:***
  Gaining access to the ciphertexts for specific plaintexts of the attacker's choice to study patterns and vulnerabilities.
- ***Differential Cryptanalysis:***
  Analyzing the differences in plaintext-ciphertext pairs to deduce patterns in the encryption process.
- ***Side-Channel Attacks:***
  Accidental data revealed by physical attributes, like timing or power usage, can be used to deduce the cryptographic key.

Cryptographic algorithms are rigorously tested and examined, frequently subjected to peer review and public scrutiny, to protect against cryptanalysis. Standards and methods for encryption are updated to maintain their resistance to new threats as cryptanalytic techniques advance.

Cryptanalysis is essential to the development of cryptographic systems because it promotes innovation and boosts security. Cryptographers can protect communication against unwanted access, preserve the privacy and trust of people and organizations, and guarantee the safety and security of sensitive data in an increasingly linked world by anticipating potential vulnerabilities and taking proactive measures to fix them.

5.4 Side-Channel Attacks: Stealthy and Insidious

One kind of cryptanalytic technique called a side-channel attack takes advantage of unintentional data leaks that occur during the physical implementation of a cryptographic system. These attacks take advantage of information exposed to the side channels during cryptographic calculations, like changes in time, power consumption, and electromagnetic emissions. They can be executed remotely, are frequently stealthy and sneaky, and function regardless of the cryptographic techniques' strength. Timing attacks and power analysis attacks are two common types of side-channel attacks.

Because side-channel assaults are feasible and resource-constrained, they pose a particular risk. To counter side-channel attacks, a comprehensive security plan is required. Side-channel leakage can be significantly decreased by hardware security modules (HSMs), and during cryptographic operations, protections like masking and blinding add randomization and hide critical data.

System designers, cryptographers, and security researchers must collaborate to create reliable and secure implementations. Cryptographers and system designers can strengthen the resilience of cryptographic systems against covert threats, protecting data secrecy and upholding confidence in the digital era by implementing secure implementation techniques and thorough evaluations.

5.5 Fault Attacks: Exploiting Implementation Weaknesses

Fault attacks are advanced cyberattacks that use implementation flaws in cryptographic systems. Fault attacks use flaws in how cryptographic algorithms are implemented in hardware or software, as opposed to conventional attacks that aim for the theoretical underpinnings of these algorithms.

Fault attacks' central tenet is to purposefully inject "faults"—controlled errors—into the cryptographic system. Various techniques, such as tampering with the power supply, changing the clock signals, or putting the hardware in harsh environments, can be used to introduce these defects. Attackers hope to gain insights into private data by analyzing how these inserted flaws affect the cryptographic computation.

Figure 5.3 illustrates the different types of fault attacks on cryptographic systems. The figure provides a comprehensive overview of how various fault injection methods, such as voltage glitches and electromagnetic interference, can compromise the integrity of cryptographic operations. This visual representation highlights the mechanisms through which attackers exploit faults to bypass security measures and gain unauthorized access to encrypted data.

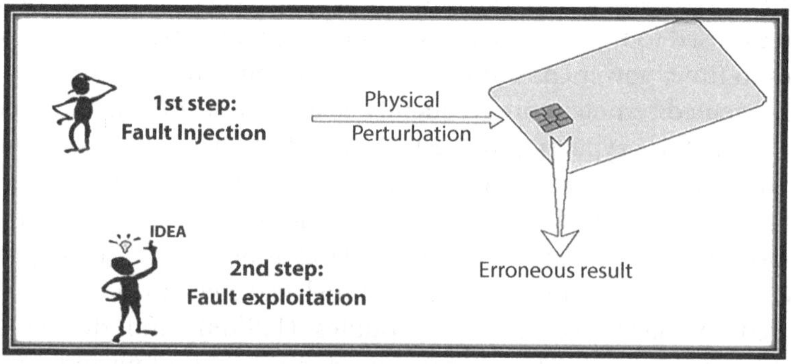

Figure 5.3 Fault attacks.

There are two primary categories of fault attacks:

5.5.1 Permanent Fault Attacks

In these attacks, the introduced fault persists throughout the cryptographic computation. This could involve permanently altering a specific bit or value within the hardware, causing consistent erroneous behavior.

5.5.2 Transient Fault Attacks

These attacks introduce a fault that is temporary and occurs during a specific instance within the cryptographic computation. Attackers carefully time their interventions to exploit the altered behavior precisely when it can reveal helpful information.

Fault attacks can compromise a range of cryptographic operations, including encryption, decryption, and digital signatures. Their effectiveness stems from their ability to target vulnerabilities that might not be apparent in the design of cryptographic algorithms themselves but become apparent during execution.

Fault attack defense calls for a multifaceted strategy. Implementers must incorporate robust redundancy and error-detection techniques into their designs for cryptographic systems. Even when flaws are introduced, methods like error-correcting codes and cryptographic redundancy can assist in guaranteeing the integrity of cryptographic operations.

Furthermore, employing advanced analysis methods like side-channel analysis and secure hardware components might strengthen the resistance of cryptographic systems to these assaults.

Fault attacks highlight how important it is to create robust cryptographic algorithms and make sure they are executed securely. Finding and addressing vulnerabilities throughout the installation phase could help us maintain confidence in electronic transactions and communication, safeguard sensitive data, and significantly increase the overall safety of cryptographic systems.

5.6 Hardware Security Modules (HSMS)

Hardware security modules (HSMs) are specially designed hardware components made to manage cryptographic keys, carry out cryptographic operations, and guarantee the general security of sensitive data in a safe and impenetrable environment.

Figure 5.4 provides a detailed depiction of hardware security modules (HSMs) and their role in securing cryptographic processes. The figure

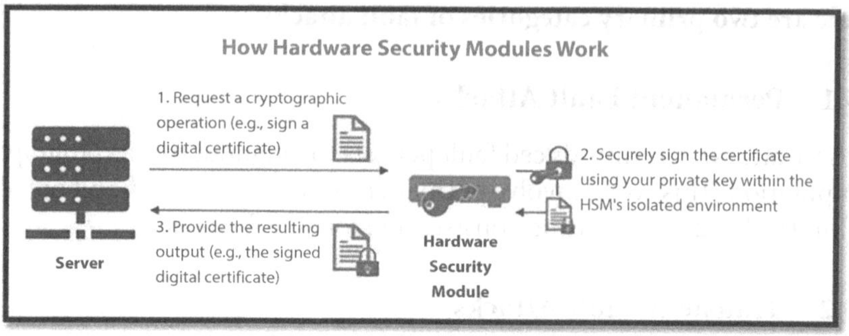

Figure 5.4 Hardware security modules.

highlights the architectural components and functional elements of HSMs, illustrating how they protect cryptographic keys and perform encryption and decryption operations in a secure environment. This visual aid underscores the importance of HSMs in safeguarding sensitive information and ensuring robust security in various applications.

5.6.1 HSMs Offer a Range of Features that Make Them a Critical Component of Modern Information Security Systems

Cryptographic keys are generated, stored, and managed securely by HSMs. Digital signatures, encryption, decoding, and other cryptographic processes all require these keys. HSMs guarantee that keys are shielded against manipulation and unwanted access. HSMs carry out a range of cryptographic tasks, such as digital signatures, hashing, encryption, and decryption. Since these processes take place inside the HSM's secure perimeter, it is more difficult for hackers to intercept or alter private information. Robust cryptography functions frequently depend on superior random numbers. HSMs offer a reliable source of randomness for creating safe keys and initialization vectors.

To guard against unwanted access or manipulation, HSMs are constructed with physical tamper-resistant safeguards. They might have sensors to identify physical assaults, such as prying open the gadget or tampering with its parts. Strict access controls are implemented by HSMs to guarantee that the device can only be used by authorized users or apps. It is frequently necessary to use multi-factor authentication to access cryptographic features.

All activities, including crucial usage, operations carried out and attempted security breaches, are recorded in logs kept by HSMs. Forensic analysis, compliance, and monitoring all depend on these audit logs.

HSMs connect to external systems through secure communication protocols. This guarantees the confidentiality and security of any data transferred between the HSM and other components.

5.6.2 HSMs Applications in Various Industries and Scenarios

To safeguard sensitive financial data, manage encryption keys, and secure transactions, HSMs are widely employed in banking and other financial institutions. To guarantee the integrity and authenticity of electronic documents and transactions, HSMs are essential for creating and managing digital signatures. Digital certificates, which are necessary for secure Internet communication, are issued and managed by Certificate Authorities (CAs) using HSMs. Organizations can benefit from secure key management in cloud deployments using cloud based HSMs, which guarantee the secrecy of cryptographic credentials even in virtualized environments.

5.7 Secure Implementations: From Theory to Reality

Converting cryptography theory into practical applications requires secure implementations. They entail picking suitable cryptographic algorithms that meet the application's security requirements, comprehending their advantages and disadvantages, and adhering to particular coding standards. To maintain security, developers must also foresee and fix side-channel vulnerabilities. To ensure that the system is functioning as intended, thorough testing—which includes security assessments, unit testing, and integration testing—is necessary. Secure creation of keys, storage, and distribution are crucial since even a single security breach can compromise the system's overall security. To handle new threats and keep a solid security posture, regular updates, patches, and vulnerability monitoring are required. It is difficult to strike a balance between usability and robust security measures; therefore, companies need to work with professionals in development, cybersecurity, and cryptography to bridge the knowledge gap. Secure implementations effectively translate theoretical advantages into operational safeguards, maintaining data availability, confidentiality, and integrity in the face of modern cyber threats.

5.8 A Holistic Approach to Cryptography

A holistic approach to cryptography encompasses a comprehensive and interconnected strategy that goes beyond individual cryptographic techniques, integrating them into a broader framework of security, risk management, and operational efficiency. This approach recognizes that cryptography is just one component of a multifaceted security ecosystem.

It is critical to comprehend the particular risk profile of each firm. This entails locating necessary resources, possible dangers, and weak points. These realizations guide the use of cryptography where it is most required. The overall security architecture should smoothly include cryptographic methods. Building a layered defense entails working in tandem with other security measures like firewalls, intrusion detection systems, and access controls. The organization's unique security requirements should be taken into consideration while selecting the appropriate cryptographic algorithms and protocols. This selection is influenced by various factors, including strength, efficiency, and potential vulnerabilities. Using coding standards, best practices, and frequent code reviews to find weaknesses that attackers could exploit are all part of secure implementation. Secure key management is essential to efficient cryptography. It covers the creation, distribution, rotation, storage, and disposal of safe keys. Key management is necessary for the duration of their lives.

To identify security breaches, cryptography solutions must be monitored in real-time. Cryptography and data protection laws frequently overlap, so making sure they adhere to industry standards and legal requirements requires a thorough plan. Every stakeholder, including developers and end users, needs to be aware of how cryptography contributes to security. Cryptographic procedures must be continuously assessed and modified due to a changing threat landscape. If third-party solutions are employed, they must go through a rigorous assessment process to guarantee that they satisfy security specifications and complement the goals of the organization. Enhancing adoption and reducing dangerous workarounds require balancing security measures with user demands. To match cryptographic measures to the organization's objectives and risk profile, a comprehensive approach necessitates cooperation between the IT, security, development, and management teams. Fast action, containment, recovery, and lessons gained are guaranteed by a well-defined incident response plan. Sustaining security requires regular audits, updates, and retirement of antiquated protocols. Organizations can secure sensitive data, foster a culture of security awareness, make full use of encryption, and remain compliant with regulations by taking a comprehensive strategy.

5.9 Quantum Key Distribution (QKD)

With the use of cutting-edge cryptography technology called quantum key distribution (QKD), parties can share encryption keys in a safe and secure manner. It accomplishes this by applying ideas from quantum physics. Unlike typical encryption techniques that rely on complex mathematical calculations, QKD allows for a secure key exchange that is theoretically immune to eavesdropping.

To create a secure communication channel, QKD depends on the characteristics of quantum states, such as superposition and entanglement. It is only possible to replicate these situations by changing their characteristics, which makes any attempt at listening obvious. QKD makes use of the Heisenberg Uncertainty Principle, which asserts that it is impossible to measure two physical quantities precisely at the same time, such as momentum and location. This idea serves as the foundation for identifying any eavesdropping attempts. A phenomenon known as quantum entanglement occurs when particles, even when isolated by great distances, develop an innate correlation. Entanglement is used by QKD to establish a shared key among parties and identify any possible illegal access.

Figure 5.5 illustrates the principles and mechanisms of quantum key distribution (QKD). The figure provides a detailed overview of how QKD protocols utilize quantum mechanics to securely exchange encryption keys between parties. It highlights key elements such as the use of quantum entanglement and the measurement process, demonstrating how these techniques ensure secure communication even in the presence of potential eavesdroppers.

A key QKD protocol is the BB84 protocol, which was put forth by Charles Bennett and Gilles Brassard in 1984. It involves the transmission of qubits (quantum bits) with polarization states. RITA sends qubits encoded in randomly chosen bases, and RAM measures them in randomly chosen bases. After public discussion and error correction, they derive a shared key while detecting potential eavesdropping. In QKD, RITA transmits a sequence of qubits to RAM over a quantum channel. They then compare

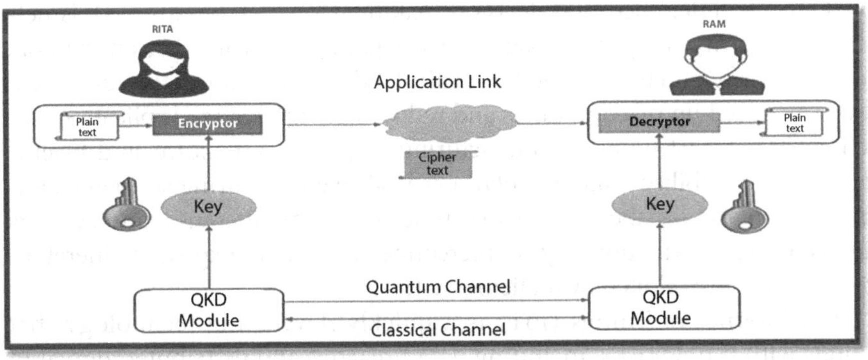

Figure 5.5 Quantum key distribution.

information about the bases used for encoding. Through error correction and privacy amplification, they derive a shared secret key while identifying any potential interception.

QKD offers an unparalleled degree of security and is founded on the fundamental principles of quantum physics. If these concepts hold true, then any attempt to listen in will unavoidably damage the quantum states, revealing the presence of an attacker. QKD systems are vulnerable to noise and channel loss, among other external factors. Cutting-edge technology, such as quantum repeaters and photon detectors, are needed for practical implementations to extend the reach of secure communication. With the potential to undermine conventional cryptographic techniques, quantum key distribution (QKD) offers great promise for communication security in the age of quantum computers. It creates the foundation for "quantum-safe" encryption, which guards against upcoming quantum attacks on data. The intriguing features of quantum mechanics present new difficulties for conventional encryption due to the capabilities of quantum computers; QKD promises a significant advancement in achieving robust data security by establishing secure communication channels impervious to eavesdropping.

5.10 Internet of Things in Cryptography

Cryptography is crucial for preserving the integrity, confidentiality, and resiliency of IoT ecosystems because the Internet of Things grows increasingly interconnected, and the requirement to defend against new threats increases. Internet of Things (IoT) devices can communicate with other systems worldwide through Bluetooth, cellular networks, Wi-Fi, and Low Power Wide Area Networks (LPWAN) since they are internet-connected. Using the vast amounts of data generated through Internet of Things devices can improve productivity, predictive maintenance, and decision making. However, because IoT is networked, security and privacy issues are brought up. Ensuring data encryption, device security, and user privacy are critical. Edge computing at the equipment level can speed up reaction times and reduce network stress. Applications for IoT include smart homes, manufacturing, logistics, agriculture, and healthcare. Interoperability standards play a crucial role in ensuring seamless communication and collaboration between devices from different manufacturers and ecosystems. The ubiquity of interconnected devices exposes vulnerabilities that can be exploited by malicious actors.

The Internet of Things (IoT) is a quickly developing technology that brings with it new risks, including data breaches and distributed denial of service (DDoS) assaults. An essential part of IoT security is cryptography, which is necessary to protect identity, data, and communication. It preserves the integrity of the ecosystem, authenticates and authorizes devices, and employs encryption to guarantee data secrecy. Quantum-resistant algorithms offer long-term security against adversaries, while techniques such as Transport Layer Security (TLS) safeguard data transfer. Moreover, cryptographic techniques guard against insider threats, guaranteeing that data manipulated by hacked systems cannot be altered. A secure IoT foundation requires cooperation between parties and adherence to cryptography best practices. It is imperative to maintain consistent upgrades and oversight of cryptographic implementations.

5.11 Artificial Intelligence in Cryptography

Artificial intelligence (AI) and encryption are bringing us a new era of secure communication and data security. By exploiting AI's processing power, capacity for pattern recognition, and flexibility, new security concerns are being addressed while traditional cryptographic techniques are being improved.

By locating holes and weaknesses in cryptographic systems, AI algorithms speed up the cryptanalysis process. This proactive strategy facilitates the early identification and mitigation of possible dangers. Models driven by AI help create and maintain cryptographic keys. This guarantees the generation of robust, erratic keys that are necessary for safe communication. Based on the properties of the data, AI algorithms dynamically modify the encryption and decryption procedures. Security and effectiveness are both improved by this modification.

AI can help in the design and development of quantum-resistant cryptography algorithms, protecting against potential future assaults as the threat posed by quantum computing grows. Artificial Intelligence is particularly good at spotting unusual patterns in encrypted network traffic, which makes it easier to detect possible attacks or illegal access early on.

AI helps create sophisticated cryptographic techniques that protect privacy, such as homomorphic encryption, which allows computations on encrypted data without jeopardizing privacy. By evaluating behavioral and biometric data, AI improves authentication techniques and guarantees robust user identity verification even if cryptographic keys are compromised. AI strengthens security against new threats by enabling real-time modifications to cryptographic settings based on changing threat environments. Artificial intelligence (AI) finds robust candidates and explores large solution spaces to speed up the search for post-quantum cryptography methods. The ability of AI to recognize patterns helps identify side-channel attacks, in which attackers breach security by leaking confidential information. AI's capacity for modeling and learning aids in the creation of novel cryptographic algorithms that prove more resistant to changing threats. AI optimizes intrusion detection and firewall systems, identifying irregular traffic patterns and potential threats within encrypted communications. The integration of AI in cryptography raises ethical concerns, including transparency, fairness, and accountability in decision-making processes.

5.12 Cryptarithmetic

A mathematical challenge called cryptarithmetic, often referred to as alphabetic or cryptarithms, involves performing arithmetic operations while utilizing letters or symbols to represent the numbers. The tricky part of answering the arithmetic equation is figuring out how the letters and numbers correspond. To make the equation true, the problem solver must determine the proper assignment of digits to letters. Each letter represents a different digit.

Constraint Satisfaction Problem (CSP)
The following problem comprehensively emphasizes the concept of constraint satisfaction.

S E N D
\+ M O R E
M O N E Y

Initial state:

1. Every letter has a unique value.
2. The challenge requires that the digit's total be displayed.

In the above problem, each letter represents a number (0-9), and the goal is to find the correct numerical order for the letters that make the equation valid.

- M=1, considering that the sum of two single-digit digits with carry cannot exceed 19.
- S=8 or 9, when S+M+C3> 9 to provide the carry; however, since M=1 and S+1+C3 >9, S+c3>8 and C3 can only be 1.

- O=0, Since S+M(1)+C3(<=1) must be at least 10 to generate carry and can be at most 11. But M is already 1, So O must be 0.
- Based on the value of C2, N=E or E+1. However, N and E cannot have the same values. N=E+1 and C2=1 as a result.
- N+R must be larger than 8 for C2 to equal 1. The total of N+R+C1 must also be greater than 9.
- Even with a carry-in, N+R cannot exceed 18, so be 9.

Crypto-arithmetic problems require logical reasoning, trial and error, and sometimes algebraic manipulation to solve. They act as entertaining brain teasers and have educational value in developing logical thinking and problem-solving skills.

5.13 The Road Ahead: Future Trends and Prospects

"The Road Ahead: Future Trends and Prospects in Securing the Future: Emerging Threats and Countermeasures in Cryptography" explores the future of cryptography, focusing on quantum-resistant evolution, homomorphic encryption, zero-knowledge proofs, and blockchain-cryptography nexus. Quantum-resistant encryption aims to counter quantum computing threats, while homomorphic encryption enhances data privacy and security. Zero-knowledge proofs enhance privacy in transactions and data sharing, benefiting industries like finance and healthcare. The fusion of cryptographic principles with blockchain technology revolutionizes data security and accountability.

AI-enhanced cryptanalysis and quantum key distribution (QKD) are revolutionizing cybersecurity by combining artificial intelligence and cryptographic analysis. AI's rapid pattern recognition and adaptive learning enhance cryptanalysis efficiency, driving faster threat identification and strengthening cryptographic defenses. QKD uses quantum principles to exchange cryptographic keys, addressing challenges like system stability and key distribution over long distances. Multi-party computation (MPC) transforms collaborative data analysis by enabling multiple parties to jointly compute over encrypted data, ensuring privacy and extracting valuable insights. Privacy-preserving technologies like differential privacy and secure enclaves enhance data analysis by safeguarding individual privacy.

Standardization and regulatory landscape in cryptography encompass globally recognized norms and legal frameworks, ensuring uniformity, compatibility, and best practices across cryptographic implementations. The quantum-safe transition strategy involves replacing vulnerable cryptographic systems with quantum-resistant alternatives, with user education and system validation ensuring a smooth transition. Empowered cybersecurity education equips individuals with knowledge and skills to navigate digital threats, fostering cyber hygiene habits and critical thinking.

Ethical cryptography ethics addressesdual use, privacy, and data protection issues while juggling security and responsible use. It encourages open-source cooperation, international standards, and user confidence, preparing for long-term security as quantum computing approaches. Ethical cryptography promotes a safe online setting that upholds individual privacy, human rights, and responsible innovation.

5.14 Conclusion

To conclude, "Securing the Future: Emerging Threats and Countermeasures in Cryptography" has illuminated the intricate interplay between cryptography, evolving threats, and the imperative for proactive countermeasures. From the quantum realm to AI, the multifaceted landscape demands continual adaptation.

This study emphasizes how crucial it is to stay ahead of emerging threats, whether by moral considerations, technology that protects privacy, or quantum-safe strategies. Policymakers, scholars, and professionals need to collaborate to plan a complete defense.

As technology develops, cryptography will always remain the foundation of data security and internet confidence. We provide the groundwork for a more dependable and secure digital future by promoting cybersecurity awareness, fostering creativity, and upholding moral principles. Upholding the principles of security and privacy while safeguarding information is crucial to the ongoing effort to secure the future in this interconnected society.

Bibliography

Journal Reference:

Kaafar, M.A. and Kamal, A.E., Securing the Future: Emerging Threats and Countermeasures in Cryptography. *IEEE Commun. Mag.*, 56, 72–78, 2018.

Zhang, X., Fan, X., Tang, X., Emerging Threats and Countermeasures in Cryptography: A Survey. *Secur. Privacy*, 17, 45–54, 2019.

Sadeghi, A., Dastjerdi, M.V., Shokri, R., Securing the Future of Cryptography: Emerging Threats and Countermeasures. *Advances in Cryptology - EUROCRYPT 2020*, 12105, 347–375.

Wang, X. and Yu, H., Quantum-Resistant Cryptography: A Survey. *Found. Trends Theor. Comput. Sci.*, 11, 1–139, 2016, arXiv: https://arxiv.org/abs/1504.07624.

Leurent, G. and Peyrin, T., Side-Channel Attacks: A Survey. *J. Cryptogr. Eng.*, 8, 239–269, 2018.

Patrascu, I.A., Bader, D.A., Malik, S., Hardware Trojans: A Survey. *ACM Comput. Surv.*, 46, 1–31, 2013.

McGrew, D.A., Peyrin, T., Courtois, N.T., Artificial Intelligence for Cryptography: A Survey. *Found. Trends Theor. Comput. Sci.*, 15, 1–119, 2020.

Waters, B., Secure Computation with Untrusted Devices: A Survey. *Found. Trends Theor. Comput. Sci.*, 7, 1–96, 2013.

Courtois, N.T., Klimov, A., Shoup, A., Post-Quantum Cryptography: A Survey. *Found. Trends Theor. Comput. Sci.*, 15, 1–95, 2019.

Peyrin, T. and Leurent, G., Cryptography for the Internet of Things: A Survey. *Found. Trends Netw.*, 12, 1–102, 2018.

Edited Volume:

Wiener, M.J., Fisher, M.J., Yung, M., *Securing the future: Emerging threats and countermeasures in cryptography*, Springer, Heidelberg, Germany, 2014.

Authored Book:

Anderson, R., *Security engineering: A guide to building dependable distributed systems*, 2nd ed. Pearson Education, Harlow, England, 2008.

Schneier, B., *Applied Cryptography: Protocols, Algorithms, and Source Code in C*, John Wiley & Sons, Hoboken, New Jersey, USA, 2011.

Katz, J. and Lindell, Y., *Introduction to modern cryptography*, 2nd ed. Chapman & Hall/CRC, Boca Raton, Florida, USA, 2014.

Chapter in Edited Volume:

Stinson, D.R., *Cryptography: Theory and practice*, 3rd ed. CRC Press, Boca Raton, Florida, USA, 2006.

Web Citation:

Cracking of Cryptographic Attack, URL: https://ijrpr.com/uploads/V4ISSUE5/IJRPR13303.pdf.

Cyber Crime and Forensic Computing: Modern Principles, Practices, and Algorithms, URL: https://www.degruyter.com/document/doi/10.1515/9783110677478/html.

Cyber Security in IoT-Based Cloud Computing: A Comprehensive Survey, URL: https://doi.org/10.3390/electronics11010016.

A Critical Cybersecurity Analysis and Future Research Directions for the Internet of Things: A Comprehensive Review, URL: https://doi.org/10.3390/s23084117.

6

Cyber Threats and Its Impact on Electronic Transactions

Ramalingam Dharmalingam* **and Vaishnavi Dharmalingam**

Majan University College, Muscat, Sultanate of Oman
Srinivasa Ramanujan Centre, SASTRA Deemed to be University, Kumbakonam, India

Abstract
Undisputedly, cyber threats and attacks are rising despite governments and organizations worldwide continuing to fight and contain them. Studies indicate that billions of dollars belonging to large financial organizations are being skimmed off by cyber-attacks across the globe. The COVID-19 pandemic has also accelerated digitalization and transformation, where people are going for cashless transactions. It is worth noting that the data of technologically savvy banks has also been breached in recent attempts. This phenomenon poses a question about who is responsible for cyber security and how to secure future transactions and build confidence among the stakeholders. The main topics of this chapter are the growth of digital transformation, the development of cyber threats, current cyberattacks, and the numerous frameworks and standards often employed globally to combat cyberattacks. Finally, it also suggests a comprehensive approach that needs to be followed by all the stakeholders in combating cyberattacks.

***Keywords*:** Cyberattacks, security of e-transactions, cybersecurity in e-banking

6.1 Introduction

Digital transformation has become a buzzword because it provides opportunities for increasing business efficiency and effective customer management by adapting customer intimacy.

**Corresponding author*: ramalingam.d@majancollege.edu.om

Kavita Sharma, Vishnu Sharma, Parma Nand, Anil Kumar Sagar and Gulshan Shrivastava (eds.) Securing the Digital Frontier: Threats and Advanced Techniques in Security and Forensics, (109–132)

To better serve their customers' distinctive requirements, businesses have understood the significance of customized information in shaping their goods, communication plans, and customer interactions. According to Chaturvedi *et al.*, in their 2021 study, recent research shows that the banking and financial services sector is expected to follow this general trend. Numerous financial transaction channels have emerged because of this paradigm change, offering clients a level of convenience in handling their finances that has never been possible. But simultaneously with this digital transition, the terrifying specter of cyber-attacks has emerged, possibly having catastrophic repercussions. Focusing on the consequences of financial transactions, this chapter aims to provide an in-depth knowledge of cybersecurity in digital transformation.

First, this introduction lays the groundwork for a thorough investigation of the complex link between digital transformation and its significant effects on the ever-changing environment of cyber threats. The author set out on a quest to discover the fundamentals of digital transformation. By doing this, some light is shed on how it has come to define today's commercial and societal spheres. It highlights how digital transformation has affected many businesses, causing a paradigm change in operational strategy and consumer interaction.

Second, a compelling story about the development of cyber threats is interspersed with crucial historical turning points. A thorough review of how cyber threats have developed over time, looking at how they now express themselves and even offering a few predictions about how the assault landscape may change. A fuller understanding of the constantly evolving techniques and strategies used by cybercriminals is made possible by this historical contextualization.

Third, the real-world effects of cyberattacks on the financial industry are covered in this chapter. How these threats affected financial institutions, the safety of client information, and the general health of the financial sector are also illustrated.

Then, this chapter focuses on the standards, protocols, and benchmarks that support cybersecurity activities. The author demonstrates how these precautions are essential for protecting the digital environment from the barrage of cyber threats and proposes establishing a multi-stakeholder collaborative approach to combating cyber risks. Further, the author states that this strategy promotes group efforts by several organizations, including enterprises, governments, and the cybersecurity community, to strengthen our defenses against a landscape of digital threats that are becoming increasingly sophisticated.

Overall, this chapter builds knowledge on the role of cybersecurity in digital transformation with a focus on financial transactions.

6.2 Digital Transformation and Cybersecurity

Digital transformation started as an option in the 1990s to promote digital products, services, and media. Mass media advertising campaigns over digital channels were considered desirable during that time [1]. The surge of mobile devices and social media from 2000 to 2015 drastically changed consumer habits. Customers have started using digital channels to communicate with businesses since they provide quick responses and 24/7 availability [2].

Nowadays, the trend is to use artificial intelligence-based mobile apps and create business value. In this process, businesses try to collect customers' data using cookies to get insight into customer behavior and sentiment, claiming to provide an improved customer experience. Unfortunately, this process also collects sensitive personal data and metadata about the customers and uses it for business development and targeted marketing activities [3].

As various dimensions of society become increasingly connected and digitally transformed, there is a growing risk of cybercrime [4]. Cybercriminals exploit multiple devices, from complex industrial machines to simple, smart home devices, which are Internet-connected, otherwise called the Internet of Things (IoT). The inherent vulnerabilities, such as non-regular software updates and inefficient security controls, enable hackers to exploit the weak spots of such devices [5]. Studies state that successful cyberattacks can have devastating consequences for individuals and businesses. Businesses sometimes face substantial economic losses, which can even result in bankruptcy. According to the "The Top Global Business Risks for 2021 report" (2021), cyber incidents are globally ranked as the third most significant business risk [6]. Cyber-attacks damage not only a particular business or country but also the world. A study states that over 90% of Fortune 500 companies suffered digital attacks in 2021 [7].

Fitchratings.com [8] states that financial institutions continue to be concerned about cyber risk, shifting the focus to include systemic and idiosyncratic risks. Focusing on systemic risk aims to improve industry preparedness and cyber resiliency, reduce single points of failure, and reduce the negative consequences of cyber-attacks. Increasing geopolitical tensions motivate regulators, as a global cyberattack on the financial system could have far-reaching implications.

The banking industry is better prepared to deal with cyber threats than other industries but is not immune to cyber threats like the recent Log4j zero-day vulnerability. The interconnection of banks, such as the core banking system, mergers, and connections through application program interfaces (API) with third-party service providers, evolves into the new attack vector in the financial supply chain. A critical third-party vendor's failure could result in significant economic losses throughout the financial system. The report titled *Attacks from All Angles: 2021 Midyear Security Roundup*, published by TrendMicro, states that ransomware remains one of the most severe risks in the year's first half and that perpetrators target well-known victims. It goes on to say that the most recent assaults used Advanced Persistent Threat (APT) tools and tactics to enter targeted networks, take data from victims, and encrypt that material. In the first half of 2021, the banking industry was adversely impacted, with ransomware attacks up 1,318%. Another example is the theft of $81 million from the central bank in Bangladesh due to a fraudulent cyber-attack against the SWIFT international transactions system in February 2016 [9].

The World Economic Forum and the Carnegie Endowment for International Peace's report, "International Strategy to Better Protect the Financial System Against Cyber Threats," were released in 2020. It claims that malicious actors use digital transformation to their advantage, endangering the financial system's integrity, economic stability, and public confidence [10]. Using cyberspace, malicious actors threaten, disrupt, and steal from investors, financial institutions, and the public. More troublingly, state-sponsored and state-sponsored attackers commit such crimes in addition to bold criminals [8]. More harmful attacks and their impacts should be predicted in the future, suggest Maurer & Nelson [10]. There are few technical solutions for attacks that endanger the trustworthiness of financial data, such as databases, algorithms, and events; these incidents potentially erode trust and confidence more generally. KPMG [11] reports the following as the key reasons for the security breaches in the financial sector: the top one is the poor security configurations of the endpoint devices, followed by lack of user awareness, application vulnerabilities, and poor incident management systems businesses have experienced some cybercrime.

6.3 Evolution of Cyber Threats

The development of cyber threats parallels that of technology. Cybercrime is evolving, from phone bugging in the 1970s to crypto-jacking in 2021. The technological society and security professionals face highly coordinated and persistent cyberattacks on electronic infrastructure assets every 10 years when the cyber defense mechanisms fail to thwart the constantly evolving attack vector [12]. A glimpse of the evolution of cyber threats is given below to help you understand their evolution.

6.3.1 Telephone Hacks in the 1950s

Pre-millennial cybercrime was conducted on telecommunications networks. That was the time when the Internet was not even conceptualized. During the 1950s and 1960s, landlines were ubiquitous in most developed nations. This decade saw the emergence of the first digital-based crime, dubbed "Phreaking," in which criminals took advantage of the tone system employed in telephone networks. Phreaks, short for "Phone Freaks," attempted to use reverse engineering strategies to access telephone networks for long-distance calls in the late 1950s, which led to the incident [13].

6.3.2 Introduction of Computer Virus in the 1970s and 1980s

Though self-replicating programs have been studied since the 1950s, the first actual implementation, in the form of a computer virus attack, happened in the early 1970s. To gain access to the ARPANET networked computers, Bob Thomas, an engineer at BBN Technologies, created a self-replicating program [12].

The first virus discovered to be extensively propagated using floppy discs was the "Elk Cloner" program, created in 1981 by a ninth-grade student from Pittsburgh and attached to the Apple DOS 3.3 OS [14].

Adleman [15] created the phrase "computer virus" and published the article *Computer Viruses—Theory and Experiments*, co-authored by his student Fred Cohen [15]. In 1986, the PC platform was hit by the first-ever "Global epidemic" known as the "brain virus" as the Internet-connected many systems around the world allowed the virus to spread faster [16]. The spread of the brain virus demonstrated a lack of system security and was followed by the "Vienna virus" in the late 1980s, the first-ever virus designed to destroy data [17].

Robert Tappan Morris released the first-ever worm, "Morris Worm," in November 1988. Morris had no idea what his brainchild could do because it was not built with malice. The Morris worm quickly duplicated itself and became the first large-scale Denial-Of-Service (DOS) assault in 1988. It swept around the globe, bringing down numerous corporate servers and personal computers. Eventually, in 1989, Morris was accused of breaking the Computer Fraud and Abuse Act and prosecuted [18].

The "Aids Trojan," used to hide files, was first utilized in a ransomware assault in 1989. It was written by Joseph Popp and coded to encrypt the files with their names before displaying a notice that said, "User license to use the software has expired." PC Cyborg Corporation demanded 189 dollars from the victims for the repair tool to decrypt the encrypted files [19]. Even though encrypting data with names backfired and was easy to restore, this gave rise to the idea of extortion using encryption, which quickly gained traction.

Ransomware assaults have progressed and become more sophisticated, as evidenced by subsequent incidents [20].

6.3.3 Widespread Malware Attacks in the 1990s

Malware established a foothold as companies began to modernize and strategize using ICT. Numerous viruses, like stealth, polymorphic, macro, and others, had evolved by 1996. They continued to develop and spread uncontrolled, with over five million viruses and malware in 2007 [21]. The Melissa Virus reportedly emerged in 1999 and was spread through a Word document. It replicated itself and emailed it to the first 50 email contacts in MS Outlook. It is still one of the most widely disseminated viruses, with an estimated repair cost of $80 million [22].

6.3.4 The Turn of the Century

Viruses become much more complex and sophisticated as years move on, as evidenced by the 2000s. Viruses that targeted system components started to appear using networks, cyberspace, and various methods, from keyboard logging to intricate attacks like ransomware.

A distributed denial of service (DDOS) attack on well-known online shopping portals, including Amazon and eBay, was launched in February 2000 by a school student found to be originating from Canada. 1.7 billion USD was lost due to the attack, and businesses were forced to shut down their websites to monitor visitor flow [23].

During the beginning of the new millennium, the malware "I LOVE YOU" was spread with emails serving as entry points for criminals looking to wreak further devastation. The worm infected approximately 50 million computers, corrupting data and propagating through the victims' email contacts [24].

Data breaches soon took center stage in the infosec landscape due to the emergence of modern threat and attack vectors and methods of dissemination, targets, and counter-cybercrime initiatives.

6.3.5 Threat to the Connected "Things" in the 2020s

Because of the creative applications of present attack types and attacks across upcoming technologies, such as IoT technology, cloud technology, virtual machines, and blockchain, the future of cyber threats is predicted to be more severe than that of the prior decade [25]. Blockchain and Internet of Things (IoT) technology have made the crypto-jacking cyber threat possible. To mine cryptocurrency, criminals who engage in crypto-jacking get unauthorized access to their victims' computers, tablets, phones, and company servers. In this attack, a bot was injected into the targeted devices and used to mine cryptocurrency. Crypto jacking's primary objective is to make money from cryptocurrency mining without bearing the steep expenditures of the public blockchain (mining hardware, high electricity prices). It installs itself on the targeted computer and uses its resources to mine cryptocurrency [26].

6.4 Emerging Cyber Threats

Emerging digital identity theft is the primary concern of Internet users. Stolen credentials and private information are used to impersonate people in cyberspace, resulting in financial and property losses or entangling the victims' identity in dubious or unlawful activity [10]. Identity thieves typically get access to publicly available information, notably on social media, corporate networks, public databases, government services, social security, health care networks, e-commerce websites, virtual marketplaces, e-payment networks, Automated Teller Machines (ATMs), and stock exchanges. If the devices and systems used to carry out e-transactions are penetrated, taken, or damaged, the interests of users and the future of e-services might be gravely jeopardized [27]. Ransomware is the most common attack type, according to IBM Security [28], followed by supply chain and phishing threats observed in 2021.

Recently, extremely dangerous cyberattacks have been reported that target ICT infrastructure and essential industrial control systems, particularly in critical infrastructures like nuclear power, oil, natural gas, and electricity, as well as critical national databases, government services, health care, and emergency aid services. These cyberattacks use a variety of channels, including mobile memory and wireless networks. As a result, they have the potential to harm the use of critical infrastructure devices and their services and businesses that rely on them. According to IBM Security [28], assaults using Linux ransomware increased by 146% in 2021, while

IoT-based attacks on SCADA systems and industrial automation devices increased by 2204%.

Identity thieves frequently access publicly available data, particularly on social media, business networks, public databases, government services, social security, health care networks, e-commerce websites, virtual markets, e-payment networks, Automated Teller Machines (ATMs), and stock exchanges. The interests of users and the future of e-services could be seriously jeopardized if the tools and systems used to conduct e-transactions are breached, stolen, or damaged [27].

One of the critical reasons for the emergence of sophisticated attacks is the growing use of modern technologies, monopolized by a few countries and classified as top-secret and cannot be exported. Some of the exportable versions of the software itself contain backdoors and vulnerabilities. Another reason for the emerging cyber threats is state-sponsored cyber activities. Since they are state-sponsored, they can access complex and sophisticated tools and techniques to attack and cause extreme damage to the target [29].

The Microsoft Digital Defense Report [30] Classifies the top 18 state-sponsored hacker groups as follows (Table 6.1):

According to the survey, the US (46%), Ukraine (19%), and the UK (9%) were the top three nations targeted between July 2020 and June 2021. During July 2020 and June 2021, the sectors most explicitly targeted were government (48%), followed by NGOs (31%) and think tanks (31%). Between July 2020 and June 2021, the nation-state activity groupings that were most active were PHOSPHORUS (9%), THALLIUM (16%), and NOBELIUM (59%).

According to the Kaspersky Security Bulletin [31], since most open banking systems rely on APIs and Web API queries carried out by financial institutions, more attacks against them in the future are possible. Open banking is the practice of banks and other financial institutions allowing regulated providers to access, use, and exchange data.

6.4.1 Malware Delivery

Emails are used to achieve this technique's goals. Email is the primary mechanism used by malware types, including "Agent Tesla," "IcedID," "Trickbot," and "Qakbot," to spread [32]. These emails frequently employ methods that overlap with phishing emails to spread malware through links or attachments. Malware delivery can be less obvious to users because it does not require user engagement as phishing does. For example, while distributing malware using attachments, attackers might use a fictitious

Table 6.1 Top 18 state-sponsored hacker groups listed in microsoft digital defense report 2021.

Activity group name	Other names	Industries targeted
STRONTIUM	APT28. Fancy Bear	Think tanks, NGOs, higher education, defense companies, IT software and services providers, government, diplomatic, and military organizations.
NOBELIUM	UNC2452	Think tanks, non-governmental organizations (NGOs), defense contractors, IT services, and organizations associated with the government and diplomacy. the public sector, business, civil aviation, and the military
BROMINE	Energetic Bear	Government, industry, civil aviation, and defense
MANGANESE	APT5, Keyhole Panda	Infrastructure for the defense sector, the software industry, and telecommunications
ZIRCONIUM	APT31	Departments, agencies, and services of the government, as well as diplomatic and commercial organizations
HAFNIUM		Think tanks, NGOs, law firms, defense industries, higher education, and medical research.
NICKEL	APT15, Vixen Panda	Departments, agencies, and diplomatic missions of the government
CHROMIUM	ControlX	Infrastructure for telecommunications, education, governmental entities, and services

(*Continued*)

Table 6.1 Top 18 state-sponsored hacker groups listed in microsoft digital defense report 2021. (*Continued*)

Activity group name	Other names	Industries targeted
GADOLINIUM	APT40	Groups in municipal government, healthcare, higher education, and the marine industries
PHOSPHORUS	Charming Kitten	Academics, journalists, and anyone involved in nuclear and diplomatic policy
CURIUM	Houseblend Tortoise Shell	Middle Eastern governments, US defense and military contractors, and IT services
RUBIDIUM	Fox Kitten Parasite	Israeli defense, IT, and logistics companies
ZINC	Lazarus Labyrinth Chollima	Academics, think tanks, and diplomats.
THALLIUM	Kimsuky Velvet Chollima	Think tanks, diplomats, and scholars
CERIUM	Kimsuky Think tanks	Academics, defense and aerospace industries, and diplomats
OSMIUM	Konni	Formal diplomatic channels think tanks.
BISMUTH	APT32 OceanLotu	Civic organizations and human rights
SILICON	Sea Turtle UNC1326	Middle Eastern and Balkan telecommunications firms

document containing macros that silently and automatically download the infection when accepted by the recipient. Because security systems cannot check password-protected archive files like 7z, RAR, and ZIP, malware typically spreads via these. In these situations, the user may believe that the document is flawed or irrelevant to them, and they may be unaware that harmful malware has been installed on their computer.

6.4.2 Fileless Malware

Detecting and removing "fileless" malware poses significant challenges due to its nature. Unlike traditional malware, fileless malware's components are derived from system processes or legitimate programs already on a device [33]. This characteristic makes it harder to identify and eliminate as it lacks a distinct file to target.

Persistent techniques utilized by fileless malware leverage registries, date stamps, and startup folder persistence. By using these methods, the malware avoids relying on static files on the disk, making it more resilient to traditional removal techniques. Examples of malware employing these techniques include banking trojans, offensive toolkits like "Cobalt Strike," and remote access trojans (RATs) that are freely available.

Organizations must go beyond relying solely on antivirus solutions to effectively clean up and counter such behaviors. Security teams need to evaluate their incident response and malware eradication protocols to ensure they comprehensively address common malware persistence strategies. This evaluation is crucial in combating the sophisticated nature of fileless malware and its ability to hide within legitimate system processes.

6.4.3 Legitimate Service Abuse

Malware distribution techniques include the use of legitimate websites, as well as controlling and commanding, exfiltration, malicious advertisements, and mining of cryptocurrency [34]. The initial delivery of malware is notoriously carried out by well-known cloud services like Microsoft One Drive, Google Drive, Adobe Spark, Dropbox, and others, while content "pasting" websites like "Pastebin.com," "Archive.org," and "Stikked.ch" are becoming more and more popular.

6.4.4 Botnet Renovations

The phrase "botnet" has also changed over time. In the past, it referred to a computer network that carried out an operator's duties. However, most malware families today may be categorized as having botnet behaviors or components. Other malware families took their place when the once-common malware botnet infrastructures Trickbot and Emotet were destroyed [35]. In their place, more severe secondary components started to be delivered at higher speeds by older botnets and a new class of evasive malware. The "European Union Agency for Criminal Justice Cooperation (EUROJUST)" carried out a takedown in January 2021, which resulted in the death of the Emotet malware family and a correspondingly sharp decline in Emotet encounters [36]. To monetize their behavior, botnets like Phorpiex15 transmitted multiple ransomware and secondary malware components, including the Avaddon ransomware, to an increasing number of infected base hosts. This past year saw a rise in botnets, including Sysrv-Hello, Purple Fox, and Lemon Duck, which used new infrastructure, programming languages, and infection techniques. Lemon Duck uses over ten unique ways of infection across Windows and Linux platforms, like most newly discovered botnets [37].

6.4.5 Search Engine Optimization and Malicious Advertising

Another effective mode of malware delivery is through search engines. Search engine optimization (SEO) tools and pre-existing infectious cookies are mainly used to deliver the malware to the end user.

The Adrozek16 is a browser extension that replaces the initial search results with malicious URLs that pretend to be Microsoft goods and other trustworthy software [38]. To manipulate search engines in 2020, the creators of Gootkit, a malware infection that can result in ransomware, adopted a slightly different method by paying for advertising to promote links to infected websites hosting the malware [39]. Other data-stealing malware, such as Jupyter or SolarMarker, used a different method to appear in search results by utilizing documents hosted on services such as AWS and Google, pointing users searching for standard terms to PDF pages that would eventually gain persistence on their device [40]. Browser alterations and search results are increasingly used for information theft, data exfiltration, and other virus delivery methods. As a result, malware is still spreading through SEO tactics in both the consumer and business sectors.

6.4.6 Security Tools as a Malware

Malware has developed to use the security tools that are currently accessible. Cobalt Strike, a for-profit penetration testing tool, is a good example. While Cobalt Strike is intended for penetration testing, it is increasingly utilized in various attacks, including ransomware, system, network discovery actions, and lateral network traversal. Cobalt Strike is specifically made to avoid being detected using conventional methods. It gives the operator a variety of choices for hiding their attack commands.

6.4.7 Web Shells Deep Dive

A web shell uses malicious code installed on the webservers. Such malicious code is run using remote access methods to steal data from the web server and utilize the site as a launchpad for more attacks against the target company. These web shell techniques are part of advanced persistent threats (APT). Microsoft's Detection and Response Team (DART) reported that web shell usage continued to rise during 2019-21 [41].

6.4.8 Domain-Generating Algorithms

Domain-generating algorithms (DGAs) are now commonly included in malware by cybercriminals, offering a fallback method if hardcoded malicious domains are confiscated by law enforcement. The technique generates domain names that appear to be random. The notion is that two machines using the same algorithm will communicate with the same domain simultaneously, allowing them to share data or fetch instructions. DGAs enhance the expense and difficulty of interrupting cybercriminal communications infrastructure since disruptors must monitor hundreds of thousands of potentially dangerous domains, whereas cybercriminals only need one [42].

6.4.9 AI-Enabled Cyber Attacks

Current cybersecurity concerns artificial intelligence and machine learning, which are providing new difficulties. Cybercriminals utilize machine learning to conduct their assaults by studying defensive countermeasures and taking advantage of recently discovered security vulnerabilities before the defenders can close them [43]. These attacks range from altering medical photos using false cancer detection using adversarial machine learning to creating adversarial traffic signals affecting autonomous vehicles' safety. Marketers and manufacturers will gather more personal data, with or without consent, as linked home gadgets evolve using the Internet of Things (IoT) to understand customer patterns and behavior better and increase their profit [44]. McAfee [45] states that machine learning algorithms are expected to create an arms race between attackers' and defenders'.

6.5 Impacts of Data Breaches in the Financial Sector

The maximum impact and the immense benefit are the main reasons cybercriminals choose their victims. As the financial sector deals with precious data with the increasing volume of online transactions, this sector remains the top priority in the target sector, followed by the health sector due to its sensitive data.

One of the best methods to prevent data breaches and others from using a data protection system specifically designed for financial services is to learn from other's mistakes. The following list of notable financial industry data breaches serves as an example to show the scope of their effects.

- In August 2020, a cyberattack on Experian, a global company with over 125 years of experience in the financial sector, affected 24 million clients and about 800,000 businesses. Experian's South African office employee was coerced into providing sensitive company information by a threat actor posing as a representative for one of the company's clients [46].
- In May 2019, First American Financial Corp. suffered a significant data breach that made over 855 million real estate and mortgage records available to the public. Users could look for personal information quickly because of a data management issue. Among the stolen goods were social security numbers, tax and mortgage information, license numbers, and other private data. Attackers might be able to view those data by altering a nine-digit transaction record [47].
- Over 100 million account holders, including their social security numbers, names, addresses, and credit card ratings, were compromised in a significant data breach assault on a US bank, Capital One, in March 2019. The attacker used a weak Web Application Firewall to access public cloud services [48].

IBM Inc [49] states that the cost of a data breach in the UK averages $3.9 million (approximately £2.76 million), an increase of 10% over the preceding 5 years. The cost of a data breach is accumulated from various expenditures. Some of the critical expenditure categories are discussed below.

The settlement amount paid to the impacted parties is the most significant expense. If a cyberattack compromises personal data, the affected consumers must compensate for the loss of information control, the sadness they experienced, and the financial hardship they faced. For instance, following a massive data breach employing Apache Struts in 2017, the Federal

Trade Commission ordered Equifax, a global credit reporting company, to pay up to $125 million in customer compensation. Due to the loss of information control, the sorrow triggered, and the financial pain experienced, affected consumers may be paid if a cyber-attack compromises personal data [50].

The second expense relates to breach investigation operations. A data breach investigation is necessary after that. Finding out what triggered the breach is essential to stop it from happening again. The inquiry will involve several phases: obtaining information, interviewing the personnel who found and reported the breach, analyzing the incident, and producing breach reports. The procedure will be expensive, time-consuming, and laborious, hindering employee productivity. Hiring a company to conduct a cyber-forensic investigation can cost between £10K and £100K [49].

Penalties for breaching the law are the third cost. Another price is the penalty for breaching legislation like the General Data Protection Regulation (GDPR). The GDPR is a regulatory framework establishing guidelines for collecting and processing personal data. The maximum penalties for violations of the UK GDPR and the Data Protection Act 2018 are £17.5 million or 4% of the annual worldwide revenue, whichever is higher. For instance, British Airways, which received one of the most considerable GDPR fines in recent years, paid a $26 million fine as restitution for failing to put security measures in place, which resulted in a breach that affected 400,000 customers.

A tarnished reputation is a severe hit to an organization's image and harms the bottom line in the long run; thus, it is the fourth cost. Customer and investor distrust leads to higher costs and a possible drop in sales. For example, after a cyber-attack in 2016, TalkTalk lost over 100,000 clients and a third of its corporate worth. This negative publicity can be difficult, if not impossible, to recover for small organizations, which is a significant factor in the high failure rate of smaller companies following a breach [51].

Downtime is the fifth cost. If recovery is not swift, the cost of downtime might quickly grow. Aside from the cost of repairing the downtime (paying a ransom, recovering data), there is also the loss of revenue, which can be devastating if most sales are conducted online. However, the loss of production is likely the most significant expense associated with downtime. Organizations suffer financial losses when collaborators cannot function during downtime, and the longer this condition persists, the higher the cost [52].

6.6 Cybersecurity Standards, Frameworks, and Benchmarks

There always needs to be clarity regarding standards and frameworks. As the name implies, standards are the most well-known practices, whereas frameworks are those used when there are no well-defined or standard procedures. ISO has established standards in every business industry worldwide, and conformance to ISO entails adhering to internationally recognized best practices [53]. A framework is, at best, a frame that can be utilized as a practice, whereas a standard is frequently rigorous and widely acknowledged as the best manner of doing anything. While a standard has only one way of doing things, a framework can evolve a person's methodology because it is adaptable and allows for experimentation.

Systems, data, and users are exposed to traditional and cutting-edge security threats because security technology has yet to keep up with the fast evolution of IT. Political rivals, financially motivated crooks, shady attackers, and unskilled or malicious authorized users are just a few of the threats to systems and technology that might be compromised. Other concerns include cybersecurity, economic security, consumer identities, and national security.

The security Standards for Cryptographic Modules specify one set of standards for all cryptographic-based security systems used by federal institutions to protect sensitive or priceless data. The creation of cryptographic modules can then be checked for conformity by users against the standard.

Security standards make exchanging information and best practices easier by ensuring everyone converses with the same terminology, definitions, and concepts. This aids in mistake prevention. Cybersecurity rules are becoming more prevalent. More commonly, both enterprises and governments are demanding its adoption. Many producers and merchants produce and market items and services that follow regulations. A cybersecurity framework, on the other hand, comprises standards, principles, and suggested techniques for countering cyber threats in the online environment. Business entities that seek to comply with national, industrial, and international cybersecurity standards typically need to use cybersecurity frameworks, or at the absolute least, it is highly recommended. For instance, a company must pass an audit demonstrating compliance with the Payment Card Industry Data Security Standards (PCI DSS) framework to process credit card transactions. Table 6.2 lists some of the most well-liked and commonly applied standards.

Table 6.2 Summary of cybersecurity standards, frameworks, and benchmarks.

Sl. no.	Name of the standard	Description
1	ISO/IEC 27031	A global standard on cybersecurity management
2	ISO 22301	In the case of a disaster, businesses can maintain operations while minimizing business impact.
3	Minimum Cyber Security Standard	The UK government established the first standard with the National Cyber Security Centre (NCSC).
4	Cyber Essentials,	The program's certification procedure enables businesses of all sizes to showcase their approach to cyber security while making the process easy and cost-effective.
5	Health Insurance Portability and Accountability Act (HIPAA)	Its objectives are to make it simpler for patients to maintain their health insurance when they move jobs, protect patient information's privacy and security, and help the healthcare industry cut administrative costs.
6	Standard Criteria (ISO/IEC 15408):	The certification of IT products is the focus of this standard. It ensures that IT products are evaluated using acceptable means and are widely used by industry and government. Part 1 (Introduction and general model), Part 2 (Security functional requirements), and Part 3 (Functional requirements for security) make up ISO/IEC 15408. (Security assurance requirements).
7	NIST Cybersecurity Framework (CSF)	Framework is based on existing best practices for managing and mitigating cybersecurity risk in critical infrastructure enterprises.
8	PAS 555	A holistic framework for adequate cyber security.

(*Continued*)

Table 6.2 Summary of cybersecurity standards, frameworks, and benchmarks. (*Continued*)

Sl. no.	Name of the standard	Description
9	ISO/IEC 18043	This standard focuses on selecting, deploying, and operating intrusion detection systems.
10	ISO 28000	This ISO standard outlines the requirements for supply-chain security management systems.
11	Payment Card Industry Data Security Standard (PCI DSS)	This regulation sets the standards for financial institutions and merchants to process credit card payments securely.
12	CSA CCM	A collection of rules called the CCM (Cloud Controls Matrix) by the CSA (Cloud Security Alliance) is intended to maximize information security for cloud computing users. The matrix gives businesses a series of recommendations for enhancing the security of their data without just depending on the Cloud provider's guarantees.
13	FISMA	Cybersecurity architecture protects the federal government's systems and data against Internet attacks. Third parties and contractors that provide services to federal agencies are also covered under FISMA. The FISMA framework, which requires organizations and outside parties to keep track of their digital assets and report any network and system connections, is closely related to the NIST standards.
14	GDPR	This regulation covers the processing of personal data entirely or in part.

(*Continued*)

Table 6.2 Summary of cybersecurity standards, frameworks, and benchmarks. (*Continued*)

Sl. no.	Name of the standard	Description
15	CIS Benchmarks	CIS benchmark statements aim to protect systems against today's increasing cyber threats. Over 100 configuration standards spread over 25+ vendor product families are available in these benchmarks.
16	COBIT	It is a framework for controls used with IT systems in financial accounting. It complies with the Sarbanes-Oxley Act.
17	PAS 555:2013, Cyber security risk - Governance and Management - Specification	This publicly accessible specification (PAS) lays a framework for managing and governing cyber security risks. The standards of this PAS specify the implications of good cyber security, which include technological, physical, cultural, and behavioral measures and strong leadership and governance. It is scalable, so it is suitable for companies of all sizes.

6.7 Innovative Approaches to Cyber-Incident Management

6.7.1 International and Multistakeholder Collaboration

Despite the rising use of various cybersecurity standards and frameworks, ambiguity still exists in managing cyberattacks. Research states that it is an organizational issue to secure better the global financial system [54]. Efforts to increase defenses and tighten rules are critical, but more is needed to keep up with the growing hazards. Unlike many others, the financial services industry has sufficient resources and experience to implement technological solutions.

The central dilemma is in choosing the collective action: how to best structure the system's protection among government entities, banking institutions, and industry, as well as how to deploy these resources effectively and efficiently. The chasm between the financial, national security, and diplomatic communities is widening. Financial institutions are especially vulnerable to cyber threats, but their partnerships with national security agencies, which are essential to address those threats effectively, are strained.

Risks are exacerbated by this duty imbalance and continued misunderstanding over roles and responsibilities for securing the global financial system. Part of this ambiguity originates from the current geopolitical environment, characterized by high levels of distrust, and inhibits international cooperation. Cybersecurity collaboration has been hampered because it addresses sensitive national security matters [55].

Because it covers sensitive national security issues, cybersecurity cooperation has been hampered, divided, and confined to the most trusted groups. Collaboration between international and multi-stakeholder groups is a "must-have" rather than a "nice-to-have."

6.7.2 Cognitive Analytics in Cybersecurity Management

As a result of the digital revolution, technical and non-technical workers will need to master new skills. Human error and a lack of knowledge frequently contribute to cyber incidents despite a company's investment in costly security measures. According to the Global Cybersecurity Outlook 2022 published by the World Economic Forum, social engineering is employed in 80% of successful hacks [56]. The likelihood of catastrophes caused by cyberattacks can be mitigated by supporting regular training for all staff and senior executives on how to perform tasks in the new digital world. An innovative method for gathering information and making decisions is cognitive analytics. It can bridge the gap between the intent of big data and the practicality of actual decision making because it is motivated by how the brain processes information, draws conclusions, and codifies instincts and experiences into learning. Artificial intelligence, natural language processing, and machine learning systems are no longer simply cutting-edge ideas; they are now potential corporate disruptors that might provide real-time decision-making insights [57].

6.7.3 Security Automation for Combating Cyberattacks

Organizations can employ security orchestration, automation, and response (SOAR) technology to quickly monitor, comprehend, choose, and react to security threats. The way security teams are organized, evaluate threats, and respond to alarms can all be significantly changed by SOAR [58].

6.8 Conclusion

This book chapter provides an overview of cybersecurity attacks in the financial sector and their exponential growth due to digital transformation strategies adopted by enterprises. The impacts of the cyberattacks and key state-sponsored cyberterrorist groups are explored. Finally, it discusses contemporary methods of handling cyberattacks.

It has been found that companies dealing with cyber-attacks are also experiencing a skills shortage. According to a poll done by the Information Systems Security Association (ISSA) and Enterprise Strategy Group (ESG), 95% of respondents believe the gap has remained relatively high in recent years [59]. Edward Humphreys, an IT security specialist, told the ISO that education is a company's most potent weapon against cybercrime. The necessary skills protect firms from security risks [60].

References

1. Nadkarni, S. and Prügl, R., Digital transformation: a review, synthesis, and opportunities for future research. *Manag. Rev. Q.*, 71, 2, 233–341, 2021.
2. Ahluwalia, S., Mahto, R.V., Guerrero, M., Blockchain technology and startup financing: A transaction cost economics perspective. *Technol. Forecast. Soc. Change*, 151, 119854, Feb. 2020, doi: 10.1016/j.techfore.2019.119854.
3. Zulfa, A.A., Sihabuddin, S., Widhiyanti, H.N., Utilization of Personal Data Through Cookies Using Artificial Intelligence from Human Rights Perspective. *Int. J. Multicult. Multireligious Underst.*, 9, 3, 293–303, 2022.
4. Paulsen, J.E., Hazelett, M.B., Schwartz, S.B., CIED cybersecurity risks in an increasingly connected world. *Circulation*, 138, 12, 1181–1183, 2018.
5. Resul, D.A.S. and Gündüz, M.Z., Analysis of cyber-attacks in IoT-based critical infrastructures. *Int. J. Inf. Secure. Sci.*, 8, 4, 122–133, 2020.
6. Risk, D. and Advisory's, F., The Top Global Business Risks for 2021.
7. Humayun, M., Jhanjhi, N.Z., Alsayat, A., Ponnusamy, V., Internet of things and ransomware: Evolution, mitigation and prevention. *Egypt. Inf. J.*, 22, 1, 105–117, 2021.
8. Fitchratings.com, Exploratory Research: Exploring Bank Cybersecurity Risk (Better Insights into Growing Risk with Cybersecurity Scores from Security Scorecard), 2021, https://www.fitchratings.com/research/banks/exploring-bank-cybersecurity-risk-13-04-2021.
9. Bouveret, A., *Cyber risk for the financial sector: A framework for quantitative assessment*, International Monetary Fund, 2018.
10. Maurer, T. and Nelson, A., International Strategy to Better Protect the Financial System Against Cyber Threats - Carnegie Endowment for

International Peace, 2020, https://carnegieendowment.org/2020/11/18/international-strategy-to-better-protect-financial-system-against-cyber-threats-pub-83105.
11. KPMG, Digital payments-Analysing the cyber landscape, 2017, https://assets.kpmg/content/dam/kpmg/ca/pdf/2017/04/digital-payments-analysing-the-cyber-landscape-kpmg-canada.pdf.
12. Chen, T.M. and Robert, J.-M., The evolution of viruses and worms. *Stat. Methods Comput. Secur.*, 1, 1–16, 2004.
13. Brenner, S. W. (2010). *Cybercrime: Criminal Threats from Cyberspace* (1st ed., Vol. 1). Bloomsbury Academic, Santa Barbara, CA, https://ecommons.udayton.edu/law_fac_pub/115
14. Touchette, F., The evolution of malware. *Netw. Secur.*, 2016, 1, 11–14, 2016.
15. Adleman, L.M., An abstract theory of computer viruses, in: *Conference on the Theory and Application of Cryptography*, pp. 354–374, 1988.
16. Highland, H.J., The BRAIN virus: fact and fantasy. *Comput. Secure.*, 7, 4, 367–370, 1988.
17. Parikka, J., *Digital contagions: A media archaeology of computer viruses*, vol. 44, Peter Lang, New York, United States of America, 2007.
18. Eisenberg, T., Gries, D., Hartmanis, J., Holcomb, D., Lynn, M.S., Santoro, T., The Cornell commission: on Morris and the worm. *Commun. ACM*, 32, 6, 706–709, 1989.
19. Gazet, A., Comparative analysis of various ransomware virii. *J. Comput. Virol.*, 6, 1, 77–90, 2010.
20. McIntosh, T., Kayes, A.S.M., Chen, Y.-P.P., Ng, A., Watters, P., Ransomware Mitigation in the Modern Era: A Comprehensive Review, Research Challenges, and Future Directions. *ACM Comput. Surv.*, 54, 9, 1–36, 2021.
21. Mat, S.R.T., Ab Razak, M.F., Kahar, M.N.M., Arif, J.M., Mohamad, S., Firdaus, A., Towards a systematic description of the field using bibliometric analysis: malware evolution. *Scientometrics*, 126, 3, 2013–2055, 2021.
22. Garber, L., Melissa virus creates a new type of threat. *Comput. (Long. Beach. Calif.)*, 32, 06, 16–19, 1999.
23. Marion, N.E. and Twede, J., *Cybercrime: An encyclopedia of digital crime*, ABC-CLIO, California, United States of America, 2020.
24. Hopper, I., Destructive 'I LOVE YOU'Computer virus strikes worldwide. *CNN Interact. Technol.*, 1, 1–5, 2000.
25. Choo, K.-K.R., Gai, K., Chiaraviglio, L., Yang, Q., A multidisciplinary approach to Internet of Things (IoT) cybersecurity and risk management. *Comput. Secur.*, 102, 102136, 2021, Elsevier.
26. Caprolu, M., Raponi, S., Oligeri, G., Di Pietro, R., Cryptomining makes noise: Detecting cryptojacking via Machine Learning. *Comput. Commun.*, 171, 126–139, 2021.
27. Thangavel, M., Divyaprabha, M., Abinaya, C., Threats and Vulnerabilities of Mobile Applications, in: *Research Anthology on Securing Mobile Technologies and Applications*, pp. 560–580, IGI Global, Hershey, PA, 2021.

28. IBM Security, X-Force Threat Intelligence Index 2022, Armonk, NY 10504, 2022, https://www.ibm.com/downloads/cas/ADLMYLAZ.
29. Akoto, W., International trade and cyber conflict: Decomposing the effect of trade on state-sponsored cyber attacks. *J. Peace Res.*, 58, 5, 1083–1097, Jan. 2021, doi: 10.1177/0022343320964549.
30. Microsoft, The 2021 Microsoft Digital Defense Report, 2022, https://thecyberwire.com/podcasts/security-unlocked/49/notes.
31. Kaspersky Security Bulletin, Kaspersky Security Bulletin 2021. Statistics | Securelist, 2022, https://securelist.com/kaspersky-security-bulletin-2021-statistics/105205/.
32. Aaron, G., Chapin, L., Piscitello, D., Strutt, C., Malware Landscape 2021, 2021.
33. Kumar, S. and Sudhakar, An emerging threat Fileless malware: a survey and research challenges. *Cybersecurity*, 3, 1, 1–12, 2020.
34. Goswami, M.P., Fake News and Cyber Propaganda: A study of manipulation and abuses on Social Media, in: *Mediascape 21st Century Emerging Perspect*, pp. 535–544, 2018.
35. Gezer, A., Warner, G., Wilson, C., Shrestha, P., A flow-based approach for trickbot banking trojan detection. *Comput. Secur.*, 84, 179–192, 2019.
36. Eurojust, World's most dangerous malware EMOTET disrupted through global action, Europol, 2022, https://www.europol.europa.eu/media-press/newsroom/news/world's-most-dangerous-malware-emotet-disrupted-through-global-action.
37. Bijalwan, A., Botnet forensic analysis using machine learning. *Secur. Commun. Netw.*, 9302318, 1–9, 2020, doi: 10.1155/2020/9302318.
38. Khanday, S.A., Fatima, H., Rakesh, N., Deep learning offering resilience from trending cyber-attacks, a review, in: *2021 International Conference on Computational Performance Evaluation (ComPE)*, pp. 741–749, 2021.
39. Han, X. and Olivier, B., Interpretable and adversarially-resistant behavioural malware signatures, in: *Proceedings of the 35th Annual ACM Symposium on Applied Computing*, pp. 1668–1677, 2020.
40. Fui, N.L.Y., Asmawi, A., Hussin, M., A Dynamic Malware Detection in Cloud Platform. *Int. J. Differ. Equations*, 15, 2, 243–258, 2020.
41. Hannousse, A. and Yahiouche, S., Handling webshell attacks: A systematic mapping and survey. *Comput. Secur.*, 108, 102366, 2021.
42. Akhila, G. and Gladston, A., A machine learning framework for domain generating algorithm based malware detection. *Secur. Priv.*, 3, 6, e127, 2020.
43. Yamin, M.M., Ullah, M., Ullah, H., Katt, B., Weaponized AI for cyber attacks. *J. Inf. Secure. Appl.*, 57, 102722, 2021.
44. Kuzlu, M., Fair, C., Guler, O., Role of Artificial Intelligence in the Internet of Things (IoT) cybersecurity. *Discov. Internet Things*, 1, 1, 1–14, Feb. 2021, doi: 10.1007/S43926-020-00001-4.

45. McAfee, McAfee Labs 2018 Threats Predictions Report, Previews Five Cybersecurity Trends, 2018, https://www.mcafee.com/blogs/other-blogs/mcafee-labs/2018-threats-predictions/.
46. Mund, B. and Bailey, L., Privilege in Data Breach Investigations. *Dep. Justice J. Fed. Law Pract.*, 69, 39–57, 2021.
47. Islam, R., The Impact of Data Breaches on Stock Performance, 2020.
48. CapitalOne, 2019 Capital One Cyber Incident | What Happened | Capital One, 2022, https://www.capitalone.com/digital/facts2019/.
49. IBM Inc, Cost of a data breach, 2020, https://www.ibm.com/security/digital-assets/cost-data-breach-report/1Cost%20of%20a%20Data%20Breach%20Report%202020.pdf.
50. Dongre, S., Mishra, S., Romanowski, C., Buddhadev, M., Quantifying the costs of data breaches, in: *International Conference on Critical Infrastructure Protection*, pp. 3–16, 2019.
51. Labrecque, L.I., Markos, E., Swani, K., Peña, P., When data security goes wrong: Examining the impact of stress, social contract violation, and data type on consumer coping responses following a data breach. *J. Bus. Res.*, 135, 559–571, 2021.
52. Wang, S.S. and Franke, U., Enterprise IT service downtime cost and risk transfer in a supply chain. *Oper. Manag. Res.*, 13, 1, 94–108, 2020.
53. Morikawa, M. and Morrison, J., Who Develops ISO Standards? A Surv. Particip. ISO's Int. Stand. Dev. Process. Oakl. Pac. Inst., 2004.
54. Sallos, M.P., Garcia-Perez, A., Bedford, D., Orlando, B., Strategy and organisational cybersecurity: a knowledge-problem perspective. *J. Intellect. Cap.*, 20, 4, 581–597, 2019, doi: 10.1108/JIC-03-2019-0041.
55. Boes, S. and Leukfeldt, E.R., Fighting cybercrime: A joint effort, in: *Cyber-physical security*, pp. 185–203, Springer, Cincinnati, Ohio, USA, 2017.
56. World Economic Forum, Global Cybersecurity Outlook 2022 J A N U A R Y 2 0 2 2 In collaboration with Accenture, 2020.
57. Petrenko, S., Makoveichuk, K., Olifirov, A., New methods of the cybersecurity knowledge management analytics, in: *International Conference on Convergent Cognitive Information Technologies*, pp. 296–310, 2018.
58. Brooks, C., Security Orchestration, Automation and Response (SOAR)-The Pinnacle For Cognitive Cybersecurity. Secur. Essentials, ed AlienVault, 2018.
59. Jon Oltsik, B. and Principal Analyst, S., A Cooperative Research Project by ESG and ISSA The Life and Times of Cybersecurity Professionals 2020 ESG RESEARCH REPORT, 2020.
60. Humphreys, E., *Implementing the ISO/IEC 27001: 2013 ISMS Standard*, Artech House, Norwood, MA, United States of America, 2016.

7

A Robust Model for Enabling Insider Threat Detection and Prevention: Techniques, Tools, and Applications

A. Sheik Abdullah[1]*, Shivansh Dhiman[1] and Arif Ansari[2]

[1]*School of Computer Science and Engineering, Vellore Institute of Technology, Chennai, Tamil Nadu, India*
[2]*Department of Clinical Data Sciences and Operations, University of Southern California Marshall School of Business, Los Angeles, California, USA*

Abstract

In today's era, cybersecurity is essential as data breaches and cyber-attacks become more prevalent. Insider threats, which are security risks from within an organization, involve employees or contractors who possess access to information and exploit it to harm the organization. Simultaneously, new methods and technologies are emerging that leverage tools like machine learning, artificial intelligence, and behavioral analytics to identify and mitigate insider threats accurately.

As technology advances rapidly, malware also evolves in sophistication. This challenges cybersecurity professionals who strive to keep up with the changing landscape. Modern malware utilizes techniques, such as polymorphism and metamorphism, enabling it to modify its code to evade detection by traditional antivirus programs. Consequently, detecting and removing malware from compromised systems has become increasingly difficult for security experts. We can evolve these measures into more robust threat detection and prevention tools. This will enable us to better protect against potential security breaches and ensure the safety and security of our systems and data.

Keywords**:** Cyber security, insider threats, machine learning, artificial intelligence, behavioural analytics, threat detection, prevention tools

**Corresponding author*: aa.sheikabdullah@gmail.com

Kavita Sharma, Vishnu Sharma, Parma Nand, Anil Kumar Sagar and Gulshan Shrivastava (eds.) Securing the Digital Frontier: Threats and Advanced Techniques in Security and Forensics, (133–168)

7.1 Introduction

In the digital age, where security and privacy are pivotal to organizational success, a concealed danger lurks in the shadows of organizations. This danger is the insider threat, a term that denotes the perilous actions of those within an organization who may misuse their access to sensitive data [1]. Surprisingly, many organizations need to pay more attention to these threats, either underestimating their potential impact or misunderstanding their nature [2]. The spectrum of insider threats is vast and varied, encompassing unintentional accidents by trusted insiders to calculated and malicious attacks by disgruntled employees or collaborators [3]. Historically, tools designed to detect and prevent these threats were limited in scope, often relying on predefined rules and needing more flexibility to adapt to a rapidly changing threat landscape [4]. In our changing world, technology is advancing at a pace that is as both technology and human interactions become more complex, and the old models need to be more effective. This creates a demand for innovative solutions. Enter the robust model—a cutting-edge framework integrating supervised machine learning algorithms and Complex Event Processing (CEP) [5]. This synergy between data-driven techniques and real-time processing offers an unparalleled advantage in precision, allowing for accurate, real-time detection and mitigation of insider threats [6]. While existing models have struggled to keep pace with evolving challenges, the robust model demonstrates a new era in insider threat detection, harnessing the potential of advanced computational methods to protect organizations from the insidious risks posed by those within. By exploring insider threats' nature, evaluating current detection tools' limitations, and unveiling the innovative, robust model, this chapter aims to provide a comprehensive overview of an urgent yet often neglected aspect of modern cybersecurity. The ideas and approaches discussed in this chapter are essential for theoretical comprehension, and they provide multiple ideas for organizations to protect themselves from the danger that lies within.

The chapter further discusses the nature of insider threats and how they affect various parts of the organization. How it plunges into the deep recesses of these dangers, untangling their intricate appearances across various spheres within establishments. Unpacking the different types and categories of insider threats provides a rich understanding of the motivations and mechanisms behind these often insidious actions [7]. The complexity of human behavior intertwined with technological advancements makes insider threat detection a non-trivial task, hence the realization that traditional detection methods are becoming increasingly obsolete [8].

Analyzing traditional insider threat detection tools and current tools helps assess certain inefficiencies. While effective in their time, prior models needed more foresight and adaptability in an ever-evolving cyber environment [9]. They were marred by their static nature, unable to learn and adapt to new, more sophisticated insider threats [10]. The ineffectiveness of these approaches is made worse by the changing world, where traditional boundaries are getting blurry, and trust dynamics are shifting quickly.

The chapter's primary focus is to create a robust model that helps mitigate most Insider threats and prevent organizations from getting attacked by malicious Insiders. Supervised learning leverages data-driven techniques' power, enabling the model to learn from historical data and predict future anomalies [11]. Complex Event Processing (CEP) integration takes this a step further, providing real-time analysis and detection, which needed improvement in many prior models [12]. This combination fails to ensure the model's accuracy. Also, allowing real-time detection helps in mitigating threats.

Furthermore, the chapter highlights the significance of taking an approach. Insider threats are not just a technological problem but are equally rooted in human psychology and organizational culture [13]. By combining machine learning algorithms with Complex Event Processing, this model offers a way for organizations to perceive and address insider threats.

7.2 Structure

To achieve this, the chapter is structured as follows:

- **Understanding Insider Threats:** In-depth look into the types and motivations behind insider threats, establishing a foundational understanding.
- **Challenges in Insider Threat Detection:** Discuss organizations' inherent complexities and challenges when identifying insider threats.
- **Techniques for Insider Threat Detection:** Exploration of various methodologies, from behavior-centric to data-centric approaches, to detect malicious or negligent activities.
- **Tools for Insider Threat Detection:** Review the leading tools, both commercial and open-source, available to organizations. The structured mapping of the chapter is illustrated in Figure 7.1.

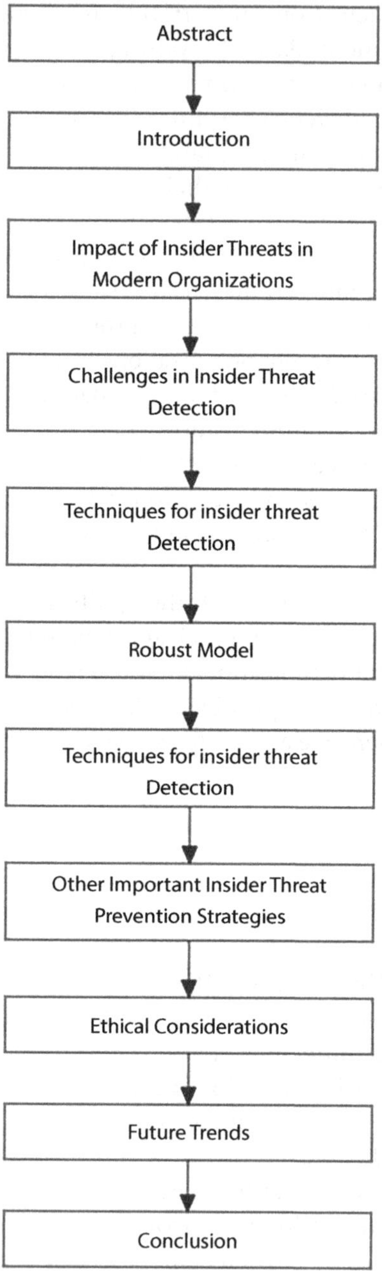

Figure 7.1 Structure-mapping of the chapter.

- **Robust Model for Insider Threat Detection and Prevention:** Creating a Robust model by combining different techniques to create a newer and better model for Insider Threat detection.
- **Applications and Case Studies:** Real-world examples to provide practical insights into the implications and outcomes of insider threats.
- **Prevention Strategies:** Recommendations on proactively curbing the threat from insiders, focusing on both technological measures and organizational best practices.
- **Ethical Considerations:** A discourse on the ethical challenges when monitoring employees, ensuring a balance between security and personal privacy.
- **Future Trends:** Speculation on the future trajectory of insider threats and the evolving methodologies to counter them.

This chapter explains insider threats, emphasizing their significance, and creates a robust model for Insider Threat detection and prevention. We intend to provide readers with a comprehensive understanding of all the methods and tools available to detect and prevent these threats. We also explore real-world applications and case studies to contextualize the theoretical knowledge. By highlighting ethical considerations and future trends, we also seek to present a balanced view that considers the issue's technological and human-centric aspects [14].

7.3 Impact of Insider Threats on Modern Organizations

The nature of insider threat needs to be explored to enhance the understanding of insider threat. Therefore, the many different types of insider threats need to be distinguished. Definitions vary from the misuse of privilege abuse to broader definitions involving the effect on the confidentiality, integrity, and availability of corporate data [1].

7.3.1 Types of Insider Threats

1. Malicious Insiders:
Malicious insiders intend to misuse access and insider knowledge to harm the organization. This harm might include stealing sensitive data, sabotaging the system, fraud, or other disruptive or criminal activities. For

example, an employee under malicious motivation starts selling confidential company information to competitors, or a dissatisfied staff member deliberately deletes data or introduces malicious code into systems.

2. Negligent Insiders:
Negligent insiders are individuals within an organization who unintentionally cause security risks or breaches through careless or uninformed behavior. Unlike malicious insiders, who actively seek to harm the organization, negligent insiders may inadvertently create vulnerabilities or expose sensitive information. For example, if a working employee accidentally sends an email with sensitive information to the wrong recipient, a staff member or an employee has a weak password, or has fallen prey to phishing schemes, it may cause compromised security.

3. Infiltrators (Compromised Insiders):
Infiltrators or compromised insiders refer to individuals within an organization who are either external entities posing as legitimate members or actual insiders whose credentials or systems have been compromised by an external threat actor. These situations can create serious security risks for the organization. For example, cybercriminals use phishing attacks to obtain a particular employee's login details and exploit any personal or critical information for malicious intents, or it can be a case of advanced persistent threats (APT) where an external actor passively maintains a long-term presence in a network using insider credentials.

4. Third-Party Insiders:
Third-party insiders refer to individuals or entities accessing an organization's systems, information, or facilities through a third-party relationship. These relationships might include vendors, suppliers, contractors, service providers, or business partners. For example, a contractor installing unauthorized or malicious software on a company's system introduces vulnerabilities, or a vendor unintentionally shares access details and other insider information.

5. Insider Threats for Espionage:
Insider threats for espionage refer to the deliberate use of authorized access within an organization to gather confidential or classified information for unauthorized purposes, often intending to deliver this information to a foreign government, rival company, or other unauthorized entity. For example, an employee may try to steal research data to share it with rival or foreign entities, or even a staff member may try to leak critical strategy to a competitor organization [15].

6. Insider Intellectual Property (IP) Theft:
Employees or partners who use unethical or illegal methods to acquire the organization's intellectual property. The motivation can be personal reasons, such as starting for personal gain, starting a competing venture, or selling to a third party. For example, an engineer may leak blueprint designs to a rival company, or a researcher may copy patented information just before resigning.

While the lines between these categories might sometimes blur, understanding these types helps organizations frame their risk assessment and mitigation strategies more effectively. It is essential to recognize that, in many cases, the threat is not from malicious intent; negligence and lack of awareness can be equally damaging. Hence, a comprehensive approach to insider threat management should address intentional and unintentional threats.

7.3.2 Importance of Understanding the Impact of Insider Threats

Understanding insider threats is crucial for businesses and organizations in our modern and technology-centered world. This understanding cares for safeguarding sensitive information. Organizations store massive amounts of confidential data, possibly ranging from unique business practices to private client information. The damages can be irreparable if it is accidentally revealed or misused from within the company. Such incidents can cause the company to face financial setbacks and lose the trust of existing and potential clients. Even worse, the fundamental functions of the business that are formed can become endangered by internal interference. It damages vital systems through intentional manipulation or errors, harming revenue streams and efficiency. The observations are more than just fixated on numbers and systems. The damages caused to the company's public image question the years of trust and confidence placed by clients and the public.

Another layer of complexity comes from the legal side of things. Strict regulations on data protection govern most industries, and failing to do so could lead to harsh legal consequences. Organizations should extend their security approaches beyond defending against external threats to navigate these challenges. Recognizing and combating threats from within is equally vital. Using a complete Insider and external security approach helps strengthen an organization's defenses, often leading to notable savings by warding off potential breaches. By investing in a more profound comprehension of these internal threats, organizations can further enable the feeling of trust and lead the employees to act with integrity and responsibility.

Organizations should keep evolving security infrastructure to succeed in a technically changing world. By doing so, the company is ensured to flourish and maintain clients' trust in their personal information, which is highly unlikely to do so with other companies [16].

7.3.3 The Magnitude of the Threat

Insider threats in the ever-evolving world are substantial and have grown significantly over the years. Statistically speaking, many cybersecurity reports and studies have consistently observed the increasing prominence of insider threats over the past few years. For instance, according to the 2020 Verizon Data Breach Investigations Report, insider threats accounted for about 30% of all data breaches. These data highlight that 30% of security incidents come from within the organization, concerning emphasized external threats.

Another poignant finding, as cited by the Poniman Institute's Cost of Insider Threats study, is the rising financial burden associated with these threats. The research highlighted that a company's average annual cost of insider-related incidents was around $11.45 million in 2020, a 31% increase from 2018. This monetary growth emphasizes the direct financial implications and the extended ramifications of system downtimes, reputational damage, and recovery processes. Additionally, the time taken to contain these incidents has also seen a spike. Quantitatively examining the situation reveals a pressing need for organizations to realign their cybersecurity

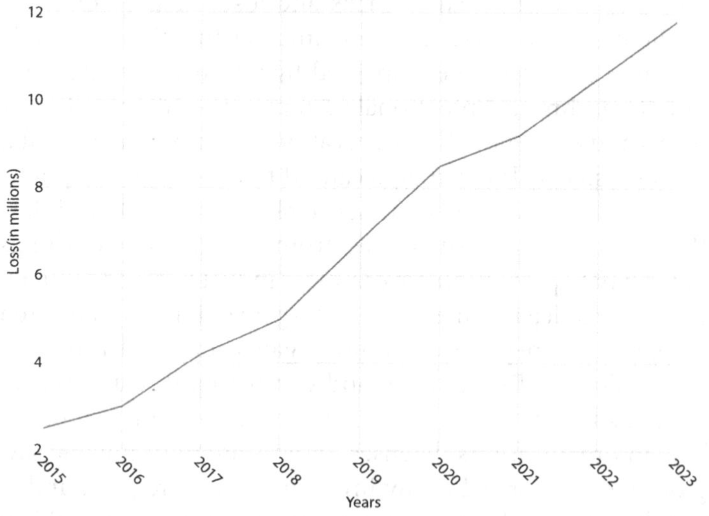

Figure 7.2 Represents the financial implications of insider attacks and provides a direct insight into the tangible impacts on organizations (the year 2015-2023).

strategies, giving insider threats the emphasis they warrant. The financial implications of inside attacks is represented in Figure 7.2.

7.3.4 Why are Insider Threats so Dangerous?

Insider threats pose a danger to the organizations that are hidden. Unlike external threats, which attempt to breach from the outside, insiders possess a vantage point from within the company's walls. Their authorized entry into information and vital infrastructure grants them an edge. More alarmingly, they are aware of the organization's weaknesses in technological defenses and procedural blind spots. The combination of their ability to operate covertly without triggering security alarms and the knowledge they possess amplifies the risks they bring. Motivations behind threats can vary widely, ranging from grudges and financial incentives to ideological differences or external influences. Addressing insider threats requires organizations to tackle a variety of challenges that can go beyond security considerations. Financially, organizations can find themselves grappling with direct losses from actions like fraud or theft and the ancillary costs of remediation, investigation, and system fortification post-incident. Moreover, with insiders' deep-rooted understanding of operational systems, the potential for disturbances in day-to-day functions looms large, manifesting as productivity lapses or even outright service halts. One of the consequences of these threats is compromising confidential data, which can include valuable assets or critical strategic plans. When this information falls into hands, it could disrupt the balance and put future business endeavors at risk. The impact caused by the breaches on an organization's reputation can be devastating. Stakeholders may question the company's integrity and dependability, while potential collaborators may become hesitant due to concerns about security incidents.

Compounding this is the legal quagmire that insider incidents might precipitate, especially in sectors bound by stringent data protection regulations. The internal organizational climate is not immune either. News of an insider threat quickly spreads, causing unease and doubt within the organization, thereby influencing employee workflow. This environment can lead to increased attrition rates within the organization. After such incidents, organizations often channel resources into bolstering security measures, investing in advanced tools, and initiating comprehensive training modules to prevent future occurrences. The diverse impacts of insider threats deepen their capability to disturb the state and hinder the advancement of an organization. It is necessary to tackle such acts of sabotage and execute tactics to safeguard against them to guarantee the enduring victory of any organization [17].

7.5 Challenges in Insider Threat Detection

We know that in this ever-evolving world, cybersecurity evolves too, which comes with more intricate types of challenges, and among them is the most denied but most damaging issue: insider threats. While it might seem paradoxical to use security within this challenge, it is far more complex than guarding against the outside because, in Insider Threats, the chances of being wrong and missing are way more than outside comparatively. Detecting and mitigating insider threats presents a unique set of challenges, which can be outlined as follows:

1. Distinguishing Malicious from Benign Activities:
The problem that often arises is that distinguishing between job-related tasks and harmful activities takes time and effort. For example, an employee may access an extensive database and do a routine backup or steal information. The loss of discrepancy makes creating that specific variable in an algorithm difficult, making it complex and leading to many errors.

2. Dynamic Nature of Organizational Roles:
We know that employees usually get promoted to higher ranks after some time, leading to higher access privileges. Someone promoted might require access to more sensitive data. This constant changing of profiles makes it difficult to maintain in the system, which means changes in the algorithm, however small it may be, complicate the model.

3. Volume and Complexity of Data:
Modern organizations generate vast amounts of data. Every day, new registrations, new logins, new files, different access controls, and numerous network activities increase the window to more potential hazards or threats, so sifting through this voluminous data to identify patterns indicative of a threat is difficult.

4. Evolving Tactics of Malicious Insiders:
Just as a refinement of security protocols is managed, malicious insiders evolve their tactics. This game of ever-development means that threat detection mechanisms should be continuously upgraded, a challenge given many organizations' resource constraints [18].

5. Privacy and Ethical Concerns:
Monitoring employees too closely can cause an invasion of privacy rights and can lead to damage to trust within the organization. Creating

a balance between usual surveillance and respecting privacy is a tough challenge.

6. False Positives and Their Consequences:
Over-intensive threat detection models can lead to false positives. Such scenarios can have multiple negative repercussions: potentially damaging an innocent employee's reputation, ill-use of security resources, and inducing "alert fatigue" in security teams.

7. Lack of Comprehensive Training and Awareness:
Negligence is the cause of most Insider Threats. However, organizations usually need help to form effective cybersecurity awareness programs, leading insider threats to be untouched or unnoticed.

8. Technological Fragmentation:
Most organizations deploy a lot of security tools and platforms. The lack of proper integration between some tools leads to vulnerabilities that malicious insiders might exploit.

9. Legacy Systems and Inconsistent Policies:
Many organizations still operate legacy systems with known vulnerabilities. Additionally, improper security policies can leave exploitable gaps. Insiders familiar with these weaknesses can exploit them and make detection harder.

10. Third-party and Supply Chain Complexities:
Modern businesses often rely on a vast network of third-party vendors, partners, and contractors. Ensuring that the used software comes under the same security standards can be difficult, and breaches on their end can be harder to detect.

11. Psychological and Behavioral Variabilities:
Human behavior is very unpredictable. At the same time, some behavioral patterns malicious insiders might exhibit, such as behavioral changes, lack of input, downloading of unnecessary data, etc., Relying solely on them can be misleading and unfair.

12. Whistleblower Protection and Fear of Repercussions:
Employees might notice suspicious activities coming from other colleagues but might be scared or threatened to report it, which might lead to others losing their trust. Ensuring whistleblower protection and anonymity, at least for the investigation, is a challenge but is a critical detection. The total number of vulnerabilities with regard to the organization is depicted in Figure 7.3.

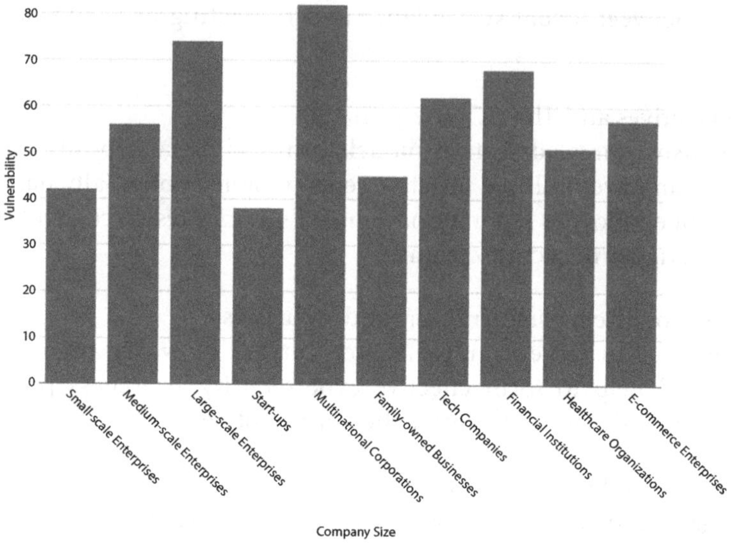

Figure 7.3 Number of vulnerabilities based on different types of organization.

Insider threat detection is a technological challenge and an organizational, ethical, and human-centric puzzle. While machine learning and AI can offer an advanced and promising future for Insider threat detection, the multifaceted nature of this challenge requires a holistic approach. Organizations must use top-notch and best technology or models with robust policies, real data training, and a culture of trust and accountability.

Given the stakes involved from financial losses and reputational damage to potential national security implications - tackling these challenges is not optional. It is a quintessential aspect of modern cybersecurity, demanding attention, resources, and continual adaptation.

7.6 Techniques for Insider Threat Detection

The insider threat landscape, characterized by its complexities and the proximity of error, requires diverse detection techniques. As technology has evolved, so have the attackers and their weapons, and using old and traditional approaches will only lead to insider attacks. Using advanced analytics models and AI-driven solutions with some conventional approaches also works. Before creating a Robust model, given are the models used to make Insider Threat detection and prevention:

1. User Behavior Analytics (UBA):
UBA solutions use machine learning algorithms to establish a basis of "normal" behavior for users in an organization. The model can identify deviations from normal daily activities by continually monitoring user activities, potentially signaling malicious actions. If an employee suddenly tries to access a large amount of data outside of office hours and downloads sensitive files, UBA can flag this as a threat and lead to further investigation. UBA's strength lies in its adaptability, ability to adjust to evolving user behaviors, and ability to offer dynamic threat detection.

2. Log Analysis:
Logs are records of events and transactions within a system. By analyzing these logs, organizations can detect suspicious activities or policy violations. Log analysis tools can signal multiple failed login attempts, trying for unauthorized access to sensitive areas, or changes made to critical system configurations outside office hours or within official commit. Even though it is essential, log analysis can be pretty complex, and it may require advanced tools or trained staff to derive meaningful insight.

3. Data Loss Prevention (DLP):
DLP solutions usually monitor data whether in transit, rest, or use. They help prevent any unauthorized or unusual data transfer between insiders and outsiders and provide an alert for potential breaches. Suppose an employee tries to email sensitive documents to someone not part of the organization or uploads them to a standard interface such as the cloud. In that case, DLP can block the action and notify security staff. DLP is especially effective against both malicious and inadvertent data exfiltration attempts.

4. Endpoint Monitoring:
This technique monitors individual user devices like computers, smartphones, and tablets. Observing organizations can detect any suspicious activity at the source. Endpoint models can detect unauthorized software installations, malicious code executions, or other policy violations done on user devices. Direct monitoring at the source helps provide a fundamental level of oversight, making endpoint solutions highly effective and potentially invasive (spreading at an alarming rate).

5. Network Traffic Analysis:
By analyzing patterns in network traffic, organizations can identify potential security threats. This might involve looking for unusual data transfer rates, unauthorized remote access, or connections to suspicious IP

addresses. If a user uploads a large amount of data to an unknown server or an outsider, the model will flag the reason as network traffic differences. It provides a bird's eye view of the organization's data flow, showing it as a warning against potential breaches [19].

6. Psycholinguistic Analysis:
Mechanism: This model analyzes language use and looks for psychological indications such as stress, malintent, and any unusual behavior in written communications. This method can raise alarms if an employee's emails suddenly exhibit signs of stress or use language like past trained insider threats. While still a field in its infancy, psycholinguistic analysis offers a unique angle of threat detection, focusing on the psychological dimension.

7. Access Control and Role-Based Monitoring:
By pre-defining user roles and their respective access privileges, organizations can monitor and control data accessibility. Any deviation from the given roles can signal potential threats. If a junior employee out of the blue accesses data reserved for senior management, this technique would flag the activity. A foundational security practice, role-based monitoring remains a robust defense against unauthorized data access.

9. Honeytokens and Decoys:
Honeytokens are digital entities, like fake data or systems, that are put inside to serve as bait for potential malicious insiders. Any accidental interaction with this data indicates that the individual has malicious intent. An organization can use it in its database with fake, deceiving data. If these data are accessed, it means a breach. It is a safe and powerful defense strategy; honeytokens can detect and act against potential insider threats.

The complexity of insider threats provides multiple approaches to detection. By exploiting a mixture of traditional monitoring techniques with cutting-edge AI-driven solutions, organizations can fortify their defenses, ensuring the sanctity of their data and systems. As the threat landscape evolves, continuous adaptation and innovation in detection techniques remain imperative.

7.7 Robust Model

To create, we must understand the shortcoming that comes with old or current models and try to overcome these problems with the new model.

7.7.1 Shortcomings in Current Insider Threat Detection Models

Current Threat Detection Models, whether they usually use supervised learning, unsupervised learning, or a combination of different algorithms, face several shortcomings given as follows:

1. **Lack of High-Quality Labeled Data:**
Labeled data containing benign and malignant activities must use a supervised learning model. Collecting and labeling data can be complex as it is peculiar to specific organizations, making it harder to generalize the process.

2. **False Positives and negatives**
Models sometimes mistake everyday routines for a threat for several reasons, causing False positives; sometimes, they can even overlook an entire malicious act and cannot detect false negatives. This inefficiency can lead to a very major drawback.

3. **Adaptation to new threats**
Some static models get a massive disadvantage in a dynamic and ever-evolving world. If, by any chance, the model is not trained for a new threat and has not been trained to face it, then it is, by default, a false positive.

4. **Class Imbalance**
In many models, the dataset contains many benign threats compared to malicious threats, which causes a discrepancy in the model. The model has been trained more for benign threats that may cause the model to get biased and give a false positive to a malicious Insider attack [20].

5. **Model Interpretability**
Many machine learning models nowadays use deep learning, which makes it complex and lacks transparency. This "Black Box" nature makes it hard to understand why a particular activity got flagged or got the positive, leading to a question of validity and trust in the model.

6. **Context Sensitivity**
Insider Threats are highly context-sensitive. It depends on the user's role, the access control assigned to a user, and the nature of the data. Models that need to incorporate this context may need help to distinguish between legitimate and malicious activities.

7. Integration and Existing Systems
Implementing machine learning for Insider Threat detection requires integration with existing security infrastructure, workflows, and data sources. This can be challenging and time-consuming.

8. Ethical and Legal Considerations
Monitoring and analyzing various user activities helps detect insider threats, which can lead to serious privacy concerns. Following legal requirements and ethical norms is vital but complicates the system's design.

9. Resource Intensive
Training and running large and complex machine learning models require significantly higher computational resources. This can be a more significant issue, especially for smaller organizations.

10. Real-time Processing Challenges:
If the model includes real-time algorithms, detecting threats will require high-speed data processing and analysis, which will be technically demanding, meaning we will have to provide massive data and storage of data, especially when dealing with large and complex datasets.

11. Collaborative Insider Threats:
When multiple insiders collaborate, their activities might not be flagged as threats, but collectively, they represent a severe risk. Detecting these coordinated actions is a complex task that current models need to handle better.

12. Human Behavior Complexity:
Human behavior is unimaginably complex and can be influenced by many factors that are hard to justify as variables or models. This complexity can lead to a decline in the model's accuracy, leading to inaccurate detection.

13. Reliance on Historical Patterns:
Current models usually rely on historical patterns of malicious behavior known as behavioral models. Still, insider threats can be unique and completely different from previous instances, making them hard to detect.

7.7.2 Required Algorithms and Tools for Robust Model

As mentioned, a well-suited machine-learning algorithm and a traditional model are required to create a machine-learned model. Requirements of the new model are described as follows:

7.7.2.1 *Supervised Learning Model*

Supervised learning is a machine learning method where a model is trained using a dataset containing both inputs and the corresponding expected outputs or "labels." Using this, the algorithm finds a function or a model that closely relates the relationship between the inputs and the labels in the training data. This model can then predict the output for new and unseen data. Types of supervised learning include regression (predicting continuous values) and classification (predicting categorical labels). The model's performance is analyzed using a separate dataset, and if the predictions are not acceptable, the model can further be adjusted and retrained.

Supervised learning models are potent and practical tools for Insider threat Detection. Here are some steps to how the model can be applied and used:

- **Training on Historical Data:** To train the model many times, historical data are preferred; training the model with historical data can recognize patterns and indicate behaviors of such threats.
- **Feature Extraction:** Usual features consist of user activities, such as login times, file accesses, network usage patterns, and more. Supervised learning can help determine which features are most needed to identify insider threats.
- **Anomaly Detection:** Supervised models help identify activities deviating from a behavioral pattern. A sudden change in the user's behavior may lead to a potential threat, and further continuation can trigger the alert. The flowchart corresponding to supervised learning model is depicted in Figure 7.4.

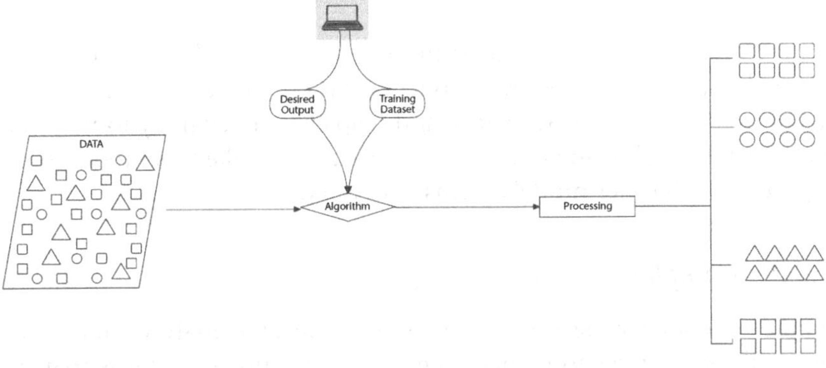

Figure 7.4 Flowchart of supervised learning model.

- **Real-Time Analysis:** Once trained, these models can analyze real-time data to detect potential insider threats, allowing organizations to respond swiftly and mitigate any possible damage.
- **Continuous Improvement:** As the model is trained, the organization still gathers more data on insider threats and false alarms, if there seems to be any. The model then gets regularly retrained and refined, improving its accuracy increases effectiveness slowly but gradually.
- **Compliance and Reporting:** These models are also capable of helping regulate meeting compliance requirements. The model is provided with a consistent approach to Insider Threat Detection and detailed reports or audits.
- **User Behaviour Profiling:** This is one of the best features of Supervised Learning. Supervised learning models create or build profiles based on expected user behavior. Any significant or unusual deviation from this profile, especially if it aligns with known insider threat indicators, can get flagged for further investigation.
- **Reduction of False Positives:** The supervised Learning model is trained by learning from labeled data that include both actual threats and benign activities; a well-trained supervised model can reduce false positives, focusing attention on the most likely threats without overwhelming security teams with false alarms.
- **Integration with Existing Security Measures:** These models can be integrated into a broader security system, and working together with other models and tools helps provide an extra layered defense against insider attacks.

Therefore, the Supervised learning model is undoubtedly suitable for Insider threat detection. As mentioned above, it solves most of the problems older or existing models face and helps boost accuracy to the maximum. Even though it solves most of the issues to make this model robust, integration with other models seems necessary.

7.7.2.2 Complex Event Processing

Complex Event Processing (CEP) is a method used to analyze data streams from multiple sources to identify meaningful events or patterns that suggest more complicated circumstances.

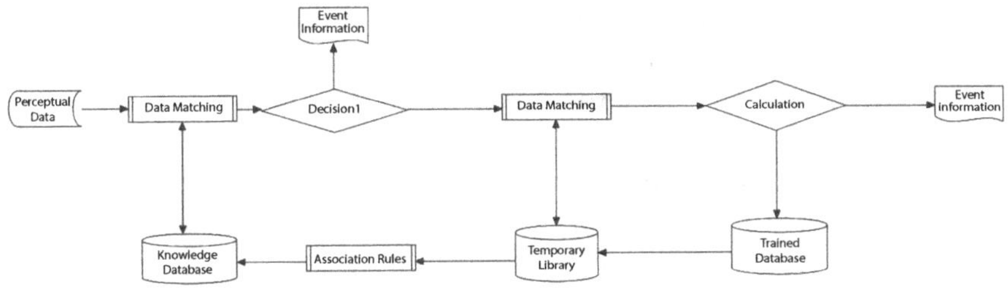

Figure 7.5 Flowchart of complex event processing model.

It is instrumental in insider threat detection, as it can process and analyze large amounts of data in real time. Working of the model in the context of Insider Threat detection is given as follows:

- **Collecting Data:** CEP, when integrated, starts to gather needed or necessary data from various sources within the organization's network. This includes logins, file accesses, email activity, network connections, and more. The flowchart for complex event processing model is represented in Figure 7.5.
- **Event Identification:** Event refers to individual actions or occurrences within a data flow. An event here can be a trigger, for instance, someone disrupting data flow by downloading a large amount of data unusually or accessing information outside of the accessed domain.
- **Event Correlation:** CEP is known to relate multiple unusual activities and finds any pattern to signify whether it is a threat or not. For instance, if a user logs in at an extraordinary time, accesses sensitive files, and then sends a large email, these events might be correlated as a potential threat.
- **Real-Time Analysis:** One of the critical features of CEP is its ability to analyze these events in real-time. This means that it can detect potential threats as they are happening, allowing for immediate investigation or response.
- **Pattern Detection:** As discussed before, by correlating two or more unusual activities, CEP can find a pattern. The model also learns these patterns, and if that pattern or behavior triggers the alert, and if required, it can continuously scan for that specific stream of pattern and alert if it is triggered.
- **Contextual Analysis:** CEP also considers the context of events, such as the user's role, the time of day, the files

accessed, etc. Understanding the context can help differentiate between actual activities and potential threats.
- **Integration with Other Systems:** Similar to supervised learning, CEP can be integrated with other security measures to create a robust insider threat detection system.
- **Response Automation:** In some instances, CEP can also be linked to automated response systems that can take immediate action if a threat is detected, such as locking user accounts or alerting security personnel.

Therefore, complex event processing or CEP is very suitable for integrating to create a new and robust insider threat detection and prevention model.

7.7.3 Integration Model

Integration of Supervised learning and Complex Event processing is feasible; it can be a more comprehensive and robust model for threat detection. Both models have different functions. The CEP model is designed to analyze and process multiple data streams in real-time, making it perfect for insider threats. Meanwhile, supervised learning is trained using labeled data and helps classify behavior as benign or malicious based on patterns. Merging the strengths of both approaches can compensate for each individual's limitations, creating a multi-faceted detection system.

Here is how we can integrate them:

1. **Initial Data Processing with CEP:** It is known that in CEP, the data are streamed in real-time, due to which preliminary patterns or anomalies based on predefined rules can be filtered, aggregated, and identified. This immediately alerts the machine of known threat patterns and reduces the data volume needing more intensive processing.
2. **Deep Analysis with Supervised Learning:** The pre-processed data or flagged events taken from the CEP can be labeled data in the supervised learning model. When trained using historically labeled data, this model can provide a more accurate analysis, identifying potential threats based on learned patterns. It can also classify flagged events as benign or malicious with higher accuracy.
3. **Feedback Loop:** As the supervised model makes classifications, this output can continuously refine and update the CEP

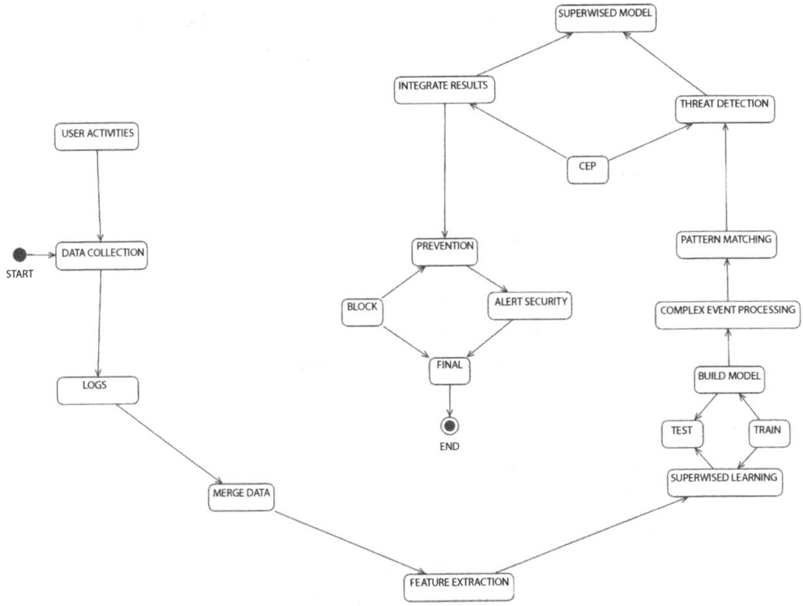

Figure 7.6 Process modeling of integration model.

rules. For example, if specific patterns repeatedly lead to false positives, CEP rules can be adjusted accordingly. Therefore, if the supervised model continuously identifies new threat patterns, rules can be added to the CEP to catch these in real-time. The integrated processing model is represented in Figure 7.6.

4. **Adaptability:** As the model has an integrated approach, the system benefits from the real-time responsiveness of complex event processing and deep learning capability of the supervised model. Moreover, as new threat patterns emerge, labeled data can be added to retrain the supervised model, and CEP rules can be updated simultaneously.
5. **Reduced False Positives/Negatives:** Combining both methods can reduce false positives and negatives. While CEP might flag a broad range of events based on predefined patterns, the supervised model can further refine these alerts, reducing the chances of overlooking genuine threats or flagging benign activities.
6. **Contextual Analysis:** The combination allows for more contextual analysis. While CEP might identify a sequence

of events as suspicious, the supervised model can analyze it in the context of historical data to determine its actual risk level.

7.7.4 Pseudocode

```
Step 1: Data Collection
  function collect_data_from_systems():
        logs = fetch_system_logs()
        user_activities = fetch_user_activities()
        return merge_data(logs, user_activities)

Step 2: Feature Extraction
  function extract_features(data):
        processed_features = []
        for record in data:
                features = process_record(record)
                processed_features.append(features)
        return processed_features

Step 3: Supervised Learning
  function split_data(features):
        return training_data, testing_data
  function train_supervised_model(train_data):
        // e.g., SVM, Decision Trees, etc.
        model = initialize_model()
        model.train(train_data)
        return model

Step 4: Complex Event Processing
  class CEP:
        function process(event, context):
                pattern = match_pattern(event, context)
                return pattern

Step 5: Threat Detection
  function detect_threat(live_events, model, event_processor):
        for event in live_events:
                context = get_context(event)
                processed_event = event_processor.process(event, context)
```

```
            prediction = model.predict(processed_event)
            if prediction == 'threat':
                    respond_to_threat(event)

Step 6: Prevention & Response
   function respond_to_threat(event):
        if event.type == 'access_violation':
                block_access(event.user)
        elif event.type == 'unusual_file_transfer':
                alert_security(event.user, event.details)

        Additional responses as needed

Main Function
   function main():
        data = collect_data_from_systems()
        features = extract_features(data)
        train_data, test_data = split_data(features)
        model = train_supervised_model(train_data)
        event_processor = CEP()
        detect_threat(live_events, model, event_processor)

Execute the main function
   main()
```

Explanation of the functions:

- collect_data_from_systems: Combines logs and user activities.
- extract_features: Converts raw data into a format suitable for machine learning.
- split_data: Divides data into training and testing sets.
- train_supervised_model: Trains a supervised learning model such as SVM or Decision Trees.
- CEP class: Contains methods for complex event processing, identifying patterns using context-aware rules.
- detect_threat: Processes live events, predicting whether they signify a threat.
- respond_to_threat: Contains the necessary actions to respond to a detected threat, such as blocking access or alerting security personnel.

This extended pseudo code provides an overall view of an insider threat detection system integrated with the Supervised Learning model and Complex Event processing by detailing each function involved. It offers flexibility to adapt specific techniques or technologies in each step, making it suitable for various industrial applications.

7.8 Application and Case Studies

The fusion of guided education and Elaborate Episode Processing (CEP) for internal danger spotting and safeguarding offers an inventive resolution to a pervasive cybersecurity issue encountered by establishments in contemporary times. Hereafter, we shall delve into the mechanics of this assimilation and emphasize a handful of theoretical instances where this amalgamated tactic has been employed.

7.8.1 Introduction

Insider menaces embrace malevolent conduct executed by persons within an establishment. These menaces may be deliberate, akin to pilfering or exposing information, or inadvertent, akin to bungling delicate data. Spotting insider menaces necessitates grasping both explicit assault blueprints and inconspicuous, atypical demeanor. In this context, the harmonious combination of tutored enlightenment and CEP can manifest as highly efficacious.

7.8.2 How the Integration Works

Complex Event Processing (CEP): CEP facilitates the real-time monitoring of numerous activities within an organization's IT infrastructure. By establishing precise rules or patterns, CEP can rapidly identify atypical conduct that could indicate an internal security risk.

Supervised Learning: This approach to machine learning necessitates a dataset that has been labeled, wherein known occurrences of internal threats have been classified. The model acquires knowledge from this information to identify if there are any potential threats. It offers a Complete analysis and alleviates false positives by understanding the intricate patterns of behavior linked to internal threats.

7.8.3 Case Studies

Case Study 1: Protecting Intellectual Property in a Tech Company
Application: A leading technology company was grappling with the loss of intellectual property due to insider threats. A system was required to identify uncharacteristic entries or alteration of confidential data.
Implementation: The corporation executed a mechanism that amalgamated CEP, which provides real-time scrutiny of file access and network actions, with a supervised learning framework with historical data encompassing recognized inside hazards.
Outcome: The integration furnished an advanced cautionary mechanism that spotted irregularities instantaneously, followed by an extensive examination employing guided education. Therefore, implementing the measures was worthy of reducing the number of examples of unauthorized access and leakage of information, effectively protecting valuable intellectual property.

Case Study 2: Healthcare Data Security
Application: A significant hospital needs to ensure the privacy and security of patient data, protecting it from external hackers and insider threats.
Implementation: The hospital integrated CEP to monitor access to patient records, coupled with a supervised learning model trained to recognize patterns associated with previous insider threats.
Outcome: The hospital uses quick detection and in-depth study to avoid unauthorized entry into patient records. This properly ensured loyalty to lawful pre-requirements and the level of confidence among patients and personnel.

Case Study 3: Financial Insider Trading Detection
Application: A financial regulatory agency began scrutinizing voluminous transaction data to uncover and avoid illegal insider trading activities within investment firms. This attempt is made to clarify any peculiar patterns that might raise suspicion.
Implementation: Organizations often use complex event processing (CEP) to conduct real-time analyses of trade data and include them with a supervised learning model that has received training on previous instances of insider trading.
Outcome: The system could identify trading patterns in time, while the supervised learning model provided a detailed understanding of whether these patterns indicated insider trading. The system's effectiveness in reducing alarms and promptly detecting threats proved extremely valuable in preserving the market's integrity.

Therefore, detecting and preventing insider threats are crucial challenges for organizations. By combining Complex Event Processing with learning, we have developed a solution that combines real-time alerts with thorough historical analysis.

Through hypothetical case studies across sectors, such as technology, healthcare, and finance, we have observed how this integrated approach efficiently safeguards sensitive information. The success of this combined model relies on factors such as using quality historical data for supervised learning, accurately defining rules in CEP, continuously updating to adapt to new threat patterns, and ensuring compliance with legal and ethical considerations.

Integrating CEP with learning marks a significant advancement in combating insider threats by providing both detection capabilities and in-depth analysis. This approach can be customized to suit contexts, showcasing its broad applicability and potential for enhancing security across diverse domains.

7.9 Other Important Insider Threat Prevention Strategies

Insider threats pose a challenge for organizations in terms of security. These threats arise from individuals with insider knowledge of systems, policies, and data who can cause harm through malicious or negligent actions. To address this issue effectively, it is vital to establish measures. This section focuses on exploring strategies to prevent insider threats.

1. Comprehensive Background Checks:
Before hiring an individual, it is crucial to understand their actions and affiliations. Conducting background checks that delve into history, previous employment records and online activities can help employers identify potential risks. In sectors, conducting rechecks after the hiring process may also be beneficial.

2. Robust Access Controls:
One of the principles in security management is the Principle of Least Privilege (PLP), which suggests that users should only have access to data and systems for their job functions. Regularly auditing and updating access permissions ensures that individuals cannot access data irrelevant to their roles.

3. Regular Training and Awareness Programs:
Employees often unintentionally become threats due to a need for more awareness regarding security practices. Regular training sessions on practices emphasizing the importance of data protection and raising awareness about threat vectors can significantly reduce inadvertent insider threats.

4. Data Loss Prevention (DLP) Technologies:
Implementing data loss prevention (DLP) tools within an organization allows for monitoring data transfers across channels. These tools help prevent the sharing or downloading of information. They can be set up to avoid the transfer of information to drives or unauthorized cloud storage, providing a real-time security measure.

5. Multi-Factor Authentication (MFA):
Implementing verification forms, MFA ensures that even if someone with insider access has the credentials, they still require an extra step of verification to access systems. This reduces the chances of access.

6. Anomaly Detection Systems:
These systems utilize AI and ML to establish user behavior patterns and send alerts when deviations are from this norm. For instance, if an employee suddenly downloads vast amounts of data or accesses systems at odd hours, the system can flag this for investigation.

7. Session Recordings:
When users try to access sensitive data or systems, there is a chance that it can be accounted for as malicious activity. If an insider knows their actions are being recorded, they may think twice before engaging in harmful activities.

8. Secure Communication Platforms:
Using encrypted and secure communication tools ensures that sensitive information shared within the organization remains confidential. It also prevents the system from data leaks and unauthorized data sharing.

9. Whistleblower Policies:
Employees often witness suspicious activities but may hesitate to report them because they fear repercussions. Establishing clear whistleblower policies where individuals can safely report concerns can bring potential threats to light.

10. Psychological Support and Monitoring:
Dissatisfied employees can be potential risks. Offering support, open channels for grievances, and monitoring significant changes in employee behavior or demeanor can help proactively identify and address potential threats.

11. Regular System and Network Audits:
Periodically conducting audits can assist in detecting vulnerabilities, unapproved entries, or alterations to the system that could imply illicit insider behavior. In conjunction with careful and precise logging, audits offer a detailed and overall view of the well-being and security status of the system.

12. Restricting Use of Personal Devices:
Limiting or monitoring the use of personal devices for official purposes ensures that sensitive data does not move to uncontrolled environments and is susceptible to leaks or breaches.

Insider dangers weaved into their very essence are intricate, owing to institutions' innate reliance on their insiders. Nevertheless, a complicated and manifold preventive tactic, which amalgamates technological instruments with human-focused approaches, holds the capacity to alleviate these hazards materially. Endowing employees with awareness regarding conceivable risks and the significance of their responsibility in averting insider dangers becomes a vital imperative. Technological resolutions, such as data loss prevention (DLP), multi-factor authentication (MFA), and anomaly detection systems amplify the fortified infrastructure. In contrast, human-focused strategies encompassing training, psychological assistance, and whistleblower guidelines ensure that the human factor garners attention.

7.10 Ethical Considerations

Implementing systems to detect insider threats goes beyond technical and operational tasks. It is closely connected to ethical considerations involving the personal rights of workers, the duties of organizations, and the broader impact on society. In this article, we explore the numerous ethical issues that companies must face and tackle when they embark on initiatives to detect insider threats.

1. Privacy Rights and Surveillance:
One of the primary ethical obstacles we must address is the issue of privacy. The constant surveillance can swiftly cross boundaries, particularly

if workers perceive that their every move, interaction, or slightest detour from their habits is being closely observed. We should ensure upholding an individual's right to privacy policy.

2. Data Access and Confidentiality:
Surveillance systems may seize personal data or discussions unrelated to security worries. Our ethical responsibility is to ensure this information is managed cautiously and not exploited.

3. Profiling and Discrimination:
Sometimes, when utilizing machine learning models or heuristic methods for detection, there is a possibility that unintentional profiling may occur based on race, gender, nationality, or other personal characteristics. Consequently, biased outcomes may arise, resulting in unfair targeting or increased scrutiny of specific groups.

4. Transparency and Openness:
Workers are entitled to be aware of the magnitude they are being observed. Even though achieving complete openness might not be practical due to security anxieties, establishments should endeavor to attain equilibrium wherein employees comprehend the fundamental outlines of the monitoring realm.

5. Whistleblower Protections:
Although whistleblower systems encourage employees to disclose dubious activities, there is a moral duty to guarantee that these individuals are shielded from retaliation. They must be assured that their deeds will not have detrimental personal or vocational consequences.

6. Proportionality and Necessity: Any surveillance or monitoring system must be balanced about the potential risks that the organization may encounter. Imposing excessively stringent systems that are disproportionate to the level of risk can encroach upon the rights of individuals without any valid justification.

7. Redress Mechanisms:
No system is foolproof. There will be occurrences of incorrect identifications. Establishing a mechanism that allows individuals to question and correct unjust allegations is ethically crucial.

8. Use of Third-party Vendors:
Frequently, when detecting insider threats, there may be a need to rely on third-party remedies or vendors. It is essential to guarantee that these external parties comply with identical moral principles, particularly about safeguarding data privacy and maintaining confidentiality.

9. Psychological Well-being:
An all-encompassing monitoring atmosphere may cultivate a sense of doubt, ultimately harming the overall workplace ambiance and employees' mental health. Achieving a harmonious equilibrium between safeguarding and promoting an encouraging work setting holds immense ethical importance.

10. Long-term Data Retention:
When organizations keep surveillance data for a long duration, ethical issues arise. The more time the data are stored, the greater the likelihood of potential misuse. To address these concerns, it is essential to establish transparent guidelines regarding data retention and to delete outdated information regularly.

11. Legal Compliance:
Although organizations may possess the necessary technical capacity for substantial observation, they must guarantee adherence to regional, provincial, or national legislation and privacy rules.

The conclusion is that detecting and managing internal hazards while considering ethical considerations to safeguard the establishment can be quite a hefty process. Achieving this type of equilibrium between the compulsion of security policy and upholding the rights and policy of employees is quite an important task. Organizations must approach this realm with a finely crafted ethical framework, unwavering transparency, and unwavering devotion to principles of justness and egalitarianism. Furthermore, engaging in ceaseless dialogues with stakeholders, including employees, regulatory bodies, and civil society organizations, can furnish diverse perspectives and steer ethical practices in the right direction. At its essence, managing internal hazards transcends the mere prevention of breaches or leaks of information; it inherently includes upholding the fundamental ethical principles upon which the establishment is rooted.

In the digital transformation era, where data are abundant, and surveillance capabilities are expansive, ethical considerations are not mere afterthoughts. They form the bedrock of any robust and sustainable insider threat detection system, ensuring organizational security and preserving and enhancing organizational integrity.

7.11 Future Trends

The ever-evolving digital landscape can present both challenges and opportunities in the field of insider threat detection. As organizations adapt to new technologies, threat actors refine their techniques. It is crucial for industries to, therefore, anticipate and prepare for emerging trends and future threats for insider threat management. Here is an exploration of the future trajectories this domain might take.

1. Integration of Advanced AI and Machine Learning:
While AI and ML have profoundly contributed to insider threat detection, their application will become even more sophisticated. Advanced algorithms will predict threats based on dynamic behavioral patterns, promising improved accuracy and reducing false positives. These systems will learn and adapt continuously from the vast amounts of data they process.

2. Predictive Analytics:
Beyond just detection, the future will include prediction as a step ahead of attackers. Systems will sense and act from merely identifying potential insider threats to predicting them before they manifest. These systems will forecast anomalies by analyzing historical data and user behavior, allowing organizations to intervene proactively.

3. Adaptive Authentication:
As user behavior becomes central to threat detection, it will also play a significant role in authentication. Adaptive authentication will evaluate the context of a user's login attempt - location, device, time, and more - to assess risk. If an effort appears risky, additional authentication steps will be triggered.

4. Increased Focus on the Human Element:
Comprehensive strategies will combine solutions emphasizing understanding human behavior to manage insider threats effectively. This will involve profiling, regular training sessions, and programs dedicated to employee wellbeing.

5. Data Privacy Enhancements:
In response to growing concerns about privacy and increased regulations, future systems will prioritize privacy as an aspect rather than an afterthought. Innovative techniques like privacy will ensure that individual user data remains anonymous while providing insights for threat detection.

6. Cross-platform Threat Detection:
As employees access data through devices and platforms, the evolution of threat detection systems will enable tracking of user activity across diverse access points. This holistic approach offers a view of threats.

7. Quantum Computing and Cryptography:
The emergence of quantum computing poses challenges and opportunities in insider threat management. While it may grant threat actors capabilities, it also brings advancements in quantum cryptography that reshape the security landscape, ultimately transforming how we detect and manage insider threats.

8. Collaborative Insider Threat Management:
Collaboration among organizations will become increasingly common as they collectively share insights, threat intelligence, and best practices to combat insider threats. This collective defense approach allows entities to work together in unison against attacks.

9. Augmented Reality (AR) and Insider Threats:
Organizations are set to enhance their collaboration efforts by exchanging insights, sharing threat intelligence, and adopting practices.

As augmented reality (AR) becomes more widespread in settings, it will create opportunities for insider threats. In response, collective defense strategies will gain popularity to counter these attacks and present a front against them.

10. Decentralized Security Systems:
Technologies like blockchain are revolutionizing the way we handle internal hazards. Through the establishment of logs that cannot be manipulated and access controls that are fully transparent, these groundbreaking technologies have the potential to provide heightened protection against unauthorized meddling by insiders.

11. Evolution of Regulatory Frameworks:
With the increasing dangers and their consequences, regulatory entities across the globe will enhance and implement fresh frameworks and guidelines. Conformity will not solely revolve around adhering to present standards but will also involve constantly adjusting to the ever-changing regulatory environment.

The future of insider threat detection and management is a blend of advanced technology and a deeper understanding of the human element. As the digital and physical worlds become increasingly intertwined, organizations must adopt a multifaceted approach, merging technological solutions with human-centric strategies. While challenges are on the horizon, so are opportunities. The next generation of insider threat management will be proactive, predictive, and deeply integrated into the organizational fabric. It will be about countering threats and building resilient systems that adapt, learn, and continuously improve.

Anticipating these trends and investing in the future is not just a strategic move but a necessity. In an interconnected world, the stakes are high, but with foresight and preparedness, organizations can navigate the complexities of the future, safeguarding their assets and preserving trust.

7.12 Conclusion

In the changing landscape of cybersecurity, developing a framework for detecting and preventing insider threats represents a significant step forward. The combination of learning and Complex Event Processing in time offers a fresh and innovative approach that has the potential to revolutionize how organizations safeguard themselves against internal vulnerabilities. However, despite its nature, this model is now at a stage where theory needs to be put into practice. The effectiveness of any machine learning model relies heavily on the quality and quantity of training data it receives. In detecting insider threats, data must be obtained from within organizational environments [11]. Although the model is well designed, it requires tuning with real-world data that captures the intricacies and nuances associated with insider threats. This encompasses not only forms and manifestations of these threats but also considers subtle aspects of human behavior and organizational dynamics. Moreover, achieving success with this model demands testing. Genuine organizational data are the benchmark against which we can validate the model's predictions by applying it to real-world scenarios that have yet to be encountered before we can identify both its strengths and areas where improvements may be necessary. We can assess the model's accuracy in a manner that provides insights into its ability to handle new instances of insider threats effectively. However, accessing such data poses a challenge. Organizations may be cautious about sharing information that could potentially expose their vulnerabilities. Overcoming this obstacle requires efforts among researchers, practitioners, and organizational leaders. To ensure confidentiality and integrity, it is crucial to prioritize transparency, trust, and ethical considerations when collecting data.

In summary, developing a model for detecting and preventing insider threats represents a breakthrough in a constantly evolving field. Its creation reflects the progress made in understanding and combating insider threats. However, there is still potential waiting to be realized. By obtaining quality training and testing data from organizations, we can uncover the true capabilities of this model. This opens opportunities for collaboration and research, bridging the gap between advancements and practical implementation. The journey towards a resilient digital landscape continues with this robust model's role in guiding us towards a future where insider threats are detected and prevented—fostering a culture built on trust, transparency, and technological excellence.

References

1. Eric D. Shaw, The role of behavioral research and profiling in malicious cyber insider investigations, Digital Investigation, 3, 1, 2006, 20–31, ISSN 1742-2876, https://doi.org/10.1016/j.diin.2006.01.006.
2. Stolfo, S.J., Bellovin, S.M., Keromytis, A.D., Hershkop, S., Smith, S.W., Sinclair, S., *Insider Attack and Cyber Security, Beyond the Hacker*, Springer New York, NY, 2008.
3. Probst, C.W., Hunker, J., Gollmann, D., Bishop, M., Aspects of Insider Threats, in: *Insider Threats in Cyber Security*, pp. 1–15, 2010.
4. Shen, A., A Bayesian Network Model for Predicting Insider Threats. *Security and Privacy Workshops (SPW)*, pp. 82–89, 2013.
5. Chandola, V., Banerjee, A., K., Anomaly Detection: A Survey. *ACM Comput. Surv. (CSUR)*, 41, 3, 15, 2015.
6. Juba, B., Kulkarni, S.R., Valetto, G., Creating a Model of Insider Threat by Simulation.," *Simul. Ser.*, 50, 1, 237–244, 2018.
7. Moore, A.P., Hanley, M., Mundie, D., A Pattern-Based Method for Identifying and Investigating Insider Threats to Digital Repositories, *Reliab. Eng. Syst. Saf.*, 96, 2, 224–231, 2011.

8. Greitzer, F.L. and Frincke, D.A., Combining Traditional Cyber Security Audit Data with Psychosocial Data: Towards Predictive Modeling for Insider Threat Mitigation, in: *Insider Threats in Cyber Security*, pp. 85–113, 2010.
9. Hunker, J., Probst, C.W., Gollmann, D., Bishop, M., Insider Threats in Computing Systems: A Survey. *Comput. Secur.*, 25, 2, 70–89, 2008.
10. Mathew, S., Petropoulos, M., Ngo, H.Q., Upadhyaya, S., A Data-Centric Approach to Insider Attack Detection in Database Systems. *Recent Advances in Intrusion Detection*, pp. 382–401, 2010.
11. Bishop, C.M., *Pattern Recognition and Machine Learning, Information Science and Statistics*, Springer-Verlag, New York, 2006.
12. Coyle, F.P., *Review of 'The power of events: An introduction to complex event processing in distributed enterprise systems,'* by David Luckham, Addison Wesley Professional, 2003, https://doi.org/10.1145/766760.764027
13. Silowash, G., Cappelli, D., Moore, A., Trzeciak, R., Shimeall, T., Flynn, L., Common Sense Guide to Mitigating Insider Threats, in: *CERT Insider Threat Center*, 4th Edition, 2012.

Authored Book

14. Muruganandham, R. S. A. A. S. S., A hybrid web analytic approach through click enabled vision based page segmentation in quest software for school students. *J. Intell. Fuzzy Syst.*, 43, 5, 6863–6875, 2022.

References

15. S.A.A.A.R.D.S. a. R.S.A.S., A Novel AI-based chatbot Application for Personalized Medical Diagnosis and review using Large Language Models, in: *2023 International Conference on Research Methodologies in Knowledge Management, Artificial Intelligence and Telecommunication Engineering (RMKMATE)*, pp. 1–5, Chennai, India, 2023, doi: 10.1109/RMKMATE59243.2023.10368616.
16. V.S.R., A.L.H.D., A.S.A., Shashank V, N.P., An Efficient Decision Support System for Stock Market Prediction using Technical Indicators as Features by Machine Learning Approaches, in: *International Conference for Emerging Technology (INCET)*, pp. 1–6, Belgaum, India, 2023, doi: 10.1109/INCET57972.2023.10170137.
17. Kishore, G. M. A. S. G. V. T. A. A. S. S. and Dutta, P. C. S. B. A. D. S. S. C., Sentiment Analysis of User Groups in an Working Environment Using CNN for Streaming Data Analysis, in: *Emerging Technologies in Data Mining and Information Security*. Lecture Notes in Networks and Systems, vol. 490, Springer, Singapore, 2023, https://doi.org/10.1007/978-981-19-4052-1_48.

18. Shrivastava, G., Gupta, D. and Sharma, K., Cyber Crime and Forensic Computing, Modern Principles, Practices, and Algorithms, in: *De Gruyter Frontiers in Computational Intelligence*, vol. 11, Germany.
19. Shrivastava, G., Peng, S.-L., Bansal, H., Sharma, K. & Sharma, M., *New Age Analytics: Transforming the Internet through Machine Learning, IoT, and Trust Modeling*, AAP & CRC Press, Taylor & Francis Group, 2020.
20. Abdullah, A.S., *Swarm Intelligence and Its Applications in Biomedical Informatics*, CRC Press, Taylor and Francis, New York, 2024.

8

Digital Vulnerabilities Unveiled: A Multidisciplinary Exploration of Emerging Threats to Security and Privacy in the Age of Networked Communication

Priya Sachdeva[1]* and Archan Mitra[2]

[1]Amity School of Communication, Amity University, Noida, India
[2]School of Media Studies, Presidency University, Bangalore, India

Abstract

In the era of networked communication, this chapter offers a multidisciplinary analysis of digital vulnerabilities, exposing new risks to privacy and security. Using a mixed-methods approach, the research forgoes intricate statistical analysis, favoring a detailed account gleaned from expert interviews, case study reviews, and surveys. The expert commentary adds scholarly profundity to the conversation, case studies contextualize real-world situations, and surveys offer insights into popular perception. This triangulation of data sources highlights the multiple facets of digital vulnerability. The chapter emphasizes the value of using an interdisciplinary approach to comprehend and solve the complex aspects of digital threats, focusing on the interplay between socio-technical factors underlying these security issues. The results support the book's overarching ideas by calling for ongoing scholarly investigation and a transdisciplinary approach to the intricate problems surrounding digital security and privacy.

Keywords: Digital security, media and communication studies, misinformation and fake news, data breaches, social engineering and phishing

**Corresponding author*: sachdevapriya35@yahoo.in

Kavita Sharma, Vishnu Sharma, Parma Nand, Anil Kumar Sagar and Gulshan Shrivastava (eds.) Securing the Digital Frontier: Threats and Advanced Techniques in Security and Forensics, (169–196)

8.1 Introduction

The rise of digital technology and networked communication has ushered in previously unimaginable possibilities for spreading information, sharing cultural experiences, and establishing social connections. However, this interconnection also exposes systemic vulnerabilities to security and privacy, challenges that are becoming increasingly pertinent as society struggles to come to terms with the negative aspects of the digital revolution. The current investigation is a rallying cry for a comprehensive grasp of the new dangers that threaten our digital existence.

This chapter intersects numerous academic disciplines, pulling from media and communication studies, cybersecurity studies, information technology studies, psychology, ethics, and legal studies. Because these domains are converging, we now have a rich tapestry to investigate the subtle and complicated nature of digital vulnerabilities. According to Floridi's hypothesis, the information age has ushered in a new ethical environment, which he calls the "infosphere" [1]. Conventional notions of privacy, security, and autonomy are being tested and redefined in this environment.

An excellent illustration of these rising dangers is the proliferation of false information and fake news. According to Marwick and Lewis, the ability of traditional gatekeeping organizations to govern and verify content in networked communication has fallen behind the rapid distribution of information made possible by networked communication [2]. Consequently, disseminating false information has developed into a weapon that can manipulate public opinion, undermine democratic institutions, and exacerbate social divisions. Findings of Lazer *et al.* on the propagation and effect of fake news on social media are reflected in this research's survey results, which suggest that an alarming majority of internet users have come across and, at times, accidentally perpetuated misleading information [3]. This research's findings are consistent with those of Lazer *et al.* [3].

In addition, the frequency of data breaches indicates a systemic problem inside the digital infrastructure responsible for maintaining personal and institutional data. According to the Identity Theft Resource Centre, the rise in such events indicates technology flaws and a broader societal failure to prioritize and enforce stringent data protection rules [4]. This failure has been noted. These breaches have significant repercussions for the trust that can be placed in digital networks and bring to light the unstable nature of our combined digital identities.

Phishing and social engineering are examples of complex combinations of technology intrusion and psychological coercion. According to the analysis of cyber events, the high success rate of these attacks highlights the need for a more profound knowledge of the human components of cybersecurity. This is a feeling that Ferguson shared in his discussion on the psychological dimensions of digital security [5].

This study used a mixed-methods approach, which proved to be very helpful in triangulating the many different aspects of digital vulnerabilities. Incorporating qualitative studies of cyber incidents and interviews with industry experts with quantitative survey data creates a complete and empirically sound base to derive conclusions [6]. This methodology reflects an expanding consensus on the significance of interdisciplinary research in handling complicated problems.

In terms of classroom instruction, this chapter has several vital repercussions for journalism and mass communication. The findings that have been provided in this article argue in favor of an updated curriculum that provides aspiring media professionals with the means to negotiate and combat the ethical, technological, and communicative problems that are posed by digital dangers. This is at the request of Potter and Thai for educational programs to adapt to the shifting landscape of media and technology [7].

This investigation of the weaknesses of digital systems makes a valuable contribution to an essential discussion about the foundation of networked societies. It is consistent with the concept of "surveillance capitalism" as articulated by Zuboff, according to which the gathering and processing personal data have given rise to new power dynamics that exploit individual weaknesses for financial benefit [8]. From such a viewpoint, the findings of this study highlight the crucial need to establish comprehensive solutions drawn from various academic fields to protect individuals' security and privacy in the digital era.

In the context of the broader Media and Communication Studies field, this chapter examines the consequences of digital dangers for democratic engagement, individual autonomy, and societal cohesiveness. This will be accomplished by attempting to integrate theoretical frameworks with practical problems. It is an endeavor that is both vital and urgent as we traverse the intricacies of the digital world of the 21st century, and it is a reflection of the need for a recalibrated moral compass in an age of digital vulnerabilities.

8.1.1 Objectives

The primary aim is to methodically analyze the present state of digital risks, with specific emphasis on the propagation of misinformation and fake news, instances of data breaches, and the utilization of social engineering techniques such as phishing. This task entails the examination of the evolutionary trajectory of these threats from 2020 to 2023, as well as the identification of the foremost vulnerabilities encountered by persons and institutions in the realm of digital technology. The act of mapping in question will serve as a fundamental basis for acquiring a comprehensive comprehension needed in formulating efficient remedies. The second aim of this study is to evaluate the quantitative and qualitative consequences of these vulnerabilities on different stakeholders. This encompasses the assessment of the impact of misinformation on public opinion and political processes, the comprehension of the repercussions of data breaches on personal privacy, institutional credibility, and economic stability, and the analysis of the psychological ramifications of social engineering on its victims. This study aims to establish associations between the prevalence of digital dangers and their tangible consequences in the physical world, thus emphasizing the imperative nature of resolving these vulnerabilities. The ultimate goal is to utilize the research discoveries to provide insights and suggest improvements to the teaching methods employed in Journalism and Mass Communication curricula. The objective is to provide upcoming media professionals with the essential abilities in critical thinking, ethical frameworks, and technological competencies, enabling them to address and minimize the difficulties arising from digital vulnerabilities effectively. This includes the development of teaching modules that specifically tackle the ethical considerations associated with digital security and privacy. It also involves formulating optimal strategies for recognizing and countering misinformation and social engineering techniques.

The aforementioned aims contribute to the project's primary aim: to facilitate a multidisciplinary discourse and develop well-informed policies that enhance digital resilience in an era characterized by substantial security and privacy concerns.

8.2 Theoretical Foundation

8.2.1 Conceptual Foundations

Because the conceptual underpinnings of the study are relevant to digital security and privacy, an interdisciplinary approach is required to accommodate the research project's theoretical framework. The Theory of Information Ethics, as stated by Floridi, is a crucial component of this paradigm [9]. This theory maintains that information in and of itself possesses inherent ethical value and, as a result, ought to be protected. This theory provides a philosophical backbone for studying digital vulnerabilities by advocating for preserving the "infosphere," which may be seen as the collective environment of information analogous to the natural environment, requiring preservation and respect.

In conjunction with this, the research uses Castells' Network Society Theory, which elucidates the nature of social structures and behaviors in the era of digital technology [10]. The idea of the network society proposed by Castells is essential to understanding how digital vulnerabilities can spread through interconnected digital and human networks. This highlights the ease with which data breaches can occur in a world that is becoming more networked [34].

Barnes (2006) came up with the term "Privacy Paradox," which explores the dichotomy between individuals' claimed worries about privacy and their behavior on digital platforms [11]. This dichotomy is examined via the lens of privacy, which is framed through the lens of the Privacy Paradox. This paradox is essential to understanding how users feel about their privacy in light of the numerous data breaches.

The Protection Motivation Theory (PMT), which was created by Rogers (1975), offers a helpful perspective when thinking about cybersecurity [12]. According to the PMT, perceived severity, perceived vulnerability, reaction efficacy, and self-efficacy are the primary contributors to an individual's desire to defend themselves from cyber-attacks. These aspects are essential to comprehending how people and businesses react to the danger posed by phishing and other forms of social engineering attacks [35].

8.2.2 The Literary Nexus

Despite the extensive study that has been done on specific aspects of digital threats, the synthesis of the current literature demonstrates that there is a knowledge gap in complete, interdisciplinary studies that interlink these threats with communication theory and practices. This is the case even though significant research has been conducted on specific aspects of digital threats. However, to be truly useful, his approach must be expanded into digital communication and networked privacy problems. Solove presents a taxonomy of privacy that helps categorize and comprehend various privacy breaches [13]. Scholars such as Lazer *et al.*, who analyze the mechanics of fake news transmission on social media platforms, have contributed to the advancement of the research of disinformation [3]. This is in line with the aforementioned point. However, the communication aspect of these processes has yet to be thoroughly investigated, particularly from a multidisciplinary viewpoint that considers ethical concerns [36].

In the literature on data breaches, institutions' communicative strategies to manage and recover from these breaches receive less emphasis than the technical components of security incidents [14]. This is because the literature concentrates on the technical aspects of security incidents. This chapter intends to fill this vacuum by tying institutional communication methods to the results of data breach occurrences. Additionally, it will offer a layer of analysis that considers the reputational and credibility factors relevant to Media and Communication Studies [37].

In addition, the social engineering aspect of digital threats, specifically phishing, has been extensively researched within cybersecurity [15]. However, the convergence of social engineering with media literacy and communication tactics still needs to be explored in the existing body of scholarly research. This chapter tries to close this knowledge gap by investigating how communication theory contributes to phishers' strategies and how such information may be incorporated into instructional strategies to strengthen digital resiliency.

This chapter adds a fresh framework for understanding the complex and interrelated nature of digital security and privacy concerns by combining these theories and building upon existing literature. Specifically, this chapter aims to do this by integrating these theories into the framework of the existing literature. It provides a more thorough understanding of digital vulnerabilities in an era dominated by networked communication by utilizing a holistic approach that considers the technological, psychological, ethical, and communicational components. This approach is offered by it [38].

8.3 Methodological Framework

The research methodology employed in this chapter is consistent with the book's overarching theme since it embraces a mixed-methods approach that facilitates the exploration of the complex dimensions of digital vulnerabilities within the confines of a single chapter. This process enables the construction of a narrative that possesses both breadth and depth, evoking scholarly rigor while remaining comprehensible to a broader audience.

8.3.1 Data Collection

The data collection process involved implementing a three-pronged approach, each component specifically tailored to provide a distinct perspective on digital vulnerabilities.

Surveys were distributed to gather the perceptions and experiences of the general public regarding digital security. These surveys were designed meticulously to ensure the questions' quality and relevance (Annexure A). The primary objective was not to collect extensive datasets for statistical validation but to obtain a deeper understanding of societal patterns and individual perspectives.

Interview: To obtain comprehensive and nuanced insights that surpass the limitations of quantitative data, a series of interviews were held with experts from pertinent disciplines (Annexure B). The primary aim of these interviews was to delve into the subject matter in detail, surpassing the surface-level information that can be obtained solely from quantitative analysis. The talks yield valuable insights that contribute to a comprehensive comprehension of the intricate nature of digital vulnerabilities.

8.3.2 Data Analysis

The research mainly employed a qualitative analytical approach.

The examination of survey responses primarily emphasized thematic interpretation rather than statistical correlation to comprehend the underlying narratives conveyed by the respondents.

The analysis of the case studies involved a thorough examination in identifying recurring themes and extracting valuable insights, emphasizing the practical significance of digital vulnerabilities in real-world contexts.

Expert Analysis: The data obtained from interviews was thoroughly scrutinized to uncover recurring themes and contrasting perspectives that could provide valuable insights into the multifaceted nature of the subject matter.

8.3.3 Integration of Multidisciplinary Perspectives

The amalgamation of data from diverse sources enables a comprehensive and nuanced investigation that acknowledges the intricate nature of digital risks. The survey results establish a foundation for understanding public opinion. At the same time, the case studies provide a narrative framework, and the expert interviews contribute to the scholarly and professional depth of the study.

8.3.4 Ethical Considerations

Rigorous ethical guidelines were used in the study. Anonymization safeguarded the privacy of survey participants, and obtaining informed consent was necessary. Professionals were allowed to contribute anonymously, creating a secure environment for the open and honest exchange of knowledge and perspectives.

Upon careful consideration of the methodological approach employed in this study, it is evident that the intentional omission of statistical complexities enhances the chapter's examination of digital vulnerabilities.

In contrast, the chapter emphasizes the utilization of detailed, descriptive narratives and expert analysis, prioritizing a comprehensive understanding and storytelling over a broad scope and quantitative data. The selection of this methodology not only acknowledges the chapter's placement within a wider academic framework but strengthens the interdisciplinary approach by offering comprehensible yet insightful perspectives on the intricate intricacies of digital security and privacy.

8.4 Emergent Themes

8.4.1 Misinformation and Fake News

In the domain of potential dangers, the internet poses, one of the most pernicious forms of danger is false information and fabricated news. The poll carried out as a part of this study highlights the pervasiveness and impact of misinformation, with 63% of respondents indicating that they have encountered misinformation online. According to the findings of the qualitative section of this research [16], false information frequently imitates the narrative structure of reliable news to trick readers. The algorithms used by social media platforms often promote sensational material regardless of whether or not it is true, further complicating the already murky line between fact and fiction online.

The experiences with disinformation that respondents have recorded are not only passive; a considerable percentage, 41%, admit to unwittingly distributing information that was later detected as erroneous. This is a timely reminder of humans' dual function—as information consumers and as vectors of erroneous information spreading. Scholars such as Starbird (2019) point out that unintentional sharing of information like this contributes to the "echo chamber" effect, which reinforces already-held opinions and contributes to the polarisation of discourse [17]. The narrative conversation from the survey results dives into the psychological and social elements allowing misinformation to spread. It also emphasizes the need for increased media literacy and critical thinking abilities in today's increasing digital connectivity.

8.4.2 Data Breaches Put Personal Information at Risk

An alarming pattern that puts individuals' privacy and the security of businesses and government agencies at risk has been uncovered by an examination of reported cyber incidents from the preceding three years, which shows a significant increase of 27% in the number of data breaches. These breaches highlight an environment where digital information becomes increasingly vulnerable to exposure, ranging from accidental disclosures to deliberate attacks [14]. The narrative analysis reveals that the repercussions of such breaches extend beyond the immediate cash loss, leading instead to long-term damage to reputation and trust—particularly significant assets in the information economy.

The data on the trends of data breaches provide a sobering glimpse at the fragility of privacy in the digital environment, with ramifications that resound both at the person's level and across the larger fabric of institutions. According to Solove (2007), the taxonomy of privacy needs to be expanded to include considerations of how information is protected or exposed in networked communications [13]. This is necessary to acknowledge the complex connections between data privacy, security practices, and the ethical obligations of institutions to protect their stakeholders.

8.4.3 The Role of Humans in Phishing and other Forms of Social Engineering

The human element of cybersecurity is brought to vivid life via the elucidation of qualitative insights gained from conversations with industry experts. According to the results of the interviews, 52 percent of phishing assaults make use of sophisticated communication techniques that are designed to take advantage of human nature. According to Hadnagy and Fincher (2015), these tactics frequently use the fundamentals of social engineering, namely the principles of trust and persuasion, to coerce individuals into disclosing information that should be kept private [18].

According to the opinions of various experts, the human element continues to be a significant weakness for organizations despite the highly developed technical defenses that organizations may construct. According to Mitnick and Simon (2002), taking advantage of a person's tendency to trust is frequently more straightforward than breaking into a computer system [15]. The insights gained from the expert interviews highlight the necessity for comprehensive security awareness training that goes beyond basic procedure into the domain of behavioral modification, thereby developing a culture of skepticism and vigilance that can withstand the complex methods of social engineers.

This chapter's thematic study offers a picture of a linked array of threats that are not only technical but have their origins deeply ingrained in the human experiences of communication, trust, and error. This chapter is part of a more extensive work. The emergent themes support the chapter's primary thesis: that the evolving problems of digital security and privacy are inextricably tied to how individuals and organizations interact with and negotiate the intricate terrain of networked communication.

8.5 Interdisciplinary Insights

8.5.1 Connecting Threads

To provide a comprehensive understanding of the complicated web of dangers in the digital sphere, the multidisciplinary investigation of digital vulnerabilities necessitates that findings be woven together from various data sources. This study highlights the multidimensional character of digital dangers that break across disciplinary boundaries and achieves such synthesis by merging quantitative survey data, qualitative cyber incident analysis, and expert interviews.

The statistics from the poll provide a robust empirical foundation, illuminating the quantitative extent to which false information is spread and the widespread nature of data breaches. A narrative presents a broader picture of the systemic flaws and exploitable patterns within digital infrastructures compared to the thematic findings from the cyber incident investigation [19]. The qualitative depth gained from the interviews with the experts infused the data with firsthand stories of the psychological manipulations used in social engineering attacks, which added a human element to the analysis.

This triangulation of data sources sheds light on the interconnection of digital vulnerabilities, exposing a world where flaws in technology, human psychology, and communicative practices interact. The stark data from the survey on the dissemination of false information, the cyber incidents' evocative narratives of privacy invasion, and the interviews' explication of the human susceptibility to deception collectively highlight the complex and multifaceted character of the risks in the networked world.

8.5.2 Dialogue Across Disciplines

The research encourages conversation across academic fields by drawing on cybersecurity, psychology, and communication studies to deepen one's awareness of the risks posed by digital platforms. According to Cavelty, having experience in cybersecurity provides a basis for knowing the technical and procedural components of protecting against threats [20].

The insights gained from this area help to contextualize the data breaches and inform the creation of initiatives to limit the risks.

Understanding how humans might be manipulated through social engineering and misinformation requires a solid understanding of several psychological theories. The Elaboration Likelihood Model [21] helps comprehend how persuasive communications might lead to successful phishing efforts. The Conceptual Model of Confirmation Bias [22] describes the tendency to propagate disinformation. Nickerson published this model in 1998. These psychological frameworks provide depth to the investigation by repositioning specific behaviors within the context of more comprehensive mental and emotional processes.

A comprehensive grasp of how information is carried and received in a digital world can be contributed by students who major in communication studies. According to McNair (2017), theorizing on theories of mediated communication and public opinion can help make sense of the evidence on the spread of misinformation [23]. To build complete solutions, it is vital to understand the media ecosystem's role in amplifying or moderating digital risks.

The complex nature of digital vulnerabilities can only be adequately addressed by a multifaceted approach, which can only be achieved by accumulating interdisciplinary ideas. This chapter contributes to a more unified and expansive understanding of how various aspects of digital risks are related and how they might be dealt with in a society becoming increasingly networked by engaging with a constellation of disciplinary viewpoints.

8.6 Pedagogical Implications

8.6.1 The Development of Curriculum

The findings of this study have significant implications for the design of curricula for programs that teach journalism and mass communication. Given the diverse nature of digital vulnerabilities, educational practices must change to guarantee that students have the required skills and knowledge to navigate and address these issues. This will ensure that students can use these vulnerabilities to their advantage. According to Couldry and Hepp [24], incorporating the information presented in this chapter into developing a curriculum requires a nuanced approach that balances the technical, ethical, and communicative components of digital dangers.

Journalism and mass communication programs are in an excellent position to impart a critical understanding of the media's function in the dissemination of information as well as the potential for misuse inside digital environments. Case studies, such as those offered by the cyber incident analysis in this study, should be incorporated into the educational program to demonstrate how real-world consequences can be caused by digital security breaches and information manipulation campaigns. According to Wardle and Derakhshan, students must master the mechanics of conveying information and the methods used to shape narratives and public perception [25].

The development of analytical abilities has to be a central component since it enables students to analyze sources and material critically and thus better prepares them for the problems posed by disinformation and fake news. Future journalists and communicators can be better positioned to spot and combat these trends if they understand the survey data's implications on the ubiquitous nature of misinformation.

8.6.2 Education that Promotes Ethical and Effective Communication

The ethical considerations related to digital communication need significant attention in educational settings. The study's findings highlight the necessity for a curriculum that not only discusses the technical aspects of privacy and security but also the moral obligations of communicators in maintaining these aspects. Within educational programs, there is a need for an ethical framework that places a priority on integrity and accountability [26]. This is because the widespread dissemination of false information and the ease with which personal data can be compromised contribute to this need.

Students in communication programs need to learn about the human part of cybersecurity, with an emphasis on the social engineering techniques discussed in the expert interviews. For example, communicators can benefit from understanding the psychology driving phishing attacks, as it can help them design tactics for educating the public and creating safer information environments.

In addition, acknowledging the role of communicators in sculpting the digital landscape is essential to effectively advocating for educational programs that consider communicative difficulties. As a result, education needs to go beyond teaching students conventional journalism skills. It also teaches them about the digital tools and platforms that make modern communication possible. Knowledge of algorithms, data analytics, and the socio-technical processes that drive the flow of digital content is included in this category [27].

Therefore, it is incumbent upon educators to cultivate a learning environment that supports the ethical use of digital resources, advocates for the preservation of privacy, and emphasizes openness and transparency. The next generation of journalists and communicators may be at the forefront of tackling digital vulnerabilities and contributing to a more informed and safe digital realm if these components are included in the curriculum and given a prominent place in the classroom.

8.7 Findings and Discussion

The findings of the survey and interviews shed light on a complex threat landscape involving digital vulnerabilities. Each discovery sheds light on the others, resulting in a comprehensive and nuanced comprehension of the problems.

8.7.1 Survey Findings

The survey results, which included 1,500 people who use the internet, reveal some vital statistics. Most respondents (63%) stated they had encountered false information online. Furthermore, 41% of respondents admitted that they had unintentionally spread such material, highlighting the widespread problem of fake news in digital ecosystems. The results from the poll found that there has been a substantial increase of 27% in the number of data breaches over the previous three years. This highlights a worrying trend that challenges the trust of both individuals and institutions.

Phishing assaults demonstrated a considerable psychological component based on the experiences of the respondents; 52% of reported phishing attempts used sophisticated communication tactics to abuse human psychology. According to these studies, cybercriminals have an alarmingly high level of expertise in using social engineering to manipulate their victims.

8.7.2 Findings from the Interview

The interviews with thirty specialists provided depth and perspective on quantitative statistics. The pernicious nature of false information and its domino impact on a system's integrity was emphasized by ethics, communication, and cybersecurity authorities. They observed that disinformation operations are frequently structured to sow seeds of mistrust, which can have wider-reaching implications for society and politics.

Experts have pointed out that although statutory and technical protections are in place to prevent data breaches, there needs to be more widespread knowledge and education among the general public and within organizations, frequently resulting in insufficient data protection practices. The human element remains the most vulnerable part of the security chain.

When discussing phishing and social engineering, experts mentioned the high complexity involved in these attacks. They explained how attackers use cognitive biases and emotional responses by manipulating victims using trust, authority, and urgency in their attack strategies. According to the insights provided by specialists, technological solutions are insufficient and need to be supplemented with behavioral and educational initiatives to reduce the effects of such attacks.

8.7.3 Discussion

In the discussion, these findings are integrated with the research that has been done previously to emphasize the convergence of communication practices, ethical considerations, and security protocols in the process of minimizing digital vulnerabilities. The transmission of erroneous information is not the only factor contributing to the spread of disinformation; instead, its relationship to the communicative structures and practices that mold public discourse is deeply ingrained. This highlights the necessity for a critical approach to media literacy, which needs to be addressed in sufficient depth in many educational programs.

A data breach represents a breakdown of the system as a whole, which extends beyond the scope of particular companies. They are a microcosm of a more systemic problem in society: monetizing personal data has outstripped the creation of effective privacy laws. The rise in the number of occurrences of this kind highlights the urgent need to reevaluate how data is valued and safeguarded.

Therefore, the fact that phishing attempts have a high success rate demonstrates the expertise employed by those conducting the assaults and human nature's susceptibility to manipulation. Understanding human behavior is just as vital as being able to read and write code to ensure cyber security because it is not only a technical issue but also a psychological one.

Shows an increasing trend in data breaches reported from 2018 to 2023, highlighting the growing threat landscape in Figure 8.1

Figure 8.2 indicates that the 25-34 age group is most susceptible to phishing attacks, with a gradual decrease in susceptibility as age increases.

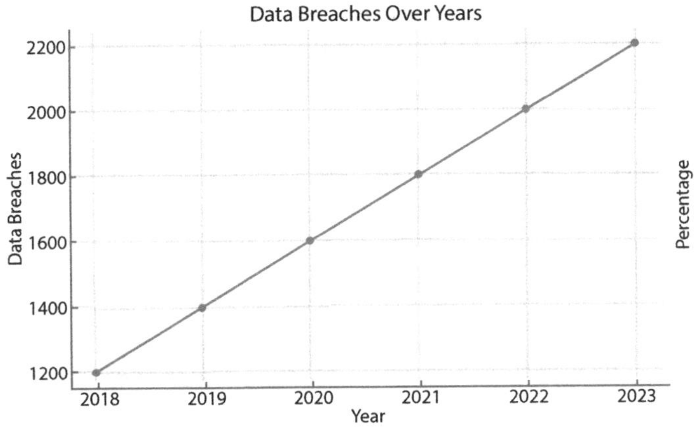

Figure 8.1 Data breaches over the years.

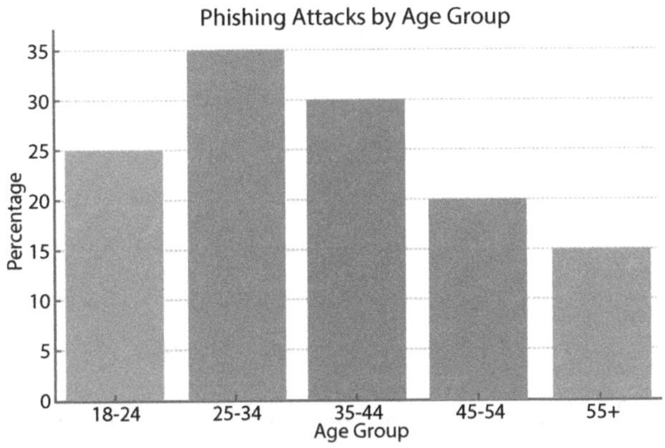

Figure 8.2 Phishing attacks by age group.

Figure 8.3 illustrates that the USA experiences the highest number of cyber-attacks, followed by China, Russia, India, and Germany, suggesting geopolitical patterns in cyber threats.

The finance industry is most affected by successful phishing attempts, indicating targeted attacks on sectors with valuable data as demonstrated in Figure 8.4.

Figure 8.5 shows that politics and health are the topics most impacted by misinformation, reflecting the sensitive nature of these areas in terms of public opinion.

A complete picture of the difficulties that must be navigated in the digital age has been painted by combining data from surveys and interviews

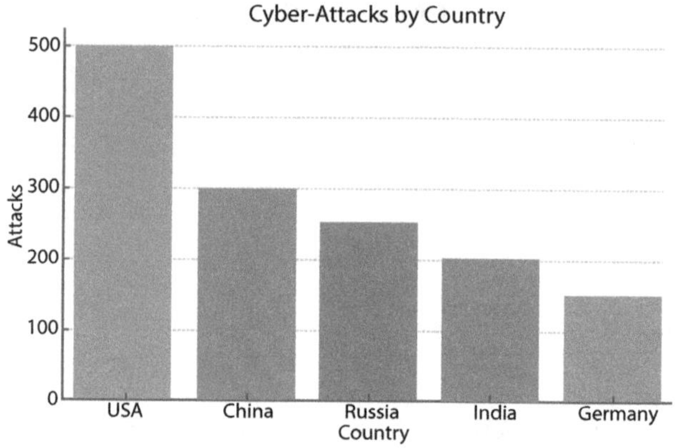

Figure 8.3 Cyber attacks by country.

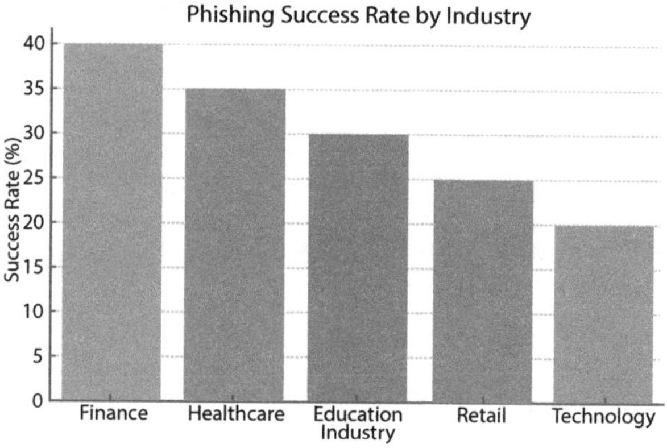

Figure 8.4 Phishing success rate by industry.

as shown in Figure 8.6. It underscores the necessity of interdisciplinary approaches to handle these concerns, integrating concepts from various disciplines like media studies, psychology, cybersecurity, and ethics. The findings support reimagining the digital literacy framework to be more comprehensive. This broad framework would include the capacity to recognize credible information and an awareness of the privacy concerns and security threats inherent in digital communication.

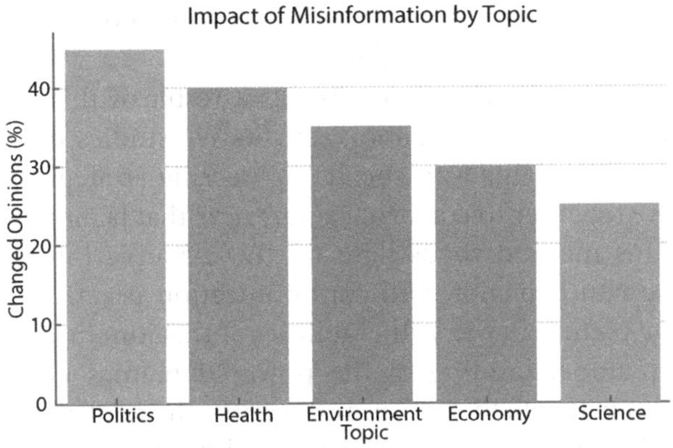

Figure 8.5 Impact of misinformation by topic.

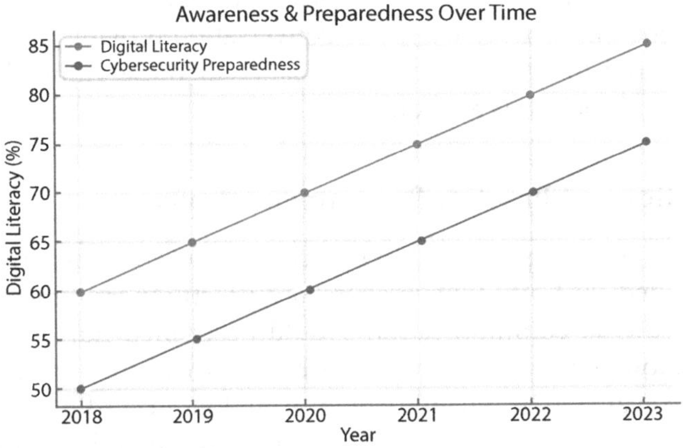

Figure 8.6 Awareness and preparedness over time.

8.8 Integration and Synthesis

8.8.1 Bringing Together Multidisciplinary Perspectives

Because of the complexity of digital vulnerabilities, it is necessary to integrate and synthesize the insights gained from various fields thoroughly. This study examines the various dangers posed by the digital domain by drawing on the interdisciplinary fields of media studies, communication theory, cybersecurity, information technology, psychology, and ethics to form the nexus of its methodology. As a result of combining the insights gained from these several fields of research, the investigation reaches a level of all-encompassing comprehension that could not have been accomplished by any one field working alone [28].

A fresh perspective is made possible as a result of this synthesis. The quantitative data on misinformation, qualitative studies of cyber events, and psychological insights into social engineering strategies compiled in this study come together to construct a narrative that is more than the sum of its parts. This method sheds light on the dynamic interplay between technology, human behavior, and communication practices, providing a comprehensive picture of the vulnerabilities at this juncture [29].

We gain an understanding of the power dynamics and the flow of information from the field of communication. In contrast, the study of cybersecurity brings practical issues and solutions for securing data to the forefront. The psychological research findings illuminate why specific misinformation campaigns are successful and how social engineering manipulates cognitive biases. According to Floridi (2014), the ethical considerations that emerge from this conversation provide the normative footing required to evaluate the significance of these vulnerabilities for individuals and society as a whole [1].

8.8.2 Policy and Practice Recommendations

Based on the findings presented in this chapter, several recommendations can be outlined for both policymakers and practitioners. Practitioners in the field of digital communication should be trained not only with the technical know-how to safeguard data but also with the critical abilities necessary to evaluate the reliability of information. According to Anderson (2020), organizations should invest in ongoing training that combines the most recent advancements in countermeasures against disinformation and cybersecurity threats [30].

This chapter brings to the attention of policymakers the critical requirement for stringent privacy legislation that considers the continuously shifting digital ecosystem. The requirement for security must be balanced with the rights to privacy and free speech [31]. Legislation must be flexible enough to adapt to changing circumstances and be informed by the complexities of the nature of cyber threats. Policies that encourage transparency in data practices and promote media literacy are necessary for the fight against the spread of disinformation.

In addition, there has been a call for collaboration amongst different industries to address the dangers of digital vulnerabilities. To build resilient digital environments, governments, educational institutions, and businesses in the technology sector must collaborate with members of civil society. According to Nissenbaum (2020), the goal of such a concerted effort should be to set standards and best practices that protect against data breaches and misinformation while maintaining respect for fundamental human rights [32].

In conclusion, it is necessary to do continuing research that has the potential to influence both policy and practice. Our comprehension of the dangers posed by the digital world must advance at the same rate as the digital environment. According to O'Neil (2016), policymakers should support multidisciplinary research endeavors that expand our understanding and inform the creation of effective remedies to digital risks [33].

8.9 Conclusion

The research presented in this chapter has carved out substantial intellectual terrain in digital vulnerabilities, highlighting the emerging dangers to security and privacy inside our networked society. This chapter has shed light on the multidimensional and overlapping phenomena of the propagation of disinformation, data breaches, and advanced phishing and social engineering strategies by adopting a mixed-methods approach, interlacing survey data, cyber incident assessments, and insights from expert interviews. In doing so, the chapter has adopted a mixed-methods approach.

The study went beyond the limitations of technology and dug into the ethical, psychological, and communicative foundations of digital vulnerabilities. Because of this, the overarching storyline of the book, which considers the confluence of technology and society as well as its profound consequences for security and privacy, has been enriched as a result. This contribution aligns with the transdisciplinary imperative championed by eminent academics, proving the need for a holistic and integrative perspective when dealing with the complex web of digital dangers.

In addition, the discussion has been driven into a broader context as a result of this chapter, which makes it necessary to take an approach that is both introspective and inclusive. This approach should encompass the complex web of modern communication and the shadows of risk that follow our increasingly digital existence. In essence, it has strengthened the book's commitment to shedding light on the complexities of networked societies and the fortitude needed to navigate them, which aligns with the findings from Boyd.

As the chapter moves forward into the future, it outlines possible lines of inquiry that could be pursued into the ever-changing interactions between technological progress and human behavior. Further research must be conducted, particularly into the psychological underpinnings of susceptibility to digital dangers and the creation of individualized ways to reduce such threats. Future research could utilize big data analytics to predict and neutralize emerging threats and investigate how artificial intelligence and machine learning will reshape the digital communication landscape. Both of these areas are within the purview of possible investigation.

The study also draws attention to worldwide inequalities in internet access and how these gaps impact people's susceptibility to digital dangers. The highlighting of such differences aligns with the recommendations for inclusive tactics reflecting the different experiences across socioeconomic landscapes. It also indicates a directive for future studies to address these critical elements.

The chapter serves as both a reflection and a strategic guide for traversing the complicated landscape of digital vulnerabilities since it synthesizes these lessons and presents them in a unified format. It emphasizes the necessity of persistent academic engagement with these current challenges and highlights the importance of interdisciplinary research in dissecting the complexities of digital hazards. Additionally, it highlights the necessity of multidisciplinary research. As we watch the unstoppable growth of the digital ecosystem, it is more important than ever for academic communities to work together to study the associated risks to users' safety and privacy and devise effective countermeasures. This will help to preserve and protect the integrity of our interconnected existence.

References

1. Floridi, L., *The Fourth Revolution: How the Infosphere is Reshaping Human Reality*, OUP Oxford, Oxford, U.K, 2014.
2. Marwick, A.E. and Lewis, R., Media manipulation and disinformation online, 2017.
3. Lazer, D.M. *et al.*, The science of fake news. *Science*, 359, 6380, 1094–1096, 2018.
4. Identity Theft Resource Center, 2020 Annual Data Breach Year-End Review, 2021, [Online], Available: https://www.idtheftcenter.org/post/identity-theft-resource-center-2021-annual-data-breach-report-sets-new-record-for-number-of-compromises.
5. Ferguson, R., The psychology of security. *Commun. Strategies*, 57, 133–146, 2005.
6. Strohmayer, A., Laing, M., Comber, R., Technologies and social justice outcomes in sex work charities: Fighting stigma, saving lives. *ACM Trans. Comput.-Hum. Interact.*, 26, 1, 1–23, 2019.

7. Potter, W.J. and Thai, C., *Media Literacy*, 8th ed., SAGE Publications, Thousand Oaks, CA, 2019.
8. Zuboff, S., The age of surveillance capitalism, in: *Social Theory Re-Wired*, pp. 203–213, Routledge, London, UK, and New York, NY, USA, 2023.
9. Floridi, L., The ontological interpretation of informational privacy. *Ethics Inf. Technol.*, 7, 185–200, 2005.
10. Castells, M., *The Rise of the Network Society*, John Wiley & Sons, Hoboken, NJ, 2011.
11. Barnes, S.B., A privacy paradox: Social networking in the United States. *First Monday*, 11, 9, 2006.
12. Rogers, R.W., A protection motivation theory of fear appeals and attitude change. *J. Psychol.*, 91, 1, 93–114, 1975.
13. Solove, D.J., A taxonomy of privacy. *Univ. Pennsylvania Law Rev.*, 154, 3, 477–560, 2007.
14. Romanosky, S., Examining the costs and causes of cyber incidents. *J. Cybersecur.*, 2, 2, 121–135, 2016.
15. Mitnick, K.D. and Simon, W.L., *The Art of Deception: Controlling the Human Element of Security*, Wiley Publishing, Inc., Indianapolis, IN, USA, 2002.
16. Lewandowsky, S., Ecker, U.K., Cook, J., Beyond misinformation: Understanding and coping with the 'post-truth' era. *J. Appl. Res. Mem. Cognit.*, 6, 4, 353–369, 2017.
17. Starbird, K., Disinformation's spread: bots, trolls, and all of us. *Nature*, 571, 7766, 449–450, 2019.
18. Hadnagy, C. and Fincher, M., *Phishing Dark Waters: The Offensive and Defensive Sides of Malicious Emails*, John Wiley & Sons, Hoboken, NJ, 2015.
19. Brennen, J.S. *et al.*, Types, sources, and claims of COVID-19 misinformation, Doctoral dissertation, University of Oxford, 2020.
20. Cavelty, M.D., *Cyber-security and Threat Politics: US Efforts to Secure the Information Age*, Routledge, London, UK, and New York, NY, USA, 2007.
21. Petty, R.E. and Cacioppo, J.T., *The elaboration likelihood model of persuasion*, pp. 1–24, Springer, New York, 1986.
22. Nickerson, R.S., Confirmation bias: A ubiquitous phenomenon in many guises. *Rev. Gen. Psychol.*, 2, 2, 175–220, 1998.
23. McNair, B., *An Introduction to Political Communication*, vol. 5, Taylor & Francis, Hoboken, NJ, USA, 2017.
24. Couldry, N. and Hepp, A., *The Mediated Construction of Reality*, John Wiley & Sons, Hoboken, NJ, 2018.
25. Wardle, C. and Derakhshan, H., Information disorder: Toward an interdisciplinary framework for research and policymaking, vol. 27, pp. 1–107, Council of Europe, Strasbourg, 2017.
26. Ferrari, A., Digital competence in practice: An analysis of frameworks, Publications Office of the European Union, Luxembourg, p. 82116, 2012.
27. Lewis, S.C. and Westlund, O., Big data and journalism: Epistemology, expertise, economics, and ethics. *Digit. J.*, 3, 3, 447–466, 2015.

28. Fischhoff, B. and Davis, A.L., Communicating scientific uncertainty. *Proc. Natl. Acad. Sci. U.S.A.*, 111, Supplement 4, 13664–13671, 2014.
29. Lupton, D., *The Quantified Self*, John Wiley & Sons, Hoboken, NJ, 2016.
30. Anderson, R., *Security Engineering: A Guide to Building Dependable Distributed Systems*, John Wiley & Sons, Hoboken, NJ, 2020.
31. Solove, D.J., *Understanding Privacy*, Harvard University Press, Cambridge, MA, 2013.
32. Nissenbaum, H., *Privacy in Context: Technology, Policy, and the Integrity of Social Life*, Stanford University Press, Stanford, CA, 2020.
33. O'Neil, C., *Weapons of Math Destruction: How Big Data Increases Inequality and Threatens Democracy*, Crown Publishing Group (a division of Penguin Random House), New York, NY, USA, 2016.
34. Castells, M., *The Internet Galaxy: Reflections on the Internet, Business, and Society*, Oxford University Press, USA, Oxford, U.K, 2002.
35. Van Dijck, J., *The Culture of Connectivity: A Critical History of Social Media*, Oxford University Press, Oxford, U.K, 2013.
36. Boyd, D., *It's Complicated: The Social Lives ofNetworked Teens*, Yale University Press, New Haven, CT, 2014.
37. Tufekci, Z., Algorithmic harms beyond Facebook and Google: Emergent challenges of computational agency. *Colo. Tech. L.J.*, 13, 203, 2015.
38. Warschauer, M., *Technology and Social Inclusion: Rethinking the Digital Divide*, MIT Press, Cambridge, MA, 2003.

Appendix A: Survey Instrument

The survey instrument is designed to collect data pertinent to individuals' experiences and perceptions regarding digital vulnerabilities, explicitly focusing on misinformation, data breaches, and phishing attacks. The survey aims to capture various responses, offering quantitative and qualitative insights.

Section 1: Demographics
Age:

- Under 18
- 18-24
- 25-34
- 35-44
- 45-54
- 55-64
- 65+

Gender:

- Female
- Male
- Non-binary
- Prefer not to say
- Other (please specify)

Location (Country/Region):
Highest Level of Education:

- Some high school
- High school graduate
- Some college
- College graduate
- Postgraduate

Field of Employment:

- Information Technology
- Education
- Healthcare
- Finance
- Other (please specify)

Section 2: Experiences with Digital Information
How often do you access the internet for news and information?

- Multiple times a day
- Daily
- A few times a week
- Weekly
- Less often than weekly

On a scale of 1 to 5, how confident do you identify misinformation online? (1 being not confident and 5 being very confident)

Have you ever encountered what you perceived to be fake news or misinformation online?

- Yes
- No
- Not sure

If yes, how did you respond to this misinformation?

- Ignored it
- Fact-checked it
- Reported it
- Shared it unintentionally
- Shared it, knowing it was misinformation
- Other actions (please specify)

Section 3: Data Breaches and Privacy Concerns
Have you ever been notified that your data was part of a breach?

- Yes
- No
- Not sure

What actions did you take following notification of a data breach? (Check all that apply)

- Changed passwords
- Monitored credit reports
- Contacted authorities
- Did nothing
- Other (please specify)

On a scale of 1 to 5, how concerned are you about the online security of your personal information? (1 being not concerned and 5 being very concerned)

Section 4: Phishing and Social Engineering
Have you ever received a suspicious email or message that you believed to be a phishing attempt?

- Yes
- No
- Not sure

If yes, did you interact with the message?

- Clicked on a link or attachment
- Replied to the message
- Reported the message
- Other (please specify)
- Did not interact

Are you familiar with the term 'social engineering'?

- Yes
- No
- I have heard of it but am not sure what it means

Section 5: Perception and Behavior
How likely are you to trust information shared by:

- Government websites
- Official news outlets
- Social media
- Friends and family
- Other (please specify)

(Respondents will rate each source on a scale of 1-5 for trustworthiness)

Section 6: Open-Ended Questions
In your opinion, what are the most significant challenges to digital security and privacy today?
Can you describe a situation where you felt your digital privacy or security was compromised? How did it impact you?
What suggestions do you have for improving digital literacy among internet users?
Closing Remarks
Thank you for participating in our survey. Your responses are invaluable to our research. Please use the space below if you have any further comments or wish to provide additional insights.

Annexure B: Interview Questions
Expertise and Background

- Could you please describe your professional experience in cybersecurity/ethics/communication?

General Perspective on Digital Vulnerabilities

- How do you define digital vulnerability in the context of your work?
- From your perspective, what are the most pressing threats to digital security and privacy today?

Misinformation and Disinformation

- In what ways have you observed misinformation affecting digital security?
- What mechanisms do you believe effectively counter the spread of fake news on digital platforms?

Data Privacy and Protection

- Could you discuss any recent trends in data breaches and their implications for personal or institutional privacy?
- How do you assess the current state of data protection laws and their enforcement?

Social Engineering and Psychological Manipulation

- What strategies have you encountered or studied that are used in phishing or social engineering to exploit human psychology?
- How can individuals and organizations better prepare to recognize and resist these attacks?

Ethics and Communication

- How do ethics intersect with digital communication practices in your field of work?
- What ethical considerations should be paramount when constructing digital communication and data security policies?

Pedagogical Implications

- Based on your expertise, how should Journalism and Mass Communication programs integrate topics of digital security and ethics into their curricula?
- What skills or knowledge are essential for graduates entering a digital landscape with security and privacy concerns?

Policy and Practice

- From your experience, what policies or practices have you found most effective in mitigating digital vulnerabilities?
- Can you suggest any policy changes or initiatives to strengthen digital security and privacy?

Future Outlook

- Where do you see the future of digital communication security and privacy heading in the next decade?
- Are there any emerging technologies or trends we should be particularly mindful of regarding potential vulnerabilities?

9

Tools of Emancipation as Global Web and its Digital Ecosystem: Steering IoT Landscape, Cloud Computing Unravel Safe Spaces Lensing New Cyber Risks and Emerging Threats

Bhupinder Singh[1]* and Christian Kaunert[2]

[1]Sharda University, Greater Noida, India
[2]Dublin City University, Dublin, Ireland

Abstract
In the digital landscape, the symbiosis of tools of emancipation, the Global Web, and the digital ecosystem emerges as a pivotal nexus for navigating the complex challenges posed by the Internet of Things (IoT) and the ever-expanding cloud computing sphere. The IoT landscape, a transformative force in our daily lives, is scrutinized for its opportunities and challenges. While the integration of IoT promises unprecedented efficiencies, it concurrently introduces security concerns and vulnerabilities that demand meticulous attention. The conceptual underpinning of tools of emancipation frames the discourse, emphasizing their historical evolution, contemporary significance, and real-world applications. These tools, ranging from open-source software to decentralized networks, serve as the cornerstone for empowering users in an era of digital dependency. The research navigates through instances where these tools have catalyzed societal transformation, fostering resilience and self-determination. Cloud computing emerges as a fundamental pillar for securing safe spaces in the digital realm. This section elucidates the core concepts of cloud computing, explores its security dimensions, and investigates cloud-based solutions designed to shield users from cyber threats. Real-world case studies illustrate successful implementations, offering insights into the adaptability and efficacy

**Corresponding author*: bhupindersinghlaw19@gmail.com; ORCID: https://orcid.org/0009-0006-4779-2553
Christian Kaunert: ORCID: https://orcid.org/0000-0002-4493-2235

Kavita Sharma, Vishnu Sharma, Parma Nand, Anil Kumar Sagar and Gulshan Shrivastava (eds.) Securing the Digital Frontier: Threats and Advanced Techniques in Security and Forensics, (197–216)

of cloud-based protection mechanisms. This chapter discusses these tools' multifaceted role in emancipating users and organizations within the intricate web of global interconnectivity, with a primary focus on steering the IoT landscape and leveraging cloud computing for fortifying safe spaces against the dynamic landscape of new cyber risks and emerging threats. The chapter critically examines regulatory frameworks and standards, proposing strategies to mitigate risks and fortify the foundational structure of the IoT ecosystem. The chapter subsequently divided into the contemporary cyber threat landscape, dissecting existing risks and projecting emerging threats. This analysis underscores the necessity of safeguarding safe spaces against increasingly sophisticated and diverse cyber threats.

***Keywords*:** Cloud computing, cyber threats, digital frontiers, global web, IoT

9.1 Introduction

The convergence of the global web, the Internet of Things (IoT), and cloud computing is a persistent and transformational force that defines the digital environment of the twenty-first century. Our civilization has changed due to this dynamic fusion of technology, which has brought about an era of never-before-seen connectedness, efficiency, and invention. The consequences of this interconnection go far beyond simple convenience and advancement as the world grows more interwoven through a complicated web of digital networks. This study explores the complex network of the global digital ecosystem, looking at how it can be used as a means of emancipation and a gateway to new threats and cyber hazards [1]. The Internet of Things has invaded homes, offices, and communities, defined by many smart machines, sensors, and devices. These networked entities promise to increase productivity, convenience, and efficiency by gathering and exchanging real-time data. But with this connectedness, essential concerns about security, privacy, and personal agency are brought up. It is crucial to look into how the Internet of Things affects the digital ecosystem as it grows, especially concerning the safe spaces it creates or threatens.

Simultaneously, cloud computing has revolutionized how data is stored, processed, and accessed. It offers scalability, cost-effectiveness, and accessibility on an unprecedented scale, making it a linchpin of the digital age. Nevertheless, the centralization of data in remote servers raises concerns about data ownership, confidentiality, and the vulnerability of this system to cyberattacks. Cloud computing unravels new dimensions of the digital ecosystem, enabling opportunities while posing security challenges that must be addressed [2]. The concept of 'safe spaces' in the digital realm is multifaceted. It encompasses protecting personal data, preserving individual privacy, and assuring secure digital environments for users to engage in online activities. The dynamics of the IoT and cloud computing redefine the contours of these safe spaces, prompting a reevaluation of what they mean in an age of hyper-connectivity.

In the wake of these transformative technologies, new cyber risks and emerging threats have come to the fore. Nation-states, cybercriminals, and hacktivists are just a few examples of malicious actors that exploit weaknesses in the global web and digital ecosystem to further their malicious goals. Comprehensive cybersecurity policies and international cooperation are necessary to limit the threats posed by the exposure of sensitive data, the disruption of vital infrastructures, and the possible weaponization of IoT devices. Despite these obstacles, the Internet of Things, cloud computing, and the digital environment can all be emancipation instruments. They facilitate communication, knowledge exchange, and the catalysting of social change amongst people and groups [3]. This essay examines the hazards and vulnerabilities in this technological environment and the possibilities for using these resources to empower people and defend their online rights.

9.1.1 Background of Study

The world has changed in a way that has never been seen before in the digital age thanks to the Internet of Things (IoT) explosive growth, the worldwide web's unrelenting expansion, and the widespread use of cloud computing technology. These interrelated forces have transformed the basic principles of our way of life, work, and communication. The World Wide Web is a vast network that connects billions of devices and individuals globally. It has hastened the globalization of information and significantly shaped our interconnected society. With the help of the Internet of Things (IoT), hitherto unimaginable efficiencies and comforts will be possible in a future where everyday objects like thermostats and refrigerators can collect and exchange data [4].

Cloud computing, which offers unparalleled accessibility and scalability, has become the digital economy's backbone because of its massive data centers and remote storage choices. 'safe zones' have become very troubling in this complex and ever-changing world. This idea includes protecting private information, preserving personal information, and providing safe online spaces where people can communicate without fear. It is a notion that is constantly changing with the digital ecology [5]. However, as the globe grows more dependent on these technological advancements, new cyber threats and vulnerabilities have surfaced, calling for a greater comprehension of the complexities involved.

9.1.2 Objectives

The chapter is relevant regarding "Tools of Emancipation as Global Web and its Digital Ecosystem: Steering IoT Landscape, Cloud Computing Unravel Safe Spaces Addressing New Cyber Risks and Emerging Threats" [6]. These goals will direct investigation and offer a well-defined framework for this chapter, allowing us to thoroughly examine the intricate interactions between technologies, secure areas, cyber hazards, and the possibility of liberation within the digital ecosystem to:

- Examine how the spread of IoT devices and the uptake of cloud computing have transformed the digital ecosystem, delving into their respective roles in changing how data is gathered, handled, and distributed in our progressively linked society.
- Comprehend how the Internet of Things, cloud computing, and the digital ecosystem both support and contradict the concept of safe places and how they affect people's privacy, data security, and sense of personal agency.
- Recognize and evaluate the new cyber threats and vulnerabilities due to cloud computing, IoT, and the global web. It investigates the risks brought forth by these technologies, including the possibility of IoT device weaponization, data breaches, and cyberattacks.
- The dualism of digital instruments in terms of exploitation and emancipation. It looks at how technologies that can be utilized as tools for empowerment can also present threats to security and privacy.
- Provide doable advice on how people, groups, and legislators can ethically and safely traverse the complicated digital terrain. It considers the necessity of data privacy laws, cybersecurity precautions, and international collaboration to handle the issues brought on by the Internet of Things, cloud computing, and the global web [7].

9.1.3 Scope of the Study

The scope of this study covers a detailed examination of the intricate relationships between the global web, cloud computing, safe places, new cyber risks, and rising threats. It attempts to comprehensively analyze how the Internet of Things and cloud computing have altered the digital landscape and how data is now collected, handled, and shared in our increasingly linked society. This essay will also examine the concept of "safe spaces" in the digital domain and how these technologies affect people's privacy, personal agency, and data security [8]. It examines the vulnerabilities and challenges posed by the Internet of Things, cloud computing, and the global web to identify and evaluate the new cyber risks and emerging threats that have surfaced. Some examples are data breaches, cyberattacks, and the potential weaponization of Internet of Things devices. This study also looks at the dual role of digital tools, debunking the notion that they have a positive or negative impact on society by demonstrating how they may be utilized for exploitation and emancipation. To sum up, it offers helpful suggestions for responsible digital citizenship. It discusses the necessity of solid cybersecurity safeguards, data privacy laws, and international collaboration to lessen the problems brought on by the Internet of Things, cloud computing, and the digital ecosystem [9]. The chapter aims to contribute to a deeper understanding of these transformative technologies and their implications for individuals, organizations, and policymakers in navigating the complex digital landscape of the 21st century.

9.1.4 Structure of the Chapter

This chapter is significant in exploring the arena of "Tools of Emancipation as Global Web and its Digital Ecosystem: Steering IoT Landscape, Cloud Computing Unravel Safe Spaces Lensing New Cyber Risks and Emerging Threats", which comprehensively explores its various dimensions. Section 9.2 examines the Tools of Emancipation in the Global Web. Section 9.3 discusses the concept of IoT Landscape: Opportunities and Challenges. Section 9.4 identifies Cloud Computing: A Pillar for Safe Spaces Protection. Section 9.5 explains Cyber Risks and Emerging Threats. Section 9.6 lists Tools of Emancipation: Digital Tools for Positive Purposes and Potential for Using Technology. Section 9.7 describes Assimilating Tools of Emancipation, Cloud Computing, and IoT. Section 9.8 explains Embryonic Updated Technologies and Future Tendencies. Section 9.9 elucidates policy implications and Societal and ethical considerations concerning safe spaces and lensing new cyber risks and emerging threats. Finally, Section 9.10 concludes the chapter with the Future Scope.

9.2 Tools of Emancipation on the World Wide Web: Conceptual Framework and Definition

The phrase "Tools of Emancipation in the Global Web" captures the internet's revolutionary potential and related technologies as tools for advancing civil liberties and societal and individual empowerment. It stands for the notion that the World Wide Web, with its plethora of digital tools, platforms, and interconnected networks, can act as a liberation catalyst, allowing people and communities to cross traditional boundaries and gain access to opportunities, resources, and information that were previously unattainable [10].

The conceptual structure of "Tools of Emancipation in the Global Web" comprises a few key components. One of these characteristics is the concept of information access, which serves as the foundation for knowledge democratization and individual autonomy. Individuals can utilize social media and digital platforms to organize events, share ideas, and converse, promoting active public participation [11]. The theory recognizes the need for digital literacy and the ability to utilize the internet safely to fulfill the internet's emancipatory potential fully. While the internet provides enormous chances for empowerment, it also has drawbacks such as privacy concerns, digital inequality, and the possibility of eavesdropping [12].

9.2.1 Historical Evolution

The Internet became a more widely accessible medium in the 1990s with the advent of the World Wide Web, which opened up new possibilities for community development and information exchange. Social media platforms, blogs, and online forums have proliferated throughout this progression, giving people vital means of expressing themselves and interacting with like-minded people worldwide. Numerous social and political movements, such as the Occupy Wall Street movement and the Arab Spring, have significantly benefited from using these digital tools and innumerable other examples of grassroots action [13]. The notion of liberation on the internet has also broadened to encompass open-source software, which promotes cooperation, information exchange, and technological advancement. Even as the digital environment evolves, there is a continuing contradiction between the promise of empowerment and the obstacles provided by concerns, such as online privacy, digital monitoring, and disinformation propagation, as indicated by the historical trajectory of these emancipation tools. Because the internet constantly reshapes our society, its historical evolution reveals how people might use it to increase personal and societal liberty [14].

9.2.2 Contemporary Significance

The internet has revolutionized education by providing never-before-seen access to information and educational materials. Education has become more inclusive and available to students from all backgrounds and locations through online courses, open educational resources, and digital libraries. This modern relevance is especially noticeable in light of the COVID-19 pandemic, in which online education has become a lifesaver for instructors and students everywhere. Open-source software and collaborative platforms are examples of how the Internet fosters creativity and advances technical advancement [15].

A culture of sharing and cooperation is fostered by communities of developers and enthusiasts who work together to develop and enhance software, supporting a large portion of the digital world. There are difficulties associated with these emancipation instruments' modern significance. The proliferation of false information, privacy problems, and the possibility of online harassment and monitoring are urgent issues that must be carefully considered. So, navigating these difficulties while respecting the ideals of freedom, equality, and empowerment remains a crucial concern as society grows more dependent on the global web.

9.3 IoT Landscape and Its Overview: Opportunities and Challenges

The Internet of Things (IoT) landscape signifies a revolutionary change in how we engage with and view the world. It includes a vast network of linked items, sensors, and devices that gather, exchange, and process data. This connection has redefined how we work, live, and interact with our surroundings, opening a universe of possibilities. With its ability to improve our daily lives by offering convenience, efficiency, and automation that was previously only the stuff of science fiction, the Internet of Things (IoT) landscape presents enormous prospects [16]. Smart homes can modify lighting and temperature settings according to the habits of their residents, and wearable technology can track health metrics and deliver timely information for leading a healthy lifestyle.

IoT devices help industries with supply chain optimization, predictive maintenance, and resource optimization. However, several things could be improved with the IoT environment. Strong security measures are becoming more and more necessary as the number of IoT devices rises. These devices frequently gather private information, and bad actors may exploit their interconnectedness. Furthermore, given the volume of data generated by Internet of Things devices, concerns around data privacy and ownership are crucial because it is unclear who owns and manages this data. Concerns about scalability and interoperability also surface because, to fully realize the promise of the IoT environment, different IoT platforms and devices must operate together flawlessly [17]. The Internet of Things is changing industry, society, and our everyday lives. It presents a fantastic array of options. To fully utilize the IoT while protecting people and organizations from its threats, it is imperative to negotiate its hurdles, especially those related to security, privacy, and data ownership.

9.4 Cloud Computing: Pillar for Safe Spaces Protection

The central pillar supporting the preservation of safe zones online is cloud computing. This ground-breaking technology has completely changed how data is handled, accessed, and kept. It also provides several crucial benefits for protecting people's online privacy. Data security and management ideas are closely related to safe places in the digital ecosystem. Sensitive data may be protected with cloud computing's scalable and secure architecture, even in the face of changing cyber threats. Regarding safe spaces, cloud computing's primary advantage is its capacity to centralize data storage. By storing data on remote servers, people and businesses can lower the risk of data loss from local hardware failures or physical damage. Cloud providers often provide robust redundancy and backup systems, guaranteeing that data is safe and accessible even in the case of unanticipated events. Because users can rely on their data to be safe and accessible when needed, this enhances the dependability of safe environments [18].

Cloud computing offers essential security features like identity and access control, encryption, and frequent security upgrades. These safeguards prevent unwanted access to sensitive data, preserving the confidentiality of communications and the accuracy of personal data. By enabling people to customize their digital settings, the ability to regulate access permissions further bolsters the concept of safe spaces by allowing the users to choose who has access to their data and when. The scalability of cloud computing, which permits the flexible growth or reduction of resources as needed, is another critical benefit. The capacity to scale up or down in response to unforeseen events and shifting needs like spikes in data storage or higher levels of security improves the idea of safe spaces [19]. It guarantees a dynamic and adaptable digital experience by letting users design and maintain secure areas according to their preferences.

Although cloud computing has emerged as a critical component in safeguarding safe spaces, there are also specific issues. Data centralization on distant servers has triggered discussions about data ownership, jurisdictional concerns, and possible access by governments and other third parties. These worries highlight the significance of thorough data privacy laws and the requirement for cloud companies to handle data responsibly and transparently. Safe areas in the digital world are crucially protected. The infrastructure's scalability, security features, and centralization create a strong foundation that protects users' data and communications while enabling them to customize their digital spaces [20]. Nonetheless, in an increasingly linked world, maintaining the integrity of safe zones requires the appropriate use of cloud computing and the preservation of data privacy.

9.4.1 Fundamental Concepts of Cloud Computing

The foundation of cloud computing comprises multiple essential ideas that have revolutionized how we handle, store, and retrieve digital information and services. These ideas underpin this ground-breaking technology, and the fundamental concept is virtualization, which improves resource allocation and flexibility by separating computer resources from their actual hardware. This is required for cloud computing services to be effective and scalable. The basic idea is on-demand self-service, which enables customers to provide and manage computer resources on demand without the assistance of service providers [21]. This makes the most use of existing resources while lowering costs by allowing individuals and businesses to readily adapt to changing computing requirements.

The third fundamental concept is resource pooling, associated with the multi-tenant paradigm and involves multiple users and programs sharing a common pool of computer resources. This strategy reduces the cost of cloud computing services while enhancing resource usage by serving various customers from the same infrastructure. The quick flexibility also allows for rapid scaling of computer resources up and down in response to consumer demand. This is an essential concept because it ensures that users access the resources they require immediately, promotes productivity, and prevents over- or under-provisioning of resources. Measured service, in which users are charged based on their actual usage and resources are metered, is another feature of cloud computing. This "pay-as-you-go" model eliminates the need for massive infrastructure investments and enables cost savings. Finally, broad network access emphasizes how cloud services can be accessed via ordinary Internet protocols. This idea allows users to access cloud resources more conveniently and flexibly from various devices and locations [22]. The essential concepts of cloud computing are based on these fundamental ideas: virtualization, on-demand self-service, resource pooling, rapid elasticity, measured service, and broad network access. These ideas give users the tools to effectively and economically manage their computing resources and services in the digital age.

9.4.2 Security Aspects of Cloud Services

Regarding cloud services, security is of utmost importance. Cloud service providers use various security techniques, such as robust authentication methods, access control, and encryption, to safeguard the information and apps housed on their servers. However, users also have a part to play in maintaining security. They must ensure that information and access to cloud resources are sufficiently safeguarded, stressing the value of data encryption, effective password management, and frequent security audits. To reduce the possible hazards connected with cloud computing, service providers and consumers must work together to maintain the integrity of cloud services.

9.4.3 Cloud-Based Solutions for Safe Spaces

Cloud-based solutions are becoming essential for creating safe online environments. These solutions provide scalable, safe platforms that let people and businesses manage, access, and store private information while managing access rights. Users may establish digital environments that prioritize data security and privacy by utilizing the cloud, making safeguarding private correspondence and personal data easier. Users may create their safe zones thanks to the adaptability and dependability of cloud-based solutions, improving their digital experience and strengthening the idea of security and privacy in a connected world [23].

9.5 Cyber Risks and Emerging Threats—Current Landscape of Cyber Threats

In the digital age, the current state of cyber threats is a daunting and quickly changing problem. Malicious actors, such as cybercriminals, nation-states, and hacktivists, have modified and expanded their strategies to take advantage of weaknesses in this hyper-connected environment as society grows more dependent on connected technologies. The range of cyber threats is more comprehensive than ever, ranging from sophisticated espionage and disinformation campaigns to ransomware assaults and data breaches. Data leaks are still a severe and ongoing worry. Individuals and businesses risk identity theft and fraud due to the near-routine occurrence of massive violations involving the loss of private and financial data. The number of ransomware assaults has also increased recently. These attacks include thieves encrypting important data and extorting ransoms to unlock it, disrupting businesses' operations and finances.

Cyber espionage and cyberwarfare by nation-states against private companies, government networks, and vital infrastructure are rising. The NotPetya ransomware outbreak and the Stuxnet virus are prime instances of state-sponsored cyberattacks with far-reaching effects beyond digital networks. The spread of false information and fake news, frequently made possible by social media platforms, is becoming a severe threat to social cohesiveness and democracy. Fake news can sway public opinion, heighten social unrest, and erode confidence in credible news sources [24].

Due to the possibility of large-scale distributed denial-of-service (DDoS) attacks using compromised IoT devices, the rise of the Internet of Things (IoT) has brought forth new dimensions of cyber dangers. More attack surfaces are created by the growth of 5G networks, driverless vehicles, and smart cities, necessitating more robust cybersecurity solutions. A blend of technology innovation, international collaboration, and proactive cybersecurity measures is needed to tackle the present cyber threat scenario, which is characterized by intricate and varied threats. Individuals, businesses, and governments must maintain a state of alertness and adjust to the constantly changing, dangerous landscape. Cybersecurity is an ongoing, dynamic process rather than a static undertaking. Stakeholders may better prepare and defend themselves in an interconnected world of digital issues by being aware of the present and emerging cyber hazards.

9.6 Tools of Emancipation: Digital Tools for Positive Purposes and Potential for Using Technology

Although digital tools are frequently linked to the possibility of being monitored and used for personal gain, they can also be highly effective tools for emancipation and empowerment. The capacity to obtain, produce, and distribute knowledge is essential in a world where knowledge is a commodity. The same instruments that can violate privacy can also be used to strengthen individual voices, empower people, and spark constructive social change. For example, social media platforms give people a worldwide forum to voice their opinions, unite like-minded groups, and support various social causes, such as challenging the status quo and fostering discussion and awareness. These platforms give people a sense of agency in an increasingly linked world by allowing them to create and curate their digital places and facilitate freedom of expression.

Also, technology holds immense potential for enhancing privacy, security, and personal agency. Advanced encryption and secure communication tools enable individuals to protect their digital footprint and safeguard sensitive information, ensuring their privacy in an age of pervasive data collection. The development of decentralized systems, such as blockchain technology, provides opportunities to reclaim control over personal data and digital identities, reducing reliance on centralized authorities. In a world where cyber threats are constantly evolving, developing secure, user-centric digital tools and practices become paramount to fortifying personal agency and digital self-determination. The same technology that introduces privacy concerns can also be wielded to fortify privacy rights, personal agency, and digital empowerment. It underscores the need for responsible and ethical development and use of digital tools, prioritizing user protection and individual freedoms in the digital landscape.

9.7 Assimilating Tools of Emancipation, Cloud Computing, and IoT

Fusing these tools facilitates the creation of smart environments that respond to users' needs and preferences in real time. For example, IoT devices make smart homes and smart cities possible, facilitating automation and data-driven decision-making [25]. When paired with cloud computing, it is possible to centrally gather and process data from various sources, improving our capacity to manage resources and effectively enhance several daily activities. Combining cloud computing, IoT, and tools of emancipation is a potent combination of technologies that can transform our digital environment and promote social advancement and empowerment. Fundamentally, this integration aims to create safe spaces where people can take more control over their digital lives by utilizing the democratizing and liberating powers of the Internet of Things (IoT), cloud computing, and the global web.

Through active engagement in public conversation, this integration guarantees data security and privacy while empowering individuals to create their digital spaces. These technologies' interconnection makes it easier to disseminate information, organize social movements, and magnify individual voices on a global scale. For instance, social media platforms work as virtual forums where people may connect with others who share their opinions and voice them, encouraging cooperation and sharing ideas. Numerous difficulties are also brought about by integrating various technologies, especially regarding digital literacy, privacy, and data security [26].

Strong cybersecurity measures and data protection methods are needed to protect personal data due to the massive amount of data created by IoT devices. Similarly, data ownership and control concerns arise as cloud computing centralizes data storage and processing, necessitating a delicate balance between user agency and service provider responsibilities [27]. While it offers incredible opportunities for individuals to curate their digital experiences, participate in societal discourse, and leverage technology for empowerment, it also calls for a vigilant approach to data security, privacy, and responsible digital citizenship. The responsible and ethical use of these integrated technologies is essential to harnessing their full potential while mitigating the associated risks and challenges in the digital age [28].

9.8 Embryonic Updated Technologies and Future Tendencies

The evolving information technology technologies are set to shape our digital landscape [29] profoundly. There are several key areas and trends are expected to define the future of technology and drive innovation-

Artificial intelligence (AI) and machine learning: AI and machine learning will continue to evolve, enabling machines to learn from data, make predictions, and solve complex problems. Future applications include more advanced virtual assistants, personalized healthcare, and autonomous systems in various domains.

Quantum computing: Quantum computing promises to revolutionize data processing by exploiting the principles of quantum mechanics. Problems like complicated simulations, cryptography, and optimization that are now unsolvable for conventional computers may be solved with this technology.

5G and beyond: It is anticipated that the introduction of 5G networks and the advancement of 6G will result in quicker and more dependable connectivity, opening up new possibilities for telemedicine, augmented reality, virtual reality, and the Internet of Things. There will be an ongoing increase in the number of connected devices.

Privacy and cyber security: With the increasing sophistication of cyber threats, cybersecurity will remain paramount. Safeguarding digital ecosystems will need the development of enhanced security mechanisms and the protection of personal data.
Edge Computing: As edge computing becomes more popular, data processing will be able to take place closer to the data source, which will lower latency and enhance real-time decision-making. This is particularly valuable in applications like IoT and autonomous vehicles.
Biotechnology and Genomics: Advances in biotechnology and genomics are poised to revolutionize healthcare. Precision medicine, gene editing, and biopharmaceuticals are areas to watch as they offer more personalized and effective treatments.
Sustainability and Green Tech: Sustainable technologies will continue to gain traction as the world seeks eco-friendly solutions. This includes renewable energy sources, electric vehicles, and the development of greener manufacturing processes.
Augmented Reality (AR) and Virtual Reality (VR): AR and VR are set to transform industries like gaming, education, healthcare, and remote work. Enhanced immersive experiences will become more accessible and practical.
Blockchain: Beyond cryptocurrencies, blockchain technology finds applications in supply chain management, voting systems, and digital identities, ensuring transparency and security in various sectors.
Biometrics and Digital Identities: Biometric authentication and digital identities will likely replace traditional passwords, enhancing security and user convenience.
Space Technology: Space exploration and commercialization, including missions to Mars and asteroid mining, will continue to evolve, opening up new opportunities in satellite communication and space travel.

These evolving technologies and future trends will shape the way we live, work, and interact with the world in the years to come. Adapting to these changes, ensuring ethical and responsible use of technology, and addressing the accompanying societal, moral, and regulatory challenges will be crucial as we navigate the future of technology [30].

9.9 New Cyber Risks and Emerging Threats

The number of cyber attacks is increasing as digitalization accelerates, and organizations appear to be under-equipped to handle IT security and address security threats to their commercial operations. Cyber attacks can negatively influence enterprises because they can compromise critical data and disrupt operations, resulting in negative consequences [31]. Hackers now understand these cyber weaknesses and how to exploit them. So, organizations must reconsider their cyber security strategy to deal with the growing threat of cybercrime and reduce cyber risk. Cybersecurity continuously evolves, and IT security departments must stay current on the latest threats. Understanding security risks in the context of business is a critical step in cybersecurity management. Companies must set proper controls over their infrastructure security [32]. With the IT landscape in enterprises becoming more complicated, data security teams must select the appropriate methods and technologies to protect themselves from potential cyber threats. The requirement for safe and secure network architecture is unavoidable. Important data should be backed up on an external hard disk. Given the increased rates of cybercrime worldwide, suppliers/vendors/third parties should also be required to test their networks regularly for vulnerabilities and potential security threats. They should invest in technologies such as antivirus, spyware, intrusion prevention, and an effective firewall [33].

9.9.1 Policy Implications, Societal and Ethical Considerations Concerning Safe Spaces Lensing New Cyber Risks and Emerging Threats

The policy implications concerning safe spaces lensing new cyber risks and emerging threats carry significant weight in the digital age. Governments and international bodies are responsible for crafting effective policies that balance safeguarding individual privacy and security while facilitating innovation and digital progress. One of the critical policy implications is the need for comprehensive data protection and privacy regulations. Policymakers must define precise data collection, storage, and usage rules, ensuring individuals control their personal information [34]. Regulatory frameworks like the European Union's General Data Protection Regulation (GDPR) are models for asserting individual rights while holding organizations accountable for data handling practices. Additionally, policies should encourage transparency and accountability among cloud service providers and IoT device manufacturers, fostering responsible practices that prioritize user safety [35].

Societal considerations in this context revolve around the impact of emerging cyber threats on our communities and daily lives. The rapid growth of IoT devices and cloud services has generated concerns about surveillance, data breaches, and cyber attacks that can disrupt essential services. Educating individuals on these technologies' potential risks and benefits is crucial in promoting digital literacy and responsible online behavior [36]. Moreover, society must grapple with the ethical implications of AI-driven surveillance, the spread of disinformation, and the potential weaponization of digital tools for political or social manipulation. To increase awareness and give people the skills and techniques to defend themselves online, policymakers, educators, and tech corporations must collaborate [37].

Ethical issues are crucial when discussing emerging threats, cyber risks, and safe spaces. The ethical concerns surrounding data ownership, spying, and the correct application of AI are becoming increasingly complicated as technology advances. Digital rights, consent, and individual autonomy are the three most important ethical principles that policymakers and tech executives should follow. Preventing bias and discrimination requires responsible AI and machine learning development, emphasizing justice, accountability, and openness [38]. In addition, ethical considerations include forbidding the creation or deployment of cyber weapons capable of causing disproportionate harm and the responsible disclosure of security flaws to thwart malevolent use. Effective laws should balance security and privacy, educate and equip society to navigate the digital world, and ensure that technical improvements are guided by moral standards. These elements create a more responsible and safe digital environment [39].

9.10 Conclusion and Future Scope

The revolutionary potential of the Internet of Things (IoT), cloud computing, and the global web as tools for both exploitation and emancipation is highlighted in this study. Safe spaces are crucial because they highlight the need to safeguard people's privacy and data integrity while promoting a safe and empowered digital environment. The article has examined the changing nature of cyber dangers and new threats, acknowledging the difficulties brought about by hacking, data breaches, and using technology as a weapon.

The future scope of this chapter is promising as the digital ecosystem continues to evolve rapidly, and future research can explore more deeply the interplay between these transformative technologies, addressing emerging issues such as quantum computing, which holds the potential to revolutionize encryption and data security. The ethical considerations surrounding AI-driven surveillance, deepfakes, and digital disinformation campaigns present a fertile ground for further examination. Moreover, the chapter's policy implications underscore the importance of regulatory frameworks that balance privacy and innovation, and future studies can delve into the effectiveness and adaptability of such regulations in a constantly changing technological landscape. In the coming years, the scope for research in this domain should encompass a proactive approach to cybersecurity, emphasizing the need for cyber security education, incident response strategies, and international collaboration to tackle global cyber threats collectively. Additionally, digital citizenship should be explored further, promoting responsible and ethical use of technology, especially among younger generations.

References

1. Kumar, S., *The digital frontier: Infrastructures of control on the global web*, Indiana University Press, USA, 2021.
2. Blikstein, P., Travels in Troy with Freire: Technology as an agent of emancipation, in: *Social Justice Education for Teachers*, pp. 205–235, Brill, Leiden, Netherlands, 2008.
3. Allmer, T., *Critical theory and social media: between emancipation and commodification*, Routledge, UK, 2015.
4. Eglash, R., Bennett, A., Cooke, L., Babbitt, W., Lachney, M., Counter-hegemonic computing: Toward computer science education for value generation and emancipation. *ACM Trans. Comput. Educ. (TOCE)*, 21, 4, 1–30, 2021.
5. Elder-Vass, D., Ethics and emancipation in action: Concrete utopias. *J. Crit. Realism*, 21, 5, 539–551, 2022.
6. Seibt, D., Schaupp, S., Meyer, U., Toward an analytical understanding of domination and emancipation in digitalizing industries, in: *Digitalization in Industry: Between Domination and Emancipation*, pp. 1–25, 2019.
7. Uzelac, A., How to understand digital culture: Digital culture-a resource for a knowledge society, in: *Digital Culture: The Changing Dynamics*, pp. 7–21, Institute for International Relations, Zagreb, 2008.
8. Maor, D., Ensor, J.D., Fraser, B.J., Doctoral supervision in virtual spaces: A review of research of web-based tools to develop collaborative supervision. *Higher Educ. Res. Dev.*, 35, 1, 172–188, 2016.
9. Castañeda, L. and Villar-Onrubia, D., Beyond functionality: Building critical digital teaching competence among future primary education teachers. *Contemp. Educ. Technol.*, 15, 1, ep397, 2023.
10. Casilli, A.A., Global digital culture| Digital labor studies go global: Toward a digital decolonial turn. *Int. J. Commun.*, 11, 21, 2017.

11. Ortega, N.R., Five central concepts to think of Digital Humanities as a new digital humanism project. *Artnodes: Rev. Arte Ciencia Tecnología*, 22, 1–6, 2018.
12. Doerr, N. and Svatoňová, E., Emphasised, feared, despised and hegemonic: images of femininity in the US far-right digital ecosystem on Telegram channels. *Eur. J. Polit. Gender*, 1, 11, 1–21, 2023.
13. Papantoniou, A.A., Regtech: steering the regulatory spaceship in the right direction? *J. Bank. Financ. Technol.*, 6, 1, 1–16, 2022.
14. Pal, P., The adoption of waves of digital technology as antecedents of digital transformation by financial services institutions. *J. Digit. Bank.*, 7, 1, 70–91, 2022.
15. Arun, J.S., Cuomo, J., Gaur, N., *Blockchain for business*, Addison-Wesley Professional, US, 2019.
16. Govindarajan, U.H., Singh, D.K., Gohel, H.A., Forecasting cyber security threats landscape and associated technical trends in telehealth using Bidirectional Encoder Representations from Transformers (BERT). *Comput. Secur.*, 1, 103404, 2023.
17. Aithal, P.S., Advances and New Research Opportunities in Quantum Computing Technology by Integrating it with Other ICCT Underlying Technologies. *Int. J. Case Stud. Bus. IT Educ. (IJCSBE)*, 7, 3, 314–358, 2023.
18. Radanliev, P., The Rise and Fall of Cryptocurrencies: Defining the Economic and Social Values of Blockchain Technologies, assessing the Opportunities, and Defining the Financial and Cybersecurity Risks of the Metaverse, arXiv preprint arXiv:2309.12322, 2023.
19. Brass, I. and Sowell, J.H., Adaptive governance for the Internet of Things: Coping with emerging security risks. *Regul. Governance*, 15, 4, 1092–1110, 2021.
20. Ahmad, W., Rasool, A., Javed, A.R., Baker, T., Jalil, Z., Cyber security in IoT-based cloud computing: A comprehensive survey. *Electronics*, 11, 1, 16, 2021.
21. Choo, K.-K.R., Cloud computing: Challenges and future directions. *Trends Issues Crime Crim. Justice*, 400, 1–6, 2010.
22. Onwubiko, C., Security issues to cloud computing, in: *Cloud computing: Principles, systems and applications*, pp. 271–288, 2010.
23. Ramgovind, S., Eloff, M.M., Smith, E., The management of security in cloud computing, in: *2010 Information Security for South Africa*, IEEE, pp. 1–7, 2010.
24. Buyya, R., Srirama, S.N., Casale, G., Calheiros, R., Simmhan, Y., Varghese, B., Gelenbe, E. *et al.*, A manifesto for future generation cloud computing: Research directions for the next decade. *ACM Comput. Surv. (CSUR)*, 51, 5, 1–38, 2018.
25. Hossain, M., Fotouhi, M., Hasan, R., Towards an analysis of security issues, challenges, and open problems in the Internet of Things, in: *2015 IEEE world congress on services*, IEEE, pp. 21–28, 2015.

26. Ibrahim, A.S., Hamlyn-Harris, J., Grundy, J., Emerging security challenges of cloud virtual infrastructure, arXiv preprint arXiv:1612.09059, 2016.
27. Carroll, M., Van Der Merwe, A., Kotze, P., Secure cloud computing: Benefits, risks and controls, in: *2011 Information Security for South Africa*, IEEE, pp. 1–9, 2011.
28. Yang, C., Huang, Q., Li, Z., Liu, K., Hu, F., Big Data and cloud computing: innovation opportunities and challenges. *Int. J. Digit. Earth*, 10, 1, 13–53, 2017.
29. Muhammad, T., Munir, M.T., Munir, M.Z., Zafar, M.W., Integrative Cybersecurity: Merging Zero Trust, Layered Defense, and Global Standards for a Resilient Digital Future. *Int. J. Comput. Sci. Technol.*, 6, 4, 99–135, 2022.
30. Plachkinova, M., Vo, A., Alluhaidan, A., Emerging trends in smart home security, privacy, and digital forensics, 2016.
31. Kandias, M., Virvilis, N., Gritzalis, D., The insider threat in cloud computing, in: *Critical Information Infrastructure Security: 6th International Workshop, CRITIS 2011, Lucerne, Switzerland, September 8-9, 2011, Revised Selected Papers 6*, pp. 93–103, Springer Berlin Heidelberg, Cham, 2013.
32. Kuyoro, S.O., Ibikunle, F., Awodele, O., Cloud computing security issues and challenges. *Int. J. Comput. Netw. (IJCN)*, 3, 5, 247–255, 2011.
33. Kumar, P., Sehgal, V.K., Chauhan, D.S., Gupta, P.K., Diwakar, M., Effective ways of secure, private and trusted cloud computing, arXiv preprint arXiv:1111.3165, 2011.
34. Nicolescu, R., Huth, M., Radanliev, P., De Roure, D., Mapping the values of IoT. *J. Inf. Technol.*, 33, 345–360, 2018.
35. Banerjee, M., Lee, J., Choo, K.-K.R., A blockchain future for Internet of Things security: a position paper. *Digit. Commun. Netw.*, 4, 3, 149–160, 2018.
36. Reetz, M.A., Prunty, L.B., Mantych, G.S., Hommel, D.J., Cyber risks: Evolving threats, emerging coverages, and ensuing case law. *Penn St. L. Rev.*, 122, 727, 2017.
37. Shrivastava, G., Peng, S.L., Bansal, H., Sharma, K., Sharma, M. (Eds.), *New age analytics: Transforming the internet through machine learning, IoT, and trust modeling*, CRC Press, US, 2020.
38. Shrivastava, G., Gupta, D., Sharma, K. (Eds.), *Cyber Crime and Forensic Computing: Modern Principles, Practices, and Algorithms*, De Gruyter, Germany, 2021.
39. Panda, D., Mishra, B.K., Sharma, K., A Taxonomy on Man-in-the-Middle Attack in IoT Network, in: *2022 4th International Conference on Advances in Computing, Communication Control and Networking (ICAC3N)*, IEEE, pp. 1907–1912, December, 2022.

10

IoT and Smart Device Security: Emerging Threats and Countermeasures

Geo Francis E.[1*], S. Sheeja[2], Antony John E.F.[3] and Jismy Joseph[4]

[1]*Dept. of Computer Science, Karpagam Academy of Higher Education, Coimbatore, India*
[2]*Dept. of Data Science, Sri Krishna Adithya College of Arts and Science, Coimbatore, India*
[3]*Dept. of Mathematics, St. Thomas College (Autonomous), Thrissur, India*
[4]*Dept. of Mathematics, Carmel College (Autonomous), Mala, India*

Abstract
This chapter delves into the ever-evolving Internet of Things (IoT) and its security challenges. In the context of the increasing number of interconnected smart devices, the chapter explores the rising potential for cyber threats, covering emerging threats, IoT vulnerabilities, attack vectors, and security best practices. It aims to assist individuals and organizations in safeguarding their IoT ecosystems and ensuring data privacy and integrity. The chapter begins by introducing IoT and smart devices. It further investigates common IoT vulnerabilities, highlighting the importance of addressing insecure designs and weak authentication for security. The chapter then addresses emerging threats in IoT and their implications for IoT systems. It concludes by presenting measures to fortify IoT security, encompassing secure device design, robust authentication, encryption, network segmentation, vigilant monitoring, and timely security updates, emphasizing best practices.

***Keywords*:** Security, threats, IoT, network, vulnerabilities, communication

10.1 Introduction to IoT and Smart Devices

The globe is undergoing a technological revolution that is redefining our interactions with our surroundings and reshaping the fundamental fabric

**Corresponding author*: edakulathur@hotmail.com

Kavita Sharma, Vishnu Sharma, Parma Nand, Anil Kumar Sagar and Gulshan Shrivastava (eds.) Securing the Digital Frontier: Threats and Advanced Techniques in Security and Forensics, (217–242)

of our everyday existence. The Internet of Things (IoT) and smart gadgets are central to this digital transition, two interconnected pillars that promise a future of unparalleled connectedness and data-driven innovation. The Introduction lays the groundwork for delving into the complexities of these cutting-edge technologies, clarifying their significance as revolutionary forces that connect disparate devices and enable seamless data transmission. The Internet of Things is an idea that defies categorization, building a linked ecosystem of physical items outfitted with sensors, software, and connections. These smart devices can gather, analyze, and communicate real-time data via the internet, ranging from smart household appliances and wearable gadgets to industrial machinery and intelligent city infrastructure. The Internet of Things allows objects to become thoughtful, proactive, and context-aware, allowing for new levels of data-driven decision-making [1, 2].

The physical and digital worlds combine in the age of IoT, opening up new opportunities for increasing efficiency, optimizing operations, and improving quality of life. The importance of IoT goes beyond the sheer quantity of connected devices; it is found in the symbiotic interaction between these devices, in which data created by one device may impact the behavior of another, resulting in a continuous flow of information and insights. IoT's revolutionary potential is manifesting across several areas, influencing people's lives and revolutionizing industries. IoT supports a data-driven culture in sectors and enterprises, where operational efficiency is optimized, and real-time insights enable informed decision-making. The IoT enables companies to monitor assets, follow supply chains, and better understand customer behavior than ever before. IoT is transforming industries such as manufacturing, where smart sensors integrated into machinery enable predictive maintenance and real-time monitoring, resulting in less downtime and more production. IoT-enabled gadgets in the healthcare industry improve patient outcomes and resource optimization by monitoring patient health, facilitating remote consultations, and streamlining medical operations. Furthermore, the disruptive influence of IoT extends into people's lives, improving convenience, safety, and personalization. IoT-enabled gadgets in smart homes provide unrivaled control and automation, allowing occupants to operate appliances, lights, and security systems remotely. Voice-activated virtual assistants offer a sophisticated touch, making houses intelligent and intuitive, seamlessly reacting to inhabitants' wants and preferences.

Wearable gadgets, such as fitness trackers and smartwatches, have become commonplace in health and fitness, allowing consumers to monitor their activity levels, heart rate, and sleep habits. Smart gadgets are the critical conduits of data exchange and communication and are at the heart of the IoT revolution. The smart device landscape is a vast ecosystem with a diverse range of networked devices; each meant to improve lives and expedite operations. An abundance of IoT-powered gadgets operate in tandem to offer a seamless living experience in smart homes. Indoor temperatures are adjusted by smart thermostats depending on tenant preferences and real-time weather conditions, resulting in energy conservation and cost savings. Smart lighting systems adapt to changing occupancy patterns, increasing energy economy while improving user comfort [3, 4]. Wearable gadgets have come to symbolize the influence of the Internet of Things on personal health and fitness. Fitness trackers measure users' daily activity, calories burnt, and sleep quality, encouraging them to adopt healthier habits and achieve their fitness objectives. In addition to maintaining time, smartwatches work as small communication centers, displaying call alerts, messaging, and other smartphone capabilities on users' wrists.

The Introduction to IoT and Smart gadgets lays the groundwork for an engrossing voyage into networked gadgets and data-driven innovation. This chapter emphasizes the revolutionary potential of IoT and urges readers to investigate the emerging difficulties and intriguing possibilities that

Figure 10.1 Overview of IoT structure.

lie ahead. Individuals and companies can exploit the full potential of this innovative technology to design a smarter and more connected future by grasping its significance, scope, and numerous uses. To realize the goal of a genuinely linked and efficient society, stakeholders must embrace cooperation, innovation, and cybersecurity as the IoT ecosystem evolves. IoT-enabled decision-making and intelligent gadgets will interconnect to revolutionize how we live, work, and flourish in a world of limitless possibilities. Figure 10.1 provides an overview of the IoT structure.

10.1.1 Definition and Scope

A technological turning point called IoT has created a seamless communication network between actual physical items and the digital world. IoT essentially entails giving physical objects connectivity, software, and sensor capabilities so they can interact and share information online. These gadgets cover a wide range, from wearable technology like fitness trackers to factory machinery to everyday home products like smart refrigerators and thermostats. Even the infrastructure of smart cities is progressively incorporating intelligent technology to improve urban services, contributing to the IoT ecosystem. The capacity of IoT to collect and interpret real-time data from several networked sources gives it its actual potential. IoT provides decision-makers priceless insights through this data-driven approach, encouraging data-driven decision-making. The Internet of Things has the potential to completely alter industries by enabling efficiency, automation, and optimization across several sectors. IoT-driven sensors integrated into manufacturing equipment continually track performance indicators, enabling predictive maintenance and reducing downtime. Industries may plan maintenance of breakdowns by foreseeing future equipment failures, which minimizes production interruptions and boosts overall productivity [5].

The potential of IoT is limitless and promises a future where connectivity and intelligence will significantly improve our quality of life. IoT gadgets have influenced many facets of daily life, improving comfort, security, and energy efficiency. IoT-enabled equipment and gadgets cooperate in smart homes to provide seamless automation and remote control. Through smartphone applications, homeowners may increase comfort while reducing energy use by adjusting thermostats, locking doors, and even getting real-time data on energy use. Wearable IoT devices have made it possible for people to continuously monitor their heart rates, activity levels, and sleep patterns for personal health and fitness. With this information, people may proactively adjust their lifestyles for better health and well-being. IoT has also opened up the possibility of more innovative, more sustainable urban landscapes. IoT solutions enhance service and infrastructure management in smart cities, optimizing resource allocation and eliminating waste. Smart traffic management systems use real-time data from the linked cars to improve traffic flow while reducing congestion and pollution [6]. Waste management systems outfitted with IoT sensors have the potential to optimize waste collection schedules, minimizing superfluous collections and boosting environmental sustainability.

As the impact of IoT grows, there are still difficulties that require careful study and practical solutions. Given the enormous volume of sensitive data generated and processed by IoT devices, security and privacy issues are at the top of the list. It is vital to have robust data encryption, authentication, and access control systems to protect against cyberattacks and unauthorized acccss to sensitive information. Furthermore, interoperability and standardization across various IoT devices are required for smooth integration and communication across multiple platforms and applications.

As a result, IoT has ushered in a new era of interconnection and data-driven intelligence that transcends industries and everyday lives. Its transformational potential is already evident in the manufacturing, healthcare, transportation, and urban planning industries. IoT enables individuals and organizations to make informed decisions, automate processes, and optimize resource utilization by utilizing real-time data. IoT's scope is expanding exponentially, offering revolutionary applications and services that improve efficiency, safety, and convenience. To retain consumer trust and confidence in this networked environment, stakeholders must address security and privacy concerns as the IoT landscape evolves. Standardization initiatives are critical to ensuring interoperability across various IoT devices, allowing for accessible communication and data sharing. Collaboration, creativity, and responsible development will be essential in designing a connected world that benefits societies, companies, and individuals equally as we navigate the potential future of IoT [7]. By embracing the possibilities of IoT, we can create a future in which technology enables us to address global concerns and create a more sustainable and affluent world for future generations.

10.1.2 Growth and Importance of IoT

IoT growth has been exponential in recent years, driven by technology improvements, lower sensor and connectivity costs, and more cloud computing use. IoT offers variousconsumer electronics, healthcare, logistics, and agriculture applications. One of the primary motivators for IoT adoption is its potential to revolutionize industries. IoT in manufacturing provides predictive maintenance, process optimization, and product quality improvement. IoT devices and wearables in healthcare monitor patient health and provide remote medical help, resulting in better patient outcomes. Smart infrastructure enabled by IoT has the potential to improve urban services, efficient energy usage, and optimize traffic management.

The significance of IoT adoption is apparent in its ability to improve numerous industries and quality of life. Rapid technological improvements have reduced the size, efficiency, and cost-effectiveness of IoT devices, making them more accessible to companies and consumers alike. With the emergence of 4G and 5G networks, data transmission rates and latency have considerably increased, allowing for real-time data interchange between devices. Cloud computing has been critical to IoT scalability, providing ample storage capacity and robust data analytics tools for dealing with the massive volumes of data created by IoT devices. Edge computing has increased the effect of IoT by decentralizing data processing, allowing for real-time reactions in applications such as autonomous cars and industrial automation. IoT applications cover a wide range of sectors. IoT-powered machine sensors enable predictive maintenance in the industrial industry, lowering downtime and improving productivity. IoT-enabled remote patient monitoring and personalized health management via wearable devices boost healthcare. Smart infrastructure enabled by IoT optimizes energy usage, waste management, and city transportation, promoting sustainability. Data-driven decision-making enabled by IoT adoption optimizes resource utilization and improves efficiency in agriculture and transportation. The capacity of IoT to revolutionize industries and increase resource utilization is driving its uprising relevance. Its potential to transform manufacturing processes, healthcare, and urban life underscores the need to adopt IoT technologies [8]—furthermore, the implementation of IoT results in a more sustainable and resource-efficient future. Incorporating IoT into daily life through smart homes and energy-efficient gadgets helps conserve resources. Collaboration among technology providers, organizations, and legislators will be critical as we move forward in the IoT age to ensure responsible and secure integration of IoT technologies. Harnessing the revolutionary power of IoT creates previously unimagined prospects for advancement, establishing a linked society that values sustainability, efficiency, and wealth for future generations.

10.1.3 Smart Device Landscape

The smart device landscape includes networked gadgets to improve our daily lives and industrial processes. Smart household appliances, wearable gadgets, linked automobiles, industrial sensors, and smart city infrastructure are all examples of these technologies. Smart home products like smart thermostats, lighting systems, and voice-activated assistantsgive homeowners better control, energy efficiency, and convenience. Wearable technologies, such as fitness trackers and smartwatches, providehelpful health and fitness data, encouraging users to live better lives. IoT-enabled sensors and actuators in the industrial sector make gathering and analyzing data in real timemore accessible, enhancing predictive maintenance and increasing operational effectiveness. Vehicle-to-vehicle (V2V) and vehicle-to-infrastructure (V2I) communication are made possible by connected automobiles using IoT technology, opening the door to safer and more effective transportation. Interoperability and security are now top priorities as the smart device ecosystem changes [9]. According to manufacturers and developers, users' privacy and data must be protected while enabling smooth communication between various devices. As a result, the Introduction to IoT and Smart Devices offers a thorough introduction to IoT as a disruptive technology and its vast applicability across several sectors. Understanding the definition, range, development, and landscape of smart devices paves the way for a deeper investigation of the issues and solutions related to IoT and smart device security, which is covered in the following sections.

10.2 Vulnerabilities in IoT Devices

IoT has made significant strides into industrial areas outside the home realm, spurring extraordinary breakthroughs in real-time monitoring and predictive maintenance. For instance, manufacturing facilities are outfitted with sensors that continually collect information on the functioning of the gear, seeing possible problems before they snowball into expensive failures. This preventative maintenance strategy guarantees improved productivity, reduced downtime, and simplified operations. The proliferation of IoT devices has brought unprecedented ease and efficiency to our lives. IoT has altered how people interact with technology, from smart homes with automatic lighting and thermostats to industrial systems with real-time monitoring. However, this fast proliferation has revealed a dark underbelly - the vulnerabilities that beset IoT devices [10]. Figure 10.2 illustrates the structure of Vulnerabilities in IoT Devices. This part will examine three primary vulnerabilities in IoT devices: unsecured device design and setup, inadequate authentication and authorization, and a lack of device updates and patch management.

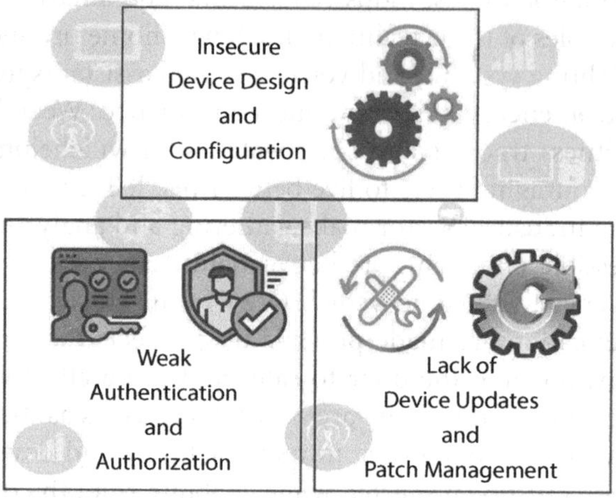

Figure 10.2 Structure of vulnerabilities in IoT devices.

10.2.1 Insecure Device Design and Configuration

The absence of safe design and setup is a crucial problem plaguing IoT devices. Manufacturers oftenprioritize speed-to-market over security, resulting in gadgets rife with flaws. Insecure design decisions can range from hardcoded default passwords to exposed ports that expose the device to assaults. Furthermore, incorrect setup settings might have disastrous implications. Insecure network setups, for example, might allow unauthorized access to the device, while poor encryption practices can expose critical data to eavesdroppers. Attackers take advantage of these defects in design and configuration to obtain unauthorized access to IoT devices, affecting their operation and potentially inflicting substantial harm. Manufacturers mustprioritize security throughout the design and development phase to overcome this issue. Conducting rigorous security assessments, applying safe coding practices, and adhering to industry best practices for device setup are all part of this. Additionally, manufacturers should urge users to change default passwords at initial setup and upgrade their device's firmware regularly to avoid known vulnerabilities.

10.2.2 Weak Authentication and Authorization

Insufficient authentication and authorization protocols are a significant area for improvement in IoT devices. Authentication refers to confirming the identity of people or devices attempting to access the system, whereas authorization determines what actions those verified users or devices are permitted to conduct. Authentication systems in many IoT devices need to be better built or nonexistent, relying exclusively on default credentials or basic passwords. Such low-security procedures make it simple for attackers to get unauthorized access to IoT devices and exploit them for harmful purposes. For example, an attacker who obtains access to a smart home security camera might breach the user's privacy, perhaps leading to more severe crimes. Robust security mechanisms, such as multi-factor authentication (MFA), should be deployed to improve authentication and authorization [11]. MFA requires users or devices to submit several forms of identity, dramatically lowering the danger of unauthorized access. Furthermore, adopting role-based access restrictions ensures that each person or device has access to the resources required for its intended purpose.

10.2.3 Lack of Device Updates and Patch Management

Another area for improvement with IoT devices is the absence of frequent patch management and device upgrades. Manufacturers frequently undervalue the need for regular software upgrades to fix security problems, leaving devices vulnerable to new dangers. IoT devices may experience software obsolescence as they age, leaving them open to vulnerabilities for which no updates are available. Furthermore, many consumers need more knowledge to update their gadgets. This negligence poses a severe security concern because of unpatched devices' continued susceptibility to known vulnerabilities that attackers might exploit. Manufacturers pledge to regularly release firmware upgrades that rapidly fix security flaws to counteract this risk. Automated update systems can make the procedure easier for consumers while maintaining their devices' security. Manufacturers should also actively participate in vulnerability disclosure programs so that security researchers may disclose and appropriately repair such issues. It is essential to be aware of and take steps to address IoT devices' vulnerabilities as they continue to influence our connected world. The security and privacy of IoT ecosystems are seriously threatened by poor authentication and authorization, unreliable device design and setup, and a lack of device upgrades and patch management. Manufacturers must prioritize security during the design and development phases, with robust authentication methods and frequent software upgrades included [12]. They can protect the promise of IoT by proactively addressing weaknesses, paving the road for a secure and linked future.

10.3 Emerging Threats in IoT Security

The fast growth of Internet of Things (IoT) devices has provided our lives with unparalleled ease and efficiency. This networked ecosystem, however, has given rise to a new set of security dangers that pose severe hazards to both persons and organizations. This section delves into three developing IoT security threats: botnets and Distributed Denial of Service (DDoS) assaults, data breaches and privacy hazards, and physical harm and safety concerns.

10.3.1 Botnets and DDoS Attacks

Botnets constitute a significant cybersecurity risk to IoT devices and the more extensive internet infrastructure. A botnet is a network of infected devices controlled by a hostile person known as a botmaster. Cybercriminals frequently recruit IoT devices into their botnet army by exploiting poor security measures such as default passwords and unpatched vulnerabilities. Botnets may be used to execute devastating Distributed Denial of Service (DDoS) assaults after they have been constructed. During a DDoS attack, the botnet floods a target server or network with massive traffic, rendering it inaccessible to genuine users [13]. These assaults can potentially impair internet services, resulting in financial losses, loss of reputation, and disruption of crucial infrastructure. IoT device suppliers must prioritize security during the design and development to protect against botnets and DDoS assaults [14]. Device breach risk may be considerably decreased by implementing robust authentication methods, ensuring frequent firmware upgrades, and encouraging users to modify default passwords. Additionally, network managers should use DDoS mitigation techniques like rate limiting and traffic filtering to defend their infrastructure from these persistent assaults.

10.3.2 Data Breaches and Privacy Risks

The networked nature of IoT devices poses some of the most severe hazards, including data breaches and privacy issues. These devices generate and transmit enormous volumes of sensitive data, making them appealing targets for hackers looking to steal important data. The potential repercussions of a data breach are severe, regardless of whether it involves personal data from wearable devices, valuable corporate information from industrial sensors, or even medical records from healthcare equipment. In addition to compromising people's privacy, data breaches may cause identity theft, financial fraud, and business reputational harm. Furthermore, combining data from many IoT devices can create a detailed portrait of individuals' actions and routines, presenting severe privacy issues. Manufacturers of Internet of Things (IoT) devices must use strong data encryption and secure communication protocols to reduce the danger of data breaches. Encryption of data is recommended for both in-transit and at-rest security. Strict access controls and user authentication procedures may also be implemented to guarantee that only authorized people can access sensitive data.

10.3.3 Physical Damage and Safety Concerns

The risk of physical harm and safety issues increases as IoT devices merge with vital infrastructure and industrial systems, which pose a severe security risk. A hacker accessing IoT devices in charge of vital infrastructure, like water treatment facilities or power grids, might cause havoc. For instance, tampering with smart city traffic management systems might result in collisions and traffic jams, putting public safety at peril. When hacked, industrial IoT (IIoT) equipment can seriously endanger the safety of both users and the environment. A cyberattack on industrial control systems in the manufacturing industry may result in the malfunctioning of the equipment, which may result in accidents or injuries. When IoT devices that monitor oil and gas pipelines are compromised, it can result in spills or explosions that negatively affect the environment and public safety. IoT device makers must put rigorous precautions in place to prevent unauthorized access and manipulation and address physical damage and safety issues. Additionally, network segmentation helps separate industrial systems and vital infrastructure from less essential devices, minimizing the attack surface. IoT device proliferation offers previously unheard-of prospects for innovation and connection. However, it also makes us vulnerable to many new security risks that call for quick response and preventative action [15]. Among the biggest problems with IoT security are botnets and DDoS assaults, data breaches and privacy risks, physical damage and safety issues, and data breaches and privacy hazards. To protect IoT's potential, manufacturers, enterprises, and people must prioritize security at all levels. Robust authentication systems, regular software upgrades, and encryption practices are required to secure IoT devices. Furthermore, regular monitoring and prompt incident response are critical in efficiently recognizing and mitigating security breaches. We can manage the hazards of connection and harness the full promise of IoT in a safe and linked society by recognizing these growing challenges and taking joint action. Embracing a culture of cybersecurity awareness and applying best practices will be critical in ensuring that the promise of IoT is preserved for future generations.

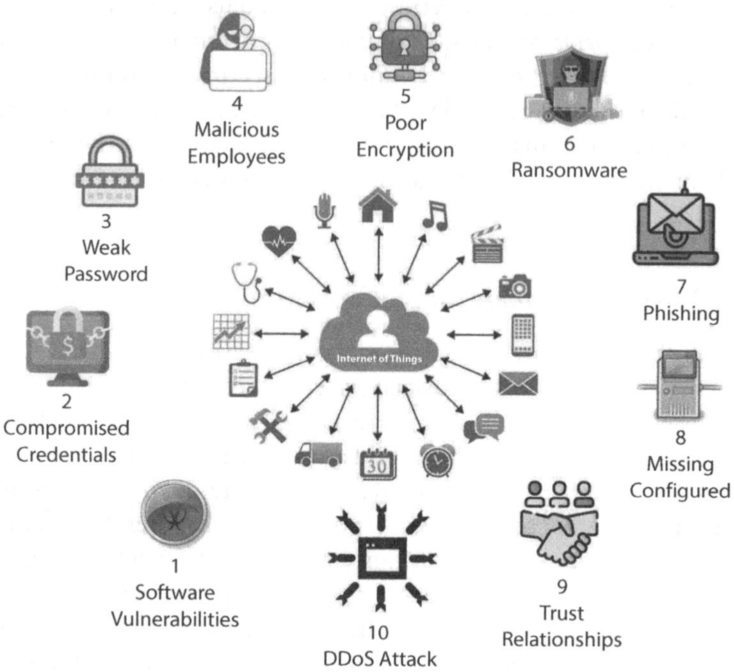

Figure 10.3 Attack vectors in IoT.

10.4 Attack Vectors in IoT

As the Internet of Things (IoT) permeates our daily lives and vital infrastructure, it exposes us to many attack vectors that hostile actors may exploit. This section delves into the three most common IoT attack vectors: network exploitation, firmware and software exploits, social engineering, and phishing. Figure 10.3 shows the attack vectors in IoT.

10.4.1 Network Exploitation

In the global arena of IoT, network exploitation is a powerful attack vector that exploits weaknesses in the communication paths between devices and backend systems. IoT devices frequently use wireless communication protocols such as Wi-Fi, Bluetooth, Zigbee, or Z-Wave to connect and share data. These communication routes may be vulnerable to eavesdropping and manipulation by adversaries due to encryption, authentication, or authorization flaws. Cybercriminals can use these flaws to intercept sensitive data exchanged between IoT devices, resulting in privacy violations and unauthorized access. Furthermore, attackers may conduct man-in-the-middle attacks, impersonating genuine devices or backend systems to modify data transmitted between devices, resulting in disruptive or deadly repercussions [16]. Regular firmware updates that address security vulnerabilities can help strengthen the resilience of communication pathways and can help mitigate network exploitation. Network administrators must also watch network traffic for suspicious activities and deploy intrusion detection systems to identify potential breaches quickly.

10.4.2 Firmware and Software Exploits

Firmware and software vulnerabilities are other important attack vectors in IoT security. Many IoT devices rely on embedded firmware and software to work, and these components may have unpatched vulnerabilities or obsolete libraries, rendering them vulnerable to exploitation. When attackers identify such flaws, they can create and disseminate malware to exploit them. Once within the device's firmware or software, the virus obtains control, allowing unauthorized access, data theft, or even total device takeover. In some situations, infected devices might join botnets, contributing to large-scale cyberattacks.

Manufacturers must prioritize security in the development process and undertake frequent security audits and vulnerability testing to mitigate firmware and software attacks. Maintaining the integrity of IoT devices requires using safe coding practices, following industry security standards, and providing timely firmware upgrades.

10.4.3 Social Engineering and Phishing

While technology flaws represent substantial risks, attackers frequently target the human element via social engineering and phishing attempts. Social engineering entails tricking people into disclosing sensitive information or acting in ways that jeopardize security. Phishing is a typical social engineering approach that involves sending false emails or messages that look to be from reputable sources, deceiving recipients into clicking harmful links, or disclosing sensitive information. Social engineering assaults in the context of IoT may target users, workers, or even manufacturers themselves. Attackers can acquire control of IoT devices or the infrastructure to which they are linked by enticing people to provide login credentials, give unauthorized access, or overcome security controls.

User education and awareness are critical in combating social engineering and phishing. Training the users to recognize and report strange messages and requests can lower the success rate of these assaults dramatically. Manufacturers and organizations must also implement multi-factor authentication and other security measures to protect against unauthorized access [17]. Understanding the many threat vectors in IoT is critical to protecting our interconnected world. Network exploitation, firmware and software exploits, social engineering, and phishing pose substantial risks to IoT devices' security, privacy, and operation. We can fortify the IoT ecosystem and ensure a safer and more resilient linked future by installing robust security measures, executing frequent upgrades, and educating the users about possible hazards. Collaboration among manufacturers, organizations, and consumers is critical for preventing harmful activities and reaping the full benefits of IoT's transformational capacity.

10.5 Countermeasures for IoT Security

The ever-expanding Internet of Things (IoT) environment provides enormous ease and efficiency to our lives, but it also offers a complicated security scenario that needs strong responses. This section examines four critical IoT security countermeasures: safe device design principles, authentication and encryption, network segmentation and monitoring, security updates, and patch management.

10.5.1 Secure Device Design Principles

Prioritizing security during the device design and development is a vital countermeasure in IoT security. Secure device design concepts include proactively identifying potential vulnerabilities and mitigating hazards before devices are released to the public. Manufacturers must follow secure coding practicesto prevent typical hazards such as buffer overflows and injection attacks. Devices should also have techniques to secure sensitive data, such as encryption and access restrictions. Hardware-based security features such as Trusted Platform Modules (TPMs) and hardware root of trust can improve IoT device security. Manufacturers may construct robust and trustworthy devices by including security in the design process, lowering the risk of exploitation throughout the device's lifespan.

Table 10.1 Countermeasures for IoT security.

Countermeasure	Description
Secure Device Design	Implement robust security in device development.
Strong Authentication	Require strong and multi-factor authentication.
Encryption	Encrypt data in transit and at rest.
Network Segmentation	Isolate IoT devices on separate network segments.
Vigilant Monitoring	Continuously monitor for abnormal activities.
Timely Security Updates	Regularly update and patch devices and software.
Best Practices	Implement industry best practices and standards.
User Training and Awareness	Educate users about security risks and practices.

10.5.2 Authentication and Encryption

Authentication and encryption are essential lines of defense against unauthorized access and data breaches in IoT. Robust authentication techniques validate the identity of individuals or devices seeking to access the IoT ecosystem, preventing bad actors from getting unauthorized access. MFA, which integrates numerous kinds of identity, considerably increases the authentication process. For example, users may be required to submit a password and a one-time authentication code emailed to their registered device to get access [18]. Encryption, on the other hand, safeguards data integrity and secrecy throughout transmission and storage. Implementing robust encryption techniques, such as the Advanced Encryption Standard (AES), guarantees that data, even if intercepted, remains unreadable to unauthorized persons. Authentication and encryption work together to build a powerful barrier against unauthorized access and data interception, protecting the privacy and integrity of IoT data. Table 10.1 provides the countermeasures for the security of IoT.

10.5.3 Network Segmentation and Monitoring

Network segmentation is a powerful defense strategy that isolates important IoT ecosystem components, lowering the potential attack surface for hackers. The effect of a breach can be reduced by segmenting the network into distinct sections, each with its own security rules, limiting lateral attacker movement across the network. Continuous network monitoring is equally essential as segmentation in identifying possible security issues. Intrusion detection (IDS) and intrusion prevention (IPS) systems actively analyze network traffic for abnormalities and suspicious activity, setting off alarms or initiating preventative action as needed. Networksegmentation and monitoring improve situational awareness, allowing quick reactions to new threats and lowering the possibility of sustained attacks.

10.5.4 Security Updates and Patch Management

Over time, the robustness of IoT devices must be maintained, which requires security upgrades and patch management. Manufacturers must promptly deliver updates and fixes to address new vulnerabilities when security experts find them. Device performance and dependability are both increased by regular security upgrades, which help shield devices from new threats. As many IoT devices operate in settings where manual updates are unfeasible, providing fast updates can take time and effort. Manufacturers should provide over-the-air (OTA) update technologies that allow devices to get updates automatically to solve this problem. Furthermore, user-friendly update procedures and alerts may persuade users to install fixes quickly.

A rigorous and proactive security strategy is needed to protect the Internet of Things. Strong IoT security practices are built on secure device design principles, authentication and encryption, network segmentation and monitoring, security updates, and patch management. The full potential of linked technologies may be unlocked while reducing the constantly changing dangers posed by the digital environment by including these countermeasures in IoT device design, deployment, and maintenance [19]. Collaboration between manufacturers, organizations, and users is crucial in developing a culture of security awareness and responsible IoT use and ensuring a safer and more successful connected future for everybody.

10.6 Case Studies in IoT Security

Real-world experiences, including both achievements and failures, have a significant impact on the IoT security space. We go into case studies in this area that showcase important IoT security events and effective IoT security initiatives.

10.6.1 Notable IoT Security Incidents

- **Mirai Botnet and Dyn DDoS Attack:** 2016 one of the most significant Distributed Denial of Service (DDoS) assaults was carried out using the Mirai botnet. This malware version targets IoT devices with default passwords. When the botnet took over hundreds of thousands of IoT devices with weak security, it launched a coordinated attack on Dyn, a significant Domain Name System (DNS) provider. Widespread internet disruptions brought on by the hack affected services for well-known websites, including Twitter, Netflix, and Reddit. The industry received a wake-up call from this tragedy, highlighting how crucial it is to protect IoT devices against botnet recruiting and DDoS attacks.
- **Stuxnet Worm:** Stuxnet was a sophisticated cyber weapon that targeted industrial control systems, including IoT devices. However, it wasn't only an IoT event. Stuxnet used holes in Siemens' Supervisory Control and Data Acquisition (SCADA) systems to attack Iran's nuclear program. The malware seriously damaged Iran's nuclear facilities, highlighting the possible repercussions of IoT device security breaches in crucial infrastructure sectors. Stuxnet differs from regular malware and viruses that had been around before its discovery in 2010. Owing to its extreme sophistication, nation-states rather than lone hackers may have been involved. The uranium enrichment facilities in Iran employ SCADA systems, which are precisely the target of the virus. To covertly infect its targets, it usedseveral zero-day vulnerabilities and a combination of cutting-edge tactics, such as rootkit capabilities and stolen digital certificates. One of Stuxnet's main targets was Siemens SCADA systems, which are widely used in industrial settings to control and monitor crucial activities. The worm entered and controlled the programmable logic controllers (PLCs) in charge of managing the centrifuges at Iran's nuclear sites by exploiting the flaws in these systems.
  Stuxnet modified the speed of the centrifuges by interfering with the PLCs' programming, forcing them to spin at erroneous speeds. The goal of this covert sabotage was to obstruct Iran's uranium enrichment activities without drawing attention to itself. The effectiveness and sophistication of Stuxnet's attack showed how hackers may affect actual physical

operations in crucial infrastructure sectors. Although Iran's nuclear program was Stuxnet's main aim, its devastating power was not limited to any particular region or sector. The worm unintentionally infected systems worldwide, including those in nations unconnected to its initial target, as it moved through the internet and infected USB devices. The risks posed by cyber weapons and the difficulty in controlling their effects were underlined by this inadvertent proliferation.

Although Stuxnet was not only an Internet of Things event, its assault on industrial control systems should serve as an eye-opener in IoT device security. IoT devices are employed in critical infrastructure and several modern industrial systems for remote monitoring and automation. Since these devices are networked, any flaws in their setup or design may be taken advantage of, as Stuxnet did with SCADA systems. The Stuxnet attack highlighted the possible consequences of failing to secure IoT devices appropriately in crucial infrastructure sectors. It emphasized the value of thorough security reviews, regular updates, and speedy vulnerability mitigation to guard against the manipulation and interruption of physical processes. It is crucial to acknowledge the worldwide implications and lessons the Stuxnet episode offers when we think about it. Protecting the fundamental elements of contemporary society and preserving the trust and integrity of linked systems depend on a proactive and cooperative approach to IoT device security. We can create a more secure and resilient future for the connected world where cyber-attacks face staunch defenses, and responsible cyber behavior prevails by taking lessons from previous tragedies like Stuxnet.

- **Vulnerabilities in IoT Smart Locks:** According to researchers, Smart locks used in homes and businesses have flaws. Owing to these issues, attackers could get access without authorization using lock bypassing methods such as replay assaults, brute force, and lock jamming. Such occurrences emphasize the requirement for strong security controls in the Internet of Things devices that influence physical access and user safety.

10.6.2 Successful IoT Security Implementations

- **Medical IoT Devices in Healthcare:** Owing to their direct influence on patient health, devices like pacemakers and insulin pumps must be protected with strong security measures. Strong firmware signatures, secure update procedures, and strong encryption have all been used by reputable medical device makers to guard against possible security flaws. Additionally, ongoing surveillance and cooperation with the cybersecurity community have made it possible to respond quickly to new threats, boosting patient safety and security.

- **Industrial IoT (IIoT) in Manufacturing:** IoT has been adopted by the manufacturing industry for process automation and proactive maintenance. Secure edge computing, which ensures that the crucial data is handled closer to the source and lowers the risk of data breaches, is critical to successful deployments. To stop attackers from moving laterally, IIoT networks are frequently segmented, separating operational technology (OT) from information technology (IT) environments. Manufacturers also give priority to routine security upgrades to quickly fix problems.
- **Connected Vehicles and Automotive Industry:** Due to their reliance on communication between several electronic control units (ECUs) and external networks, connected cars pose particular security difficulties. Strong authentication and encryption techniques are used in successful implementations to protect communication connections. To protect car systems, manufacturers monitor ongoing threats, quickly fixing possible vulnerabilities and disseminating over-the-air (OTA) upgrades. Case studies in IoT security provide producers, organizations, and users with helpful learning opportunities. The necessity of prioritizing security in IoT device design, development, and deployment is underscored by notable occurrences. They draw attention to the possible repercussions of insufficient security precautions and the necessity of ongoing surveillance and quick reaction to new threats. Successful IoT security implementations, on the other hand, highlight the advantages of strong security procedures by showing how encryption, authentication, network segmentation, and routine updates can build a reliable and trustworthy IoT ecosystem. A culture of security awareness and safe IoT use depends on learning from achievements and errors. We can collaboratively negotiate the challenges of IoT security and realize the full potential of a secure and connected society by building on these experiences.

10.7 Future Trends and Challenges in IoT Security

The future of IoT security offers both encouraging trends and challenging problems as the Internet of Things (IoT) develops and permeates more facets of our lives. Regulatory and legal considerations, securing emerging IoT technologies, and artificial intelligence and machine learning in IoT security are the three key factors we cover in this section that will shape the future of IoT security. This section delves into the future trends and challenges that will shape the landscape of IoT security, paving the way for a secure and trustworthy connected world.

10.7.1 Artificial Intelligence and Machine Learning in IoT Security

Machine learning (ML) and artificial intelligence (AI) have the potential to change the IoT security industry completely. Traditional security methods need help to keep up with the changing threat picture as IoT networks grow and produce enormous volumes of data. AI and ML provide a dynamic and proactive approach to security, which can identify risks in real time and take appropriate action. AI-powered security solutions may analyze IoT device data from enormous datasets to spot patterns indicating potential attacks or unusual behavior. Machine learning algorithms can find undiscovered or zero-day vulnerabilities by learning from the past and anticipating future attack patterns [20]. By feeding AI-powered security systems with insufficient data intended to confound or go around detection algorithms, cybercriminals may try to trick the systems. To keep ahead of advanced attack methods, continual research and development are necessary to ensure the robustness of AI-based security systems.

10.7.2 Regulatory and Legal Considerations

Regulatory organizations worldwide are now addressing IoT security issues due to the growth of IoT devices and their potential impact on privacy and security. Governments and industry standards bodies are putting more and more effort into creating laws and policies to ensure the safe use of IoT technology. Regulations may require manufacturers to adhere to specific security standards and implement safeguards, including secure device design, encryption, and routine software upgrades. Additionally, more excellent compliance standards could apply to IoT devices that handle sensitive data or have the potential to affect public safety. Manufacturers and organizations, particularly those operating internationally, face difficulties navigating the complicated environment of IoT security rules. A thorough awareness of various jurisdictions' legal and regulatory landscape is necessary to ensure compliance with regional laws.

10.7.3 Securing Emerging IoT Technologies

Future IoT security will cover existing IoT hardware and software and newly developed IoT hardware and software. Security issues must advance as new technologies like 5G networks, edge computing, and quantum computing become crucial components of the IoT ecosystem. 5 G networks provide faster and more dependable connections; however, these networks also open up new attack vectors and the possibility of larger-scale DDoS attacks. To stop the growth of IoT-related security concerns, securing infrastructure and 5G-enabled devices will be essential. In IoT applications, edge computing, which analyses data closer to the source, lowers latency and improves real-time responsiveness. However, it is necessary to safeguard numerous endpoints and provide effective communication; protecting dispersed edge networks takes much work. Despite being in its infancy, quantum computing has the potential to undermine the security of existing cryptographic techniques employed in IoT [21]. Researchers are looking into quantum-resistant encryption techniques to protect IoT data from potential quantum-based attacks. A proactive strategy, including cooperation between academics, manufacturers, and governments, is needed to secure the development of IoT devices. Table 10.2 provides the future trends and challenges in IoT security. The security of these technologies has to be continually assessed and improved to counter new threats as they develop and become more commonplace.

IoT security's future holds both great potential and imposing difficulties. AI and machine learning have made powerful solutions available to guard against evolving threats and foresee potential vulnerabilities. Regulatory and legal factors are crucial to guarantee responsible IoT implementation and safeguard user privacy. Utilizing growing IoT technologies' revolutionary potential and protecting against new dangers requires their security. All stakeholders, including manufacturers, organizations, policymakers, and individuals, must work together to address these future trends and difficulties. We can pave the road for a safe and resilient IoT ecosystem by proactively adopting security technology and regulatory framework breakthroughs, unleashing the full promise of a connected world for future generations.

Table 10.2 Future trends and challenges in IoT security.

Trend/challenge	Description
Edge Computing	Increased reliance on edge devices for processing data.
AI and Machine Learning	Utilizing AI for anomaly detection and threat mitigation.
5G Connectivity	Leveraging faster and more reliable connections.
Regulatory Compliance	Adhering to evolving data protection regulations.
Blockchain for Security	Enhanced data integrity and secure transactions.
Supply Chain Vulnerabilities	Addressing security risks in IoT device supply chains.
Device Firmware Updates	Ensuring secure and timely updates for IoT devices.
Data Privacy	Protecting user data and privacy in IoT systems.
Evolving Threat Landscape	Staying ahead of new and sophisticated cyber threats.

10.8 Conclusion

Security is a top priority in the ever-changing IoT world, necessitating ongoing attention and innovation. Several significant aspects have emerged throughout our investigation of IoT security, impacting the way we approach and handle the difficulties in this linked world. As we embrace this digital revolution, it is essential to recognize that the future of IoT lies in its promise and security. In this concluding section, we recap the key points explored in this book, emphasize the critical importance of implementing robust IoT security measures, and envision a future where security remains at the forefront of IoT development.

10.8.1 Recap of Key Points

The path through IoT security has revealed the following essential points: The fast expansion of the Internet of Things has revolutionized businesses and our everyday lives, announcing enormous opportunities for efficiency and comfort. With the rise of IoT devices, new and sophisticated dangers such as botnets, data breaches, and physical harm concerns have developed. Insecure device design, inadequate authentication, and a lack of updates all pose significant risks to IoT security. Secure device design, authentication, encryption, network segmentation, and timely upgrades are critical countermeasures to protect IoT ecosystems. Notable security events and successful deployments in many industries provide valuable insights into IoT security practices' possible implications and advantages.

10.8.2 Importance of IoT Security Implementation

Implementing robust IoT security practices is not a luxury but a necessity. IoT devices and networks are critical infrastructure, impacting everything from personal safety to national security. By prioritizing security at every level, from device design to user education, we can prevent cyberattacks, protect user data, and ensure the trustworthiness of the IoT ecosystem. Moreover, a strong focus on security also preserves the potential of IoT to drive innovation and progress. By addressing security concerns, we foster an environment where individuals and organizations can confidently embrace IoT technologies, unlocking the full transformative power of the connected world.

10.8.3 Future Outlook for IoT Security

IoT security will face exciting opportunities and complicated obstacles in the future. AI and machine learning will become increasingly crucial in threat identification and response, allowing proactive and adaptive security solutions. Regulatory and legal issues will shape responsible IoT adoption, driving adherence to security standards and responsibility. To handle increasing risks, securing new IoT technologies such as 5G, edge computing, and quantum computing will need continual study and collaboration. Because of the linked nature of IoT, global cooperation in creating security standards and exchanging threat intelligence is required to build a safer digital environment. As we go through the interconnected IoT ecosystem, implementing security is not an option but a requirement. By learning from real-world incidents, applying appropriate remedies, and being alert in the face of future difficulties, we can unleash the full promise of IoT while retaining customer trust and confidence. IoT security is a shared responsibility that manufacturers, companies, governments, and individuals share. We can build a secure and resilient linked society by collaborating and emphasizing security at every stage of IoT development. This ensures a future in which IoT advances support progress and prosperity for all. We are on a mission to embrace the potential of the connected world while protecting its integrity for future generations via continuous efforts and unwavering commitment to security.

References

1. Gokhale, P., Bhat, O., Bhat, S., Introduction to IOT. *Int. Adv. Res. J. Sci. Eng. Technol.*, 5, 1, 41, 2018.
2. Hossein Motlagh, N., Mohammadrezaei, M., Hunt, J., Zakeri, B., Internet of Things (IoT) and the energy sector. *Energies*, 13, 2, 494, 2020.
3. Khan, M.A., Challenges Facing the Application of IoT in Medicine and Healthcare. *Int. J. Comput. Inf. Manuf.*, 1, 1, 39, 2021.
4. Adi, E., Anwar, A., Baig, Z., Zeadally, S., Machine Learning and Data Analytics for the IoT. *Neural Comput. Appl.*, 32, 16205, 2020.
5. Lin, T., Deep Learning for IoT. *IEEE 39th International Performance Computing and Communications Conference*, vol. 1, 2020.
6. Ding, J., Nemati, M., Ranaweera, C., Choi, J., IoT Connectivity Technologies and Applications: A survey. *IEEE Access*, 8, 67646, 2020.
7. Zikria, Y.B., Ali, R., Afzal, M.K., Kim, S.W., Next-generation Internet of Things (IoT): Opportunities, Challenges, and Solutions. *Sensors*, 21, 4, 1174, 2021.
8. Smys, S., Basar, A., Wang, H., Hybrid Intrusion Detection System for the Internet of Things (IoT). *J. ISMAC*, 2, 04, 190, 2020.
9. Farooq, M.S., Riaz, S., Abid, A., Umer, T., Zikria, Y.B., Role of IoT Technology in Agriculture: A Systematic Literature Review. *Electronics*, 9, 2, 319, 2020.
10. Valsalan, P., Baomar, T.A.B., Baabood, A.H.O., IoT Based Health Monitoring System. *J. Crit. Rev.*, 7, 4, 739, 2020.
11. Balaji, S., Nathani, K., Santhakumar, R., IoT Technology, Applications and Challenges: a Contemporary Survey. *Wireless Pers. Commun.*, 108, 363, 2019.
12. Atlam, H.F. and Wills, G.B., IoT Security, Privacy, Safety and Ethics, in: *Digital Twin Technologies and Smart Cities*, p. 123, 2020.
13. Chanal, P.M. and Kakkasageri, M.S., Security and Privacy in IoT: a Survey. *Wire. Pers. Commun.*, 115, 2, 1667, 2020.
14. Alladi, T., Chamola, V., Sikdar, B., Choo, K.K.R., Consumer IoT: Security Vulnerability Case Studies and Solutions. *IEEE Consum. Electron. Mag.*, 9, 2, 17, 2020.
15. Krishnamurthi, R., Kumar, A., Gopinathan, D., Nayyar, A., Qureshi, B., An Overview of IoT Sensor Data Processing, Fusion, and Analysis Techniques. *Sensors*, 20, 21, 6076, 2020.
16. Hussein, A.H., Internet of Things (IoT): Research Challenges and Future Applications. *Int. J. Adv. Comput. Sci. Appl.*, 10, 6, 77, 2019.
17. Brous, P., Janssen, M., Herder, P., The Dual Effects of the Internet of Things (IoT): A Systematic Review of the Benefits and Risks of IoT Adoption by Organizations. *Int. J. Inf. Manage.*, 51, 101952, 2020.
18. Mouha, R.A., Internet of Things (IoT). *J. Data Anal. Inf. Process.*, 9, 2, 77, 2021.

19. Cui, Y., Liu, F., Jing, X., Mu, J., Integrating Sensing and Communications for Ubiquitous IoT: Applications, Trends, and Challenges. *IEEE Network*, 35, 5, 158, 2021.
20. Liu, H., Han, D., Li, D., Fabric-IoT: A blockchain-based access control system in IoT. *IEEE Access*, 8, 18207, 2020.
21. Mohanta, B.K., Jena, D., Ramasubbareddy, S., Daneshmand, M., Gandomi, A.H., Addressing Security and Privacy Issues of IoT using Blockchain Technology. *IEEE Internet Things J.*, 8, 2, 881, 2020.

11

Secured IoT with LWC and Blockchain

Srishti Priya Chaturvedi[1]*, Ajay Yadav[1], Santosh Kumar[2] and Rahul Mukherjee[1]

[1]*Electronics and Communication Engineering Department, Bennett University, Greater Noida, India*
[2]*School of Physics Science and Information Technology, Liaocheng University, Liaocheng, China*

Abstract
Data transmission over the Internet is significantly increasing due to the Internet of Things. This has led to significant concerns about security and privacy, as sensitive information is being shared among these devices. However, the complexity and severity of the security concerns are significantly more severe because of the heterogeneity of Internet of Things objects. Moreover, the resource-constrained characteristics limit the use of security techniques like antivirus, firewall, and intrusion detection systems that need significant computing capabilities. Numerous methods have been explored to safeguard user privacy and security, but lightweight encryption/decryption techniques and blockchain methods have emerged as the most effective. Lightweight cryptographic algorithms ensure that private and sensitive data is kept secure while receiving, saving, and processing. Similarly, a decentralized, immutable blockchain structure enables security in the form of a ledger, lowering the data integrity risk.

***Keywords*:** Internet of Things (IoT) security, security attacks, authentication, lightweight cryptography, blockchain

**Corresponding author*: E21SOEP0015@bennett.edu.in

Kavita Sharma, Vishnu Sharma, Parma Nand, Anil Kumar Sagar and Gulshan Shrivastava (eds.) Securing the Digital Frontier: Threats and Advanced Techniques in Security and Forensics, (243–268)

11.1 Introduction

The primary function of the Internet involves accessing and exploring web page content, often known as web browsing. However, human life has become efficient and smooth with using Internet of Things (IoT) devices in various fields like agriculture, home automation, industries, and healthcare. IoT allows automation, which reduces manual interception. Users can now have the option to control their home's electronic systems, such as smart lights, smart locks, washing machines, doorbells, and other embedded sensors, remotely or through smartphone apps. Additionally, farmers can conveniently cultivate and irrigate their crop fields, as they can remotely oversee factors such as irrigation, soil quality, temperature, and more. IoT has expanded from rural to urban sectors in one form or another [1]. The embedded sensors can collect, interact, and transmit data from one place to another, assisting the users in controlling the environment. Real-time data exchange requires IoT devices to constantly communicate with the corresponding backend system servers or other devices. Furthermore, these Internet of Things (IoT) devices and embedded sensors have limited resources and can only handle a certain amount of memory and computation power.

IoT is a sophisticated, self-configuring network that uses open, standardized communication protocols to link individually identifiable "Things" to the Internet [1]. This giant network requires many technologies to work collectively to achieve its target. The fundamental blocks of IoT are sensors and actuators capable of sensing, actuating and have the potential to be programmable. However, these building blocks are supposed to be used in abundance and expandable. This gives rise to scalable characteristics of IoT [2]. The standard naming strategy might need help to handle the devices on this scale. The naming policy may need to be updated or revised to offer a distinctive naming convention. Identification and authentication methods must also be updated to reflect the growth of naming. Other significant difficulties in the design of identification and authentication technologies are transparency and reliability. Transparency is a crucial concern for IoT security. Most people need more time to complete lengthy setting requirements to activate their smart devices. Authentication procedures ought to be as straightforward as possible. Reliability is another crucial concern for the IoT ecosystem.

IoT security involves safeguarding, identifying, and monitoring security risks while fixing the vulnerabilities of various IoT devices that may be dangerous for the entire network. Initially, IoT devices were designed with little security in mind, which may provide weaknesses in a system [3]. Identification, authentication, authorization, secrecy, data integrity, and non-repudiation, shown in Figure 11.1, are all components of secure data communications. Installing security software on the device is generally impossible because of its large memory space requirement. Furthermore, it can be provided with malware that contaminates the attached network. Therefore, IoT security involves securing Internet-connected smart devices and connecting networks from threats and breaches.

IoT security threats can be classified into two groups. Similar to the conventional network environment, threats to confidentiality, integrity, and availability (CIA) exist in the first category. However, because of the IoT objects' size and diversity, the complexity and gravity of the security concerns are much more serious. The other type of threat results from the new IoT ecosystem property. It is to be expected that the data in the IoT ecosystem will be increasingly dynamic and personal as IoT equipment becomes more pervasive and starts collecting sensitive measurements like heartbeats and house temperature. The vast majority of IoT devices collect sensitive information on users. Therefore, readings about owners' private places are recognized as personal assets. If there is a breach, this

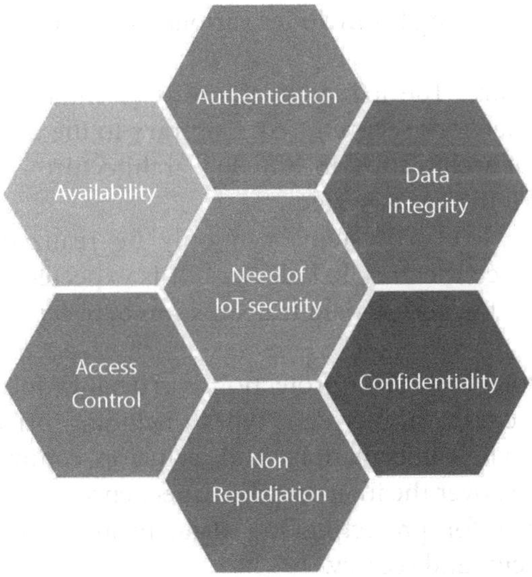

Figure 11.1 Components of a secure data communication.

information might identify the owner's location geographically, as well as their health and lifestyle choices.

According to Gartner's report [1, 2], interoperability and security are two of the biggest obstacles in developing IoT infrastructure. For real-life utilization of IoT, interoperability and security must be considered. In this regard, international standards in information and communication technology (ICT) systems offer essential guidelines and protocols to assist with developing and deploying information technologies. Similarly, other global committee for standardization including the International Organisation for Standardisation (ISO), International Telecommunication Union (ITU-T), International Electro-technical Commission (IEC), and Internet Engineering Task Force (IETF), are contributing to the formation of IoT-related standards, including architecture, framework, network protocols, and definitions [2]. They have also released several standards.

The IoT has been designed to simplify tasks and reduce manual interruptions, making the environment more intelligent and effective with minimal impact on safety and privacy for participating people and devices. An American management consulting company, Bain & Company [4], surveyed its customers' deployment of IoT infrastructure and found that security is a crucial element.

Due to the frequent occurrences of fraud, security is applicable across various domains, encompassing information flow, the Internet, devices, and other networks [5]. There are numerous methods for achieving security in ICT. The following list includes various aspects of IoT security.

- Architecture: The IoT architecture is essential for keeping the IoT network secure [4, 6]. Contrary to the conventional notion of architecture in ICT, IoT architecture is crucial to safeguard the entire system.
- Network: IoT ecosystems can only be realized through networks connecting IoT devices. It is expected to be protected for the secure data transmission between sender and receiver.
- Data Protection: Data protection is crucial in IoT environment because various data types, including private information, vital information, and actuator commands, are exchanged over the internet. This aspect encompasses several techniques for protecting IoT data, including encryption, authenticity, and secrecy.

- Secure Access: This element relates to the authentication, authorization, and access control of IoT devices, network protocols, and platforms.

11.1.1 IoT Architecture

An adaptable multi-tiered structure is essential for the IoT as it is designed to link billions or trillions of diverse things to the Internet [5]. Moreover, integrating multiple technologies results in the diversification of architectures proposed by researchers. Therefore, there is no single IoT architecture; instead, multiple IoT architectures are provided to help us understand various technologies [6–8].

11.1.1.1 Three-Layered IoT Architecture

The most typical and widely accepted IoT architecture has three layers. As seen in Figure 11.2, it consists of three layers: the perception/physical layer, the network layer, and the application layer. Each layer has its own set of protocols for communicating with others.

- Perception/Physical layer: There are numerous terminologies for this layer. It can also be called a sensory, device, or recognition layer. The bottom-most layer is responsible for sensory and actuation-related tasks [7]. Its distinctive feature is the digital representation of information obtained from the natural environment. The protocols utilized in this

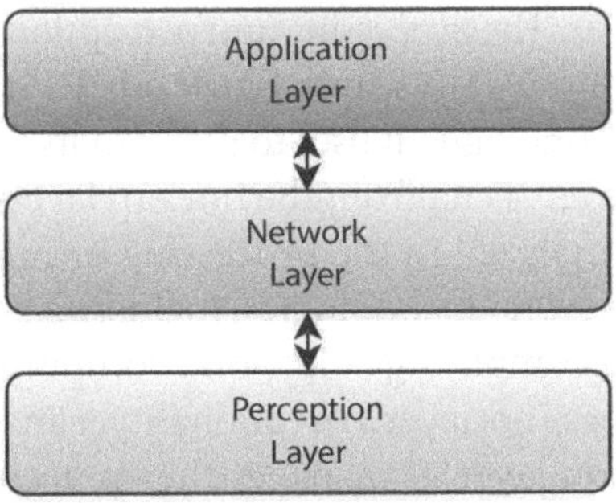

Figure 11.2 Three-layered IoT architecture.

layer are the Institute of Electrical and Electronics Engineers (IEEE) 802.15.1, IEEE 802.11 (Wireless Fidelity), Wi-Fi, Near Field Communication (NFC), etc.

- Network layer: This layer establishes communication between IoT nodes for resource sharing. It provides a path for the exchange of information and services [7]. The protocols utilized in this layer are Internet Protocol version 4 (IPv4), Transmission Control Protocol (TCP), Internet Protocol version 6 (IPv6), User Datagram Protocol (UDP), Time Synchronized Mesh Protocol (TSMP), cognitive RPL (CORPL), Computer Communications Network (CCN), etc.
- Application layer: It is the top layer in the IoT architecture and is responsible for providing user services. Utilizing the data received by the perception layer, the application layer aims to manage and deliver applications worldwide. Application protocols like Constrained Application Protocol (CoAP), Data Distribution Service (DDS), Message Queuing Telemetry Transport (MQTT), Advanced Message Queuing Protocol (AMQP), etc. are used by smart homes, smart cities, and smart agriculture.

11.1.1.2 Five-Layered IoT Architecture

Another widely accepted model is the five-layered architecture. Figure 11.3 shows five layers: perception, transport, processing, application, and business. Each IoT design has a similar overall functionality; the variances are in the display style [8]. In both architectures, the perception and application layers play identical roles. Here is an explanation of the remaining layers.

- Transport layer: The processing and perception layers exchange information through this layer. Bluetooth, RFID, and Wi-Fi are among the technologies it uses to perform its function.
- Processing layer: Data from the bottom layers is stored, processed, and analyzed in the processing or middleware layer. It combines several technologies, including big data processing, edge/fog computing, and cloud computing.
- Business layer: This layer's functionality is incorporated with the application layer. It manages the applications, business, and overall IoT system and thereby indicates the successful deployment of IoT in real life.

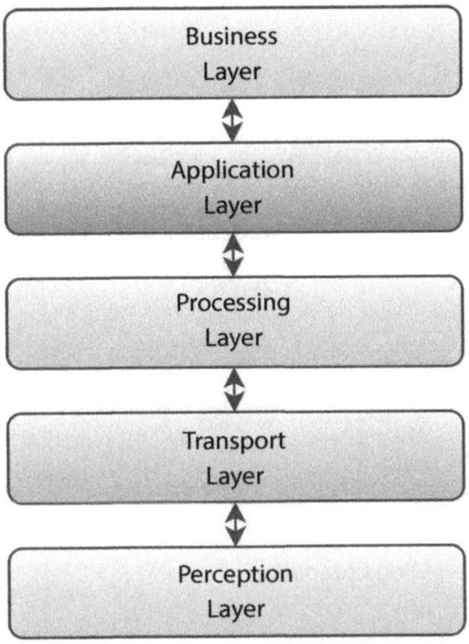

Figure 11.3 Five-layered IoT architecture.

11.1.1.3 Cloud and Fog/Edge-Based IoT Architecture

In real-life IoT implementation, the connected devices generate massive amounts of data. Data processing is a cumbersome task. The increasing rate of IoT implementation in every sector accelerates the need to store and process the collected data. The problem of storing, processing, and accessing large amounts of data is the outcome of rapid growth in IoT. To overcome this issue, methods like cloud computing and fog/edge computing, shown in Figure 11.4, are incorporated with IoT [9].

- **Cloud Computing:** Cloud computing enhances the success rate of the IoT. It allows users to store abundant data and offers a suitable platform to access them using the Internet. Cloud computers carry out the data processing in some systems in a highly centralized manner. The architecture comprises a cloud in the middle, applications above it, and a network of smart devices below it. The reason behind the popularity of this technology is its capability to offer excellent flexibility and scalability [9]. Developers can offer their software, storage, and other services for machine learning, data mining, and visualization that can be accessed via the cloud.

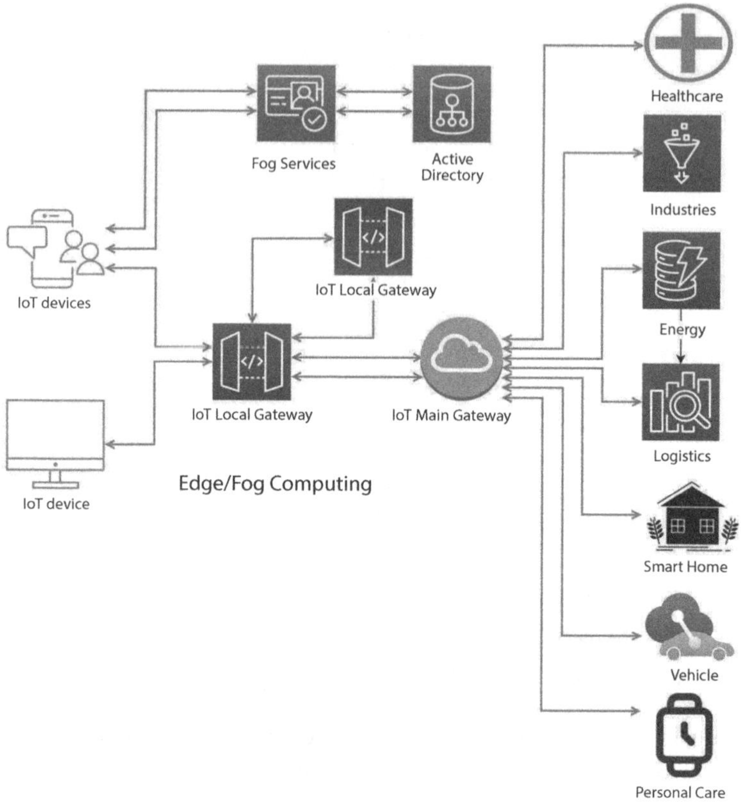

Figure 11.4 Cloud and fog/edge-based IoT architecture.

IoT cloud computing provides a range of connectivity options, suggesting a broad range of network access [10]. Users can access cloud computing resources via various devices, including mobile phones, tablets, and computers. Moreover, they can scale the service based on their requests and needs. Despite having multiple advantages, IoT cloud computing has some vital drawbacks, like the rise of security issues [10, 11]. The connected devices may lack reliable authentication while using cloud services. Therefore, it is imperative to note that effective cloud architecture is crucial for assuring security, dependability, and optimizing performance parameters.

- **Fog/Edge Computing:** To implement IoT in real-time applications, it is essential to process the generated data quickly in the cloud. This ensures that the data is efficiently managed and utilized. The current cloud computing method could be more efficient for rapidly and accurately analyzing large data sets. To tackle this problem, a novel framework called edge/fog computing has been created [11]. IoT solutions use edge computing to process data at the network edge, which speeds up processing and response time. In this technique, the network gateways and sensors conduct data processing analytics. Further, fog and edge computing are two technologies that are very closely related and frequently used interchangeably. Edge computing directly integrates processing capabilities into connected endpoints near the data generation device/point. However, it is fog if intelligence is found at a different network node, such as a local node or an IoT gateway, i.e., situated between an endpoint and the cloud. The fog is designed with a layered approach, encompassing monitoring, pre-processing, storage, and a security layer that bridges the physical and transport layers. The pre-processing layer is responsible for processing, filtering, and analytics of received data, while the monitoring layer keeps track of the power, resources, responses, and services. The temporary storage layer provides storage capabilities such as storage, distribution, and data replication. Lastly, the security layer secures the data using encryption/decryption.

11.2 Applications of IoT

IoT has much potential to adapt to benefit the economy, environment, and society [12]. Some IoT-based concepts include mobility, smart grids, smart homes and buildings, environmental monitoring for public safety, healthcare, agriculture, and independent living. Here are some IoT implementation areas.

11.2.1 Smart Home

A smart home features lighting, heating, and various electrical appliances, unlike regular living spaces. A notable distinction lies in controlling a computer or a smartphone remotely. It allows for managing energy consumption by automating tasks such as controlling temperature, turning on and off lights, opening and closing window coverings, and altering the watering schedule according to the weather.

11.2.2 Smart Healthcare

Healthcare services are now systematically linked to the Internet of Medical Things (IoMT) IT system. Earlier, the only ways that patients could communicate with doctors before IoMT were in person, over the phone, or via text. Integrating IoMT-connected devices in the healthcare sector has facilitated remote monitoring, thereby unlocking the potential to ensure the well-being of patients and enabling medical professionals to deliver timely and suitable treatments. The idea is used to allow for machine-to-machine communication by integrating Wi-Fi systems with medical devices. IoT is crucial in considerably lowering healthcare expenses and increasing treatment outcomes.

11.2.3 Industrial IoT

IoT has recently gained traction within the industrial domain. Given the rigorous demands of contemporary industrial equipment and operations, the functional capacities of IoT are either adapted or custom-tailored to align with industry requirements precisely. With the help of industrial IoT, businesses can get valuable data from their operations. The collected data helps in improving operational control when appropriately aggregated and analyzed. Industrial IoT connects and automates the devices and equipment in manufacturing, transportation, oil and gas, power production and transmission, mines, and ports.

11.2.4 Smart Agriculture

The methods and techniques used to carry out agricultural tasks have significantly changed. Modernized farming concepts have replaced conceptual farming for the modern farmer. IoT innovative agricultural solutions are developed to assist and automate crop field monitoring using sensors and actuators. As a result, farmers can readily and conveniently check field conditions from anywhere.

11.2.5 Smart Mobility

Smart Mobility is a methodology that enables convenient, efficient, and seamless travel using a variety of modes. Vehicular Ad-hoc Networks (VANETs) have recently received much attention due to the passage of time and the steadily rising social needs. Numerous cutting-edge and sophisticated solutions are being created for the automotive sector through the utilization of IoT.

11.2.6 Smart Grid

A smart grid is a system that distributes electricity and utilizes digital communication technology to observe and address fluctuations in local energy consumption. Embedded sensors allow two-way communication to express electrical demands. The energy is distributed throughout the grid by the previously calculated needs.

11.2.7 Environment Monitoring

Environmental monitoring is the practice of keeping track of features that are connected to our surroundings either directly or indirectly, such as weather patterns, water quality monitoring, conservation of endangered species, and several other parameters. Applications are used with different sensors to track changes in environmental characteristics in real time. Most current air and water safety monitoring technologies involve physical labor, innovative instrumentation, and lab processing. IoT enhances this method by reducing the need for human intervention, enabling more frequent sampling, extending the range of sampling and monitoring, and facilitating advanced local testing. It reduces the amount of human involvement in system operation, farming analysis, and monitoring.

The core usage of IoT is to link several devices together to automate the conventional situation of prevailed systems. This makes it vulnerable to security attacks; as a result, new cyber-security challenges have emerged. To reduce the impact of security attacks on IoT, various measures like securing communication protocols, implementing lightweight cryptography, enhancing security features of IoT platforms, and integrating attack detection techniques can be used. Further, there is one more emerging and promising technology that can be beneficial in protecting the data security of IoT systems. It creates an unchangeable audit trail of sensor observations by storing sensor data as transactions. The immutable records of blockchain transactions also contain information about how IoT devices interact with other network entities. Consequently, many techniques can be augmented with IoT systems to enhance security.

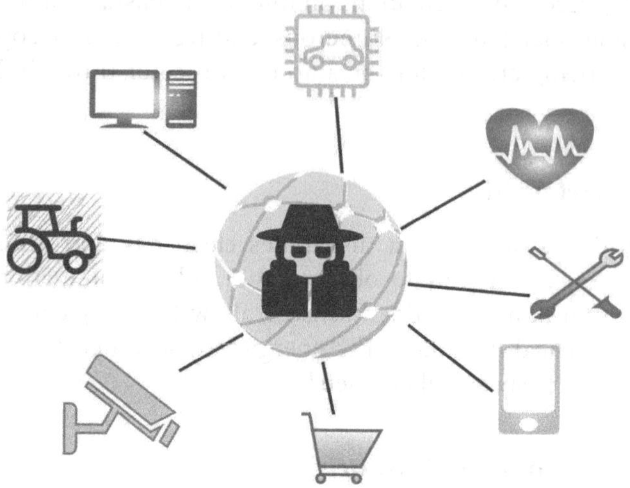

Figure 11.5 Need for IoT security.

11.3 Different Security Attacks on IoT Layers

There are numerous attacks possible on IoT, which can be briefly described in the context of the nature of the attacker and the IoT layered architecture [13, 14]. The user connects to various heterogeneous devices using the internet, which may compromise his security and privacy, as depicted in Figure 11.5. The attacker intends to harm the overall system by stealing or sniffing the data.

11.3.1 Active Attack

This attack involves creating false information or modifying the data stream. It tries to change system resources or interfere with their functionality. This attack affects the data integrity and badly impacts the data confidentiality [15]. The attacker may try to disrupt the communications and gain unauthorized access to IoT resources. Consequently, the networking services might be discontinued or degraded. Studying the impact of security attacks on various IoT layers is mandatory. Therefore, this section briefly describes the possible attacks on each layer, and its tabular representation is shown in Table 11.1.

Table 11.1 Tabular representation of layer-wise possible security attacks.

IoT layer	Possible security attacks
Perception/Physical Layer	Node capture attack, side channel attack, Malicious code injection attack, False data injection attack, replay attack/ Freshness attack, Cryptanalysis attack and Sleep deprivation attack, Eavesdropping and interference.
Network Layer/Communication Layer	Denial-of-service attacks, Man-in-the-middle attacks, Spoofing attacks, Sybil attacks, Sinkhole attacks, Wormhole attacks, Routing information attacks.
Application Layer (Database Virtualization + Data Analytics and Mining)	Phishing Attacks, Malicious scripts, Malicious viruses/worms.

11.3.1.1 Security Attacks on Perception/Physical Layer

With this layer, the physical environment can be sensed through sensors and data gathering. It comprises sensors, actuators, RFID, QR codes, etc. The selection of sensors depends on the application's requirements. Since sensors can gather information about temperature, moisture, motion, air quality, and location, the attacker can exploit them easily [16]. Common security attacks and threats on this layer are as follows:

- *Hardware tampering*: The attacker can easily damage the node if it is nearby. He can easily modify the hardware or even completely replace it. Moreover, the privacy of the data, like the routing table and cryptographic keys, is at risk if the attacker captures the gateway node. Therefore, the entire network, including all the layers, is at critical risk in this attack.
- *Node-capture*: It is one of the potentially dangerous threats on the perception layer that allows an attacker to access the key or the primary node of the system, such as the gateway. Consequently, the information could be exposed, including keys for secure communication, memory data, and communications between sender and receiver.
- *Sleep denial attack*: Nodes in the IoT network are often powered by disposable batteries, and they are designed to go to sleep when not in use to extend battery life. The attacker

provides the incorrect information to the node and keeps it awake, which consumes power and causes the node to go down.

- *Fake/Malicious node*: This attack corresponds to the addition of a node to the system, and the attacker exchanges fake data. The goal of this attack is to restrict the sharing of accurate information. The malicious node can use the legitimate nodes' energy and control the entire network.
- *Replay attack*: This attack occurs when a third party intercepts communication between a sender and a recipient and steals genuine data. The intruder provides evidence of his identity and authenticity and pretends to be a legitimate user.
- *Timing attack*: It is typically applied to resource-constrained devices. It enables an attacker to identify weaknesses and extract secrets of the system by tracking how long a system takes to reply to different requests, data, or cryptographic algorithms.

11.3.1.2 Security Attacks on Network Layer

The network layer links the application and physical layers. The application layer receives and processes the data collected by the physical layer from its surroundings. The mode of this information flow can be wired or wireless. It is also in charge of linking networks, network devices, and smart objects together. It is, therefore, particularly susceptible to security breaches. Common security attacks on this layer are as follows,

- *Man-in-The-Middle (MITM) attack*: During this attack, an unauthorized third party secretly intercepts and modifies the ongoing communication between the sender and receiver. This malicious person can manipulate the messages according to their agenda and gain complete control over the entire communication process [17]. Such attacks significantly threaten digital security by enabling attackers to gather and tamper with sensitive information.
- *Denial of Service (DoS)*: When authorized users cannot access devices or network resources, this is known as a denial of service (DoS) attack. This attack is typically executed by overwhelming the targeted devices or network resources with a high volume of repetitive requests, effectively blocking some or all legitimate users from utilizing them.

- *Sinkhole attack*: This attack targets the wireless sensor network (WSN) and directs the entire sensor node to drop the packets at a single location. Such an attack nullifies data security and discards all packets rather than sending them to their intended recipient.
- *Storage attack*: In this attack, the attackers may alter the user credentials and the stored information in the cloud. The chance of attack increases due to the replication and sharing of information with other users.
- *Exploit attack*: It occurs in software that utilizes the security vulnerabilities of any software, systems, or equipment. This attack aims to conquer the overall system and steal data stored in a network.
- *Routing information attack*: These are rapid/immediate attacks where the attacker can confuse the system, create routing loops, permit or prevent movement, issue false error signals, and replay or modify the routing data.

11.3.1.3 Security Attacks on Processing Layer

The processing layer collects data sent from the transport layer, commonly named the middleware layer. Its primary function is to eliminate unnecessary information without significance and extract the pertinent data. The processing layer is susceptible to various attacks that can impact its operations.

- *Malware*: This attack impacts the data privacy and confidentiality of the user. It describes the usage of Trojan horses, worms, spyware, viruses, and adware to interact with the system. It gets injected as scripts and executable instructions and violates the system standards by stealing the confidentiality of information.
- *Exhaustion*: It can result from previous attacks intended to deplete system resources like the battery and memory. An attacker using this attack disrupts the processing of an IoT structure.

11.3.1.4 Security Attacks on Application Layer

This layer delivers personalized services to the users. The specific services offered rely on the information obtained from sensors and may vary for each application. In this layer, lightweight and resource-constrained devices are used, which have limited computational power and are therefore susceptible to attacks. Malicious code can modify program codes with flaws, leading to application malfunctions. Consequently, the applications may be compromised, experience crashes, fail to operate as intended, or carry out authenticated services incorrectly. Some common security attacks targeting this layer include:

- *Malicious code attack*: The complete system may fail due to the insertion of malicious code. This type of attack may not be stopped or managed by anti-virus software.
- *Cross-site scripting*: This type of attack is known as an injection attack, which allows an unauthorized individual to insert a client-side script, such as JavaScript, into a well-established website with a large user base. By doing so, the attacker can completely modify the application's content to suit their needs and misuse the original data without authorization.

11.3.1.5 Security Attacks on Business Layer

The business layer oversees the entire system and dictates how an application should function. This layer oversees and controls IoT applications, business models, and revenue streams. Furthermore, it can regulate data generation, storage, and modification. Common concerns regarding the business security layers encompass.

- *Zero-Day Attack*: This type of attack involves an application with security flaws or loopholes. The worst part of this attack is that the user is unaware of the application's flaws and continues using it. The perpetrator exploits this vulnerability to gain unauthorized control over the system, unbeknownst to the user and without their consent.
- *Business Logic Attack*: The method of this attack closely resembles a zero-day attack, where the attacker capitalizes on a programming flaw. It controls and monitors the exchange of information between a user and the underlying database of an application. The business layer encounters several common issues, such as programmer errors, input validation, password recovery validation, and encryption methods.

11.3.2 Passive Attack

Passive attacks are challenging to detect. Wireless communication is more prone to passive attacks because wireless links can be easily sniffed without anyone noticing. Data confidentiality is the main target of passive attacks. Attackers use passive attacks to monitor communication, steal data, and utilize it to degrade a person's or organization's reputation. It is divided into two categories, i.e., eavesdropping and traffic analysis.

11.3.2.1 Eavesdropping

The attacker intercepts private communications like calls, messages, video conferences, and fax transmissions in this attack. It is an illegitimate real-time attack where the user is unaware that someone is stealing the communication. It makes an effort to eavesdrop on network traffic carrying data.

11.3.2.2 Traffic Analysis

In a wireless connection, the confidentiality of the data flowing through the network can be sniffed and monitored by the attacker. In this scenario, the hacker collects network data through packet sniffers or port-scanning software before attacking the specific information.

Although most current methods focus on the network layer, the IoT security architecture emphasizes that security measures should encompass all three layers of the core IoT structure: perception, network, and application. It can also be deduced that creating a suitable IoT threat model would aid in devising effective security mitigation strategies for the IoT.

11.4 Solution to IoT Security Attacks

There are two most promising solutions for securing IoT systems: one is to use cryptography techniques, and another one is implementing blockchain-based IoT systems [18]. A brief overview of both methods is as follows.

11.4.1 IoT Security Using Blockchain Technology

Blockchain technology has garnered significant interest due to its potential to address security, anonymity, traceability, and centralization [19]. Integrating blockchain technology into IoT systems offers decentralized

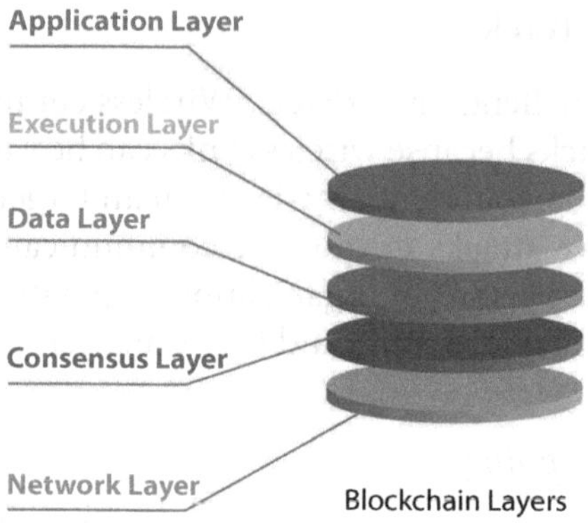

Figure 11.6 Blockchain layers.

resource management, reduced operational expenses, and enhanced security [20]. As a result, realizing an IoT platform utilizing blockchain technology is imminent, albeit with specific challenges [21]. This innovative technology, depicted in Figure 11.6, consists of five distinct layers.

11.4.1.1 Network Layer

This decentralized peer-to-peer (P2P) system enables users to share resources without relying on a central authority. Within the P2P network, there are two primary types of nodes: lightweight and full. Full nodes are accountable for maintaining duplicate ledgers and handling mining, validation, and executing consensus rules. On the other hand, lightweight nodes support the full nodes without storing the entire ledger themselves. Lightweight nodes serve as clients to send transactions while also storing block headers. The crucial network layer handles block propagation, transactions, and peer discovery [21].

11.4.1.2 Consensus Layer

A blockchain relies on consensus to function effectively. It involves a procedure that sets out the criteria for confirming a consensus regarding validating the blocks to be incorporated into the blockchain.

11.4.1.3 Data Layer

This layer encompasses most of the fundamental technology behind the blockchain. It includes various components such as the data block and chain structure, hashing, Merkle trees, and asymmetric data encryption. These elements form the backbone of the blockchain's functionality.

11.4.1.4 Execution Layer

Virtual machines (VMs), containers, and compilers are runtime environments installed on nodes for executing code. In addition, this layer implements trust through the utilization of smart contracts. In every individual node within the network, the execution of these smart contracts takes place on local virtual machines. To ensure agreement among untrustworthy parties, the network collects computer instructions capable of self-execution.

11.4.1.5 Application Layer

The uppermost stratum of the blockchain network is the application layer, which links decentralized applications and the fundamental blockchain technology [21]. Cryptocurrency stands as the most prevalent implementation of blockchain technology.

11.4.2 Blockchain-Based IoT Applications

Blockchain-based IoT, as shown in Figure 11.7, has gained much attention these days and is a general, scalable, and secure blockchain solution for IoT.

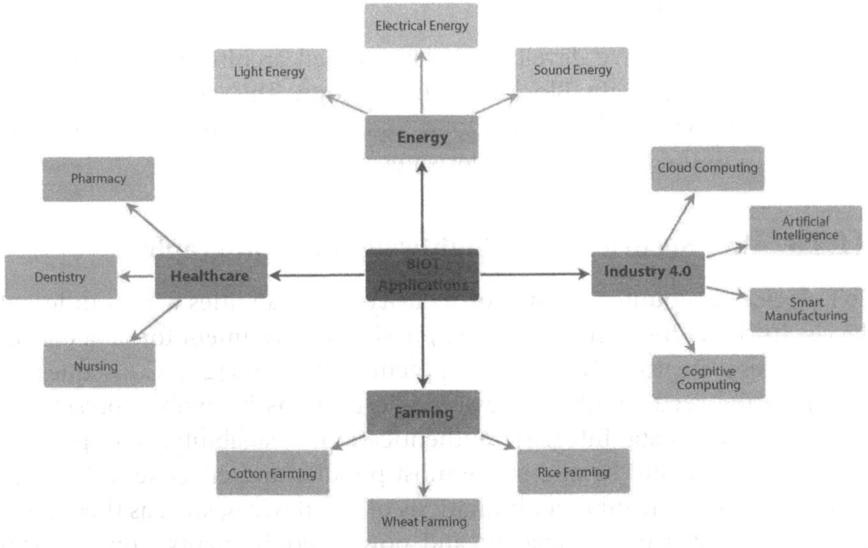

Figure 11.7 Blockchain-based IoT applications.

11.4.2.1 Cyber-Physical Systems

Blockchain has a crucial role in cyber-physical systems (CPS), where the Internet of Things is widely used to collect sensed data about the surroundings and the system under observation [22].

11.4.2.2 Intelligent Transportation System

A novel method [23] put forward for detecting and notifying vehicle accidents using a certificate-based authentication system enabled by blockchain technology.

11.4.2.3 Smart City

Unlike traditional centralized database systems, a blockchain-based solution for smart property [24] is proposed that provides security against fraud.

11.4.2.4 Supply Chain Management

Supply chain management has the potential to utilize blockchain technology [25] to monitor and trace the agricultural source of food items.

11.4.2.5 Underwater Things

Uddin *et al.* [26] have developed a layer-based architecture that utilizes specialized Lightweight Blockchain technology. This architecture incorporates components from the Cloud and Fog to handle and store data securely from the Internet of Underwater Things (IoUT).

11.4.3 IoT Security Using Lightweight Cryptography

IoT devices encounter a range of security vulnerabilities across different levels. Its direct interaction with the physical environment for data collection makes it an attractive target for potential attackers [27]. Consequently, ensuring the security of IoT devices is crucial, as it involves preserving confidentiality, data integrity, authentication, availability, and privacy. Cryptography could be one of the most popular and effective techniques [28]. Because of the inherent limitations of IoT devices, such as their computational cost, storage capacity, and power requirements, conventional cryptography methods are not suitable for these devices.

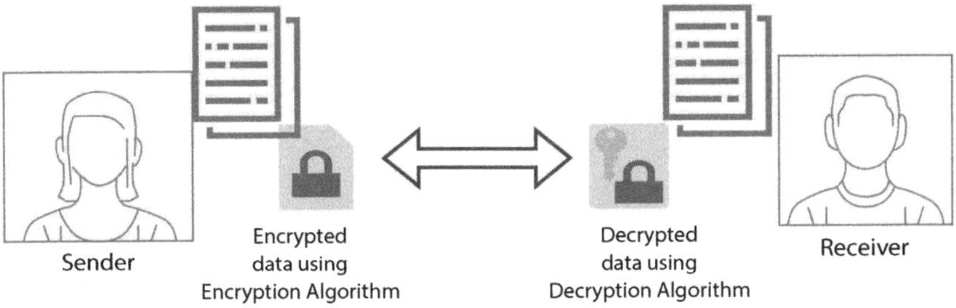

Figure 11.8 Secure data communication using cryptography.

This further gives rise to the need for lightweight cryptography to secure communication in resource-constrained IoT devices [28, 29].

Cryptography was initially developed to protect the confidentiality of diplomatic and military communications. It comprises several mathematical operations shown in Figure 11.8. The field of cryptology focuses on creating and improving techniques for encrypting and decrypting data to guarantee its security and authenticity. Cryptography involves three fundamental operations: encryption key generation and decryption. Encryption employs the conversion of plain text into unreadable and secure form, resulting in a challenging task for illegitimate users to retrieve the actual message. On the other hand, decryption involves converting a ciphertext back into its original text. This method is employed to safeguard the confidentiality of a message, preventing its unauthorized access.

Traditional cryptography is divided into two categories: private, also known as symmetric cryptography, and public, also called asymmetric cryptography.

Figure 11.9 Symmetric cryptography utilizing the same key for encryption and decryption.

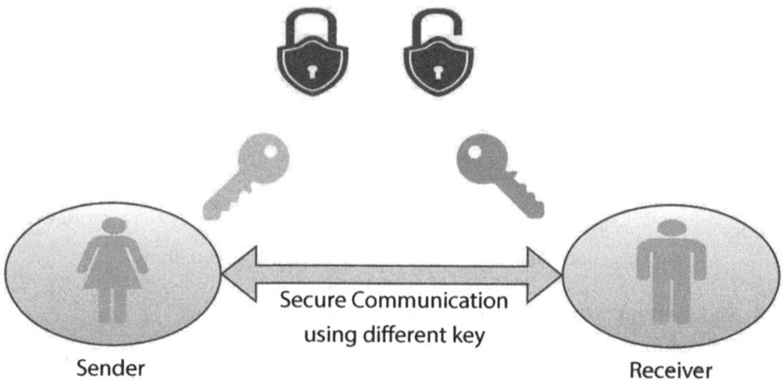

Figure 11.10 Asymmetric cryptography utilizing different keys for encryption and decryption.

Symmetric cryptography involves using a single private or secret key for secure message transmission. Conversely, asymmetric cryptography employs a pair of keys: the public and private keys, as illustrated in Figures 11.9 and 11.10, respectively, to ensure secure communication. Key size is a crucial factor in both symmetric and asymmetric approaches. Additionally, the amount of time required for computation also influences the choice of algorithm for security purposes. Asymmetric cryptography is generally more intricate and time-consuming compared to symmetric cryptography.

11.4.3.1 Lightweight Cryptography

Traditional cryptographic algorithms cannot be implemented in the context of technologies like the IoT, where the building blocks are resource-constrained devices [30]. The alternative way is to make the lighter version. The ISO standard ISO/IEC 29192 outlines the lightweight cryptography requirements and security features. This multipart international standard aims to be lightweight and address essential aspects such as data confidentiality, authentication, key exchange, identification, and non-repudiation. This standard offers standardized procedures for sensor-based networking, radiofrequency identification (RFID) tags, smart cards, secure batteries, and other lightweight cryptographic applications. These characteristics/features are used as a metric for choosing the best algorithm or algorithm-embedding device. These characteristics are the most widely used and recognized for evaluating the robustness of any lightweight cryptographic cipher. A lightweight cipher occupies as little space as possible [31]. The industry has

Table 11.2 Tabular representation of various structures of lightweight cryptographic techniques.

Structure type	Algorithm
Generalized Feistel Network (GFN)	CLEFIA, Piccolo, Twis, Twine, HISEC
Feistel Network (FN)	GOST, DESL/DESXL, Camellia, TEA/ XTEA/XXTEA, SIMON, KASUMI, SEA, Fantomas, ITUBee, MIBS, Robin, LBLOCK, FeW
Substitution–Permutation Network (SPN)	AES, Puffin-2, GIFT, Picaro, SKINNY, Midori, EPCBC, mCryption, Noekeon, Iceberg, Klein, Prince, Print, Present, Led, Pride Zorro, I-Present, Rectangle
Non-linear feedback shift register (NLFSR)	KeeLoq, KATAN/KTANTAN, Halka
Addition-Rotation-XOR (ARX)	SPECK, IDEA, Hight, BEST-1, LEA
HYBRID	Hummingbird, Hummingbird-2, Present-GRP

embraced approximately 41 lightweight symmetric cryptographic algorithms [32, 33]. The selection of appropriate encryption techniques for efficient implementation depends entirely on the application's requirements. These techniques have specialized structures that follow a particular design pattern. The most common design structures of encryption techniques are Substitution-Permutation Network (SPN), Addition-Rotation-XOR (ARX), Feistel Network (FN), and Hybrid structures. Table 11.2 summarises the structure-based categorization of lightweight cryptographic techniques.

11.5 Conclusion

IoT devices are being used by several applications with a motive to ease daily tasks without human intervention. Businesses are increasingly utilizing IoT devices to improve efficiency and raise operational visibility. Due to this, an increasing quantity of connected devices installed on corporate and local networks can access sensitive data and vital infrastructure. Hence, ensuring the security of IoT becomes a crucial concern, especially with the rapid expansion of IoT devices in various domains. Many techniques have been developed and deployed with IoT systems, but they all have certain limitations. In this context, the two most promising solutions for IoT security can be employing lightweight cryptography on IoT devices and the other is utilizing a decentralized blockchain technique. Conventional encryption techniques consume lots of processing power, memory, and space, but the lighter version can be deployed on resource-constrained devices. Much work has been done in this direction, resulting in many lightweight encryption techniques like SIMON, SPECK, TWINE, PRESENT, etc. However, choosing the most appropriate application-specific techniques is another big challenge. In addition, there is a need for a lightweight algorithm that balances cost, performance, and security, especially in domains like IoT. Lightweight authentication ciphers are incredibly prevalent in the modern world, but choosing and rating these algorithms is difficult because of the many variables and competing goals that must be considered. Conversely, blockchain can allow IoT devices to share reliable information that opposes non-cooperative organizational frameworks. The immutable decentralized characteristic of this technique can be utilized to secure communication.

References

1. Hahn, J., The internet of things (IOT) and libraries. *Lib. Technol. Rep.*, 53, 5–8, 2017.
2. Lee, E., Seo, Y.D., Oh, S.R., Kim, Y.G., A Survey on Standards for Interoperability and Security in the Internet of Things. *IEEE Commun. Surv. Tutor.*, 23, 2, 1020–1047, 2021.
3. Zhou, W., Jia, Y., Peng, A., Zhang, Y., Liu, P., The effect of iot new features on security and privacy: New threats, existing solutions, and challenges yet to be solved. *IEEE Internet Things J.*, 6, 2, 1606–1616, 2018.
4. Bosche, A., Crawford, D., Jackson, D., Schallehn, M., Smith, P., How providers can succeed in the Internet of Things, Bain & Company, 2016.
5. Kortuem, G., Kawsar, F., Sundramoorthy, V., Fitton, D., Smart objects as building blocks for the Internet of things. *IEEE Internet Comput.*, *14*, 1, 44–51, 2009.
6. Khan, R., Khan, S.U., Zaheer, R., Khan, S., Future Internet: the Internet of things architecture, possible applications, and key challenges, in: *2012 10th International Conference on Frontiers of Information Technology*, pp. 257–260, 2012.

7. Yang, Z., Yue, Y., Yang, Y., Peng, Y., Wang, X., Liu, W., Study and application on the architecture and key technologies for IOT, in: *2011 International Conference on Multimedia Technology*, pp. 747–751, 2011.
8. Wu, M., Lu, T.J., Ling, F.Y., Sun, J., Du, H.Y., Research on the architecture of Internet of Things, in: *2010 3rd international conference on advanced computer theory and engineering ICACTE*, vol. 5, pp. V5–484, 2010.
9. Omoniwa, B., Hussain, R., Javed, M.A., Bouk, S.H., Malik, S.A., Fog/edge computing-based IoT (FECIoT): Architecture, applications, and research issues. *IEEE Internet Things J.*, *6*, 3, 4118–4149, 2018.
10. Alli, A.A. and Alam, M.M., The fog cloud of things: A survey on concepts, architecture, standards, tools, and applications. *Internet Things*, *9*, 100177, 2020.
11. Hong, C.H. and Varghese, B., Resource management in fog/edge computing: a survey on architectures, infrastructure, and algorithms. *ACM Comput. Surv. CSUR*, *52*, 5, 1–37, 2019.
12. Shrivastava, G., Peng, S.L., Bansal, H., Sharma, K., Sharma, M. (Eds.), *New age analytics: Transforming the internet through machine learning, IoT, and trust modelling*, CRC Press, USA, 2020.
13. Mrabet, H., Belguith, S., Alhomoud, A., Jemai, A., A survey of IoT security based on a layered architecture of sensing and data analysis. *Sensors*, *20*, 13, 3625, 2020.
14. Ahmed, M.M., Shah, M.A., Wahid, A., IoT security: A layered approach for attacks & defenses, in: *2017 International Conference on Communication Technologies ComTech*, pp. 104–110, 2017.
15. Deogirikar, J. and Vidhate, A., Security attacks in IoT: A survey, in: *2017 International Conference on I-SMAC IoT in Social, Mobile, Analytics and Cloud, I-SMAC*, pp. 32–37, 2017.
16. Mahmoud, R., Yousuf, T., Aloul, F., Zualkernan, I., Internet of things (IoT) security: Current status, challenges and prospective measures, in: *2015 10th International Conference for Internet Technology and Secured Transactions (ICITST)*, pp. 336–341, 2015.
17. Panda, D., Mishra, B.K., Sharma, K., A Taxonomy on Man-in-the-Middle Attack in IoT Network, in: *2022 4th International Conference on Advances in Computing, Communication Control and Networking (ICAC3N)*, pp. 1907–1912, 2022.
18. Shammar, E.A., Zahary, A.T., Al-Shargabi, A.A., A survey of IoT and blockchain integration: Security perspective. *IEEE Access*, *9*, 156114–156150, 2021.
19. Ferrag, M.A., Derdour, M., Mukherjee, M., Derhab, A., Maglaras, L., Janicke, H., Blockchain technologies for the Internet of things: Research issues and challenges. *IEEE Internet Things J.*, *6*, 2, 2188–2204, 2018.
20. Khan, M.A. and Salah, K., IoT security: Review, blockchain solutions, and open challenges. *Future Gener. Comput. Syst.*, *82*, 395–411, 2018.

21. Panarello, A., Tapas, N., Merlino, G., Longo, F., Puliafito, A., Blockchain and iot integration: A systematic survey. *Sensors, 18*, 8, 2575, 2018.
22. Zhao, W., Jiang, C., Gao, H., Yang, S., Luo, X., Blockchain-enabled cyber-physical systems: A review. *IEEE Internet Things J., 8*, 6, 4023–4034, 2020.
23. Vangala, A., Bera, B., Saha, S., Das, A.K., Kumar, N., Park, Y., Blockchain-enabled certificate-based authentication for vehicle accident detection and notification in intelligent transportation systems. *IEEE Sens. J., 21*, 14, 15824–15838, 2020.
24. Bhushan, B., Khamparia, A., Sagayam, K.M., Sharma, S.K., Ahad, M.A., Debnath, N.C., Blockchain for smart cities: A review of architectures, integration trends and future research directions. *Sustain. Cities Soc., 61*, 102360, 2020.
25. Borah, M.D., Naik, V.B., Patgiri, R., Bhargav, A., Phukan, B., Basani, S.G., Supply chain management in agriculture using blockchain and IoT, in: *Advanced applications of blockchain technology*, pp. 227–242, 2020.
26. Uddin, M.A., Stranieri, A., Gondal, I., Balasurbramanian, V., A lightweight blockchain based framework for underwater iot. *Electronics, 8*, 12, 1552, 2019.
27. Acar, A., Fereidooni, H., Abera, T., Sikder, A.K., Miettinen, M., Aksu, H., Uluagac, S., Peek-a-boo: I see your smart home activities, even encrypted!, in: *Proceedings of the 13th ACM Conference on Security and Privacy in Wireless and Mobile Networks*, pp. 207–218, 2020.
28. Shrivastava, G., Gupta, D., Sharma, K. (Eds.), *Cyber Crime and Forensic Computing: Modern Principles, Practices, and Algorithms*, De Gruyter, Berlin, Gemany, 2021.
29. Ning, L., Ali, Y., Ke, H., Nazir, S., Huanli, Z., A hybrid MCDM approach of selecting lightweight cryptographic cipher based on ISO and NIST lightweight cryptography security requirements for internet of health things. *IEEE Access, 8*, 220165–220187, 2020.
30. Dhanda, S.S., Singh, B., Jindal, P., Lightweight cryptography: a solution to secure IoT. *Wireless Pers. Commun., 112*, 1947–1980, 2020.
31. Katagi, M. and Moriai, S., Lightweight cryptography for the Internet of Things, Sony Corporation, pp. 7–10, 2008.
32. Thakor, V.A., Razzaque, M.A., Khandaker, M.R., Lightweight cryptography algorithms for resource-constrained IoT devices: A review, comparison and research opportunities. *IEEE Access, 9*, 28177–28193, 2021.
33. Panda, D., Mishra, B.K., Sharma, K., Machine Learning-Based Detection for Distributed Denial of Service Attack in IoT, in: *International Conference On Innovative Computing And Communication*, pp. 637–651, 2023.

12

Social Engineering Attacks: Detection and Prevention

Rajat Singh[1], Priyanka Soni[2*] and Animaw Kerie[3]

[1]*Graphic Era (Deemed to be University), Dehradun, Uttarakhand, India*
[2]*Gurukula Kangri (Deemed to be University), Haridwar, Uttarakhand, India*
[3]*Addis Ababa Science and Technology University, Addis Abba, Ethiopia*

Abstract
With technological advancement, social engineering attacks are evolving and getting smarter. This chapter focused on various social engineering attacks, like phishing, water holing, tailgating, etc., that are being carried out in the contemporary era. In addition, detailed social engineering attack detection models such as SEADM, SEADMv2, SEADer, and SEADer++V2 have been explored. The approaches, such as Security Information and Event Management (SIEM), Next-Gen cloud-based WAF, Human-as-a-Security-Sensor framework, etc., are highlighted to prevent social engineering attacks. Preventive measures to create awareness amongst people and to fight social engineering attacks have also been discussed.

Keywords: Social engineering, phishing, OSINT, artificial intelligence

12.1 Introduction

The amelioration of digital technology has accelerated communication between individuals. Digital communication has overcome geographical boundaries and made connectivity easy and accessible to humans. People are connected on social networking platforms (like Twitter, Snapchat, Instagram, Facebook, etc.). Individuals make their personal information available to people they are not acquainted with. In addition, people

**Corresponding author*: sonipresearch@gmail.com

Kavita Sharma, Vishnu Sharma, Parma Nand, Anil Kumar Sagar and Gulshan Shrivastava (eds.)
Securing the Digital Frontier: Threats and Advanced Techniques in Security and Forensics, (269–290)

also exchange sensitive data on multiple online dating platforms, online gaming platforms, e-commerce online shopping platforms, etc. They are unaware that their information might render them vulnerable to social engineering attacks. Digital communication systems are susceptible and thus can effortlessly be accessed through attacks like social engineering by malicious users. Social engineering attacks are perilous in cyber security, primarily targeting and exploiting human vulnerabilities instead of technical ones [1].

Social engineering attacks are galloping rapidly, hence a serious concern to society. Social engineering attacks have turned ubiquitous, and the success rate of these attacks is high. Humans are regarded to be a fragile association in the security chain system. Hence, social engineering attacks are powerful and surpass various security checks (like antivirus software, fireball, intrusion detection systems, cryptographic techniques, etc.), thus posing a significant challenge to the robust security of multiple networks [2, 3].

Social engineering has evolved from exploiting social interactions and people's trust and emotions through psychological manipulation [4]. Social engineering comprises numerous malicious acts employed to psychologically influence individuals such that they promulgate their personal and sensitive information like passwords, credit card details, confidentialities of organizations, etc. [5]. Social engineering attacks are significant to attackers when they fail to unveil any technical vulnerabilities in the network and system. These attacks are unstoppable despite deploying high-level security features to the software, hardware, and network systems. Social engineering attacks are very devastating and are regarded as global cyber threats. Individuals who commit social engineering attacks are called social engineers [6]. Social engineers may comprise a person or group of people who may target a person, group of individuals, organizations, institutions, or government bodies. Social engineers employ several techniques to influence humans' cognitive ability and emotional state by exploiting their psychological vulnerabilities. David Gragg, in 2003, recognized around seven psychological vulnerabilities of social engineering [7]. These include:

12.1.1 Strong Affect

The cognitive ability of humans is severely impacted when a strong emotion in them is triggered, like fear, anger, anxiety, or excitement. The ability of an individual to make decisions wisely, provide counterarguments, analyze situations, and provide logical reasons is also strongly affected. Social engineers exploit this intense vulnerability of humans and execute their attacks [8]. An example of this technique may include phishing attacks. These attacks are carefully planned and executed by attackers. Phishing attacks are ones in which attackers, to obtain and access sensitive and confidential information of people for monetary gains, design websites to masquerade as genuine and authentic. Phishing attacks are mainly carried out through emails due to their ease of reaching a wider population [8, 9].

12.1.2 Overloading

Time is a significant element in this technique, where due to excessive and non-stop bombardment of persuasive axioms, people become cognitively propitiate and submissive and thus can be easily tricked by the attackers [8].

12.1.3 Reciprocation

Social exchange theory explains that when someone extends kindness to an individual, the individual feels indebted to reciprocate with the same. Similarly, to make individuals obligated, the social engineer might create issues for individuals and later pretend to be the helping hand of the individuals, such that the individual might disclose their credentials to the attackers in reciprocation [10].

12.1.4 Deceptive Relationship

People willingly share information with someone with whom they have an established relationship. Social engineers purposefully identify such individuals to build a relationship, extract information, and exploit the individual using the same [8].

12.1.5 Diffusion of Moral Duty and Responsibility

Through this technique, individuals are persuaded by social engineers to believe that divulging the information will lead to more benefits and financial gains for the organization. There is nothing wrong with going against policy to bring beneficial consequences [8].

12.1.6 Authority

When social engineers portray themselves as an authoritative figure, an automatic response is triggered in the individual, and they preferably feel more compliant to requests for information disclosure. The individual has a combined induced response to fulfill the authority's demand in addition to the fear of being punished by the same if the legitimacy of authority is being questioned. In this manner, social engineers, masquerading as authority figures, seek information and exploit it for their benefit [10].

12.1.7 Consistency and Commitment

People are willing to fulfill their commitments in all possible circumstances, even if they do not own them. Social engineers could utilize this kind of trigger as it would induce a sense of discomfort like anxiety, stress, or uneasiness, and thus, social engineering attacks can easily be carried out. Though this is not exceptionally ideal because humans possess rational decision-making power, at some point, it may be susceptible to errors [8].

Social engineers work on these compliance principles of friendship, reciprocity, scarcity, authority, commitment, social validation, etc., to influence individuals, gather information and induce social engineering attacks. These principles can exploit psychological vulnerabilities through direct or indirect communication. Direct communication could be unidirectional or bidirectional. The communication medium could vary and may involve email, text messages, web pages, telephone calls, etc.

12.2 Life Cycle of Social Engineering

Instead of exploiting technical vulnerabilities, social engineering attacks employ an unconventional approach to human psychology exploitation. Hence, extensive knowledge of the life cycle of social engineering would be of great significance in combating social engineering attacks. The life cycle of these attacks involves the following significant steps:

12.2.1 Selection of Target and Reconnaissance

The initial step in social engineering is extensive research about the target, an individual or organization, and reconnaissance. The target's information could be gathered from social media platforms, publicly available sources, or discarded documents. Depending on the amount of information acquired, the attack will preferably appear to be more convincing [11].

12.2.2 Planning and Preparation

Social engineers devise a well-organized plan depending on the amount of information collected. They employ the best-suited kind of social engineering attack like tailgating, phishing, etc., depending on the characteristics and susceptibilities of the selected target. Besides, they chose the suitable time and the best channel to execute the attack and maximize its chances of being successful [12].

12.2.3 Initiation of Contact

In this step, the attackers initiate contact by using different modes of communication, such as email, texts, phone calls, etc., with their targets. The attacker strives to establish a rapport and to foster acquaintance to engage the target [12].

12.2.4 Fostering Trust and Manipulation

After the contact is established with the target, the attacker strives to acquire their trust by posing themselves as an authoritative figure, service providers, colleagues, etc. In addition, the attacker could also employ deceptive techniques like instilling fear of missing out, particular stress, etc, to exploit the target's emotions to promote compliance with the target [12].

12.2.5 Elicitation and Exploitation

This is a crucial step in the cycle of social engineering as the attacker in this step acquires the credentials and sensitive information from the target [13]. The target might be directed to fake websites to input login information through phishing attacks, or the target might be compelled to divulge sensitive information for legitimate reasons through pretexting [14].

12.2.6 Launch of Attack

The attackers launch the attack with precise objectives. These could include distributing malware to the system, unauthorized access, or obtaining confidential data. The target is prevented from recognizing that the request might be malicious due to previously employed manipulative tactics [15].

12.2.7 Maintaining the Access

Some attackers aim to sustain the connection, even after obtaining the initial target. This is usually done in cases of indulging installation of malware into the system [12].

12.2.8 Covering the Trails

The attackers, upon accomplishing the attack, try to mask their tracks. This is done by deleting communication records between the target and the attacker, removing any traces that embarks the attacker's presence in the target's system, and reducing indications of unauthorized access [14]. This is critical for preserving the attacker's anonymity and prolonged access to the victim's system.

Social engineers capitalize on beliefs, emotions, and behavior to persuade individuals to reveal required information and permit unauthorized access. Thus, comprehension of the life cycle of social engineering attacks will help individuals and organizations fortify the walls of defense and prevent such attacks.

12.3 Types of Social Engineering

Social engineering attacks can be categorized into two different categories: computer-based and human-based. The attacker has restricted influence on limited victims in human-based attacks. The attacker engages in personal interaction with the victim to collect information. In comparison, computer-based attacks are executed with the aid of software or a malicious program introduced into the computer or system of the target. The computer-based social engineering attacks can target a wider population at once [16].

Based on the mode of an attack, social engineering could be grouped into three: technical, physical, and social-based attacks. Technical attacks may occur using the internet, online platforms, or social networking sites. The physical-based attacks employ physical action commenced by the attacker to acquire information. Lastly, social-based attacks imply the exploitation of psychological manipulation and emotional susceptibilities of the target by the attacker to gain information [16].

Attacks utilizing social engineering have a wide range of variations and frequently vary. The social engineering attacks comprise multiple aspects, including technology, humans, psychology, etc. Some of the social engineering attacks based on these aspects include:

12.3.1 Phishing

It is the frequently exploited kind of social engineering. The attackers send bogus messages or emails to deceive victims by masquerading as legitimate personalities, such that the victim discloses their login credentials and sensitive personal information by clicking on a link. Website and email phishing attacks are the most frequently employed [17].

12.3.2 Vishing

Phishing attacks carried out on telephone-oriented communication lines are called vishing. To prevent victims from realizing that they are being tricked, attackers employ psychological tactics like giving them anxiety, inducing fear or threat, or conveying good news. Robocall and Help Desk Impersonation attacks are typical vishing attacks [16].

12.3.3 Grooming

It is a recently evolved kind of social engineering attack in which the attacker collects subsequent information about the pedophilia victims by utilizing information technology and psychological techniques. Attackers communicate with victims through emails, text messages, or telephone, and the objective of the conversation is to entrap the victim [18].

12.3.4 Identity Theft

In this, the attacker steals another person's identity through publicly available information (like names, images, conversation styles, etc.) and impersonates someone else (authority figure, employee of an organization, customer, banker, etc.). The information about the person whose identity is taken might be gathered from multiple online platforms or social networking sites, discarded documents, etc. The attacker then utilizes this stolen identity to deceive victims so that they divulge their personal and sensitive data to the attacker [19].

12.3.5 Quid Pro Quo Attacks

The attack in which reciprocity from products and services that are free of cost is expected. For this attack to occur, there ought to be an agreement between the attacker and the victim. In Quid pro quo attacks, the victim might request the attacker to perform or execute a task that is supposedly considered to be beyond the scope of the victim's capability to perform with an agreement that in exchange for a favor, the victim would do anything or disclose any crucial data that might be required by the attacker [20].

12.3.6 Dumpster Diving Attacks

In this attack, the limitations of the victims are exploited, particularly the inefficiency of the victim to filter out the obsolete data or documents that are of no further use in either digital or physical form. People often need to be careful with their documents and data before destroying them, unaware that this data or document could be misused if it falls into the wrong hands. Hence, data or documents in the physical form that are discarded and tossed into the landfill, in addition to data in digital form that is deleted on the hard drive, prove to be an essential source of information for the attackers in the dumpster diving attacks [21].

12.3.7 Diversion Theft Attacks

These attacks are also referred to as diversionary. It is a form of attack in which an attacker introduces distractions to distract away from the targeted victim. People, organizations, and security systems are manipulated in these attacks. In the diversion theft attack, the attacker makes use of courier companies and might insert rootkits or any malware into systems utilized by the company or into their computers, such that the installed rootkits or malware remains undetected by the network and the attacker might gain easy access to the company's network [16].

12.3.8 Tailgating

It is additionally known as piggybacking and trailing. In piggybacking, the attacker might trail the victim physically into a restricted region or campus and acquire unauthorized access to that secured region by taking advantage of the victim's courtesy and confidence. The attacker carefully observes the activities conducted by the people working in an organization so that the attacker can effortlessly enter through the security checks of the organizations [22]. People unaware of being under the surveillance of the attacker unknowingly provide them with the information that turns out to be the key to their exploitation.

12.3.9 File Masquerade

File masquerade attacks often occur when the victim is unaware of the different files and folders in their computer systems or any other external storage device, such as a hard drive, pen drive, compact disk, etc. The attacker might insert the trojan horse or malware into the files and folders; the victim, unaware of the fact and thinking that the file is free from viruses and malware, executes it without any suspicion. Thus, this becomes an entry gateway for the attacker into the victim's system [23].

12.3.10 Water-Holing

In water-holing, the perpetrator observes the digital trails of the victim, identifies the most often visited website by the target organization or the target individual, and compromises those websites by embedding a trojan or malware into them. In the water-holing technique, the attacker establishes two-way communication with the victim. This connection is established when the target visits the website, downloads any application or clicks on the link. Once the connection is established, the attacker can gain unauthorized ingress into the target system [24].

12.4 Social Engineering Attacks Using Advanced Techniques

With the advancement of technology, cyber threats are increasing progressively. On the one hand, new technology or technological advancement is considered a boon for people worldwide, while on the other hand, some new technologies are becoming threatening and dangerous. Artificial intelligence (AI) technology is highly exploited for social engineering attacks. Numerous social engineering attacks could be executed by employing AI. These methods enable cybercriminals to design sophisticated manipulation strategies, which raises their chances of success and profit rates [25]. The "CyberLover" chatbot was one of the first reported hacks to exploit AI technology in social engineering attacks [26].

Another emerging technology that could have drastic adverse effects in the hands of cybercriminals is the technology of deepfake. The technology of deepfake utilizes AI to create fake images, videos, and audio. Deepfakes hold immense potential to deceive humans into believing that what exists is not real [27]. In addition, voice cloning technology could lead to industrial accidents and raise numerous potential risks [22]. Open-source intelligence (OSINT) could be utilized for both cybersecurity and cybercrime. The information gathered by OSINT may be used by criminals to manipulate online behavior and weaken their victims, as well as by intelligence agencies to combat cybercrime and terrorism. Studies have shown that the security of any business can be secretly jeopardized by acquiring employee personal information from open sources and using it in a cyberattack [28]. The best method of preventing social engineering attacks is to teach internet users about online privacy protection and how to spot and stop attacks [29].

12.5 Social Engineering Attack Detection Models

Over time, researchers have put forward various models for uncovering social engineering attacks. Some of the detection models are:

12.5.1 SEADM

This model was developed by Monique Bezuidenhout, Francois Mouton, and H.S. Venter in 2010. The model was the first of its kind in detecting social engineering attacks. It focuses on social engineering attacks targeting employees. The model was proposed as a decision tree to make it more practical for employees. The model could be described as

The very first step in the model is to describe the emotional state of the person who is the user. The emotional state could be stated as stable or unstable. In case of an unstable emotional state, the request should be elevated. The stable emotional state is followed by the question of accessing the data that was appealed for and understanding the request. The request is elevated if the individual needs to understand and access the request's information. The request is followed by the query of whether the information is already available to the public in the public domain. The request should be provided access if the information is already accessible to the public. However, if the information is not readily available to the public, it should be interrogated with the requester's identity question.

If the requester's identity can be authenticated, it should be verified based on authority level, previous interaction, credibility, and the existence of the requester. If any of the three bases of identification are met, the request could be examined under the purview of sensitivity of the information. Based on sensitivity, the information could be classified as privileged or non-privileged. Privileged information requires consent, whereas non-privileged information denotes data that is publicly accessible and does not require authorization. If the information falls under the category of non-privileged information and the individual feels an acceptable level of discomfort or no discomfort in sharing that information, the request could be entertained.

However, in case of high discomfort, the request could be elevated. In the case of privileged information, whether the requester has a mandatory ascendancy when requesting the data should be further questioned. If the requester has authority, it could be examined under the individual's discomfort when sharing the information. If the discomfort is high, the request can be elevated. If the discomfort is low, access could be provided. However, if the requester needs more authority to request the information, whether the information is necessary for performing duties should be examined. If the answer is no, the request should be elevated. If the answer is yes, the question of urgency is put forward. In case of no urgency, the request could be elevated, and in case of urgency, it could be examined under the level of discomfort. The request is entertained in case of an acceptable level of discomfort and is rejected in case of a high level of discomfort.

On the contrary, if the identity of the requester is not verifiable. The question of the sensitivity of the information is put first. The request is elevated if the information is privileged. In the case of non-privileged details, the necessity of the information to perform duties is asked. If the answer to the question is no, the request could be elevated, and if the answer is yes, it is further questioned under the urgency of the request. Suppose there is no urgency, the request can be elevated. If the information is urgent to acquire, it is scanned under the discomfort of sharing it. If the level of discomfort is high, requests could be elevated. If the discomfort is low, access to the information could be provided [30].

12.5.2 SEADMv2

This model was an upgraded version of SEADM. The model was ameliorated by Francois Mouton, Louise Leenen and H.S. Venter in 2015. The model is described as

The request is first questioned whether the individual who receives the request understands what is requested or not. The individual could persuade the requester to elaborate further and detail the request to clarify it. However, if, even after elaboration, the individual needs help to understand the request, the request is deferred or referred. It could be deferred or referred if the request is understandable, but the individual needs to learn how to perform it. If the individual understands the request and knows how to perform it, the question of authority comes into play. If the individual does not have the authority to perform or provide a request, the request could be deferred or referred.

If possessing the authority to perform or provide a request, the request should be examined whether the information is available in the public domain. The request could be performed if the information is in the public domain. The request should be performed if the request is preapproved to abstain from a life-threatening emergency. If not, the request could be examined under the four reasons for refusal: administrative, procedural, unusual, new type, or any other reason. If no such reasons exist for refusal, the request can be entertained. If appropriate reasons are found, the requester's identity should be inspected. The request can be deferred or referred when the requester's identity is not verifiable. If the requester's identity is verifiable, it should be verified under four categories: authority level, credibility, previous interaction, and the existence of the requester. The request can be deferred or referred if no such verification is met.

The requester could be verified through a third-party source for one or two verifications. The request could be deferred or referred if the identity is not verifiable from a third-party source, or the verification must reflect the data as verification necessities. If three or more verifications are possible, the question of whether the requester has the authority to request the action or information will be examined. If the requester does not have such authority, the request could be referred to or deferred. However, if the requester does possess such authority, the request could be performed [31].

12.5.3 SEADer

The SEADer model was developed by Merton Lansley, Stelios Kapetanakis, and Nikolaos Polatidis in 2019. The model utilizes natural language processing and artificial neural networks in machine learning. The model was broadly divided by researchers into 3 stages, namely, Data Pre-Processing, which was followed by Feature Extraction, and finally, the stage of Aggregation of Results.

The model was divided into a series of a total of 11 steps. Steps 1 to 5 conduct an examination of malicious links. Steps 6 and 7 check the spelling quality, whereas steps 8 to 11 examine the intent of the text. The purpose of the text is determined by utilizing a predefined denylist. These steps form the 3 features of the model, which are scored as per model. These scores are link score, spelling score, and intent score. The value of each feature could range between 0 and 1. Based on the score, the model processes the data and determines an output as an attack or no attack. The outcome of estimating an attack or no attack is determined by the Multilayer perceptron (MLP) classifier. High outcomes indicate an attack, whereas low outcomes indicate no attack [32].

12.5.4 SEADer++ V2

SEADer++V2 is a modified and improved version of the previous SEADer and SEADer++ model. Instead of an 11-step process of SEADer, the SEADer++V2 utilizes a 14-step process. These additional steps in the model create 3 new scores named Topic modeling along with the three steps from SEADer: Intent score, Spelling score, and Link score. All these scores generate the final output of attack or no attack. The SEADer++V2 model is found to be more effective as compared to the SEADer++. The accuracy of SEADer++V2, as put forward by researchers, was estimated to be 80.1%, while that of SEADer++ was 78.4%. The precision of SEADer++V2 was estimated to be 79.7% compared to 80.1% of SEADer++ [33].

12.6 Detection of Social Engineering Links

Chris Giovanni M. has described three simple steps to identify the social engineering or phishing link [34]. The first step to verifying a suspicious link is to check the uniform resource locator (URL) behavior. This could be done by utilizing the websites such as URLScan.io. A public scan of the URL will provide essential information regarding the link. The information could be used to verify the link.

The next step in the link verification is to check the domain's reputation. This could be achieved by utilizing websites like brightcloud.com. The lookup feature of the website could rank the web's reputation, ranging from trustworthy to suspicious. The last step is interacting with the URL using a virtual sandbox browser, Browserling. Interact with the link virtually to look out for any suspicious activity. Based on these 3 steps, a link could quickly be sorted into suspicious or reliable links.

12.7 Preventive Approaches

12.7.1 SIEM

Management of events and information is vital to combat social engineering attacks. SIEM stands for security information and event management. SIEM can collect, accumulate, store, and correlate events usually produced by a well-managed infrastructure [35]. The origin of the term SIEM could be traced back to "Improve IT Security for Vulnerability Management", a 2005 Gartner research study by Amrit Williams and Mark Nicolett [36].

According to Gartner IT Glossary, SIEM could be defined as "technology that supports threat detection and security incident response through the real-time collection and historical analysis of security events from various event and contextual data sources. It also supports compliance reporting and incident investigation by analyzing historical data from these sources" [37]. SIEM receives events from several sensors, such as Firewalls, intrusion detection systems, antivirus software, etc. These diverse events are correlated and presented in the form of synthetic views to stimulate alerts for threat response and reporting of security. They serve as the cornerstone of security operations centers that are modern in nature [38, 39].

To identify network incidents and irregularities in an IT system infrastructure, several businesses have designed SIEM software packages (e.g., HP, IBM, Intel, and McAfee) [40]. Over the years, the SIEM platforms have become sophisticated and efficient with technological advancement. More often, a basic SIEM comprises individual building elements called blocks. These blocks can operate separately from one another, but SIEM can only function effectively with the proper reciprocity between all blocks [40]. These basic blocks of SIEM include source device, parsing normalization, log accumulation, log repository, rule engine, and monitoring. SIEM works by gathering logs and event data. The event and log data generated by devices, networks, infrastructure, and systems are used to conduct the analysis. The analysis comprehensively presents an organization's information technology [41].

SIEMs are a combination of several integrated security techniques, such as "Log management systems (LMS)", "Security event management (SEM)" and "Security information management (SIM)". LMS is used as a central data storage in the form of a simplified log. SIM utilizes automation to generate reports based on the long-term storage and analysis of log data. At the same time, SEM works on real-time monitoring and correlating the events. In combination, SIEM systems work on the employed rules and statistical correlations. These rules and statistics are used to analyze real-time data, and during forensic investigations, they aid in generating actionable information.

SIEM could be highly beneficial in assisting security teams in promptly identifying malicious incidents, which could help mitigate cyberattacks. SIEM technology evaluates all data and sorts threat activity. The threats are classified according to their risk level [41]. The SIEM serves as an effective tool in combating social engineering attacks when powered by user and behavior analytics [42]. The fundamental elements of SIEM software have remained valuable throughout time. The SIEM has also witnessed advancements in its functioning, which are essential in the competitive environment. This has eventually resulted in more thorough and sophisticated risk rcduction methods [41].

12.7.2 Next-Gen Cloud-Based WAF

Though individuals and organizations employ firewalls for protection against various malware and viruses, the next-generation cloud-based firewall web application is mainly developed and designed to provide security and prevent social engineering attacks. The web-based WAF is quite different from the conventional WAF, which the organizations currently deploy on a large scale. The web WAF is more efficient against social engineering attacks. In addition, AppTrana, specifically, is used to keep an eye on websites or any of the web applications for suspicious activity and misconduct. Despite the modus operandi of social engineering attacks being dependent on human errors, it will provide a protective shield against any social engineering attacks by blocking the attacks and alarming individuals and organizations about the endeavors to install malware into the system of individuals and organizations. Implementing risk-based WAF is one of the most effective measures to protect oneself against any potential infiltration and prevent social engineering attacks [43].

12.7.3 "Human-as-a-Security-Sensor Framework"

The defense framework to protect individuals and organizations against social engineering attacks was devised by Heartfield and Loukas in 2018. The key feature of this framework is that it focuses on the potential of humans and regards them as sensors that can identify, detect, and report different types of social engineering attacks, hence called the "Human-as-a-Security-Sensor framework". This framework primarily depends on the users' reporting attacks on social engineering.

Heartfield and Loukas examined this framework in real cases. The architecture of "Human-as-a-Security-Sensor" comprises three primary processes: categorization, detection, and response. The framework of "Human-as-a-Security-Sensor" presents limitations primarily when used in embedded systems and smartphones. The information displayed between smartphones, computers, and embedded systems varies a great deal; for instance, the complete address of the "Uniform Resource Locator (URL)" is not displayed in the browser [44]. This might create obstacles for the users in identifying social engineering attacks and make the role of users as sensors challenging a great deal as users exhibit a crucial and essential role in the "Human-as-a-Security-Sensor framework" [44].

12.7.4 Awareness Programs

Social engineering targets the psyche and emotions of humans. Thus, social engineering attacks might be dangerous to a great extent. Hence, it is important to educate individuals and organizations about the potential hazards of social engineering and preventive measures against the attacks through awareness programs. One of the prime objectives of the awareness programs includes empowering people to identify the warning indications of social engineering by providing them with information and knowledge about the varied tactics and techniques employed in social engineering attacks.

Effective awareness programs foster the development of conscious security behavior in individuals and organizations. Furthermore, awareness programs aid individuals and organizations by enlightening them on methods to mitigate insider attacks, identify and verify unknown requests, implement security measures on social media profiles, etc. The awareness programs assist the non-technical staff in the organization to gain information about the existing cyber threats and to avoid errors on their part. Awareness programs greatly help in gaining hands-on experience pertaining to various aspects of social engineering; for example, simulation phishing exercises enlighten people in recognizing and defending phishing attacks.

12.7.5 Prevention Protocols

The co-utile disclosure of confidential information or prevention protocol could manage the flow of data between users on social networks [45]. Before evaluating the privacy functionality score, the co-utile protocol examines the privacy risk of the data on social networks. The initial phase is to analyze the privacy risks on social networks, particularly structures and data types, before releasing the data. In the second phase, participation in social networks was determined through a score of privacy functionality. The decentralization of interactions on social networks was employed in the co-utile protocol. Due to the mutual rational behavior of co-utile protocol, it can resist attacks [45].

Social engineering attacks can be prevented by the significant contribution of Artificial Intelligence by augmenting the abilities of humans, accelerating detection, and improving response mechanisms. A technique was devised by Kumar and Dabas in 2019 to identify and prevent attacks pertaining to profile cloning on social networks [46]. A type of identity theft, profile cloning, implies duplicating someone else's profile without their knowledge and consent, with authentic credentials available on social networks. The detection of clone profiles has become easy with the collaboration of similarity index components and machine learning processes. It is of immense importance to educate social network users about the potential risks in disclosing and displaying excess information on their profiles, as this information could be stolen by the perpetrators to carry out their malicious activity over social networks.

Hence, there is a dire need to introduce an education model that considers the dangers in the context of the amount of information displayed on social networks and controls profile cloning attacks. This model could provide knowledge to the users about profile settings, verifying friend requests before accepting them, allowing access to one's personal information, and learning about the potential risks on social networks due to a single click on any link whose source is unknown.

12.8 Preventive Measures Against Social Engineering Attacks

Many technical and non-technical methods exist to prevent social engineering attacks. The handful of the most common measures that could be considered to safeguard oneself from social engineering attacks are:

12.8.1 Avoid Clicking Unknown Links

Unknown links are a potential gateway to social engineering victimization. The unknown links could be received via email, text message, social media chat, etc. These links should not be opened; if they are supposed to be open, one must verify the link before clicking.

12.8.2 Use Multi-Factor Authentication

Multifactor authentication is a method that requires more than one verification, including the login credentials, such as a one-time password (OTP). Multifactor authentication effectively prevents the hijacking of accounts even when the login credentials are compromised.

12.8.3 Verify Email Sender's Identity

The phishing links are most commonly distributed via email. The verification of email addresses before opening any link or file received via email is an effective method to avoid social engineering victimization.

12.8.4 Check for SSL Certificate

Thoroughly investigate the website before handing over any private data. Examining the URLs to ensure the website's genuineness is essential. Secure Sockets Layer (SSL) certificate could be utilized for this purpose. Websites initiated with "https://" could be considered trustworthy and secured. In contrast, websites starting with "http://" fail to provide a safe and secure connection and thus are not regarded as trustworthy [43].

12.8.5 Check for Updates

The updates for apps and systems enhance security. Thus, updates should be made as soon as possible.

12.8.6 Pay Attention to Your Digital Footprint

Limit the sharing of excessive information that is personal on diverse social media platforms. Cybercriminals might use sensitive personal information like bank details, location, contact number, etc., to execute social engineering attacks.

12.9 Conclusion

Advancing technology and the internet have instigated a dreadful cyberspace threat, including social engineering. The diverse types of these attacks could hamper the security of an individual in one manner or another at multiple levels, whether it be personal level, organizational level, government level, or international level. Humans, being fragile, are the crucial key to the security of the digital system and, hence, are principal targets in social engineering. Thus, every level has the exigent necessity to play a pivotal role in expeditiously curbing such heinous attacks. This could be achieved if everyone participates at different levels and efficiently generates awareness, impeding fake websites and links and employing multi-factor authentication. At the same time, organizations and governments should improve their security infrastructure and policies to prevent themselves from falling prey to these attacks.

References

1. Rabinovitch, E., Staying protected from 'social engineering'. *IEEE Commun. Mag.*, 45, 9, 20–21, 2007.
2. Wolthuis, R., Broenink, G., Fransen, F., Schultz, S., de Vries, A., Simple & Secure: Attitude and behaviour towards security and usability in internet products and services at home, in: *ISSE 2009 Securing Electronic Business Processes*, N. Pohlmann, H. Reimer, W. Schneider (Eds.), Vieweg+Teubner, Germany, 2010.
3. Bullée, J.W.H., Montoya, L., Pieters, W., Junger, M., Hartel, P., On the anatomy of social engineering attacks—A literature-based dissection of successful attacks. *J. Investig. Psychol. Offender Profiling*, 15, 1, 20–45, 2018.
4. Fan, W., Kevin, L., Rong, R., Social Engineering: I-E based Model of Human Weakness for Attack and Defense Investigations. *IJCNIS*, 9, 1, 1–11, 2017.
5. Handoko, H. and Putri, D., Threat language: Cognitive exploitation in social engineering, in: *Proc. International Conference on Social Sciences, Humanities, Econ. Law*, 2018.
6. Chitrey, A., Singh, D., Singh, V., A comprehensive study of social engineering based attacks in India to develop a conceptual model. *Int. J. Inf. Netw. Sec.*, 1, 2, 45–53, 2012.
7. Gragg, D., A multi-level defense against social engineering. *SANS Reading Room*, 13, 1–21, 2003.
8. Broadhurst, R. and Chantler, N., Social engineering and crime prevention in cyberspace. *SSRN Electron. J.*, 1–21, 2008.
9. Dong, X., Clark, J.A., Jacob, J.L., User behaviour based phishing websites detection, in: *International Multiconference on Computer Science and Information Technology*, vol. 2008, pp. 783–790, IEEE, 2008.
10. Workman, M., A test of interventions for security threats from social engineering. *Inf. Manag. Comput. Sec.*, 16, 5, 463–483, 2008.
11. Tetri, P. and Vuorinen, J., Dissecting social engineering. *Behav. Inf. Technol.*, 32, 10, 1014–1023, 2013.

12. Wang, Z., Zhu, H., Liu, P., Sun, L., Social engineering in cybersecurity: A domain ontology and knowledge graph application examples. *Cybersecurity*, 4, 1, 1–21, 2021.
13. Tulupieva, T.V., Abramov, M.V., Tulupiev, A.L., Model of social influence in analysis of socio-engineering attacks. *Admin. Consult.*, 8, 8, 97–107, 2021.
14. Thakur, T. and Verma, R., Catching classical and hijack-based phishing attacks, in: *International Conference on Information Systems Security*, pp. 318–337, Springer International Publishing, 2014.
15. Green, B., Prince, D., Busby, J., Hutchison, D., The impact of social engineering on industrial control system security, in: *Proc. First ACM Workshop on Cyber-Physical Systems-Security and/or Privacy*, pp. 23–29, 2015.
16. Salahdine, F. and Kaabouch, N., Social engineering attacks: A survey. *Future Internet*, 11, 4, 89, 2019.
17. Hijji, M. and Alam, G., A multivocal literature review on growing social engineering based cyber-attacks/threats during the COVID-19 pandemic: Challenges and prospective solutions. *IEEE Access*, 9, 7152–7169, 2021.
18. Zambrano, P., Torres, J., Flores, P., How does grooming fit into social engineering?, in: *Advances in Computer Communication and Computational Sciences: Proceedings of IC*, vol. 4s, pp. 629–639, Springer, Singapore, 2019.
19. Hedayati, A., An analysis of identity theft: Motives, related frauds, techniques and prevention. *J. Law Confl. Resolut.*, 4, 1, 1–12, 2012.
20. Chetioui, K., Bah, B., Alami, A.O., Bahnasse, A., Overview of social engineering attacks on social networks. *Procedia Comput. Sci.*, 198, 656–661, 2022.
21. Koyun, A. and Al Janabi, E., Social engineering attacks. *Multidiscip. Eng. Sci. Technol. (JMEST)*, 4, 6, 7533–7538, 2017.
22. Wang, K., Liu, X., Chen, C.M., Kumari, S., Shojafar, M., Hossain, M.S., Voice-transfer attacking on industrial voice control systems in 5G-aided IIoT domain. *IEEE Trans. Ind. Inform.*, 17, 10, 7085–7092, 2020.
23. Yasin, A., Fatima, R., Liu, L., Yasin, A., Wang, J., Contemplating social engineering studies and attack scenarios: A review study. *Sec. Privacy*, 2, 4, e73, 2019.
24. Krombholz, K., Hobel, H., Huber, M., Weippl, E., Advanced social engineering attacks. *J. Inf. Sec. Appl.*, 22, 113–122, 2015.
25. Blauth, T.F., Gstrein, O.J., Zwitter, A., Artificial intelligence crime: An overview of malicious use and abuse of AI. *IEEE Access*, 10, 77110–77122, 2022.
26. Rossi, S., Beware the Cyberlover That Steals Personal Data, PC World, 2007, https://www.pcworld.com/article/140507/article.html.
27. Kietzmann, J., Lee, L.W., McCarthy, I.P., Kietzmann, T.C., Deepfakes: Trick or treat? *Bus. Horiz.*, 63, 2, 135–146, 2020.
28. Ball, L., Ewan, G., Coull, N., Undermining: Social engineering using open source intelligence gathering, in: *4th International Conference on Knowledge Discovery and Information Retrieval*, Scitepress Digital Library, pp. 275–280, 2012.

29. Peltsverger, S. and Zheng, G., Enhancing privacy education with a technical emphasis in IT curriculum. *J. Inf. Technol. Educ. Innov. Pract.*, 15, 1–17, 2016.
30. Bezuidenhout, M. and Venter, H., Social engineering attack detection model: Seadm, in: *Information Security for South Africa*, vol. 2010, pp. 1–8, IEEE, 2010.
31. Mouton, F., Social engineering attack detection model: Seadmv2, in: *International Conference on Cyberworlds (CW)*, vol. 2015, pp. 216–223, IEEE, 2015.
32. Lansley, M., Polatidis, N., Kapetanakis, S., Seader: A social engineering attack detection method based on natural language processing and artificial neural networks, in: *Computational Collective Intelligence, Proceedings: 11th International Conference, ICCCI 2019, Hendaye, France, September 4-6*, pp. 686–696, Springer International Publishing, Berlin, Heidelberg, 2019.
33. Lansley, M., Kapetanakis, S., Polatidis, N., SEADer++ v2: Detecting social engineering attacks using natural language processing and machine learning, in: *International Conference on INnovations in Intelligent SysTems and Applications (INISTA)*, vol. 2020, pp. 1–6, IEEE, 2020.
34. Giovanni, C., Investigate Phishing Links: How To? LinkedIn. LinkedIn, 2023, https://www.linkedin.com/posts/chrisgiovanni_how-to-investigate-phishing-links-activity-7088649532665651200-MLIa.
35. Miller, D.R., Harris, S., Harper, A., VanDyke, S., Blask, C., *Security Information and Event Management (SIEM) Implementation*, McGraw-Hill Professional, Osborne, USA, 2010.
36. Williams, A., The Future of SIEM–The market will begin to diverge, [Blog], Jan. 1. 2007.
37. Chuvakin, A., Let's define 'SIEM'! Gartner Blog Network, 2017, https://blogs.gartner.com/anton-chuvakin/2017/08/14/lets-define-siem/.
38. Granadillo, G.G., El-Barbori, M., Debar, H., New types of alert correlation for security information and event management systems, in: *8th IFIP international conference on new technologies, mobility and security (NTMS)*, vol. 2016, pp. 1–7, IEEE, 2016.
39. Bryant, B.D. and Saiedian, H., Improving SIEM alert metadata aggregation with a novel kill-chain based classification model. *Comput. Sec.*, 94, 101817, 2020.
40. González-Granadillo, G., González-Zarzosa, S., Diaz, R., Security information and event management (SIEM): Analysis, trends, and usage in critical infrastructures," *Sensors (Basel)*, 21, 14, 4759, 2021.
41. Gast, K., What is SIEM? And How Does it Work?, LogRhythm, 2021, Available at: https://logrhythm.com/blog/what-is-siem/#Gartner.
42. Gonzalez, C., Top 5 social engineering techniques and how to prevent them, Exabeam, 2022, https://www.exabeam.com/information-security/top-8-social-engineering-techniques-and-how-to-prevent-them-2022/.

43. Chinnasamy, V., Social engineering attacks: 10 ways businesses can prevent it, Indusface, 2023, https://www.indusface.com/blog/10-ways-businesses-can-prevent-social-engineering-attacks/.
44. Heartfield, R. and Loukas, G., Detecting semantic social engineering attacks with the weakest link: Implementation and empirical evaluation of a human-as-a-security-sensor framework. *Comput. Sec.*, 76, 101–127, 2018.
45. Sánchez, D., Domingo-Ferrer, J., Martínez, S., Co-utile disclosure of private data in social networks. *Inf. Sci.*, 441, 50–65, 2018.
46. Kumar, N. and Dabas, P., Detection and prevention of profile cloning in online social networks, in: *5th International Conference on Signal Processing, Computing and Control. (ISPCC)*, vol. 2019, pp. 287–291, IEEE, 2019.

13

Multilayer Perceptron of Occlusion and Pose-Sensitive Ear Attributes for Social Engineering Attack Mitigation

O. Taiwo Olaleye[1]*, Oluwasefunmi Arogundade[1], Adebayo Abayomi-Alli[1], Wilson Ahiara[2], Temitope Ogunbiyi[3], Segun Akintunde[1], Segun Dada[4] and Olalekan Okewale[5]

[1]*Department of CS, Federal University of Agriculture, Abeokuta, Ogun State, Nigeria*
[2]*Department of Systems Engineering, Michael Okpara University of Agriculture Umudike, Abia State, Nigeria*
[3]*Department of CS & IT, Bells University of Technology Ota, Ogun State, Nigeria*
[4]*Department of CS, University of Ibadan, Oyo State, Nigeria*
[5]*Directorate of Pan African University for Life & Earth Science Institute, University of Ibadan, Oyo State, Nigeria*

Abstract

Facial biometrics have emerged as a promising approach for user authentication due to their non-intrusive nature and wide availability of facial imagery. This chapter thereby focuses on enhancing user authentication in facial biometrics using multilayer perceptron for digital forensics. The study addresses the challenges posed by occlusion and pose variations, which can significantly impact the accuracy of authentication systems. By leveraging an inclusive dataset with sensitivity to identified threats in literature, the effectiveness of the Perceptron in handling these variations is investigated. One-hot encoding is employed to represent categorical data feature attributes, just as parameter optimization is implemented to maximize the model's performance. The model evaluation results demonstrate the Perceptron's effectiveness in handling occlusion and pose variations, highlighting its potential for real-world applications in digital forensics. The study emphasizes the importance of one-hot encoding and parameter optimization in improving the performance of perceptron models.

**Corresponding author*: agsobaolaleyetaiwo@gmail.com

Kavita Sharma, Vishnu Sharma, Parma Nand, Anil Kumar Sagar and Gulshan Shrivastava (eds.) Securing the Digital Frontier: Threats and Advanced Techniques in Security and Forensics, (291–314)

Keywords: Multilayer perceptron, occlusion, pose-sensitive, cybersecurity, social engineering

13.1 Introduction

In today's interconnected world, where digital interactions and transactions have become ubiquitous, the need for robust authentication mechanisms has become paramount. Traditional methods relying solely on passwords or personal identification numbers (PINs) have proven susceptible to social engineering attacks [1], compromising the security and integrity of individuals and organizations alike [2]. As a result, there is a growing demand for innovative approaches that can effectively mitigate such threats and enhance digital security. Digital forensics and cybersecurity play crucial roles in safeguarding information [3, 25], investigating cybercrimes [4], and preserving digital evidence. These fields constantly face evolving challenges as adversaries seek to exploit vulnerabilities and exploit human weaknesses to gain unauthorized access or deceive individuals into divulging sensitive information. Social engineering attacks, which exploit psychological manipulation to deceive victims, have emerged as a significant concern [3], requiring specialized attention within the digital forensics and cybersecurity landscape. This chapter addresses these challenges by proposing a novel approach to enhance authentication and mitigate social engineering attacks. By utilizing occlusion and pose-sensitive black ear images together with their respective user passwords, along with advanced data science techniques that seek to address threats to the internal and external validity of existing models in the literature, this research aims to foster inclusivity, remove biases inherent in existing frameworks, and bolster the security of digital systems. Through an exploration of the mathematical models behind the color layout and edge histogram filters, as well as an investigation of the most suitable machine learning classifier, this chapter aims to contribute to the growing body of knowledge in digital forensics and cybersecurity. By integrating biometric authentication and user-generated passwords, this research provides a comprehensive and resilient defense against social engineering attacks. In what follows, details of black ear biometrics, the methodologies employed for data collection and preprocessing, feature extraction techniques, the incorporation of user-generated passwords, the selection of appropriate machine learning classifiers, and the evaluation of the proposed framework's effectiveness are all discussed. Through experimentation and analysis, we aim to showcase the potential of this approach to mitigate social engineering attacks and enhance the overall security posture of digital systems. By embracing this innovative and inclusive approach to biometric authentication, we can pave the way for a more secure and resilient digital landscape.

13.1.1 Biometric Authentication and Social Engineering Attacks

Biometric authentication is a method of identity verification that relies on individuals' unique biological or behavioral characteristics of individuals [5]. These characteristics, often called biometric traits, are human body features.

13.1.1.1 Strengths of Biometric Authentication

i. Biometric traits are unique to individuals [1], making them difficult to replicate or forge. Unlike passwords or PINs that can be shared or stolen, biometric traits are inherent to an individual and are not easily transferable.
ii. Biometric authentication provides a convenient and user-friendly experience [6]. Users present their biometric traits for verification. This ease of use enhances user acceptance and reduces the burden of memorizing multiple passwords.
iii. Biometric traits are difficult to replicate [5], mainly when sophisticated biometric systems are used. For example, fingerprint patterns or iris structures have intricate details that are challenging to reproduce accurately, making it harder for impostors to deceive the system.
iv. Unlike passwords or physical tokens, biometric traits are always with the individual and cannot be easily forgotten or misplaced [7]. This eliminates the risk of losing or forgetting the authentication factor.

13.1.1.2 Weaknesses of Biometric Authentication

i. Biometric traits are inherently permanent and cannot be easily changed if compromised [7]. Unlike passwords that can be reset or revoked, if a biometric trait is compromised, it may have lifelong implications for the affected individual.

ii. Collecting and storing biometric data raises privacy concerns, as the biometric information is considered highly personal and sensitive [5]. If not adequately protected, unauthorized access to biometric databases can lead to identity theft or unauthorized tracking.
iii. While biometric traits are unique, some can be susceptible to spoofing attacks [8]. For example, fingerprints can be replicated using artificial means, and facial recognition systems can be tricked with high-quality photographs or 3D-printed masks. These vulnerabilities require robust anti-spoofing measures to ensure the integrity of biometric authentication systems.
iv. Biometric systems may encounter false acceptance or false rejection errors [8]. Striking the right balance between security (low false acceptance rate) and user convenience (low false rejection rate) is a challenge in implementing biometric authentication.
v. Biometric authentication systems capture accurate biometric samples and perform accurate comparisons [7]. Factors such as sensor quality, environmental conditions, or changes in the individual's biometric traits (e.g., due to injuries or aging) can impact the system's performance and accuracy.

Social engineering attacks are manipulative tactics employed by malicious individuals to deceive and exploit human vulnerabilities [3] Rather than targeting technical vulnerabilities in systems. These attacks rely on psychological manipulation [9], persuasive techniques [4], and exploiting the trust [1] to lure individuals. One significant impact of social engineering attacks is the potential for unauthorized access to sensitive information or systems. Attackers can access personal accounts, corporate networks, or sensitive databases by impersonating a trusted entity or manipulating individuals into providing confidential data. This unauthorized access can lead to data breaches, financial loss, intellectual property theft, or the compromise of critical infrastructure [7]. Another consequence of social engineering attacks is the erosion of trust [10]. These attacks exploit individuals' trust in familiar communication channels like emails, phone calls, or face-to-face interactions. When individuals fall victim to social engineering tactics, their trust in legitimate communication channels may be undermined, making it harder to discern genuine requests from malicious ones. This loss of trust can hinder effective communication, disrupt workflows, and weaken security protocols [8]. Successful attacks can also result in unauthorized actions or disclosures that damage an individual's reputation or an organization's brand image. Once trust is breached, rebuilding reputation and restoring confidence becomes a significant challenge, which can have long-lasting consequences in terms of financial and professional relationships [5]. Social engineering attacks can also serve as entry points for other malicious activities. By tricking individuals into clicking on malicious links, downloading malware-infected files, or unknowingly disclosing credentials, attackers can gain footholds within networks and launch broader cyberattacks [8]. Social engineering attacks act as a gateway for more sophisticated cyber threats [3], amplifying the overall security risks faced by individuals and organizations [6].

Biometrics can help mitigate social engineering attacks by providing a secure and unique authentication factor that is inherently tied to an individual's physical or behavioral characteristics, making it more difficult for attackers to deceive or impersonate. This requires the involvement of the biological traits of the authentic user in the authentication system. However, attacks can boycott biometric systems by exploiting vulnerabilities in the implementation [3], such as bypassing or spoofing the biometric sensors, manipulating the enrollment process, or targeting the underlying infrastructure and storage of biometric data. The vulnerabilities associated with the storage of biometric data and manipulation of the enrollment process have gained research interest [1] and are the focus of this study. Machine learning methodologies have been widely incorporated to address vulnerabilities associated with the storage of biometric data and the manipulation of the enrollment process by employing advanced data encryption techniques [11], anomaly detection algorithms [12], and pattern recognition models [13] to enhance data security, detect fraudulent activities, and ensure the integrity and authenticity of the enrollment process. However, there are threats to existing literature's internal and external validity.

13.2 Literature Review

Predictive analytics has gained traction in no small measure within cybersecurity, fraud detection, digital forensics, etc. Predictive analytics is a branch of data analysis that utilizes historical and current data to predict future events or outcomes. It involves applying various statistical and machine-learning techniques to identify patterns, relationships, and trends in data and use them to make informed predictions [14].

In the work of Achary and Shelke [4], an expert system was implemented to mitigate attacks from social engineering platforms. The study analyzed the malicious behavior of attackers for the mitigation study. The proposed approach applies to offline text and real-time scenarios to determine if a human Chatbot or offline chat is engaging in malicious activities. The method involves analyzing and validating text messages for linguistic errors, utilizing a model to identify and differentiate potential attacks. The technique is evaluated using factual and semi-synthetic datasets to achieve higher accuracy in the results.

Furthermore, using machine learning algorithms, the developed model can detect phishing links (URLs) from web pages and classify them as legitimate or illegitimate URLs. Similarly, social engineering attacks were detected in online environments using the functionalities of data science [10]. The proposed and implemented method applies to offline texts and online environments. The conversation text is first parsed for correction of grammatical errors using the functionalities of natural language processing techniques, using both real and semi-synthetic datasets. The experimentation achieved higher accuracy results, while alternative methods were employed in the study for evaluation purposes. The survey of Lansley *et al.* also mitigated social engineering attacks [9]. Artificial neural networks and natural language processing functionalities were employed in the study, which produced SEADer solutions for social engineering attack mitigation. SEADer++ v2 was likewise implemented by Lansley *et al.* [2] to optimize the performance of SEADer. Data science techniques of machine learning are similarly employed in the work of Lopez and Camargo [15] by extracting features from dialog texts, including count and report on website links, spell check and blacklist count. The features were used to train Random Forest, Neural Network, and the Support Vector Machine, all to mitigate social engineering attacks. The binary classification problem returned a 0.7899 weighted average of the accuracy metric. In another attempt, a Convolutional Neural Network and Word Embedding were employed for an early-stage recognition system for social engineering attack detection. The work conducted by Tsinganos *et al.* targets persuasions identified in chat-based cyber attacks [6].

13.2.1 Black Ear Inclusivity in Biometric Authentication Systems

The inclusion of the black ear as a biometric identifier in biometric systems offers several advantages and addresses the need for inclusivity [16]. Studies can foster a more comprehensive and representative approach to biometric authentication by incorporating black ear images. Using black ear images helps reduce biases in traditional biometric frameworks. Many existing biometric systems predominantly rely on data collected from individuals with lighter skin tones [17], leading to inherent biases and potential inaccuracies when authenticating individuals with darker skin tones. Introducing black ear-based authentication models can address this bias and create more inclusive systems that accurately represent diverse individuals. Black ear images provide a unique and distinct biometric identifier [18]. The ear's shape, contour, and structural characteristics are highly individualistic, similar to biometric traits like fingerprints or facial features. Using occlusion and pose-sensitive training data could further enhance the accuracy and robustness of black ear-based authentication systems, as it consider real-world variations in ear appearance due to factors such as accessories, hairstyles, or head positioning. The rationale for using black ear images as a biometric identifier will be rooted in the rich diversity and uniqueness of the human population [19]. Instances of pose and occlusion-sensitive ear image signals are presented in Figure 13.1. Biometric systems that solely rely on traditional features may inadvertently exclude or misidentify individuals with specific physical attributes, including darker skin tones. By incorporating other data science methodologies alongside inclusive training data, a machine learning-based authentication system could optimize existing frameworks to mitigate social engineering attacks in cyberspace [19].

This chapter, therefore, seeks to achieve the following objectives:

1. To reduce data bias in literature by introducing a black ear-based authentication model, fostering inclusivity, and addressing alleged prejudices in traditional frameworks.
2. To explore the significance of occlusion and pose-sensitive training data for enhancing the accuracy and reliability of authentication systems, considering the real-world variability in ear appearance.
3. To assess the relevance and effectiveness of MPEG7 color layout attributes in extracting feature attributes from black ear images, contributing to the understanding of color spatial arrangement for biometric recognition.
4. To examine the relevance and suitability of MPEG7 edge histogram attributes in capturing distinctive edge patterns from black ear facial images, facilitating precise feature extraction for robust authentication and classification purposes.

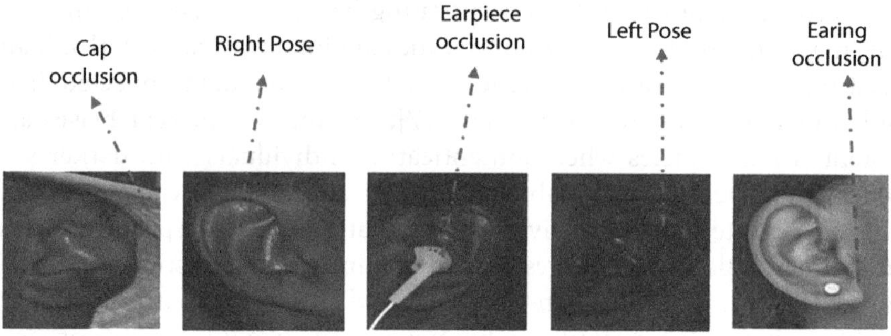

Figure 13.1 Instances of pose and occlusion-sensitive ear signals.

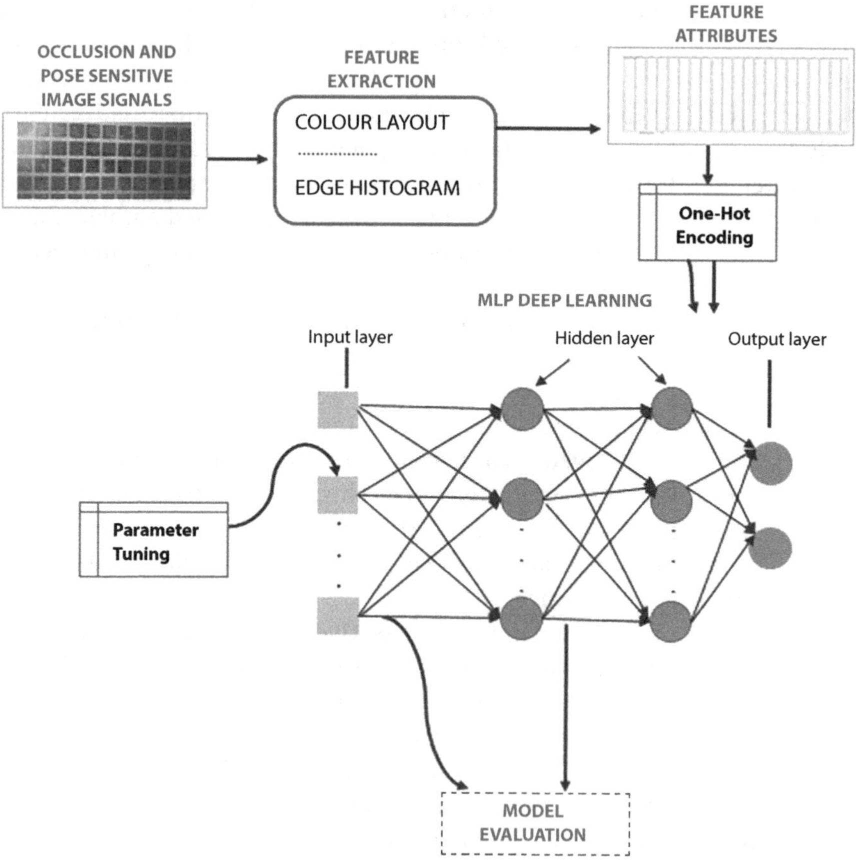

Figure 13.2 Activity sequence of the research design.

13.3 Materials and Methods

The materials and methodological approach of this study are discussed in this section of the chapter. The experimental research is a four-step approach, including acquiring primary black ear data, feature extraction through the instrumentality of the Colour Layout and the Edge Histogram Filters, the predictive analytics phase and the model evaluation phase. The phases are described in Figure 13.2.

13.3.1 Data Acquisition

This study employs black ear image signals of 152 individuals to execute the proposed framework presented in Figure 13.1. The data is occlusion and pose sensitive; hence, it improves existing datasets used in the literature. The data (OPIB) is published by Adebayo-Alli *et al.* [19], consisting of student volunteers. The population comprises 40.35% female ear instances and 59.65% of male instances. For each of the 152 instances, six ear images (left and right sides) were captured, considering different angles and illumination considerations. Therefore, 907 ear image instances are included within the age group of 18 and 35 years. The color representation is Red, Green, and Blue (RGB) with 224 x 224 resolution.

13.3.2 Feature Extraction

Image feature extraction involves analyzing and extracting pertinent information or attributes from an image to capture the unique patterns, structures, or textures that represent the objects or regions of interest in the image. This process entails extracting pixel-based features such as color histograms, intensity gradients, texture descriptors, edge attributes, and histograms of oriented gradients from the dataset consisting of 907 images. The image filters employed in the feature extraction are the Colour Layout Filter and the Edge Histogram Filter.

13.3.2.1 Color Layout Filter

The color layout filter extracts 33 image feature attributes based on the spatial arrangement of colors within the images. It captures information about the distribution and positioning of different color components or channels (such as red, green, and blue) in the black-ear images [20]. The process involves dividing each image instance into smaller regions or blocks and computing statistical descriptors for each block. These descriptors may include color moments representing each block's color distribution, such as mean, variance, and skewness. By capturing the spatial arrangement of colors, the color layout filter can extract meaningful information that distinguishes individuals based on their black ear images. The mathematical model includes the color moment discussed below.

The Colour Moment: Color moments capture the statistical properties of color distributions in each image [20]. The commonly used color moments are the mean, variance, and skewness.

- Mean: The mean represents the average value of a color component (e.g., red, green, blue) within a block or region.
- Variance: The variance measures a block's spread or dispersion of color values. It indicates how much the color values deviate from the mean.
- Skewness: Skewness characterizes the asymmetry of the color distribution. It measures the degree of distortion from a normal distribution.

13.3.2.2 Edge Histogram Filter

The edge histogram filter focuses on extracting features based on the distribution of edges in an image [21]. Edges represent abrupt changes in pixel intensity and can provide valuable information about the structural characteristics of the black ear images. To apply the edge histogram filter, each image is first processed to detect edges using edge detection techniques, such as the Canny edge detector or the Sobel operator. Then, the histogram of edge orientations or gradients is computed to capture the distribution of edge directions in the black ear image. Here's an overview of the mathematical model of the filter.

- Edge Detection: Edge detection techniques, such as the Canny edge detector or the Sobel operator, are applied to the black ear image to identify edges. These techniques calculate the gradient or intensity changes in the image to locate regions of significant variation 688-700.
- Edge Orientation: The edge orientation or gradient direction is determined once the edges are detected. Typically, the gradient orientation is quantized into discrete bins or angles (e.g., 0°, 45°, 90°, 135°) to create a histogram 688-700.

- Edge Histogram: The histogram represents the distribution of edge orientations in the black ear image 688-700. Each histogram bin corresponds to a specific edge orientation; its value indicates the frequency or count of edges with that orientation.

By constructing the histogram of edge orientations, the distribution of edge directions and their frequencies are captured, which form distinctive features for each black ear image. The color layout and edge histogram filters provide quantitative representations of the color spatial arrangement and edge characteristics of the black ear images. These mathematical models enable the extraction of meaningful feature attributes that help distinguish individuals and contribute to the classification and recognition processes in the research. The extraction of numeric features is achieved using the WEKA data mining toolkit for this study. The extracted features are then deployed for the training and testing the predictive model used in this study, which is discussed in the sub-section below.

13.3.3 One-Hot Encoding

Given the successful extraction of numeric features from the entire acquired black earset through the two filters, the class column of the dataset includes the classes of the instances. Each data instance will be represented by their respective class. However, some machine learning algorithms typically require categorical variables encoded as numerical values for optimal performance. Standard encoding techniques include one-hot encoding and label encoding. One-hot encoding creates binary columns for each category, while label encoding assigns a unique numerical value to each category. The categorical variable (class: names of individuals) is adequately encoded before training the MLP classifier. For this study, the One-hot encoding will be implemented. One-hot encoding is a technique used to convert categorical variables into a numerical representation that can be used by machine learning algorithms. It creates binary columns for each unique category in the categorical variable, where each column represents the presence or absence of individual person data point [22]. With the categorical variable class noted as "name of person 1" or "name of person 2" etc., after applying one-hot encoding, numbers of binary columns are created according to the names of individuals represented in the dataset. If a data point has the class "name of person 1", the "Class_ name of person 1" column will have a value of 1, and the other class columns will have a value of 0 at that instance. This process is repeated for each data point, resulting in a numerical representation of the categorical variable.

The mathematical model behind one-hot encoding is relatively straightforward. Given a categorical variable with n unique categories, the one-hot encoding process creates n binary columns. Each binary column represents a category, and the value in that column for a particular data point is 1 if the data point belongs to that category and 0 otherwise. Therefore, for each data point, only one binary column will have a value of 1, and the rest will be 0.

Pseudocode of the One-hot Encoding:

```
function OneHotEncoding (pose and occlusion sensitive data):
    encoded_data = empty DataFrame
    for each categorical_variable in data:
        unique_categories =
get_unique_categories(categorical_variable)
        for each category in unique_categories:
            encoded_data[category] = 0
        for index, value in enumerate(categorical_variable):
            encoded_data.at[index, value] = 1
    return encoded_data
```

In the above pseudocode:

i. *data* represents the input dataset containing categorical variables.
ii. *encoded_data* is an empty DataFrame that will hold the one-hot encoded representation of the categorical variables.
iii. *get_unique_categories* is a function that returns a list of unique categories in a given categorical variable.
iv. The algorithm iterates over each categorical variable in the dataset.
v. For each categorical variable, it retrieves the unique categories.
vi. It then creates new binary columns in *encoded_data* for each unique category.
vii. For each data point in the categorical variable, it sets the value of the corresponding category column to 1, indicating the presence of that category for that data point.
viii. The algorithm returns the resulting *encoded_data* DataFrame.

13.3.4 Predictive Analytics by the Perceptron

The Multilayer Perceptron is employed for the predictive analytics of this study. When fed with feature attributes extracted by the Colour layout and Edge Histogram filters, the MLP utilizes its layered structure and learning algorithm to process and analyze the data, enabling it to learn patterns and make predictions. It extracts meaningful representations of the image through its layers, as seen in Figure 13.1 above. The input layer receives the feature attributes as inputs, passes it to one or more hidden layers that perform computations and transformations on the input data, and to an output layer that generates the final predictions or classifications. During the learning process, the MLP adjusts the weights and biases of its connections between neurons to minimize the difference between its predicted output and the desired output [23]. This is achieved through backpropagation means, and as the MLP iteratively learns from the feature attributes, it can uncover complex relationships and patterns within the data. For example, the MLP can learn to associate specific combinations of color layout attributes with certain classes or patterns or identify distinctive edge histogram attributes that differentiate between different objects or regions in an image. The strength of the MLP lies in its ability to generalize from the learned patterns to make predictions on unseen data [23]. Once the MLP has been trained on a set of labeled data with corresponding feature attributes, it can be used to classify or predict the labels of new, unseen instances based on their extracted feature attributes. This process is implemented on all feature attributes of the input ear image signals to authenticate each instance as either legitimate or impersonation. The 10-fold cross-validation methodological approach will be implemented by Python libraries on the Anaconda Jupyter notebook and the experimental result is evaluated by the usual performance metrics.

13.3.5 Parameter Optimization of MLP

Parameter optimization refers to fine-tuning the parameters of machine learning models to improve their performance on specific tasks. In the case of the MLP, parameter optimization involves adjusting values such as the learning rate, number of hidden layers, number of neurons in each layer, and activation functions to achieve optimal results. By optimizing these parameters, the MLP can effectively learn from the extracted feature attributes and make accurate predictions in user authentication systems for cyber security. A stratified approach to parameter optimization ensures that the model is robust and reliable, considering factors such as data distribution, class imbalance, and generalization capabilities [24]. Optimizing the learning rate and network architecture can enhance the MLP's ability to detect and classify patterns while fine-tuning the activation functions can improve its ability to capture non-linear relationships in the facial dataset for user authentication. Ultimately, this parameter optimization process contributes to the development of a more efficient and secure user authentication system. Here are some of the MLP parameters and their tuning strategies:

1. Number of hidden layers: The number of hidden layers determines the depth of the network and its ability to learn complex representations [24]. Increasing the number of hidden layers can help capture more intricate patterns in the data but also increases the risk of over-fitting. Tuning this parameter involves finding the right balance between model complexity and generalization.
2. Number of neurons per hidden layer: The number of neurons in each hidden layer controls the network's capacity to learn and represent information. Adding more neurons can enhance the model's ability to capture intricate relationships but also increase computational complexity and the risk of over-fitting [24]. Tuning this parameter involves experimenting with different configurations to identify the optimal size for each hidden layer.
3. Activation functions: Activation functions introduce non-linearities to the network and help determine its ability to learn complex mappings [24]. Standard activation functions include sigmoid, ReLU, and tanh. Choosing the appropriate activation functions depends on the problem's characteristics and the model's desired behavior. Tuning this parameter involves testing different activation functions and evaluating their impact on the model's performance.
4. Learning rate: The learning rate controls the step size at which the model adjusts its weights during training process [24]. Conversely, a lower learning rate may result in slower convergence but can improve stability [24]. Tuning this parameter involves experimenting with different learning rate values to find the optimal balance between convergence speed and stability.
5. Regularization techniques, such as L1 and L2 regularization or dropout, prevent over-fitting by adding penalty terms

to the loss function or randomly disabling neurons during training [24]. Tuning the regularization parameter involves finding the optimal strength of regularization that prevents over-fitting without significantly sacrificing performance.

6. Batch size: The batch size determines the number of training samples processed before updating the model's weights [24]. A smaller batch size may result in faster convergence but also introduce more noise in the weight updates [24]. Larger batch sizes can provide more stable weight updates but may slow down convergences. This parameter involves experimenting with different batch sizes and assessing their impact on training speed and model performance.

13.4 Result and Discussion

The experimental results of the study are presented in this section. Four phases of machine learning experimentations are implemented using a 10-fold cross-validation approach. This includes MLP training with the extracted feature attributes, training of MLP after One-Hot Encoding of the feature attributes, training of MLP after parameter optimization, and the training of MLP after One-Hot Encoding and parameter optimization.

13.4.1 Performance Metrics of MLP on Occlusion and Pose Sensitive Ear Facial Dataset

The provided results in Figure 13.3 is obtained from training the MLP model with the OPIB dataset.

i. The precision of 0.8789 indicates the model's ability to correctly classify positive instances (such as authentic users) while minimizing false positives. It reflects the accuracy of the optimistic predictions made by the model.
ii. The accuracy of 0.875 represents the overall correctness of the model's predictions.
iii. The F-measure of 0.8798 provides a correct assessment of the Perceptron's performance. It combines correctly identifying positive cases (precision) and capturing all positive instances (recall).

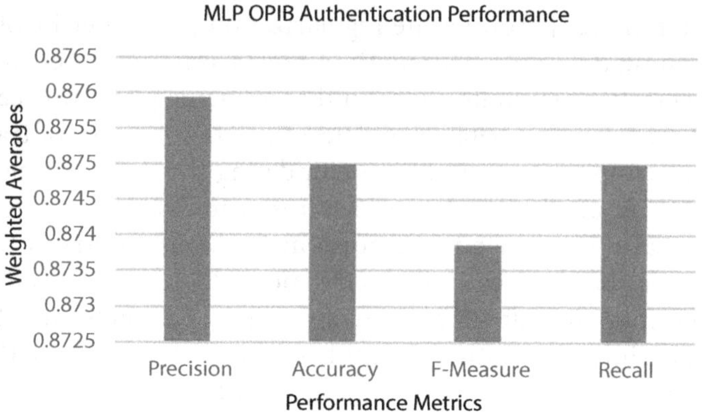

Figure 13.3 The performance of MLP on the OPIB dataset.

iv. The recall of 0.875 measures the model's ability to identify all positive instances (such as authentic users) out of the total positive instances. It indicates the model's sensitivity in detecting authentic users and minimizing false negatives.

13.4.2 Performance Metrics of MLP on Occlusion and Pose Sensitive Ear Facial Dataset After One-Hot Encoding

The provided results in Figure 13.4 correspond to the performance of the MLP model after applying one-hot encoding to the ear feature attributes.

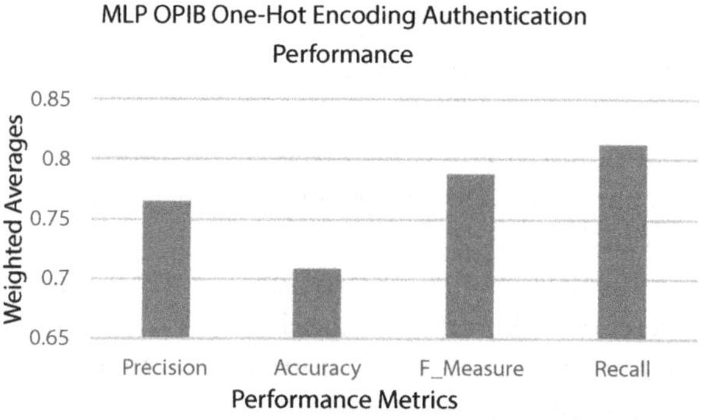

Figure 13.4 Performance of MLP on the OPIB dataset with one-hot encoding.

i. The precision of 0.754 indicates the model's ability to correctly classify positive instances (such as authentic users) while minimizing false positives. It reflects the accuracy of the optimistic predictions made by the model.
ii. The accuracy of 0.707 represents the overall correctness of the model's predictions.
iii. The F-measure of 0.77898 provides a balanced assessment of the model's performance by considering precision and recall. It combines correctly identifying positive cases (precision) and capturing all positive instances (recall).
iv. The recall of 0.826 measures the model's ability to identify all positive instances (such as authentic users) out of the total positive instances. It indicates the model's sensitivity in detecting authentic users and minimizing false negatives.

13.4.3 Performance Metrics of MLP on Occlusion and Pose Sensitive Ear Facial Dataset with Parameter Optimization

The provided results in Figure 13.5 indicate the performance of the MLP model with parameter optimization on the OPIB dataset.

i. The precision of 0.8 suggests that the model has a moderate ability to correctly identify positive cases (such as authentic users) while minimizing false positives (incorrectly classifying non-authentic users). It reflects the accuracy of the optimistic predictions made by the model.
ii. The accuracy of 0.82 indicates the overall correctness of the model's predictions. It represents the degree of correctly classified instances.
iii. The F-measure of 0.82 combines precision and recall into a single metric, providing a balanced assessment of the model's performance. It considers the ability to correctly identify positive cases (precision) and capture all positive cases (recall).
iv. The recall of 0.83 measures the ability of the model to correctly identify all positive instances (such as authentic users) out of the total positive instances. It indicates the model's sensitivity to detecting authentic users, minimizing false negatives (classifying an authentic user as non-authentic).

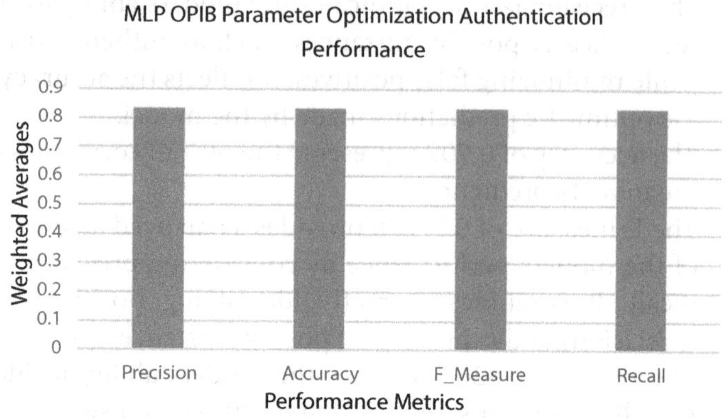

Figure 13.5 Performance of MLP on the OPIB dataset with parameter optimization.

13.4.4 Performance Metrics of MLP on Occlusion and Pose Sensitive Ear Facial Dataset After One-Hot Encoding with Parameter Optimization

The provided result in Figure 13.6 demonstrates the performance of MLP trained on the occlusion and pose-sensitive ear dataset for user authentication in this cybersecurity study. The achieved values indicate the effectiveness of the model in correctly classifying users.

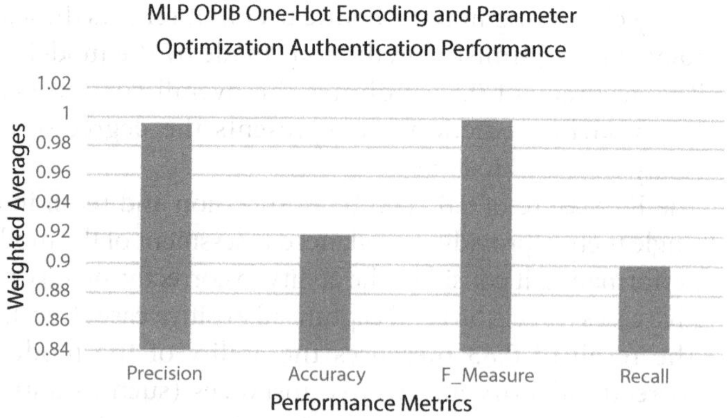

Figure 13.6 Performance of MLP on the OPIB dataset after one-hot encoding with parameter optimization.

i. The precision of 0.99567 indicates that the model can correctly identify positive cases (authenticated users) while minimizing false positives (incorrectly classifying non-authenticated users). It reflects the accuracy of the optimistic predictions made by the model.
ii. The accuracy of 0.919956 indicates the overall correctness of the model's predictions.
iii. The F-measure of 0.998887 combines precision and recall into a single metric, providing a balanced assessment of the model's performance. It is particularly useful when there is an imbalance between positive and negative cases in the dataset.
iv. The recall of 0.89987 measures the ability of the model to correctly identify all positive instances (authenticated users) out of the total positive instances. It indicates the model's sensitivity to detecting authentic users, minimizing false negatives (classifying an authentic user as non-authentic).

The results obtained from the trained MLP model demonstrate its effectiveness in accurately identifying authentic users. The achieved precision values consistently exceeded 0.75, indicating high accuracy in classifying positive instances. The accuracy values consistently surpassed 0.70, highlighting the overall correctness of the model's predictions. Furthermore, the F-measure values consistently exceeded 0.77, signifying a balanced assessment of the model's performance in terms of precision and recall. The recall values consistently exceeded 0.80, demonstrating the model's ability to capture a significant portion of the positive instances. These findings suggest that the trained MLP model, combined with the occlusion and pose-sensitive ear dataset, holds promise for reliable user authentication in cybersecurity applications. The high precision, accuracy, F-measure, and recall values indicate the model's potential to effectively distinguish between authentic and unauthorized users based on their ear features.

13.4.5 Overall Evaluation of MLP on the Experimental Measures

The obtained results provide valuable insights into the performance of MLP in relation to occlusion and pose-sensitive facial biometrics, one-hot encoding, and parameter optimization.

1. Occlusion and Pose Sensitive Facial Biometrics: The precision, accuracy, F-measure, and recall values achieved indicate that MLP effectively handles the challenges associated with occlusion and pose variations in facial biometrics. The model demonstrates its ability to learn and recognize individuals even in occlusions and changes in facial pose. This suggests that MLP can be a reliable solution for authentication tasks involving occlusion and pose-sensitive facial biometrics, making it suitable for real-world applications where such variations are common.
2. One-Hot Encoding: The results show the positive impact of one-hot encoding on the performance of MLP. MLP can effectively capture the distinct patterns and relationships in the data by encoding categorical variables, such as the ear feature attributes into binary vectors. This encoding technique enhances the model's ability to learn and discriminate between different categories, leading to higher precision, accuracy, F-measure, and recall values. The findings highlight the importance of feature encoding in maximizing the performance of MLP in biometric authentication tasks.
3. Parameter Optimization: The achieved precision, accuracy, F-measure, and recall values underscore the significance of parameter optimization in improving the performance of MLP. By fine-tuning the model's hyperparameters, such as the number of hidden layers, learning rate, and activation functions, MLP can adapt and learn from the data more effectively. This optimization process enhances the model's ability to generalize to unseen data and make accurate predictions. The results demonstrate the importance of carefully selecting and optimizing the parameters of MLP to achieve optimal performance in biometric authentication tasks.

The results suggest that MLP benefits from one-hot encoding and parameter optimization when applied to occlusion and pose-sensitive facial biometrics. These techniques enhance the model's ability to handle variations in facial features, capture meaningful patterns in the data, and improve its overall performance in user authentication tasks. The findings emphasize the potential of MLP as a reliable and effective approach for biometric authentication in real-world scenarios.

13.5 Conclusion

In conclusion, this study investigated Multilayer Perceptron's (MLP) performance in the context of occlusion and pose-sensitive facial biometrics for user authentication. The results demonstrated that MLP exhibited strong performance in handling challenges related to occlusion and pose variations, making it a suitable solution for real-world applications where such variations are common. Furthermore, the study highlighted the importance of one-hot encoding in improving the performance of MLP. MLP could effectively capture distinct patterns and relationships in the data by encoding categorical variables, precisely the ear feature attributes, into binary vectors. This encoding technique enhanced the model's ability to learn and discriminate between different categories, resulting in higher precision, accuracy, F-measure, and recall values.

Additionally, the study emphasized the significance of parameter optimization in maximizing the performance of MLP. By fine-tuning hyperparameters such as the number of hidden layers, learning rate, and activation functions, MLP adapted and learned from the data more effectively. This optimization improved the model's ability to generalize to unseen data and make accurate predictions.

The study significantly contributes to the knowledge of occlusion and pose-sensitive facial biometrics and Multilayer Perceptron (MLP) applications for user authentication. The findings demonstrate the effectiveness of MLP in handling challenges related to occlusion and pose variations, providing valuable insights into its applicability in real-world scenarios. Additionally, it highlights the importance of one-hot encoding in improving the performance of MLP. By effectively encoding categorical variables, specifically the names attached to each ear feature instance, into binary vectors 1 to 21, the model's ability to capture distinct patterns and relationships in the data is enhanced. Furthermore, the study emphasizes the significance of parameter optimization in maximizing the performance of MLP. By fine-tuning the hyperparameters, the model's ability to adapt and learn from the data is improved, leading to better generalization and more accurate predictions. Overall, the study contributes to understanding how MLP can be effectively applied in occlusion and pose-sensitive facial biometrics, providing valuable insights into the techniques of one-hot encoding and parameter optimization. These findings can inform future research and development efforts in the field, advancing the knowledge and application of MLP for user authentication and biometric systems.

References

1. Benavides, E., Fuertes, W., Sanchez, S., Sanchez, M., Classification of Phishing Attack Solutions by Employing Deep Learning Techniques: A Systematic Literature Review, in: *Developments and Advances in Defense and Security*, 2019.
2. Lansley, M., Kapetanakis, S., Polatidis, N., SEADer++ v2: Detecting Social Engineering Attacks using Natural Language Processing and Machine Learning, in: *020 International Conference on INnovations in Intelligent SysTems and Applications (INISTA)*, Novi Sad, 2020.
3. Banga, R., Bhardwaj, A., Peng, S.L., Shrivastava, G., Authorship Attribution for Online Social Media, in: *Social network analytics for contemporary business organizations*, pp. 141–165, IGI Global, 2018.
4. Achary, R. and Shelke, C.J., An Expert System for the Detection and Mitigation of Social Engineering Attacks (Sea) Using Machine Learning Algorithm. *Sentiment Analysis and Deep Learning*, vol. 1432, pp. 389–403, 2023.
5. Olaleye, T., Arogundade, O., Adenusi, C., Misra, S., Bello, A., Evaluation of image filtering parameters for plant biometrics improvement using machine learning, in: *International Conference on Soft Computing and its Engineering Applications*, 2021.
6. Tsinganos, N., Mavridis, I., Gritzalis, D., Utilizing Convolutional Neural Networks and Word Embeddings for Early-Stage Recognition of Persuasion in Chat-Based Social Engineering Attacks. *IEEE Access*, 10, 108517–108529, 2022.
7. Jain, A., Hong, L., Pankanti, S., Biometric identification. *Commun. ACM*, 43, 2, 90–98, 2000.
8. Hadid, A., Evans, N., Marcel, S., Fierrez, J., Biometrics systems under spoofing attack: an evaluation methodology and lessons learned. *IEEE Signal Process Mag.*, 32, 5, 20–30, 2015.
9. Lansley, M., Polatidis, N., Kapetanakis, S., SEADer: A Social Engineering Attack Detection Method Based on Natural Language Processing and Artificial Neural Networks, in: *International Conference on Computational Collective Intelligence*, 2019.
10. Lansley, M., Mouton, F., Kapetanakis, S., Polatidis, N., SEADer++: social engineering attack detection in online environments using machine learning. *J. Inform. Telecommun.*, 4, 3, 346–362, 2020.
11. Andrade, J.G., Progression of atrial fibrillation after cryoablation or drug therapy. *N. Engl. J. Med.*, 388, 2, 105–116, 2023.
12. Lavin, A. and Ahmad, S., Evaluating real-time anomaly detection algorithms–the Numenta anomaly benchmark, in: *2015 IEEE 14th international conference on machine learning and applications (ICMLA)*, 2015.
13. Wang, M., Yin, X., Zhu, Y., Hu, J., Representation learning and pattern recognition in cognitive biometrics: A survey. *Sensors*, 22, 14, 5111, 2022.

14. Olaleye, T.O., Arogundade, O.T., Misra, S., Abayomi-Alli, A., Kose, U., Predictive Analytics and Software Defect Severity: A Systematic Review and Future Directions. *Sci. Program.*, 2023, 1–23, 2023.
15. Bansal, H., Shrivastava, G., Nguyen, G.N., Stanciu, L.M., *Social Network Analytics for Contemporary Business Organizations*, pp. 177–181, IGI Global, USA, 2018.
16. Oyebiyi, O.G., Abayomi-Alli, A., Arogundade, O.T., Qazi, A., Imoize, A.L., Awotunde, J.B., A Systematic Literature Review on Human Ear Biometrics: Approaches, Algorithms, and Trend in the Last Decade. *Information*, 14, 3, 192, 2023.
17. Lin, C.-L. and Fan, K.-C., Biometric verification using thermal images of palm-dorsa vein patterns. *IEEE Trans. Circuits Syst. Video Technol.*, 14, 2, 199–213, 2004.
18. Alshazly, H., Linse, C., Barth, E., Idris, S.A., Martinetz, T., Towards explainable ear recognition systems using deep residual networks. *IEEE Access*, 9, 122254–122273, 2021.
19. Adebayo, A.-A., Elizabeth, B., Olusegun, F., Abayomi, D.G., Bamidele, A.J., An Occlusion and Pose Sensitive Image Dataset for Black Ear Recognition, Zenodo, 2023.
20. Stojkovic, A., Shopovska, I., Luong, H., Aelterman, J., Jovanov, L., Philips, W., The effect of the color filter array layout choice on state-of-the-art demosaicing. *Sensors*, 19, 14, 3215, 2019.
21. Mun, J., Jang, Y., Nam, Y., Kim, J., Edge-enhancing bi-histogram equalisation using guided image filter. *J. Visual Commun. Image Represent.*, 58, 688–700, 2019.
22. Rodríguez, P., Bautista, M.A., Gonzalez, J., Escalera, S., Beyond one-hot encoding: Lower dimensional target embedding. *Image Vision Comput.*, 75, 21–31, 2018.
23. Teoh, T.T., Zhang, Y., Nguwi, Y.Y., Elovici, Y., Ng, W., Analyst intuition inspired high velocity big data analysis using PCA ranked fuzzy k-means clustering with multi-layer perceptron (MLP) to obviate cyber security risk, in: *2017 13th International Conference on Natural Computation, Fuzzy Systems and Knowledge Discovery (ICNC-FSKD)*, 2017.
24. Lou, W., Xie, B., Aubril, J., Fan, Y., Luo, L., Arrivé, A., Optimized flow distributor for stabilized thermal stratification in a single-medium thermocline storage tank: A numerical and experimental study. *Energy*, 263, 125709, 2023.
25. Bottou, L., Stochastic gradient descent tricks, in: *Neural Networks: Tricks of the Trade*, Second Edition, pp. 421–436, 2012.

14

Study and Analysis of Cyberbullying Message Detection and Prevention Using Machine Learning Techniques

S. Shanmugam[1], S. Gunasekaran[2*] and N. Anusha[3]

[1]*Department of Computing Technologies, SRM Institute of Science and Technology, Kattankulathur, Chennai, Tamil Nadu, India*
[2]*Department of CSE, Ahalia School of Engineering and Technology, Pallakad, Kerala, India*
[3]*Department of Artificial Intelligence and Data Science, Vidya Jyothi Institute of Technology, Hyderabad, Telangana, India*

Abstract
The proliferation of Internet usage has facilitated the practice of networking through social media platforms while also intensifying issues such as online abuse and cyberbullying. Cyberbullying has a disproportionately lousy effect, with victims' health often deteriorating and some even resorting to suicide as a result. This chapter studies cyberbullying and classifying related messages to develop effective detection methods. We compare four machine learning approaches using Count Vectorizer and TF-IDF across two metrics. Recent advances in machine learning enable automatic cyberbullying detection, which can help mitigate the problem and assist victims. However, limitations exist in using machine learning for this task. While machine learning shows potential for cyberbullying detection, further research is required to improve accuracy and viability. This chapter discusses cyberbullying, proposes a classification framework, evaluates machine learning techniques, and suggests future research directions for developing more robust cyberbullying detection.

Keywords: Cyberbullying, machine learning, natural language processing (NLP), text classification, abusive language

**Corresponding author*: gunaphd@yahoo.com

Kavita Sharma, Vishnu Sharma, Parma Nand, Anil Kumar Sagar and Gulshan Shrivastava (eds.)
Securing the Digital Frontier: Threats and Advanced Techniques in Security and Forensics, (315–332)

14.1 Introduction

"Cyberbullying" refers to the intentional misuse of technology, like social media platforms, text messaging, or online discussion boards, to engage in acts of harassment, humiliation, or intimidation against an individual [1]. The phenomenon entails using technological means to engage in antagonistic or belligerent conduct directed at an individual [2]. The phenomenon of cyberbullying can exert a significant influence on the psychological well-being, interpersonal relationships, and holistic welfare of the individual subjected to such maltreatment. Cyberbullying can take many forms, including spreading rumors, uploading nasty remarks or photos, and sending intimidating communications [3, 4]. Cyberbullying can manifest across several channels, encompassing popular social media platforms such as Facebook, Twitter, Whatsapp, Snapchat, and online gaming groups.

One of the most pernicious elements of cyberbullying lies in its perpetual nature, as it can transpire incessantly throughout the day and night. Moreover, the perpetrator can exploit the anonymity provided by anonymous accounts or fabricated personas, impeding the victims' ability to evade the persistent torment [5]. This phenomenon may give rise to feelings of powerlessness and despondency among individuals who have experienced it. In contemporary times, the phenomenon of cyberbullying has gained significant traction, particularly within the younger demographic. Raising awareness about cyberbullying and implementing preventive measures and interventions are crucial for fostering a secure and supportive online community. The phenomenon of cyberbullying exhibits a diverse range of manifestations and can show varying degrees of severity.

The examples of cyberbullying [6] are:

1. **Sending abusive communications:** Repeatedly sending messages, threats, and foul language are examples.
2. **Spreading rumors or lies:** This includes spreading false information, posting embarrassing images/videos without consent, or creating fake profiles to imitate or mock someone.
3. **Exclusion and isolation:** Excluding someone from online chats or activities or forming cliques that shut out the victim.
4. **Posting cruel comments/photos:** Posting negative comments on social media or sharing hurtful images or memes.
5. **Doxing:** Refers to sharing personal information, such as phone numbers or addresses, without consent.

6. **Stalking:** Following someone online without their permission.
7. **Sexual harassment:** Sending unwanted sexual messages, images, or explicit content without consent.
8. **Cyberbullying can cause anxiety, depression, and suicidal thoughts:** Preventing and addressing harassment is vital.

Signs that may indicate cyberbullying:

1. **Mood changes:** Cyberbullying may make someone more emotional or agitated after using their device.
2. **Avoiding activities:** Victims may stop activities they once enjoyed or spend less time online.
3. **Changes in sleep/diet:** Cyberbullying stress may cause abrupt changes in sleep or eating habits.
4. **Poor performance:** Cyberbullying can negatively impact school or work performance.
5. **More screen time:** Victims may spend more time online to avoid face-to-face contact or monitor what's happening.
6. **Hiding social media:** Rapidly deleting or hiding accounts could signify cyberbullying.
7. **Shift in mood/behavior:** Cyberbullies can make victims feel anxious, depressed, or isolated.

Cyberharassment and cyberbullying are both forms of harmful behavior that utilize technology as a means to inflict injury, humiliation, or intimidation against an individual [7]. However, a notable distinction between cyberbullying and cyberharassment lies in the frequency and nature of the actions. Cyberbullying entails the recurrent perpetration of abusive behavior or the issuance of threats in an online environment. Conversely, cyberharassment pertains to single occurrences of such actions. Cyberharassment includes sending threatening communications, spreading libelous remarks, or sharing private photos. Gaming forums and communities also see cyber harassment. Cyberbullying is repeated internet abuse targeting vulnerable people. Both cyber harassment and cyberbullying can cause anxiety, depression, and suicidal thoughts. Preventing and managing online abuse is crucial [8].

This chapter employs an ensemble-based machine learning approach to detect and mitigate cyberbullying. The method aggregates predictions from multiple models to enhance overall algorithmic performance.

By combining the predictions of several models, the resulting predictions become more accurate and robust compared to any individual model. Some popular ensemble-based machine learning algorithms, including random forest, gradient boosting machines (GBM), Support Vector Machines, AdaBoost, and XGBoost, are employed to find the appropriate classifier model.

14.2 Literature Survey

Cyberbullying is an increasing concern in the digital era, and academics have looked into a variety of machine-learning techniques to detect and prevent it. One such technology that has shown promising results in detecting cyberbullying is ensemble learning. This section examines the current state of machine learning algorithms for categorizing and detecting cyberbullying.

14.2.1 Identifying Cyberbullies Through Twitter Data Analysis

Because of the risk of addiction and the decreased need for people to interact with one another in real life, certain people find that social media has become an indispensable tool [9, 10]. The amount of time that children spend participating in physically active pursuits is decreasing. In contrast, the amount of time adults spend using social media for positive and negative activities is increasing. The data on cyberbullying on Twitter was gathered for the study using a variety of approaches, including clustering, Naive Bayes, and Decision Tree J48, among others. Comparatively, the Decision Tree J48 approach had a success rate of one hundred percent, while the Naive Bayes method had an average success rate of ninety-two percent. On Twitter, psychological bullying is by far the most common type of cyberbullying, accounting for 31% of all reported incidences.

14.2.2 Cyber Bullying Detection on Social Media Using Machine Learning

This study [11] aims to improve Nave Bayes classifier capabilities for word extraction and model generation on text streaming. It evaluated 467 million tweets and 170,019 postings from cyberbullying Data. The Poly kernel was the most effective for identifying cyberbullying, with the highest accuracy at N-Gram 5 (92.75%). The studies [12–14] propose ensemble learning approaches for detecting cyberbullying on Instagram and Twitter. The ensemble approach outperforms individual classifiers, achieving an F1-score of 0.879 and an accuracy of 86.5%. This work [15] used Twitter to identify cyberbullying perpetrators and victims, analyze the reliability, and educate victims about the hazards of their behavior. They used a web-based tagger to analyze unlabeled tweets, identifying 257 regular users, 45 actors, 53 bullies, and 6 potential bullies. The study found that cyberbullying occurs in Indonesian tweets, with an F1 score of 67%. However, the system requires more feature extraction algorithms to differentiate between positive and negative terms. To improve feature extraction and classification precision, the researchers plan to implement an enhanced Indonesian POS labeling instrument and develop a notification system for cyber bullies.

14.2.3 Cyberbullying in Schools: A Research of Gender Differences

The articles [16], [17], and [18] examine the prevalence and type of teen cyberbullying among 264 students from three junior high schools. The study found that almost half of students were bullied, and one in four were cyberbullied, with over half of students knowing someone who was being cyberbullied. Most cyberbullying victims and bystanders did not report incidents to adults. The gender disparity in cyberbullying highlights the need for diversified approaches to research and intervention programs. The study [19] highlights the importance of regular safety measures for teenagers, as most prefer to be unobservant bystanders. Bystander education can provide essential ways to combat cyberbullying, and it is crucial to address the issue collaboratively by schools, families, communities, and society. This study has limitations, such as being gathered in a metropolis and considering cyberbullying in different age ranges, such as elementary and senior high schools.

14.2.4 Automated Detection of Cyberbullying Using Machine Learning

Cybercrime is increasing due to increased internet use and social media accessibility. Cyberbullies, anonymous and potentially damaging, can be detected using text processing, NLP, and machine learning algorithms [2, 20–23]. This project aims to automate cyberbullying detection on social media, improving moderation and response. Current methodologies include supervised learning, SVM, and Naïve Bayes.

14.3 Implementation of Cyberbullying Model

14.3.1 Dataset Description

The datasets are collected from various sources in Twitter and Formspring. The collected data are in the form of content messages, posts, or comments that contain occurrences of cyberbullying. The dataset ought to be different and contain an adequate number of cases. Figure 14.1 represents the Sample dataset, and preprocessed data are diagrammatically represented in Figure 14.2.

Information Preprocessing: Preprocess the content information by evacuating halt words and accentuations and changing overall content to lowercase. You'll moreover need to expel certain words that are not significant to cyberbullying, such as "the" and "a." Change over the content data into numerical vectors employing a vectorization method, such as TF-IDF or Word2Vec.

tweet_text	cyberbullying_type
In other words #katandandre, your food was crapilicious! #mkr	not_cyberbullying
Why is #aussietv so white? #MKR #theblock #ImACelebrityAU #today #sunrise #	not_cyberbullying
@XochitlSuckkks a classy whore? Or more red velvet cupcakes?	not_cyberbullying
@Jason_Gio meh. :P thanks for the heads up, but not too concerned about ano	not_cyberbullying
@RudhoeEnglish This is an ISIS account pretending to be a Kurdish account. Lik	not_cyberbullying
@Raja5aab @Quickieleaks Yes, the test of god is that good or bad or indifferen	not_cyberbullying
Itu sekolah ya bukan tempat bully! Ga jauh kaya neraka	not_cyberbullying
Karma. I hope it bites Kat on the butt. She is just nasty. #mkr	not_cyberbullying
@stockputout everything but mostly my priest	not_cyberbullying
Rebecca Black Drops Out of School Due to Bullying:	not_cyberbullying
@Jord_Is_Dead http://t.co/UsQInYW5Gn	not_cyberbullying
The Bully flushes on KD http://twitvid.com/A2TNP	not_cyberbullying
Ughhhh #MKR	not_cyberbullying
RT @Kurdsnews: Turkish state has killed 241 children in last 11 years http://t.co	not_cyberbullying
Love that the best response to the hotcakes they managed to film was a non-cc	not_cyberbullying
@yasmimcaci @Bferrarii PAREM DE FAZER BULLYING COMIGO =(UHAHUAH BAN	not_cyberbullying
@sarinhacoral @Victor_Maggi tadinhu de mim , sofrendo bulling viu MIMI'	not_cyberbullying
@0xabad1dea @kelseytheodore2 twitter is basically the angry letters of our ge	not_cyberbullying
Best pick up line? Hi, you're cute... ?: I love how people call James Potter is a bi	not_cyberbullying
Now I gotta walk to classss?! I officially hate the stupid bus system! -_-	not_cyberbullying
@halalcunty @biebervalue @liamxkiwi @greenlinerzjm @halalflaws I know Sa	not_cyberbullying
Kids LoveðŸ""â¤ @ Mohamad Bin Zayed City Ù…Ø¬ÙŠÙ†Ø© Ù…ØÙ…Ø¯ Ø¨Ù† Ø	not_cyberbullying

Figure 14.1 Dataset sample.

```
# preprocessing functions

# converting tweet text to lower case
def text_lower(text):
    return text.str.lower()

# removing stopwoords from the tweet text
def clean_stopwords(text):
    # stopwords list that needs to be excluded from the data
    stopwordlist = ['a', 'about', 'above', 'after', 'again', 'ain', 'all', 'am', 'an',
              'and','any','are', 'as', 'at', 'be', 'because', 'been', 'before',
              'being', 'below', 'between','both', 'by', 'can', 'd', 'did', 'do',
              'does', 'doing', 'down', 'during', 'each','few', 'for', 'from',
              'further', 'had', 'has', 'have', 'having', 'he', 'her', 'here',
              'hers', 'herself', 'him', 'himself', 'his', 'how', 'i', 'if', 'in',
              'into','is', 'it', 'its', 'itself', 'just', 'll', 'm', 'ma',
              'me', 'more', 'most','my', 'myself', 'now', 'o', 'of', 'on', 'once',
              'only', 'or', 'other', 'our', 'ours','ourselves', 'out', 'own', 're',
              's', 'same', 'she', "shes", 'should', "shouldve",'so', 'some', 'such',
              't', 'than', 'that', "thatll", 'the', 'their', 'theirs', 'them',
              'themselves', 'then', 'there', 'these', 'they', 'this', 'those',
              'through', 'to', 'too','under', 'until', 'up', 've', 'very', 'was',
              'we', 'were', 'what', 'when', 'where','which','while', 'who', 'whom',
              'why', 'will', 'with', 'won', 'y', 'you', "youd","youll", "youre",
              "youve", 'your', 'yours', 'yourself', 'yourselves']
    STOPWORDS = set(stopwordlist)
    return " ".join([word for word in str(text).split() if word not in STOPWORDS])
```

Figure 14.2 Pre-processed dataset using Python.

14.3.2 Architecture and Functionalities of the Proposed System

Figure 14.3 illustrates the three primary stages of implementing the cyberbullying model. The three main components in this context are preprocessing, feature extraction, and classification. The preprocessing stage encompasses removing noise and superfluous text to clean the data. The preprocessing stage is conducted in the following manner:

- Stage 1: This initial stage, known as tokenization, is when phrases or entire paragraphs of text are processed and transformed into individual words, then organized and presented as a list.
- Stage 2: It performs text lowering; this lowers all the letters in the list of words that escaped tokenization, such as "THIS IS AWESOME," which becomes "this is awesome."

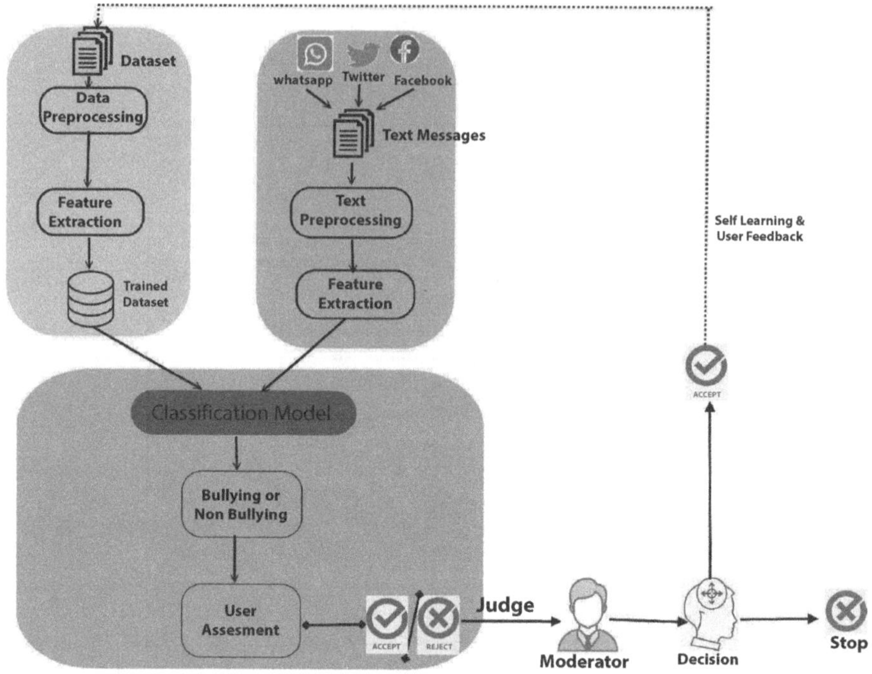

Figure 14.3 Overall architecture of proposed approach.

- Stage 3 of the data preparation procedure involves removing stop words and encoding letters like "n" and "t." The objective of this stage is to eliminate words and characters that do not contribute meaningful information to the classifiers.

The feature extraction process can be conducted by applying text processing techniques on textual data obtained from social media platforms like Twitter, WhatsApp, and Facebook. Once the feature extraction process is completed, the input is inputted into classification algorithms, categorizing the provided data into two distinct classes: cyberbullying and non-cyberbullying. The verification process can also involve a moderator, and the model can then utilize the results to further its self-learning capabilities.

14.3.2.1 NLP Toolkit for Implementation

The Python-based Natural Language Toolkit (NLTK) is the best NLP model-building tool for research and education. NLTK has a large community and offers language processing tutorials, sample datasets, and a Python language processing manual. NLTK is a great starting place for NLP skills, but it takes time to perfect. Its modular architecture allows tokenization, tagging, stemming, parsing, and classification, offering significant NLP capabilities. Despite its learning curve, NLTK is a versatile, well-supported library for NLP skills and model creation. Its modular design allows for several NLP functions.

NLP approaches are widely employed in the field of data science. Many include Bag of Words, Tokenization, Stop word removal, Stemming, lemmatization, and keyword extraction.

Assessment and testing are pivotal to creating a cyberbullying location framework utilizing machine learning. The reason for the evaluation and testing is to guarantee that the demonstration is precise, dependable, and viable in identifying cyberbullying. Here are the steps for assessing and testing a cyberbullying location framework utilizing machine learning:

1. Segment the dataset: Segment the dataset into sets for preparation, approval, and testing. The demonstration is prepared with the preparation set, the hyperparameters are adjusted with the approval set, and the model's performance is evaluated with the testing set.
2. Characterize assessment measurements: Select suitable assessment measurements such as accuracy, review, F1-score, and precision to the degree of the model's execution.
3. Prepare the demonstration: The show utilizes the preparing set and assesses its execution on the approval set. Alter hyperparameters based on executing the approval set, such as learning rate, bunch estimate, and regularization.
4. Test the show: Once the show is prepared and hyperparameters are optimized, assess its execution on the testing set. Utilize the assessment measurements characterized in step 2 to degree the model's execution.
5. Utilize a perplexity lattice: Create a disarray framework to imagine the model's execution on the testing set. A perplexity network measures the proportion of true positives, true negatives, false positives, and false negatives.
6. Analyze mistakes: Analyze the errors made by demonstrating and distinguishing common patterns. This may offer assistance in recognizing regions for change within the show.
7. Cross-validation: Perform cross-validation to approve the model's execution over distinctive information folds. Cross-validation includes dividing the information into different

folds, preparing the show on one overlay, and testing it on another. This makes a difference to guarantee that the model's execution is steady over different parts of the information.

8. Utilize real-world information: Finally, test the demonstration of real-world details to assess its execution in a real-world situation.

In outline, assessing and testing a cyberbullying location framework includes part of the dataset, characterizing assessment measurements, preparing and testing the show, employing a disarray framework, analyzing blunders, performing cross-validation, and testing the demonstration on real-world information. By taking these steps, you'll guarantee that your cyberbullying location framework is precise, dependable, and compelling in recognizing cyberbullying.

14.3.3 Performance Evaluation Measures

The performance evaluation measures considered in this work are accuracy, precision, recall, and F1Score [24]. The detailed description is given as follows:

Accuracy: Accuracy is the number of categories a model predicts correctly divided by its total predictions. Classification model accuracy is measured by True Positive (TP), True Negative (TN), False Positive (FP), and False Negative (FN). These measures are often used to evaluate machine learning algorithm efficiency. Accuracy shows how well a model performs for a dataset by aggregating numerous relevant performance measurements into a single value. Accuracy evaluates model performance holistically by considering all these factors.

$$Accuracy = \frac{TP + TN}{(TP + TN + FP + FN)} \tag{14.1}$$

Precision: Precision describes a classification model's ability to retrieve only relevant data points and filter out noise. Mathematically, precision is calculated by dividing the number of true positives by the total number of optimistic predictions, including both true and false positives.

$$Precision = \frac{TP}{(TP + FP)} \tag{14.2}$$

Recall: A model's ability to locate every relevant case in a data set. The total number of true positives divided by the total number of true positives + false negatives yields recall.

$$Recall = \frac{TP}{(TP + FN)} \quad (14.3)$$

F1Score: Precision and Recall are weighted averaged to provide the F1-Score. The formula below is used to determine the F1 Score. A single metric that encompasses both features, the F1-score aids in combining precision and recall.

$$F1Score = \frac{2 \times Precision \times Recall}{(Precision + Recall)} \quad (14.4)$$

14.4 Evaluation and Comparison of Machine Learning Techniques for Cyber Bullying

This section discusses the results of various classifiers using TF-IDF and CountVector-based feature selection approaches. A detailed discussion of the proposed approach is given as follows:

Table 14.1 presents a comprehensive comparative evaluation of seven classification machine learning models on a binary classification dataset. Providing metrics like accuracy, precision, recall, and F1 score enables data-driven assessments of each model's strengths, weaknesses, and overall suitability for the problem, which is graphically given in Figure 14.4. Analyzing these key performance metrics facilitates valuable insights into the models' efficacy in discriminating between the two classes under consideration based on the patterns gleaned from the dataset. Examining the interplay between metrics like precision and recall illuminates subtle differences in how the models perform classification. The set of models analyzed provides diversity in algorithm types - from more straightforward linear and tree models like Naive Bayes and decision tree to ensemble methods like random forest and boosted decision trees to flexible nonlinear models like SVM. This allows for determining if the evaluation dataset and problem benefit more from simple or complex models in practice.

Table 14.1 Performance measurement of classifiers using TF-IDF-based feature selection.

Classifier	Accuracy (%)	Precision	Recall	F1 score
DT	87.38	0.83	0.94	0.88
RF	89.71	0.91	0.90	0.91
XGB	87.38	0.91	0.87	0.89
NB	88.78	0.98	0.89	0.91
SVM	**89.71**	**0.94**	**0.88**	**0.91**
Bagging DT	88.08	0.87	0.91	0.89
Boosting DT	87.38	0.88	0.89	0.89

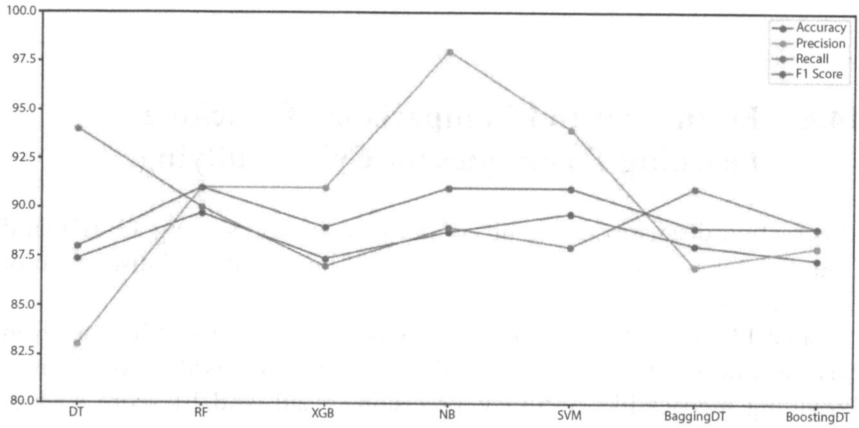

Figure 14.4 Graphical representation of performance measurement of classifiers using TF-IDF-based feature selection.

Accuracy indicates the overall proportion of correct predictions. All models achieve 87% to 90% accuracy, implying decent class separation on this dataset. The top accuracy by SVM and random forest points to the strength of nonlinear processing. However, every model has at most 90% accuracy significantly, suggesting substantial overlap between classes. Precision reveals incorrectly predicted positives out of all optimistic predictions. High precision signifies lower false positives. Naive Bayes demonstrates high 98% precision, meaning almost all its optimistic predictions were correct. Comparatively, base decision trees and bagging show poorer 83% to 88%

precision, making more false positive errors: recall or true positive rate measures the percentage of actual positives detected. Values near 100% are desired. Base decision tree and its bagged variant achieve the highest recall, exceeding 90%, meaning they correctly identify almost all positive instances despite more false positives. Random forest lags at 90% recall.

The F1 score balances both recall and precision by taking their harmonic mean. This compresses sensitivity and predictive value into a singular metric. Naive Bayes, SVM, and random forest achieve the best F1 scores, all above 90%, underlining effectiveness. The probabilistic Naive Bayes emerges as the most precise model, minimizing false positives. However, SVM and random forest match it on F1 and accuracy through slightly better recall. The nonlinear ensemble models do not confer noticeable gains over the base decision tree, implying the problem likely does not require high model complexity. With domain context, further inferences could be made about which models might be preferred for factors like interpretability, performance on unknown data, or misclassification costs. However, the critical metrics provided here enable a quantitative comparison of the real-world effectiveness of this evaluation dataset. They demonstrate how to critically analyze classification model performance in a comprehensive and unbiased data-driven manner.

Table 14.2 presents a comprehensive performance comparison of seven classification machine learning models on a binary text classification task. The models are evaluated on a shared dataset using the CountVectorizor for standard text feature extraction. The table enables an easy relative assessment of each model's capabilities by reporting accuracy, precision, recall, and F1 scores as percentages, as shown in Figure 14.5. Several key insights can be drawn from analyzing the evaluation metrics. All models achieve vital accuracy between 89% and 91%, indicating good overall predictive performance and separation between the text classes. However, each model is at most the others in accuracy on this dataset. The random forest ensemble model attains the highest recall score of 93%, which most accurately identifies the true positive cases from the class distribution. However, its precision is lower at 88%, implying it makes more false-positive errors despite detecting more actual positives. Conversely, the XGBoost model demonstrates the highest percentage precision of 94%, so most of its positive predictions are correct. However, its recall is lower at 89%, so it captures fewer true positives than random forest. SVM and logistic regression achieve the top F1 scores, which balance precision and recall. Their comprehensively strong results imply that these models may be best suited for deployment, depending on factors like interpretability needs and misclassification costs.

Table 14.2 Performance measurement of classifiers using CountVectorizer-based feature selection.

Classifier	Accuracy (%)	Precision	Recall	F1 score
LR	90.65	0.93	0.90	0.92
DT	89.71	0.88	0.93	0.91
RF	90.18	0.92	0.90	0.91
XGB	89.95	0.94	0.89	0.91
SVM	90.88	**0.92**	**0.91**	**0.92**
Bagging DT	89.25	0.93	0.88	0.91
Boosting DT	89.01	0.89	0.91	0.90

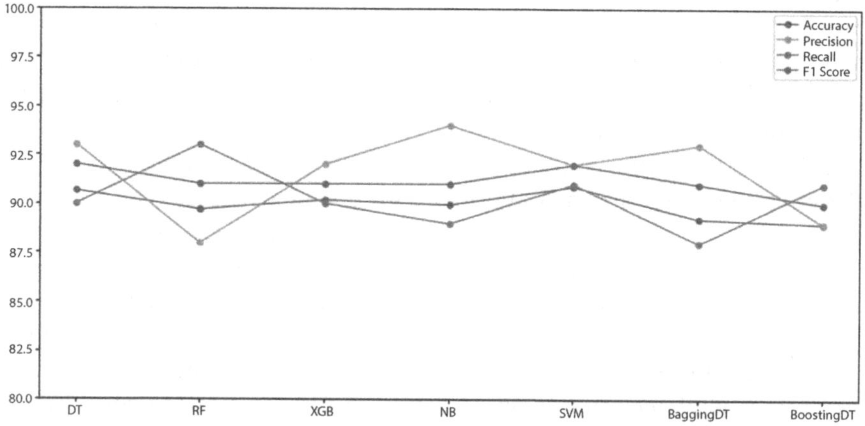

Figure 14.5 Graphical representation of performance measurement of classifiers using CountVectorizor-based feature selection.

Nonlinear ensemble models like random forest and gradient boosting do not confer significant gains over the simpler decision tree model. This suggests that the textual dataset may not require highly complex models, and linear decision boundaries may suffice for good performance. The Naive Bayes model is surprisingly strong, matching the validation set metrics of the more advanced methods. Its probabilistic foundations are well-suited for text-data applications. In summary, the percentage-based metrics enable empirical comparison of model performance with the true evaluation dataset. The insights lay the foundation for selecting the suitable model for deployment based on its precision-recall tradeoffs and overall effectiveness.

14.5 Conclusion

Cyberbullying continues to harm mental health, social lives, and safety, especially for vulnerable kids and women. Social media has expanded online harassment, abuse, and bullying. Cyberbullying detection requires automated methods. A recent study suggests that ensemble models can identify cyberbullying. Current methods lack textual feature comprehension, context modeling, generalization across populations and platforms, and abuse-type classification. Machine learning can spot cyberbullying early and implement multimodal prevention to create safe, supportive online communities with attentive collaboration. Nuanced, thorough, and ethical answers remain a research problem. The analysis and results show that SVM performs better than ensemble classification approaches.

References

1. Giumetti, G.W. and Kowalski, R.M., Cyberbullying via social media and well-being. *Curr. Opin. Psychol.*, 45, 101314, 2022.
2. Evangelio, C., Rodriguez-Gonzalez, P., Fernandez-Rio, J., Gonzalez-Villora, S., Cyberbullying in elementary and middle school students: A systematic review. *Comput. Educ.*, 176, 104356, 2022.
3. Pichel, R., Feijóo, S., Isorna, M., Varela, J., Rial, A., Analysis of the relationship between school bullying, cyberbullying, and substance use. *Child. Youth Serv. Rev.*, 134, 106369, 2022.
4. Chan, T.K., Cheung, C.M., Benbasat, I., Xiao, B., Lee, Z.W., Bystanders join in cyberbullying on social networking sites: the deindividuation and moral disengagement perspectives. *Inf. Syst. Res.*, 34, 3, 828–846, 2023.
5. Kibe, L., Kwanya, T., Kogos, A., Ogolla, E., Onsare, C., Types of Cyberbullying Experienced on Facebook by Undergraduate Students in Kenyan Universities. *J. Cyberspace Stud.*, 6, 2, 149–182, 2022.
6. Yi, P. and Zubiaga, A., Session-based cyberbullying detection in social media: A survey. *Online Soc. Netw. Media*, 36, 100250, 2023.
7. Saleem, S., Khan, N.F., Zafar, S., Raza, N., Systematic literature reviews in cyberbullying/cyber harassment: A tertiary study. *Technol. Soc.*, 70, 102055, 2022.

8. Abarna, S., Sheeba, J.I., Jayasrilakshmi, S., Devaneyan, S.P., Identification of cyber harassment and intention of target users on social media platforms. *Eng. Appl. Artif. Intell.*, 115, 105283, 2022.
9. Mangaonkar, A., Pawar, R., Chowdhury, N.S., Raje, R.R., Enhancing collaborative detection of cyberbullying behavior in Twitter data. *Cluster Comput.*, 25, 2, 1263–1277, 2022.
10. Muzakir, A., Syaputra, H., Panjaitan, F., A Comparative Analysis of Classification Algorithms for Cyberbullying Crime Detection: An Experimental Study of Twitter Social Media in Indonesia. *Sci. J. Inf.*, 9, 2, 133–138, 2022.
11. Li, X., Xie, X., Wang, J., Tang, Y., Text sentiment analysis based on improved naive bayes algorithm, in: *International Conference on Adaptive and Intelligent Systems*, Springer International, Cham, pp. 513–523, 2022.
12. Singh, N. and Sharma, S.K., Review of Machine Learning methods for Identification of Cyberbullying in Social Media, in: *2021 International Conference on Artificial Intelligence and Smart Systems (ICAIS)*, pp. 284–288, IEEE, 2021.
13. Talpur, B.A. and O'Sullivan, D., Cyberbullying severity detection: A machine learning approach. *PLoS One*, 15, 10, e0240924, 2020.
14. Perera, A. and Fernando, P., Accurate cyberbullying detection and prevention on social media. *Procedia Comput. Sci.*, 181, 605–611, 2021.
15. Gamal, D., Alfonse, M., Jiménez-Zafra, S.M., Aref, M., Intelligent multilingual cyber-hate detection in online social networks: taxonomy, approaches, datasets, and open challenges. *Big Data Cogn. Comput.*, 7, 2, 58, 2023.
16. Kasahara, G.M., Houlihan, D., Estrada, C., Gender differences in social media use and cyberbullying in Belize: A preliminary report. *Int. J. Psychol. Stud.*, 11, 2, 32, 2019.
17. Yang, B., Wang, B., Sun, N., Xu, F., Wang, L., Chen, J., Sun, C., The consequences of cyberbullying and traditional bullying victimization among adolescents: Gender differences in psychological symptoms, self-harm and suicidality. *Psychiatry Res.*, 306, 114219, 2021.
18. Zhang, D., Huebner, E.S., Tian, L., Longitudinal associations among neuroticism, depression, and cyberbullying in early adolescents. *Comput. Hum. Behav.*, 112, 106475, 2020.
19. Aizenkot, D., Cyberbullying experiences in classmates 'WhatsApp discourse, across public and private contexts. *Child. Youth Serv. Rev.*, 110, 104814, 2020.
20. Nirmal, N., Sable, P., Patil, P., Kuchiwale, S., Automated detection of cyberbullying using machine learning. *Int. Res. J. Eng. Technol. (IRJET)*, 7, 12, 2054–2061, 2021.
21. Khari, M., Shrivastava, G., Gupta, S., Gupta, R., Role of cyber security in today's scenario, in: *Detecting and mitigating robotic cyber security risks*, pp. 177–191, IGI Global, UK, 2017.

22. Shrivastava, G., Sharma, K., Khari, M., Zohora, S.E., Role of cyber security and cyber forensics in India, in: *Handbook of Research on Network Forensics and Analysis Techniques*, pp. 143–161, IGI Global, UK, 2018.
23. Shrivastava, G., Gupta, D., Sharma, K. (Eds.), *Cyber Crime and Forensic Computing: Modern Principles, Practices, and Algorithms*, De Gruyter, UK, 2021.
24. Shrivastava, G., Kumar, P., Gupta, B.B., Bala, S., Dey, N. (Eds.), *Handbook of research on network forensics and analysis techniques*, IGI Global, UK, 2018.

15

Future Directions in Digital Forensics and Cybersecurity

Elipe Arjun and Priyanka Singh*

Amity Institute of Forensic Sciences, Amity University, Noida, India

Abstract
Digital forensics and cybersecurity fields constantly change to keep up with emerging technologies and evolving threats. This chapter offers valuable insight into the prospects of these fields, with a focus on key trends and challenges. It explores the potential impact of groundbreaking technologies like quantum computing, Blockchain, and artificial intelligence on digital forensics and cybersecurity. Moreover, it highlights the growing importance of automation and machine learning in digital forensics while examining the changing nature of cyber threats. The chapter emphasizes the need for collaborative, interdisciplinary approaches to combat future threats effectively. It also stresses the ethical and human elements that require careful consideration in developing and implementing upcoming digital forensics and cybersecurity practices. As these fields evolve, professionals and researchers must stay abreast of these trends and challenges.

***Keywords*:** Cyber security, digital forensics, quantum computing, block chain, artificial intelligence

15.1 Overview of Digital Forensics and Cyber Forensics

In the rapidly evolving landscape of technology, digital forensics and cybersecurity have become indispensable fields in safeguarding sensitive information and combating the ever-increasing threat of cybercrime. The continuous advancements in digital systems and the widespread

**Corresponding author*: psingh31@amity.edu

Kavita Sharma, Vishnu Sharma, Parma Nand, Anil Kumar Sagar and Gulshan Shrivastava (eds.) Securing the Digital Frontier: Threats and Advanced Techniques in Security and Forensics, (333–366)

connectivity of devices have created new challenges that necessitate proactive measures in cybersecurity and digital forensics [1].

This chapter explores future directions in digital forensics and cybersecurity, providing insights into emerging trends, techniques, and technologies that shape the landscape of investigations and security practices. By understanding these future directions, professionals in the field can equip themselves with the necessary knowledge and tools to respond effectively to the evolving strategies employed by cyber criminals and contribute to the development of robust defense strategies.

This chapter begins by giving an overview of the present status of digital forensics and cybersecurity to lay the groundwork for the following issues. It examines the critical methodologies and tools commonly used in digital investigations and the prevailing cybersecurity practices implemented by organizations. This examination helps identify the existing gaps and limitations, which in turn necessitate the exploration of future directions in these fields.

This chapter also covers the developing trends and technologies that promise to shape the future of digital forensics and cybersecurity. Machine learning, artificial intelligence, blockchain, and platform-as-a-service forensics are investigated because these can transform investigations and strengthen defenses against online threats.

This chapter seeks to provide readers with a complete picture of the future environment by doing an extensive review of the state of digital forensics and cybersecurity now and examining potential future advances. For scholars, practitioners, and politicians attempting to negotiate the complex difficulties of the modern age, the ideas given here are an invaluable resource.

The future directions in digital forensics and cybersecurity require a multidimensional approach encompassing technological advancements, legal frameworks, and stakeholder collaboration. This chapter explores these aspects and emphasizes the importance of proactive measures in mitigating emerging threats [2].

In addition to technological advancements, legal frameworks and regulations play a crucial role in guiding the practices of cybersecurity and digital forensics. This chapter discusses the need for robust legislation and international cooperation to address global cybercrime challenges effectively. It examines legal considerations such as privacy, data protection, and the admissibility of digital evidence in different jurisdictions.

Collaboration between numerous stakeholders is necessary to determine the future of cybersecurity and digital forensics. The chapter examines the importance of information sharing, knowledge exchange, and public-private partnerships between businesses, police enforcement, and the government. These collaborations promote innovation, facilitate the development of best practices, and provide a better response from everyone to emerging dangers.

Digital forensics and cybersecurity fields require ongoing study and improvement due to the complexity and sophistication of cyber threats. The need for continual education and training is emphasized in this chapter to provide professionals with the tools they need to deal with ever-evolving threats effectively.

It emphasizes the value of academic degrees, certifications, and professional associations to promote expertise and knowledge exchange. As we explore the potential avenues for digital forensics and cybersecurity, it becomes clear that a comprehensive and interdisciplinary strategy is needed to manage the always-evolving threat landscape. We can proactively negotiate the obstacles posed by cybercriminals and create a safe digital environment for people, companies, and society by keeping up with developing trends, harnessing technology breakthroughs, improving legislative frameworks, and encouraging collaboration [3].

The future of digital forensics and cybersecurity directions provide a comprehensive understanding of the current landscape, emerging threats, and countermeasures. We can strive toward a safer and more secure digital future by anticipating and adapting to evolving challenges. Figure 15.1 shows the image of digital forensic expert witness.

15.2 Introduction

Although digital forensics may be a growing field, its roots can be found in 1970, when engineers found the lone duplicate of a database that had been accidentally wiped. Digital forensics has advanced rapidly from its foundation. Nowadays, digital investigations can address issues such as recovering deleted data or reconstructing attacks offline by dumping network traffic. The standard toolkit used for digital forensics covers all the various components of the cyber investigation process [4].

However, as previously suggested, evolutions in the ICT sector decrease its effectiveness and present risks. Numerous techniques are used to collect digital data, which raises privacy concerns. Private information about the user can be taken because there is no protection. Insiders who want to steal money and damage personal data may target the computing device. The roots of cybercrime need to be better understood and supported by evidence. Historical evidence shows that the first computer sabotage occurred

Figure 15.1 Image of digital forensic expert witness.

in the 19th century. The leading cause of escalating cybercrimes and conflicts is gathering digital evidence and information [5].

In modern times, criminals who lack digital fingerprints present a challenge for law enforcement agencies, forensic investigators, juries, and IT security experts. Organized groups utilize sophisticated techniques to commit money laundering, drug trafficking, terrorist acts, and smuggling. Digital evidence from thieves who use laptops, smartphones, and computers can be used in court proceedings. Digital data such as network traces, messages, audio, and video is crucial in crime scene investigations. Forensic principles are applied to ensure a forensically sound investigation. Cybercrime has evolved, and criminals often use sophisticated methods to breach networks, resulting in data leakage and breaches. Forensic investigations are crucial in incident replies to gather digital proof. Digital devices such as computers, smartphones, and IoT devices are analyzed using forensic principles, and acquisition-capable tools must adhere to legal criteria and be supported by computational procedures.

In today's interconnected world, digital forensics and cybersecurity play a pivotal role in safeguarding our digital lives and critical infrastructures. As technology advances at an unprecedented pace, the landscape of cyber threats becomes increasingly complex and sophisticated. Anticipating and preparing for future threats is not just a prudent approach but an imperative.

This chapter delves into the crucial task of envisioning the future of digital forensics and cybersecurity, exploring how emerging technologies, trends, collaborations, ethics, and challenges shape these fields.

15.2.1 Rapid Technological Evolution

The fusion of emerging technologies like quantum computing, artificial intelligence (AI), and the Internet of Things (IoT) transforms how humans interact with and protect digital systems. Quantum computing presents an opportunity for more excellent cryptography and a barrier to preserving data privacy because it can crack existing encryption techniques. The ability of AI to automate jobs, analyze massive amounts of information, and predict cyber dangers can transform how risks are detected and investigated [6].

15.2.2 An Ever-Changing Threat Landscape

The proliferation of linked devices and an uptick in cyberattacks are make digital forensics and cybersecurity more challenging in the future. Due to nation-state actors' exploitation of sophisticated, persistent threats and ransomware attacks on critical infrastructure, the stakes have never been higher. The success of future cybersecurity initiatives depends on our capacity to grasp these new threats and create efficient countermeasures [7].

15.3 Technologies and Their Impact

A technological revolution is about to occur in cybersecurity and digital forensics. Quantum computing can improve cryptography since it can solve complicated problems at inconceivable rates for classical computers. However, given its ability to circumvent widely used encryption systems, cryptographic techniques for protecting sensitive data must be re-examined. Artificial intelligence (AI) comprises machine learning and deep learning algorithms, revolutionizing threat identification, routine labor automation, and vulnerability prediction.

15.3.1 Balancing Opportunity and Threat

New Technologies Are Changing the Environment: A technological revolution occurs in cybersecurity and digital forensics. Quantum computing can improve cryptography since it can solve complicated problems at inconceivable rates for classical computers. However, given its ability to circumvent widely used encryption systems, cryptographic techniques for protecting sensitive data must be re-examined. Threat identification, regular work automation, and vulnerability prediction are revolutionized by artificial intelligence, including machine learning and deep learning algorithms. It is essential to anticipate and prepare for future threats. This chapter discusses the emerging technologies likely to impact digital forensics and cybersecurity soon and the emerging trends and future directions in these fields.

15.4 Impact of Emerging Technologies on Digital Forensics and Cybersecurity

Quantum computing is one of the most critical new technologies impacting digital forensics and cybersecurity. There is a chance that quantum computers can decrypt digital data that is currently encrypted. Cybercriminals may find it considerably simpler to steal sensitive data or carry out cyberattacks. Artificial intelligence is a new technology that impacts digital forensics and cybersecurity (AI). Many of the processes required in digital forensics, including data processing and pattern identification, can be automated using artificial intelligence (AI) [8]. This could aid in accelerating and improving the forensic investigation process. Cybercriminals, however, can also employ AI to create more advanced attack strategies; new technologies are constantly reshaping the digital landscape of forensics and cybersecurity. As these technologies evolve, they present opportunities and challenges for professionals in these fields. Here are some notable emerging technologies and their impact on digital forensics and cybersecurity:

15.4.1 Artificial Intelligence (AI) and Machine Learning (ML)

AI and ML are frequently used to analyze data, detect patterns, and make predictions. AI enhances threat detection in cybersecurity by identifying anomalies and adapting to new attack methods. In digital forensics, AI automates evidence analysis, making the process faster and more efficient. AI and ML automate tasks in digital forensics, such as data analysis, threat identification, and incident response [9]. This frees up analysts to investigate cases more quickly. Figure 15.2 shows how AI & machine learning using NVIDIA A40 GPU and Scikit-learn.

Figure 15.2 AI & machine learning using NVIDIA A40 GPU and Scikit-learn

15.4.2 Quantum Computing

Quantum computers have the potential to break current encryption methods, which could compromise the security of sensitive data. However, they can also be used to develop new encryption techniques resistant to quantum attacks. Digital forensics might also be affected as quantum computing could impact data recovery and encryption-related investigations. Although it is still in its infancy, quantum computing has the potential to transform digital forensics and cybersecurity. Quantum computers could break current encryption standards, making it much easier for attackers to steal data [10].

15.4.3 5G Technology

As we move towards implementing 5G networks, it's essential to consider the potential cybersecurity risks that come with it. The faster speeds and increased connectivity may require new ways to monitor and secure network traffic, while the growth of IoT devices on 5G networks can expand the attack surface. We must take more robust cybersecurity measures to ensure the safety of our data and protect against possible large-scale attacks. While 5G undoubtedly offers many benefits, we must also be prepared to tackle the new challenges it presents regarding cybersecurity and digital forensics [11].

15.4.4 Blockchain Technology

Although frequently linked to cryptocurrencies, blockchain has uses outside of the financial sector. The integrity of digital forensic evidence can be improved by using it to produce tamper-proof logs and recordings. However, it also makes it challenging to locate and detect illegal actions carried out via cryptocurrency. Data storage using blockchain technology is transparent and safe. Because it may be used to trace and confirm the legitimacy of digital evidence, it is a potential technique for digital forensics [12]. Figure 15.3 shows image of crypto currency & block chain market.

15.4.5 Biometric Technologies

Authentication systems increasingly integrate biometrics like voice, facial, and fingerprint recognition. Although these technologies provide better security, they also give rise to issues with privacy and the risk of biometric data breaches [13].

Figure 15.3 Image of crypto currency & block chain market.

15.4.6 Cloud Computing

Scalability and convenience are provided by cloud services, but they also create new attack vectors. Due to remote data storage and the complexity of virtualized systems, digital forensics and incident response in cloud environments require skills [14].

15.4.7 IoT (Internet of Things)

IoT device growth poses a challenge for cybersecurity since these devices frequently have weak security features. IoT devices that have been compromised can be used as access points into networks, which could result in data breaches and other security concerns. The internet-connected physical device network is known as the IOT. Attackers may leverage the enormous amounts of data that these devices produce to access networks and systems to investigate and respond to cyber incidents and digital forensics.

15.4.8 Automated Threats and Botnets

A growing number of cyberattacks use automated bots. Botnets can propagate malware, conduct Distributed Denial of Service (DDoS) assaults, and engage in other illegal activities. Advanced monitoring and response mechanisms are needed to identify and mitigate these dangers. Automated bots are being used in an increasing number of cyberattacks. Malware propagation, Distributed Denial of Service (DDoS) attacks, and other illicit activities are all possible with botnets. To recognize and reduce these risks, sophisticated monitoring and response systems are required. Automated bots are being used in an increasing number of cyberattacks. Malware propagation, Distributed Denial of Service (DDoS) attacks, and other illicit activities are all possible. With botnets to recognize and reduce these risks, advanced monitoring and response techniques are required [15].

15.4.9 Augmented Reality (AR) Virtual Reality (VR) and Autonomous Systems and AI-Driven Attacks

Technologies like AR and VR open new doors for cyber dangers like data leakage, unlawful entry into virtual environments, and potential psychological manipulation. It takes a combination of cutting-edge techniques and established cybersecurity methods to secure these environments [1]. The pace and sophistication of cyber threats can be increased by deploying autonomous systems and AI-driven attacks, such as automated phishing and social engineering attacks. It is necessary to use both AI-based detection and human-driven analysis to defend against these threats [16].

15.5 Cybersecurity and Digital Forensics: Threats and Opportunities

Cybersecurity and digital forensics are essential to maintaining contemporary digital technology's security, consistency, and dependability. Digital forensics and cybersecurity are exposed to opportunities and risks as new technologies develop.

15.5.1 Threats

- **Advanced Persistent Threats (APTs):** APTs are highly advanced, well-targeted cyberattacks that are frequently state-sponsored and have a long latency. Due to their intricacy and capacity to overcome conventional defenses, they present a severe challenge to digital forensics and cybersecurity experts.
- **Advanced malware:** Malware is growing more complex and challenging to find. The ability of some malware to self-destruct or remove evidence of its use makes it incredibly difficult for digital forensics investigators to identify those responsible for cybercrimes [17].
- **Data breaches:** Data breaches are increasing frequently as hackers discover new ways to exploit computer system holes. A data breach can make sensitive personal information, financial information, or intellectual property available to unauthorized people. Both people and organizations could be devastated by this [18].
- **Insider threats:** Insider dangers are frequently the most challenging to identify and avoid. Access to sensitive information may motivate employees to steal or sell it to unapproved parties. Accidental data loss or improper data handling are additional sources of insider dangers.
- **Cyberwarfare:** Nation-states are attacking their adversaries more frequently with the help of cyber warfare. Denial-of-service attacks, data theft, and disruption of vital infrastructure can all be part of this. Both military and civilian targets are susceptible to the devastation caused by cyber warfare [19]. Figure 15.4 shows the image of digital world and cyberwarfare.
- **Deepfake Technology:** The prevalence of deepfake technology makes it more challenging to believe in digital evidence. This could make it difficult to authenticate and verify digital material, affecting judicial procedures and investigations.
- **Ransomware and Extortion:** Attacks using ransomware have increased frequently, leading to data breaches and financial losses. Cybercriminals use double extortion tactics to gain leverage to demand ransom payments, in which they first take sensitive data before encrypting it [20].

Figure 15.4 Cyberwarfare.

15.5.2 Opportunities

Figure 15.5 shows digital forensics and information security in ransomware threats and data protection strategies.

- **Better detection and prevention:** As digital forensics and cyber security technologies advance, cybercrimes are becoming more accessible to identify and stop. For instance, intrusion detection systems (IDS) can monitor computer networks for unusual activities. Additionally, data can be analyzed using artificial intelligence (AI) to spot potential dangers [21].

Figure 15.5 Digital forensics and information security.

- **Enhanced forensics capabilities:** The ability to recover and analyze digital evidence is getting more accessible because of the development of robust and sophisticated digital forensics technologies. This can aid investigators in finding cybercriminals and prosecuting them. Digital forensics research advances are also a result of technological advancements. More thorough and precise investigations are made possible by new techniques for retrieving and interpreting data, even from encrypted sources [22].
- **Advanced Tools and Techniques:** Digital forensics and cybersecurity professionals can use increasingly advanced tools and approaches for identifying, assessing, and reducing threats because of technological advancements. Processing and making sense of enormous amounts of information involves using artificial Intelligence, big data analytics, and ML.
- **Blockchain for Evidence Integrity:** Digital evidence can be given a tamper-proof chain of custody using blockchain technology, preserving its integrity and legitimacy throughout the inquiry.
- **Cloud Security & Collaborative Defense:** There is a chance to create effective security measures adapted to the cloud environment as organizations depend more and more on cloud services. This offers enhanced capabilities for incident

response and real-time monitoring. Collaboration and information exchange between businesses, governments, and cybersecurity professionals can improve the effectiveness of the fight against online threats. Sharing threat intelligence can aid in thwarting attacks before they become widespread [23].

- **Cybersecurity Regulations:** Governments have enacted stronger laws and norms because of the increased awareness of cybersecurity concerns. This may result in more accountability for corporations and better security procedures.
- **Increased awareness:** People are taking precautions to protect themselves as they become more aware of the threats associated with cybercrime. This entails creating secure passwords, setting up security software, and exercising caution while sharing information online.

15.6 Future of Digital Forensics

Most digital forensic tools are designed to find the evidence anticipated to be on the suspect's device tool. Still, they have few characteristics for examining unfamiliar and complex situations, such as large-scale networks and informational sources. As a result, most forensic software's purpose is not to find anomalies. The development of tools and procedures for analysis are issues that must be dealt with soon. Most of the data and any potential digital hints are given to the examiner for additional research. Sadly, these devices and engineering methods, including appropriate visualization [24]. Figure 15.6 shows the future of digital forensics.

Figure 15.6 Future of digital forensics.

Assisting forensic examiners is challenging, given the absence of standardized norms and complex computational requirements. Cloud computing offers advantages for digital investigations, particularly for demanding tasks such as log analysis, data indexing, and multimedia processing. Forensics as a Service (FaaS) is a promising opportunity for investigators, as it allows them to access a tool Giuseppe Totara and his colleagues developed through a web interface for indexing forensic disk images. FaaS also simplifies software updates and improvements by centralizing all software in one location, which reduces complexity for end-users and allows professionals to focus on their investigations. Additionally, software-defined networking techniques provide additional abstraction layers for analyzing attacks or infections, eliminating the need for resource-intensive traffic analysis campaigns [25].

Digital forensics can prove to be crucial in certain situations. One such problem is when dealing with IoT, where the physical and cyber worlds are interconnected. Digital IoT forensics can be an effective way to gather information about the non-digital environment. For example, IoT nodes can provide evidence of someone's presence in a room by examining in-door presence sensor values. However, it is essential to note that such investigations raise privacy concerns. Since sensors can be influenced by multiple individuals, not just the potential criminal, it can complicate matters. With personal devices, appliances, and IoT nodes playing an increasingly important role in court trials, it is essential to consider how IoT and CPS can impact digital forensics in terms of challenges and opportunities [26].

15.6.1 Emerging Trends and Future Directions in Digital Forensics

In our modern world, digital forensics tools are crucial in investigating cybercrime. Cybercriminals are constantly devising new methods to commit fraud and inflict economic losses, making it imperative for digital societies to possess scalable and privacy-preserving forensics tools. IoT and CPS can further complicate matters, as nodes differ significantly in data storage, accessibility, and investigative trade-offs. To counter the increasingly sophisticated anti-forensic techniques, new tools are necessary to enhance IoT forensics, especially with the emergence of Crime as a Service (CaaS). Cloud computing, combined with intelligent automation and visualization tools, can assist forensic analysts in navigating complex environments and making sense of vast amounts of information. It is crucial to note that during forensic investigations, the location, type, and accessibility attributes of IoT devices should be analyzed on a case-by-case basis. This is particularly relevant to devices that move often, like fitness trackers, smart clothing, and smartwatches. It also applies to devices that are part of larger mobile objects, such as drones, bikes, or cars. Accessing these nodes can be challenging. For example, if a state's laws permit law enforcement to access smart devices, criminals could just park their smart cars at the closest border or send their smartwatches to another country, making them unavailable to law enforcement or delaying access. Digital forensics is a constantly evolving field that faces new challenges as technology advances. Some key themes expected to impact digital forensics include the increasing use of AI, the rise of cloud computing, the prevalence of mobile devices in criminal activity, the growing importance of international collaboration, and the need to stay current with emerging technologies [27].

15.6.2 Potential Benefits and Challenges of These Emerging Trends of Digital Forensics

Despite the swift development of the profession, progress in digital forensics is getting more and more challenging. The widespread usage of digital devices and various hardware and software platforms partly causes this. For instance, developing unified or standard tools is difficult since many distinct operating systems and file formats exist. Cryptography, digital rights management, and trusted smartphone computing frameworks can make gathering evidence difficult.

The issue of space is becoming increasingly complicated for several reasons besides merely the fact that a variety of technologies are present. Cybercrime has recently developed to encompass new "business models," such as crime as a service (CaaS). Potential adversaries find obtaining the software, frameworks, and services they want to launch a cyberattack is more straightforward. Tox, a ransomware-building kit found on the dark web in 2015, illustrates this.

Cloud computing presents challenges in digital forensics, such as reduced physical control over data, lack of standard interfaces, and issues with multiple ownerships and jurisdictions. However, it also offers advantages in data management, including load-balancing scalability and redundancy features that make evidence collection and analysis more straightforward [28].

15.6.3 Significant Challenges in Modern Digital Forensics, Both from an Ethical and Technological Perspective

- **High volume and speed.** Due to the prevalence of gigabit-class links and multimedia-rich materials, the amount of data that needs to be saved and processed for evidence gathering and occurrence detection has significantly increased. This becomes particularly crucial in cases involving live networks where it might not be feasible for investigators to record and save all necessary traffic for examination. Despite this, the challenges of obtaining, storing, and processing data for forensic purposes, particularly in massive volumes, have persisted for over a decade. This problem has only been exacerbated by the exponential growth in digital information production and accessibility.
- **Complexity explosion.** The complexity of forensics has sharply increased due to the proliferation of new services and technological advancements. Experts face the challenge of managing this complexity because the evidence is not limited to a single host. It is spread across various real and virtual locations, including online social networks, cryptocurrencies, wallets, cloud-based service infrastructure, cloud resources, and personal network-attached storage. As a result, it takes more knowledge, resources, and time to reconstruct the evidence accurately. This added complexity also impacts the duration of digital investigations and the number of resources, such as labor, required by forensic specialists or outside parties, like LEA-funded specialized experts [29]. Some chores could be automated to address these problems partially. The digital investigation community, however, has sharply criticized this because it could impair the investigation's caliber and the expertise of forensics professionals.
- **Standards Development:** Managing multiple hardware and software entities, such as RAM and USB solid-state mass storage, is essential in digital forensics. Despite technological advancements, collecting, organizing, and analyzing files remains the most common digital artifact. However, there is no consensus among the research community on standard formats, schema, and ontologies. In cases involving complex cybercrimes, collaborative information processing

or outsourced storage and computation may be necessary. Therefore, the digital forensics community must establish adequate standard formats and abstractions. The utilization of XML, as exemplified in "Automating Disk Forensic Processing with Sleuth Kit, XML, and Python," offers a potential solution for achieving this goal [30].

- **Privacy-preserving investigations & Legitimacy:** With the increasing technological advancements, more parts of our lives are being integrated into the online world through social networks and media sites. Unfortunately, this has also resulted in a rise in social engineering attacks that can have severe consequences for victims. It's essential to report and investigate these attacks promptly, but gathering information for the investigations can threaten users' privacy, particularly when cloud computing is involved. As digital infrastructures become more complex and virtualized, conducting investigations legally without violating laws is becoming increasingly challenging in borderless scenarios. We must find ways to conduct investigations that preserve privacy and are fair and legitimate for all parties involved [7].
- **Anti-forensics Techniques Rise:** Anti-forensics techniques are expected to increase as security measures progress. These techniques involve encryption, obfuscation, cloaking, and hiding information. For example, steganographic configurations can make it challenging to analyze filesystems by allowing information to be concealed in unused challenging disk areas or metadata, such as timestamps. Binary obfuscation is currently the most used technique, but other methods may soon become relevant for digital forensics investigations [31].

15.7 The Future of Cybersecurity

15.7.1 Overview of Future Directions and Emerging Trends in Cybersecurity

The discipline of cybersecurity is constantly developing to address new threats and issues as technology advances. Several developing developments are shaping the future of cybersecurity:

- **Blockchain technology:** Due to its potential to improve security in various applications, blockchain has recently attracted much attention. Blockchain can offer decentralized, tamper-proof storage for crucial data in cybersecurity. It provides a transparent and unchangeable ledger that may be applied to secure identity management, supply chain security, and other applications. Using the distributed ledger technology known as blockchain, safe and unchangeable records can be produced [32].
- **Zero Trust Architecture:** The security framework Zero Trust places a strong emphasis on the maxim "never trust, always verify." No one is given implicit trust because it is assumed that there are risks inside and outside the network. No matter where the users or devices are, this method calls for constant authentication and permission.
- **IoT & Cloud Security:** Due to the growth of the attack surface brought on by the proliferation of Internet of Things (IoT) devices, IoT security is a significant issue. The security of connected devices and the data they generate is a growing concern. The need for cloud environment security is growing as more businesses adopt cloud-based technology. Solutions for cloud security are being developed to better visibility, control, and defense against dangers peculiar to clouds [8].
- **5G Security:** The introduction of 5G networks brings opportunities as well as difficulties. Although 5G can speed up communication and innovation, it also introduces new security vulnerabilities due to increased connection and the possibility of more significant assaults.
- **Regulation observance &increased significance of human elements:** Security breaches are commonly caused by human error. Human aspects in cybersecurity become more crucial as businesses implement more complicated technologies. Governments are creating rules and regulations to safeguard data security and privacy. To avoid fines, organizations must abide by these rules.

15.7.2 Emerging Trends and Potential Benefits Include

- **Better Authentication, Data Integrity, and Threat Detection Capabilities:** The combination of blockchain, zero trust architecture, and AI can improve security.

- **Efficiency:** Automation using AI and ML can help in real-time threat detection and response, saving time and effort from manual analysis.
- **Scalability:** Scalable security choices that may change to meet the evolving needs of companies are possible with cloud-based solutions and blockchain technology.

15.7.3 Challenges in Cybersecurity

Figure 15.7 shows challenges in digital forensic technology.

- **Complexity:** These new technologies can be challenging to implement and require much knowledge. To prevent vulnerabilities, proper configuration and administration are crucial.
- **Privacy Concerns:** Concerns about acquiring and using personal information develop as AI and ML are used for data analysis.
- **Adaptation Period:** Transitioning to new security paradigms like zero trust architecture can be time-consuming and disruptive because it requires considerable system changes.

Figure 15.7 Challenges in digital forensics.

- **Misuse of Technology:** While AI might aid in threat detection, bad actors can also use it to develop more sophisticated attacks.
- **Cost:** It can be expensive to implement sophisticated cybersecurity safeguards, especially for smaller firms with fewer resources.

15.8 Collaboration and Interdisciplinary Approaches

Due to the complexity and swift evolution of cyber threats and attacks, collaboration, and interdisciplinary approaches are vital in digital forensics and cybersecurity. These methods promote the cooperation of specialists from different domains to improve the efficacy of investigations, threat detection, and mitigation measures. Appreciating the importance of digital forensics and cyber security in protecting our digital environment is crucial. The two fields are increasingly interwoven as cyber-attacks become more sophisticated and prevalent. Collaboration between digital forensics and cyber security professionals is vital to adequately protect against these assaults. By working together, specialists from these two professions may improve the general understanding of cyber risks, enhance the efficiency of investigations, and uncover and address security vulnerabilities to prevent cyber-attacks from happening in the first place. There are various ways to collaborate with these experts, including formal partnerships, attending conferences and workshops, and sharing information and resources online. An interdisciplinary approach to cybersecurity is becoming increasingly crucial as the dangers to our digital world get more complex, and by working together, people from diverse disciplines may develop more effective solutions to defend our digital systems and data [15]. Figure 15.8 shows the interdisciplinary approach of digital forensics and cyber security.

15.8.1 Ways in Which Digital Forensics and Cyber Security Might Collaborate

Digital forensics experts can assist cyber security professionals with insights into attackers' strategies. This information can be used to design new security controls and processes.

Cyber security specialists can aid digital forensics experts in collecting and preserving digital evidence in a form admissible in court. Digital forensics and cyber security professionals can work together to establish training programs for employees to defend themselves from cyber dangers.

Figure 15.8 The interdisciplinary approach of digital forensics and cyber security.

Digital forensics and cyber security specialists might collaborate on research initiatives to develop new methods for detecting and responding to cyber threats. The interdisciplinary approach of digital forensics and cyber security is vital for securing computer systems and data in the ever-changing threat landscape [33].

By working together, these two professions can build a more comprehensive understanding of computer systems' hazards and design more effective techniques to prevent and respond to such threats.

- **Computer science and Law:** This strategy combines the legal principles of evidence collection and preservation with the technical knowledge of computer scientists to ensure that digital evidence is collected and preserved in a way that is admissible in court.
- **Computer engineering and Information Security:** This technique combines information security professionals' knowledge with computer engineers' technical competence to design new security controls and processes to safeguard computer systems against assault.
- **Mathematics and Network Security:** This technique combines the knowledge of network security professionals with the mathematical foundations of cryptography to discover innovative approaches for safeguarding communications and data.

- **Criminology and Psychology:** This technique combines the knowledge of psychologists and criminologists with the technical competence of digital forensics professionals to understand the motivations and actions of cyber criminals.
- **Information exchange:** Digital forensics and cybersecurity experts deal with several facets of cyber events. Both teams can better prepare themselves and their responses by exchanging knowledge about threats, attack methods, and vulnerabilities. While digital forensics professionals can provide invaluable information about attack patterns and indicators of penetration, cybersecurity teams can offer insights into new threats.
- **Threat Intelligence:** Collaboration enables the sharing of threat intelligence data, which contains details about malicious actors, their methods, techniques, and procedures (TTPs), as well as other signs of compromise. Cybersecurity teams can actively bolster their defenses and spot potential threats early by using threat intelligence from digital forensics investigations [34].
- **Utilization of Tools and Technologies:** Exchanging Tools and Technologies can enhance both professions' capacities. Cybersecurity teams can evaluate potential breaches using digital forensics technologies, and during investigations, digital forensics teams can leverage cybersecurity tools to provide real-time monitoring and intrusion detection capabilities.
- **Cross-Training:** Training team members in cybersecurity and digital forensics can help professionals develop diverse skill sets. They can comprehend an attack's entire lifetime, from prevention to detection, investigation, and recovery.
- **Research and Innovation:** By bringing together professionals with various viewpoints, interdisciplinary collaboration promotes research and innovation. New methodologies, tools, and techniques that meet current difficulties in both domains may be developed.

By working together, professionals from different disciplines can better understand computer systems' hazards and devise more effective solutions to prevent and respond to those threats. To remain ahead of cyber threats and respond to crises successfully, teamwork and multidisciplinary methods between digital forensics and cybersecurity are crucial. Professionals from these sectors may cooperate to strengthen their combined capabilities and guarantee the overall security of digital systems and assets by exchanging knowledge, talents, tools, and viewpoints [35].

15.9 Ethics and Human Factors in Future Digital Forensics and Cybersecurity

Ethics, in its broadest sense, refers to people's interest in discovering the best way to live. As philosopher Socrates famously said in 399 B.C., "The most important thing is not just life, but living a good life."

15.9.1 Why Do we Need Ethics in Technology?

Experts have concluded that ethics is becoming increasingly relevant in technological disciplines and that engineers' vocabulary should reflect this. Technology ethics is the main focus of a division inside IEEE, the world's most significant technical professional organization. IEEE even holds international conferences on ethics in engineering, science, and technological practice. In addition to its professional code of ethics, IEEE creates ethical guidelines for cutting-edge fields, including artificial intelligence, robotics, and data management. But why is technology ethics becoming more and more important? The short answer is that technology is rapidly influencing how we live our lives, which may either make leading a fulfilling life simpler or more challenging. The distribution of vital resources like food, water, and medical care may be improved with well-designed and wisely applied technology, which can enhance our lives. Conversely, improperly developed or misapplied technology can have unfavorable effects like promoting unhealthy habits or environmental damage [36].

It is critical to keep in mind that technologies aren't morally neutral. They exhibit the attitudes of those who create, utilize, and spread them. They may, therefore, both show and shape what our society values. Why, then, is ethics a subject receiving more and more attention in technological contexts? One factor is that technological advancements drastically and quickly alter our way of life. Legislators and regulators need help keeping up with these developments, and many require more technical knowledge to formulate sensible technology policies. Technological specialists are relied upon to assist in predicting social repercussions and choosing ethical design and implementation strategies. It's a complicated and changing world, and the few existing laws must be more consistent and sufficient. To guarantee that we're creating a better society for everyone as we continue to rely more and more on technology, we must prioritize ethics in technological domains [37].

15.9.2 What Does Ethics Have to Do with Cybersecurity and Digital Forensics?

The main objective of cybersecurity practices is to ensure the safety and security of data, computer systems, and networks. However, the ultimate goal is to protect the integrity, functionality, and reliability of human institutions and practices that depend on them. Therefore, cybersecurity professionals are responsible for safeguarding the lives and welfare of individuals who rely on these institutions and practices, such as patients in hospitals, credit users, students, and inventors. The ethical aspects of cybersecurity practices are intrinsic, as these practices are now crucial in securing and maintaining the capacity of human individuals and groups to live well. With the increasing complexity of safeguarding online data and systems, the ethical obligation of cybersecurity professionals to protect others is becoming a more challenging responsibility [38].

Future digital forensics and cybersecurity methods must be developed and implemented carefully, considering many ethical and human elements to guarantee that new technologies are efficient, just, and respectful of people's rights and privacy. Here is a summary of some essential factors:

- **Consent and Privacy:** Ensure people's privacy rights are upheld throughout digital inquiry. Before gathering and analyzing individuals' digital data, get their informed consent. Limit the amount of data collected to what is required for the investigation to avoid needless intrusion.
- **Accountability and Transparency:** Keep the procedures and methods employed in digital forensics and cybersecurity investigations transparent. Give each person participating in the inquiry their specific tasks and responsibilities. Establish accountability processes for data processing errors or ethical violations [39].

- **Data management and security:** Implement robust data security procedures to protect the confidentiality and accuracy of gathered digital evidence. To avoid unauthorized access to sensitive information, abide by specified data retention and disposal standards.
- **Fairness and Prejudice:** Consider any biases in data collecting and analysis that could disproportionately affect particular people or groups and take steps to address them. Create impartial and fair tools and algorithms and periodically check them for discriminating results.
- **Cultural Awareness:** Recognize cultural variances that could influence how digital evidence is interpreted and consider cultural settings while conducting investigations. Avoid making assumptions and preconceptions that could result in misunderstandings or incorrect judgments [40].
- **Compliance with laws and regulations:** Ascertain that all digital forensics and cybersecurity procedures follow all applicable laws, rules, and professional standards. Keep abreast of changing legislative frameworks to ensure that investigations are carried out within the law.
- **Reliability and consistency:** Standardize processes and approaches to ensure consistency and dependability in investigations. Update and improve procedures regularly in light of new technological developments and problems [41].

15.9.3 Potential Benefits

Using digital forensics and cyber security's chances and difficulties might provide many advantages. These include Increased protection against cyberattacks, data breaches, and other criminal actions via more secure computer systems and networks. Enhanced capacity for cybercrime investigation and prosecution can aid in bringing offenders to justice and preventing such assaults. Improved awareness of cyber risks and vulnerabilities can assist firms in creating more effective security solutions. Increasing the general public's understanding of cyber security can help lower the likelihood that people and companies are be the target of cyberattacks [42].

15.10 Challenges and Opportunities of Digital and Cyber-Forensics

15.10.1 Challenges

The challenge of keeping up with the most recent dangers is because of the ever-increasing complexity of computer systems and networks. The level of complexity of cyber criminals is that they are always coming up with new ways to exploit weaknesses. There is a need for more experts in digital forensics and cyber security. There are difficulties in gathering and evaluating digital evidence regarding law and ethics. Despite the problems, several chances exist to use digital forensics and cyber security options [41]. New technologies can be created to automate processes and boost the effectiveness of digital forensics investigations, such as artificial intelligence and machine learning. The greater sharing of information and resources across higher education institutions, companies, and law enforcement agencies.

The creation of educational programs to educate additional experts in digital forensics and cyber security. Adopt global norms and best practices to enhance the accuracy and uniformity of digital forensics investigations. We may strengthen the security of our computer systems and networks and contribute to our protection from cybercrime by addressing the problems and possibilities associated with digital forensics and cyber security.

Cybersecurity and digital forensics are closely connected topics constantly developing in response to the shifting threat landscape. Here are some of the difficulties and chances these fields face:

- **Digital systems and device complexity:** It is difficult for forensic investigators to compile and analyze evidence of contemporary encryption techniques due to the complexity of modern digital devices and systems.
- **Advanced encryption methods:** Cybercriminals use These more often to impede forensic investigators' access to data. Digital devices create and store an ever-increasing amount of data, making it challenging for forensic IOs to sift and evaluate it.

- **Chain of Custody:** To prevent tampering with digital evidence, it is crucial to maintain the chain of custody. This can be not easy, especially when the evidence is on distant computers or the cloud.
- **User confidentiality:** Forensic investigators must balance maintaining user privacy while gathering and analyzing digital evidence.

15.10.2 Opportunities

- **Advances in technology:** The ability to retrieve and analyze digital evidence is becoming easier for forensic investigators because of technological advancements. For instance, new technologies are being created to automate specific digital forensics processes, such as data analysis and recovery.
- **Increased awareness of cyber threats:** Individuals and corporations are becoming more conscious of cyber threats. As a result, there is a rising need for digital forensics services.
- **Creation of best practices and standards:** The endeavor to create standards and best practices for digital forensics is expanding. This makes it easier to guarantee that digital evidence is gathered and examined, trustworthy and consistent.
- **Cooperation between the commercial sector and law enforcement:** In the area of digital forensics, there is growing cooperation between law enforcement and the business sector. This helps make it easier to detect and punish cybercriminals [28].

15.11 Conclusion

In conclusion, this book chapter highlights the critical importance of anticipating and preparing for future digital forensics and cybersecurity threats. Proactive steps are required to keep one step ahead of adversaries and successfully reduce possible risks, given the rapidly changing nature of technology and cyber threats. This paper emphasizes the necessity of readiness by focusing on essential issues linked to the changing nature of cyber threats, the difficulties experienced by experts in digital forensics, and the relevance of teamwork and constant learning.

15.11.1 Summary of Key Points

- **Evolving Threat Landscape:** New technologies and attack vectors continually evolve, causing the digital environment to change. Professionals must be flexible and proactive in spotting hazards in this dynamic environment.
- **Challenges in Digital Forensics:** It's possible that traditional digital forensics methods can't handle sophisticated and complicated cyberattacks. Professionals must continuously refresh their knowledge and equipment to investigate and respond to accidents appropriately.
- **Interdisciplinary Collaboration:** Digital forensics and cybersecurity are interdependent. Cooperation amongst diverse fields is essential to share information and insights about new risks. This includes law enforcement, the commercial sector, academia, and the government.
- **Continuous Learning:** Because of the speed at which technology develops, professionals must pursue ongoing education to stay abreast of the most recent cybersecurity and digital forensics developments.
- **Preparation and Proactive Measures:** To lessen the effects of potential future threats, organizations must invest in solid cybersecurity safeguards, incident response plans, and disaster recovery techniques.

15.11.2 Discussion of Importance

Anticipating and preparing for future threats in digital forensics and cybersecurity is of paramount importance for several reasons:

- **Minimizing Impact:** By being prepared, organizations can lessen the effect of cyber attacks. They can implement systems to efficiently prevent, detect, and respond by anticipating potential dangers.
- **Maintaining Trust:** Trust in digital systems is essential as society increasingly relies on them. When firms are adequately prepared, when breaches happen, they can demonstrate rapid and effective responses, maintaining their trust.
- **Staying Ahead of Adversaries:** Cyber opponents are constantly changing their strategies, methods, and tactics.

Security experts can better protect against attacks and create plans to combat new threats by anticipating their movements.

- **Resource Allocation:** Well-prepared Organizations can deploy their resources wisely, concentrating on the vulnerable or focused areas. This avoids wasting time and effort on no longer effective or necessary defenses.
- **Legal and Ethical Considerations:** The landscape's change brings Legal and ethical difficulties. Well-prepared professionals can negotiate these intricacies while abiding by the applicable laws and ethical standards.

15.11.3 Conclusion and Implications for Future Research and Practice

In conclusion, digital forensics and cybersecurity demand a proactive and adaptive approach to future threats. The implications for future research and practice are clear:

- **Research:** Future studies should concentrate on developing proactive defense systems powered by AI, cutting-edge tools for sophisticated digital investigations, and predictive threat intelligence.
- **Training and Education:** To improve professionals' readiness for upcoming difficulties, training programs should stress multidisciplinary skills, continual learning, and scenario-based exercises.
- **Collaboration:** Collaboration between government, business, and academia can promote information sharing and aid in the creation of potent defenses against new dangers.
- **Policy Development:** To create legislation that promotes the adoption of proactive cybersecurity measures while resolving legal and ethical issues, policymakers should collaborate with experts.
- **Investment:** Organizations must allocate resources to technology and personnel training to ensure they are well-equipped to anticipate, respond to, and mitigate future threats.

References

1. Alawida, M., Omolara, A.E., Abiodun, O.I., Al-Rajab, M., A deeper look into cybersecurity issues in the wake of Covid-19: A survey. *J. King Saud Univ. Comput. Inf. Sci.*, 34, 10, 8176–8206, Nov. 2022, doi: 10.1016/j.jksuci.2022.08.003.
2. Quach, S., Thaichon, P., Martin, K.D., Weaven, S., Palmatier, R.W., Digital technologies: tensions in privacy and data. *J. Acad. Mark. Sci.*, 50, 6, 1299–1323, Nov. 2022, doi: 10.1007/s11747-022-00845-y.
3. Tariq, U., Ahmed, I., Bashir, A.K., Shaukat, K., A Critical Cybersecurity Analysis and Future Research Directions for the Internet of Things: A Comprehensive Review. *Sensors*, 23, 8, 4117, Apr. 2023, doi: 10.3390/s23084117.
4. Caviglione, L., Wendzel, S., Mazurczyk, W., The Future of Digital Forensics: Challenges and the Road Ahead. *IEEE Secur. Priv.*, 15, 6, 12–17, Nov. 2017, doi: 10.1109/MSP.2017.4251117.
5. Jones, G.M. and Winster, S.G., An Insight into Digital Forensics: History, Frameworks, Types and Tools, in: *Cyber Security and Digital Forensics*, pp. 105–125, Wiley, USA, 2022, doi: 10.1002/9781119795667.ch6.
6. Gad, A.G., Mosa, D.T., Abualigah, L., Abohany, A.A., Emerging Trends in Blockchain Technology and Applications: A Review and Outlook. *J. King Saud Univ. Comput. Inf. Sci.*, 34, 9, 6719–6742, Oct. 2022, doi: 10.1016/J.JKSUCI.2022.03.007.
7. Jang-Jaccard, J. and Nepal, S., A survey of emerging threats in cybersecurity. *J. Comput. Syst. Sci.*, 80, 5, 973–993, Aug. 2014, doi: 10.1016/J.JCSS.2014.02.005.
8. Williams, P., Dutta, I.K., Daoud, H., Bayoumi, M., A survey on security in internet of things with a focus on the impact of emerging technologies. *Internet Things*, 19, 100564, Aug. 2022, doi: 10.1016/j.iot.2022.100564.
9. Kaur, R., Gabrijelčič, D., Klobučar, T., Artificial intelligence for cybersecurity: Literature review and future research directions. *Inf. Fusion*, 97, 101804, Sep. 2023, doi: 10.1016/J.INFFUS.2023.101804.
10. Buchanan, W. and Woodward, A., Will quantum computers be the end of public key encryption? *J. Cyber Secur. Technol.*, 1, 1, 1–22, Jan. 2017, doi: 10.1080/23742917.2016.1226650.
11. Rao, S.K. and Prasad, R., Impact of 5G Technologies on Smart City Implementation. *Wirel. Pers. Commun.*, 100, 1, 161–176, May 2018, doi: 10.1007/s11277-018-5618-4.
12. Wu, H. and Zheng, G., Electronic evidence in the blockchain era: New rules on authenticity and integrity. *Comput. Law Secur. Rev.*, 36, 105401, Apr. 2020, doi: 10.1016/J.CLSR.2020.105401.
13. Jain, A.K., Ross, A., Prabhakar, S., An introduction to biometric recognition. *IEEE Trans. Circuits Syst. Video Technol.*, 14, 1, 4–20, 2004, doi: 10.1109/TCSVT.2003.818349.

14. Urias, V.E., Stout, W.M.S., Loverro, C., Young, J.W., Hypervisor Assisted Forensics and Incident Response in the Cloud, in: *2016 IEEE International Conference on Computer and Information Technology (CIT)*, De Gruyter Berlin, Germany, pp. 768–775, 2016, doi: 10.1109/CIT.2016.104.
15. Dwivedi, Y.K. *et al.*, Metaverse beyond the hype: Multidisciplinary perspectives on emerging challenges, opportunities, and agenda for research, practice and policy. *Int. J. Inf. Manage.*, 66, 102542, Oct. 2022, doi: 10.1016/J.IJINFOMGT.2022.102542.
16. Sarker, I.H., Furhad, M.H., Nowrozy, R., AI-Driven Cybersecurity: An Overview, Security Intelligence Modeling and Research Directions. *SN Comput. Sci.*, 2, 3, 1–18, May 2021, doi: 10.1007/S42979-021-00557-0/METRICS.
17. Chen, Z., Roussopoulos, M., Liang, Z., Zhang, Y., Chen, Z., Delis, A., Malware characteristics and threats on the Internet ecosystem. *J. Syst. Software*, 85, 7, 1650–1672, Jul. 2012, doi: 10.1016/J.JSS.2012.02.015.
18. Hammouchi, H., Cherqi, O., Mezzour, G., Ghogho, M., El Koutbi, M., Digging Deeper into Data Breaches: An Exploratory Data Analysis of Hacking Breaches Over Time. *Procedia Comput. Sci.*, 151, 1004–1009, Jan. 2019, doi: 10.1016/J.PROCS.2019.04.141.
19. Ashraf, C., Defining cyberwar: towards a definitional framework. *Def. Secur. Anal.*, 37, 3, 274–294, Jul. 2021, doi: 10.1080/14751798.2021.1959141.
20. Dagar, D. and Vishwakarma, D.K., A literature review and perspectives in deepfakes: generation, detection, and applications. *Int. J. Multimed. Inf. Retr.*, 11, 3, 219–289, Sep. 2022, doi: 10.1007/s13735-022-00241-w.
21. Yaacoub, J.P.A., Noura, H.N., Salman, O., Chehab, A., Advanced digital forensics and anti-digital forensics for IoT systems: Techniques, limitations and recommendations. *Internet Things*, 19, 100544, Aug. 2022, doi: 10.1016/J.IOT.2022.100544.
22. Garfinkel, S.L., Digital forensics research: The next 10 years. *Digit. Investig.*, 7, SUPPL., S64–S73, Aug. 2010, doi: 10.1016/J.DIIN.2010.05.009.
23. Alouffi, B., Hasnain, M., Alharbi, A., Alosaimi, W., Alyami, H., Ayaz, M., A Systematic Literature Review on Cloud Computing Security: Threats and Mitigation Strategies. *IEEE Access*, 9, 57792–57807, 2021, doi: 10.1109/ACCESS.2021.3073203.
24. Horsman, G. and Errickson, D., When finding nothing may be evidence of something: Anti-forensics and digital tool marks. *Sci. Justice*, 59, 5, 565–572, Sep. 2019, doi: 10.1016/J.SCIJUS.2019.06.004.
25. O'Shaughnessy, S. and Keane, A., Impact of Cloud Computing on Digital Forensic Investigations, pp. 291–303, 2013, doi: 10.1007/978-3-642-41148-9_20.
26. Atlam, H.F., El-Din Hemdan, E., Alenezi, A., Alassafi, M.O., Wills, G.B., Internet of Things Forensics: A Review. *Internet Things*, 11, 100220, Sep. 2020, doi: 10.1016/j.iot.2020.100220.
27. Mugisha, D., ROLE AND IMPACT OF DIGITAL FORENSICS IN CYBER CRIME INVESTIGATIONS. *Int. J. Cyber Criminol.*, 47, 3, Mar. 2019.

28. Shrivastava, G., Gupta, D., Sharma, K. (Eds.), *Cyber Crime and Forensic Computing*, De Gruyter, Berlin, Germany, 2021, doi: 10.1515/9783110677478.
29. Kloosterman, A. *et al.*, The interface between forensic science and technology: how technology could cause a paradigm shift in the role of forensic institutes in the criminal justice system. *Philos. Trans. R. Soc. B: Biol. Sci.*, 370, 1674, 20140264, Aug. 2015, doi: 10.1098/rstb.2014.0264.
30. Mislan, R., Harrill, D.C. and Mislan, R.P., A small scale digital device forensics ontology. *Small Scale Digit. Device Forensics J.*, 1, 1, 242–248, 2007.
31. Hosgor, E., Detection and Mitigation of Anti-Forensics. *Int. J. Comput. Sci. Inf. Secur.*, 18, 46–52, Dec. 2020, doi: 10.5281/zenodo.4425257.
32. Javaid, M., Haleem, A., Singh, R.P., Suman, R., Khan, S., A review of Blockchain Technology applications for financial services. *BenchCouncil Trans. Benchmarks Stand. Eval.*, 2, 3, 100073, Jul. 2022, doi: 10.1016/J.TBENCH.2022.100073.
33. Elyas, M., Ahmad, A., Maynard, S.B., Lonie, A., Digital forensic readiness: Expert perspectives on a theoretical framework. *Comput. Secur.*, 52, 70–89, Jul. 2015, doi: 10.1016/j.cose.2015.04.003.
34. Huang, K., Siegel, M., Madnick, S., Systematically Understanding the Cyber Attack Business. *ACM Comput. Surv.*, 51, 4, 1–36, Jul. 2019, doi: 10.1145/3199674.
35. Alghamdi, M.I., Digital forensics in cyber security—recent trends, threats, and opportunities, in: *Cybersecurity Threats with New Perspectives*, 2021.
36. Dwivedi, Y.K. *et al.*, Opinion Paper: 'So what if ChatGPT wrote it?' Multidisciplinary perspectives on opportunities, challenges and implications of generative conversational AI for research, practice and policy. *Int. J. Inf. Manage.*, 71, 102642, Aug. 2023, doi: 10.1016/J.IJINFOMGT.2023.102642.
37. Macnish, K. and van der Ham, J., Ethics in cybersecurity research and practice. *Technol. Soc.*, 63, 101382, Nov. 2020, doi: 10.1016/J.TECHSOC.2020.101382.
38. Rajasekharaiah, K.M., Dule, C.S., Sudarshan, E., Cyber Security Challenges and its Emerging Trends on Latest Technologies. *IOP Conf. Ser. Mater. Sci. Eng.*, 981, 2, 022062, Dec. 2020, doi: 10.1088/1757-899X/981/2/022062.
39. Khan, M. and Haque, S., Cyber Security and Ethics on Social Media. *J. Mod. Dev. Appl. Eng. Technol. Res.*, 1, 2, 51–58, 2017.
40. scholar (2).
41. Fenech, J., Richards, D., Formosa, P., Ethical principles shaping values-based cybersecurity decision-making. *Comput. Secur.*, 140, 103795. https://doi.org/10.1016/j.case.2024.103795.
42. Li, Y. and Liu, Q., A comprehensive review study of cyber-attacks and cyber security; Emerging trends and recent developments. *Energy Rep.*, 7, 8176–8186, Nov. 2021, doi: 10.1016/J.EGYR.2021.08.126.

16

Tomorrow's Shields: Exploring Future Trends in Cyber Security and Forensics

Mridu Sharma[1]*, Ravshish Kaur Kohli[2] and Kunal Sharma[3]

[1]*Department of Forensic Science, School of Liberal Arts and Sciences, Mody University of Science and Technology, Laxmangarh, Rajasthan, India*
[2]*Amity Institute of Forensic Sciences, Amity University Noida, Uttar Pradesh, India*
[3]*Department of Regulatory Affairs for Drugs, Biologics and Medical Devices, Northeastern University, Toronto, Canada*

Abstract

As we venture further into the digital age, the landscape of cyber security and forensics is rapidly evolving. This paper explores the emerging trends and future directions in these critical fields, focusing on the technological advancements and strategic approaches necessary to protect against increasingly sophisticated cyber threats. Key areas of exploration include the integration of cloud forensics, social crime forensics, IoT, and the development of advanced forensic techniques to keep pace with new types of cybercrimes. These technologies enhance the ability to predict, identify, and mitigate cyber attacks more efficiently than traditional methods. The advent of quantum computing, while promising unprecedented computational power, also poses significant risks to current cryptographic standards, necessitating the development of quantum-resistant encryption algorithms. In cyber forensics, advancements focus on tracking and analysing cybercriminals' complex digital footprints. Enhanced forensic tools and methodologies are essential for investigating sophisticated cybercrimes, ranging from data breaches to ransomware attacks. The paper concludes by emphasising the importance of a multi-faceted approach to cyber security and forensics, combining technological innovation, regulatory frameworks, and international cooperation. As cyber threats evolve, so must our defences, protecting sensitive information and maintaining trust in digital systems.

***Keywords*:** Cybercrimes, cyber security, cyber forensics, digital forensics, IoT, social media forensics, USB

**Corresponding author*: mrdshrm@gmail.com

Kavita Sharma, Vishnu Sharma, Parma Nand, Anil Kumar Sagar and Gulshan Shrivastava (eds.) Securing the Digital Frontier: Threats and Advanced Techniques in Security and Forensics, (367–386)

16.1 Introduction

The advent of Web 2.0 technology and the substantial advancements in the digital realm have brought about a notable shift in the global paradigm. In contemporary times, individuals progressively participate in online interactions, actively contribute to collaborative initiatives, and share their written content on digital platforms. Nevertheless, concerns for trust and verifiability are raised due to the anonymity and simplicity of executing these actions [1]. The expansion of digital technologies has primarily driven the rise of novel methods for committing computer crimes. Furthermore, networks and extensively enhanced data transmission have given rise to apprehensions regarding security. Every day, malicious methodology, tools, and software are continuously developed and deployed to pose a significant threat to public and private networks. These malicious entities are specifically designed to hack data storage systems to collect valuable and sensitive information [2]. In response to the growing menace, the field of digital forensics has garnered significant interest as a means of mitigating cybersecurity risks. According to the scholarly discourse in Sharma *et al.* [3], digital forensics is the scientific discipline concerned with the systematic processes of presenting, documenting, analysing, archiving, and identifying information and evidence derived from electronic and digital devices. It is crucial to note that these activities are conducted with the utmost regard to protecting user privacy. In addition, it employs scientific methodologies to replicate and elucidate the chronological progression of the occurrences. Digital forensics accomplishments to present illicit artifacts as evidentiary material in a court of law by examining, reviewing, and documenting these sequences [3].

Undoubtedly, social networks play a crucial role in driving the modern world, and the advancements in digital technologies have further facilitated cyber crimes growth. These developments have led to new techniques, tools, and attacks enabling attackers to infiltrate highly regulated environments [4]. Digital forensics is employed by security specialists, academia, and law enforcement organizations to address the growing prevalence of cyber abnormalities. Professionals in this field employ scientific methodologies, including identification, validation, interpretation, and documentation, to gather digital evidence from various digital devices such as RAM, smartphones, memory cards, floppy discs, and flash drives. Nevertheless, as digital forensics tools progress, hackers increasingly utilize anti-forensics technologies to intentionally introduce delays or eliminate digital evidence [5]. Furthermore, even though the digital forensics framework is intended to safeguard user privacy, the widespread accessibility to the Internet, the emergence of the Internet of Things (IoT), and the prevalence of cloud computing have sparked the emergence of novel criminal phenomena. In addition, the field of digital forensics is anticipated to encounter novel and distinctive obstacles due to the incorporation of advanced and potent anti-forensics approaches within cyber threats and malware. Therefore, examining these problems while concurrently exploring contemporary developments in digital forensics is imperative.

16.2 Recent Digital Forensic Trends

16.2.1 Cloud Forensics

Cloud forensics has garnered significant interest from forensic professionals in recent times. This can be attributed to the several advantages cloud computing offers, such as a vast resource pool, cost-effectiveness, dynamicity, and extensive storage accessibility. There are various types of cloud computing, including hybrid, private, and public models. Additionally, multiple services are available, such as security as a service, database as a service, integration as a service, and software as a service [5]. Moreover, many firms and organizations use cloud computing to transfer their products and services. This practice is driven by many advantages, such as enhanced scalability, decreased expenditure on IT infrastructure, uninterrupted company operations, and the ability to access and implement automatic upgrades effortlessly. Consequently, cloud computing has garnered significant acceptance within various governmental entities and business enterprises. Similarly, Communication Service Providers (CSPs) have strategically created data centres in different jurisdictions worldwide to offer cloud services, aiming to achieve cost efficiency and ensure uninterrupted service availability [4]. Nevertheless, the increase in cybercrimes and the security concerns associated with the cloud environment provide significant challenges for organizations seeking to migrate their systems to this platform. Furthermore, security experts perceive cloud computing as a prospective domain of apprehension due to the intricate nature of forensics investigation within a cloud computing environment. As a result, cloud forensics has garnered significant attention from forensic investigators to address challenges arising from cloud computing. Cloud forensics utilizes digital forensics techniques within a cloud-based setting [6]. This discipline employs scientific concepts, established methodologies, and technological procedures to analyze events occurring in a cloud environment through reporting, analysis, preservation, gathering, and identification of digital data, aiming to reconstruct these events.

Cloud forensics is a complex field due to the inherent features of cloud computing, such as extensive virtualization, data duplication, jurisdictional considerations, and multi-tenancy. Furthermore, the specific methodologies employed in cloud forensics are contingent upon the deployment and service model utilized within cloud computing [7]. In the context of Platform as a Service (PaaS) and Software as a Service (SaaS), the level of control over network management and process monitoring is notably constrained. On the other hand, Infrastructure as a Service (IaaS) provides a greater management level and a user-friendly forensic mechanism. The field of cloud forensics presents significant challenges due to its intricate nature. However, it is indisputable that the advancement of cloud computing has given rise to apprehensions regarding privacy and security. The focus on the authentication, authorization, and accounting (AAA) protocol in cloud forensics has generated considerable interest among digital forensics officers. This interest stems from the protocol's ability to facilitate the reconstruction, investigation, and analysis of cloud attack events, ultimately enabling the swift recovery of cloud systems [8]. This approach demonstrates a significant level of efficacy. It presents a clear juxtaposition to conventional forensic methodologies that rely on log files to isolate the system to retrieve valuable information. However, it obscures the perception of the occurrence. Cloud forensics can be classified into three categories: Legal, Organisational, and Technical [9]. The legal aspect encompasses formulating agreements and regulations to ensure digital forensics methodologies adhere to legal statutes and regulations. In contrast, the organizational dimension incorporates the organizational factors of digital forensics [10]. The technological dimension encompasses the requisite methods and tools for conducting forensic investigations inside cloud computing. Therefore, it can be concluded that cloud forensics is a highly significant phenomenon within digital forensics. Using cloud computing qualities, such as distributed forensic processing, computing power, reporting, and scalability, allows forensics investigators to leverage its capabilities effectively.

16.2.2 Social Media Forensics

The proliferation of Industry 4.0 and Web 2.0 technologies has led to a notable surge in the adoption of social media platforms, which have now emerged as a predominant means of social interaction. Users actively share information, create accounts, and participate in social platforms through these websites. Consequently, hackers can abuse users' accounts [5]. Furthermore, several social media platforms, such as LinkedIn, Instagram, Facebook, and Twitter, have been susceptible to numerous cyber attacks and viruses. Cyber attacks against social media platforms can occur externally, originating from sources outside the system or network, or internally, from within the network itself. External system attacks commonly involve Distributed Denial of Service (DDoS) or Denial of Service (DoS), whereas attacks occurring within the network involve the unauthorized retrieval of cookie data [4]. Moreover, it has been demonstrated that these social media programs' databases are highly susceptible to such attacks. Given the current circumstances, there has been a notable shift in the focus of digital investigators towards social media forensics. Social media forensics is crucial in facilitating criminal investigations, as social media posts serve as precious evidence for investigators (refer to Figure 16.1). Similarly, social media platforms are valuable for obtaining information about possible criminals, suspects, and witnesses, making them highly advantageous for profiling [11]. Furthermore, integrating social media and digital forensics enables investigators to access various contemporary and varied data sources. These sources encompass demographic location, images, contact lists, geo-location, and text messages. The integration of network data and metadata holds the capacity to aid in the facilitation of digital forensics investigations. Moreover, metadata can also authenticate factual information inside online social networking. Therefore, social media forensics is an emerging phenomenon within the digital forensics field, as it can effectively furnish substantial digital evidence.

The proliferation of social media applications across many platforms has facilitated the generation of digital forensic traces or artifacts, which can serve as valuable resources in investigative processes. For example,

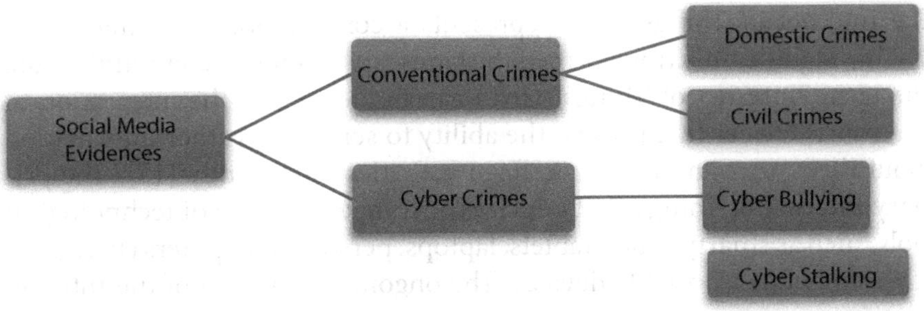

Figure 16.1 Use of social media forensics in criminal investigation [4].

a study conducted by researchers [12] revealed that conversation logs can be recovered from popular social networking platforms such as Facebook. Many digital forensic artifacts, including photographs, location data, friends, posts, passwords, and usernames, are often left behind as potential evidentiary material. The significance of these artifacts as crucial evidence positions social media forensics as a key trend within the field of digital forensics. Previous research, such as the study by Ruan *et al.* [13], comprehensively analyzed various social media platforms, namely MySpace, Twitter, and Facebook, across mobile devices such as Androids, iPhones, and Blackberries. The study reported the successful extraction of digital forensic artifacts, including posted comments, timestamps, passwords, URLs, photos, and user data in text format. This suggests that social media forensics can identify and track digital evidence dispersed throughout various social media platforms. Moreover, it effectively examines, verifies, and retrieves digital evidence. Furthermore, social media forensics encompasses three distinct features: reverse search integration, tampering localization analysis, and information visualization and extraction [14]. One notable benefit of utilizing Google Image Search is its ability to generate search results within a dedicated web browser tab. Additionally, the system integrates six distinct tampering localization maps produced using forensic algorithms. These maps are designed to identify various indicators of tampering on social media platforms. Moreover, it provides comprehensive support for metadata indexing and can showcase embedded thumbnails, if present. By utilizing these functionalities, forensic professionals can conduct a more in-depth analysis of the information to extract valuable evidence. The increasing prominence of social media forensics has emerged as a notable trend within the field of digital forensics.

16.2.3 IoT Forensics

The Internet of Things (IoT) represents a contemporary paradigm shift that has significantly transformed the landscape of mobile communication. The term "Internet of Things" (IoT) can be defined as the integration of electronic devices that possess the ability to sense and gather information about their surroundings to perform activities intelligently [15]. The primary Internet of Things (IoT) devices encompass a range of technological tools, such as smartphones, tablets, laptops, personal computers (PCs), and other embedded portable devices. The ongoing expansion of the Internet of Things (IoT) domain has facilitated consumers' ability to exchange their data across many platforms. In addition, Internet of Things (IoT) systems can establish communication by utilizing Internet application programming interfaces (APIs) or direct communication. Furthermore, these entities can also be managed via computational devices such as cloud servers. The networking capabilities and intelligence of Internet of Things (IoT) technologies offer substantial advantages for commercial and residential use [16]. Nevertheless, despite its myriad benefits, Internet of Things (IoT) systems are susceptible to various security vulnerabilities and malicious activities, including but not limited to extensive surveillance, disruption of IoT networks, Denial of Service (DoS) assaults, and the deployment of ransomware. Consequently, specialists in digital forensics have exhibited a strong inclination toward studying and practicing Internet of Things (IoT) forensics to conduct digital investigations. The emergence of the IoT forensics trend can be attributed to the intricate and distinctive issues posed by IoT systems within digital forensics [4]. Furthermore, applications based on the Internet of Things (IoT) encompass many resources and diverse devices, generating an extensive volume of data, sometimes called Big IoT data. Utilizing this data, in conjunction with digital forensics tools and techniques, allows investigators to track cybercrimes, hence aiding in preventing cyber attacks.

Although there are increasing advantages associated with IoT forensics, it is undeniable that this field generates a substantial volume of data, leading to a notable increase in the workload for data centres [17]. Consequently, forensic investigators encounter supplementary analytics, security, and capacity obstacles. In addition, the preservation and retrieval of data from Internet of Things (IoT) enabled services and devices pose problems related to protocols, data formats, and physical interfaces, adding complexity to the process of extracting evidence. Despite its various limitations, IoT forensics provides a more comprehensive and reliable source of evidence compared to traditional computer systems [18]. The field of IoT forensics is designed to respond to the needs and demands of consumers without necessitating their active involvement. Consequently, the IoT forensics ecosystem offers contextual data that aids digital forensic investigators in analyzing real-world occurrences. Therefore, the field of digital forensics is witnessing a significant rise in the prominence of IoT forensics. This may be attributed to its capacity to offer contextual and digital evidence and the numerous obstacles encountered within this sector.

16.3 Threats Faced by Digital Forensics

16.3.1 Technical Challenges

The proliferation of digital technology has presented many opportunities, yet it has also posed numerous obstacles for the field of digital forensics. Despite the extensive analysis and study conducted by various digital forensic professionals and researchers on numerous established digital forensic concerns, there remains a need to categorize these challenges [19]. This narrative reveals that digital forensic systems are susceptible to technical obstacles that jeopardize the integrity of those systems. Technical problems refer to prospective hazards that can be mitigated by utilizing established operations, protocols, and expertise. They recognize that digital forensics necessitates synergistic integration of ethical principles and technical proficiencies. Several significant technical obstacles are commonly encountered in the field of digital forensics. These challenges include encryption, managing large volumes of data, and addressing compatibility issues among various forensic tools [20]. The proliferation of communication technology has facilitated the widespread availability and ease of use of advanced encryption products and services. As a result, the complexity of encryption algorithms and standards is increasing, augmenting the temporal and cognitive challenges associated with performing cryptanalysis. This methodology combines encrypted files to extract coherent and significant data. Furthermore, implementing encryption renders electronic data illegible, providing criminals the means to conceal their illicit actions [21]. The investigation process of a digital forensic investigator can be adversely impacted by this phenomenon. Research findings indicate that around 60% of cases involving encryption need more processing, primarily due to the substantial constraints it imposes on investigators' capacity to extract information from the available evidence [22]. Hence, the ease of implementation, affordability, and widespread accessibility of encryption tools significantly challenge the integrity and credibility of the digital forensics process.

In addition to employing encryption techniques, vast quantities of data within various programs, such as enterprise resource planning systems, also present a significant challenge to digital forensic operations. The exponential growth in the amount of data generated poses a considerable challenge for legal systems and forensic investigators in effectively addressing digital risks [23]. Similarly, the advent of cloud computing has led to the substitution of many IT hardware components, including network switches, racks, and servers, with virtualized software that can be accessed remotely and adjusted based on the specific requirements of businesses. Moreover, these services and data can be administered and hosted by a third-party entity or a user from any location. Hence, it is plausible that the data and software may be physically distributed over many geographic areas [22]. The distributive nature of data significantly diminishes the level of control and visibility that forensic experts have over digital forensic artifacts. Similarly, there is variation among digital forensic tools and methodologies in terms of cost, complexity, and functionality. As a result, most digital forensic tools consist of diverse components, leading to heightened levels of incompatibility that hinder their collaborative functionality [20]. In addition, several forensic technologies exhibit limitations in effectively managing the progressively expanding storage capacity of the devices under investigation. The presence of extensive targets poses a significant technological obstacle for digital forensic investigations due to the requirement for more intricate analysis methodologies. Hence, it is asserted that various technical obstacles present a substantial risk to the efficacy and reliability of digital forensics.

16.3.2 Operational Challenges

It is widely acknowledged that digital crimes are deliberate in nature and purpose. As a result of these circumstances, digital forensics encounters a multitude of operational obstacles. Incidence prevention, response, and detection are significant focus areas within these obstacles. Traditional information technology (IT) settings that employ on-premises data processing typically incorporate internal incident management processes to prioritize the maintenance of high levels of security [20]. This procedure incorporates intrusion detection systems, log file analysis, and monitoring alongside data loss prevention systems that ascertain and identify instances of data loss, attackers, and intruders. Security events can pose significant challenges for consumers of cloud services. The reason for this is that these security incidents pose a threat to both commercial and personal data. Moreover, the attackers employ anti-forensics technology, which enables them to pilfer or obliterate any potential proof [24]. Similarly, the absence of standardized methods and protocols in digital forensics poses a significant risk to the integrity and effectiveness of evidence extraction and investigative processes. The current state of digital forensic models is characterized by a lack of standardization, which has contributed to the heightened complexity of the procedure. Moreover, scholarly research, such as the study referenced in Balogun and Zhu [22], contends that the absence of universally accepted criteria poses significant challenges in evaluating the proficiency of forensic professionals. The lack of standardized techniques was seen as acceptable during the earlier stages of digital forensics, as it was regarded as an enigmatic investigative process that allowed professionals to uncover concealed evidence and information, yielding valuable insights into illegal behaviours. Nevertheless, the proliferation of digital technologies has expanded the scope of digital forensic inquiry beyond traditional small-scale computer systems. It now encompasses virtualized environments that encompass non-standard interfaces and diverse storage devices.

In addition to the challenges mentioned earlier, the field of digital forensics is also susceptible to the issue of forensics preparedness. Forensic readiness refers to the capacity of computer networks or computer systems to accurately document data and activities in a manner deemed legitimate and adequate for forensic investigations [25]. The accelerated progress in cloud computing has compelled organizations to adapt their approaches to flexibly implement, construct, and formulate IT plans. In addition, it is essential to note that cloud computing needs to improve in terms of forensic readiness, posing additional risks to digital forensic operations. In digital forensics, the operational problem of manual investigation and intervention of physical hard discs is a significant concern. Although uncomplicated and direct with a single disc or partition, the technique becomes significantly more intricate when RAID setups are incorporated [20]. Furthermore, the complicated nature of digital forensics necessitates caution when manually examining complex disc images, as this approach may threaten the integrity of digital artifacts. Similarly, there is a prevailing belief within the field that forensic analysis should possess qualities such as validity, accuracy, completeness, and reliability. Nonetheless, balancing safeguarding user privacy and obtaining crucial digital evidence poses a significant concern for digital forensics. As a result of the expansion in storage capacity, it is typical for a limited fraction of the data to be utilized for investigative purposes. At the same time, a significant proportion of the information needs to be considered [26]. The potential consequence of this situation is a violation of the user's privacy, presenting an added difficulty for digital forensic procedures. Therefore, based on the available information, it can be asserted that operational issues pose a significant risk to the integrity and effectiveness of digital forensic analysis.

16.3.3 Personnel-Related Challenges

The integrity of digital evidence is at risk due to issues associated with personnel. One of the most significant issues in personnel management is the need for more adequately qualified forensic personnel [20]. The field of digital forensics holds considerable importance due to the prevalence of cyber crimes. However, the efficacy of digital forensics is compromised by a need for more competent forensic officers. The scarcity of adequately qualified forensic investigators can be attributed to the intense rivalry within law enforcement and the stringent qualifications necessary for digital forensics. This specialized area demands professionals with technical proficiency, certification, and training to effectively provide scientifically sound evidence [22]. Similarly, it is indisputable that digital forensics has acquired significant significance within the realm of forensic practitioners, law enforcement agencies, and computer specialists. Regrettably, the progress in this particular domain has fostered a context susceptible to semantic discrepancies. One further personnel-related obstacle that may arise is the issue of maintaining a chain of custody. The concept of chain of custody pertains to the chronological record that establishes the precise location of the evidence at each stage of its collecting process. The physical management of proof is a significant concern in digital forensic investigation, as it poses a challenge due to the absence of tangible objects in a digital context [7]. Furthermore, the successful management of the chain of custody is a significant difficulty in digital forensics, primarily due to proprietary technology, complex procedures, and multi-jurisdictional regulations. Therefore, it may be concluded that issues linked to personnel present a significant obstacle to conventional forensic procedures.

In addition to the issues mentioned earlier, it is indisputable that the field of digital forensics needs a cohesive formal representation of standardized processes and expertise for the analysis and collection of digital artifacts. The presence of incompatibility and conflict across different digital forensics technologies is an inevitable consequence [16]. Mistakes in the interpretation and analysis of digital artifacts arise when there is a need for a standardized or formalized approach to the study, preservation, and collection of digital evidence. Similarly, forensic professionals employ specialized skills and digital technologies to handle a substantial volume of data in forensic investigations effectively. Nevertheless, it is worth noting that these professionals frequently need to document their research, impeding the training process and external evaluations [22]. Using past information and experience is vital in training new digital forensic specialists, as it facilitates the cultivation of expertise and the dissemination of knowledge across detective communities. Regrettably, digital forensic practitioners exhibit deficiencies in documentation and adherence to legal protocols, exacerbating the risks associated with digital forensic investigations [4].

16.4 Opportunities

16.4.1 USB Forensics

The Universal Serial Bus (USB) is a prevalent storage technology generally recognized for its high level of effectiveness in both mobility and capacity. Typically, the USB protocol employs a USB controller command to establish and maintain security measures within the USB drive. Nevertheless, due to its convenient availability, it is frequently utilized to perpetuate cybercriminal activities. Using the controller command within the USB introduces additional vulnerabilities throughout the user certification procedure, rendering it more susceptible to potential cyber attacks [3]. Fortunately, USB can generate an IP address, which may be utilized to track efforts to evade USB security measures. This implies that as the Universal Serial Bus (USB) continues to advance in terms of its capabilities and storage capacity, it can provide an increased amount of data for examination in the field of digital forensics. The increasing importance of USB drives in digital forensics must be addressed, as they pose a significant threat to both computers and sensitive data. The USB's convenient accessibility, affordability, and compact design render it highly suitable for theft and the deliberate destruction of potential digital evidence [27]. Malicious malware and viruses have the potential to be implanted in networked or stand-alone computer systems via USB connections, whether unintentionally or intentionally. Consequently, prospective hackers can entirely eradicate or conceal their malevolent undertakings. Due to this rationale, USB forensics has emerged as an essential element in computer investigations, enabling digital forensic professionals to track USB connection activity within PreFetch, Shortcuts, and Link file directories [28]. These traces have the potential to aid forensic investigators in the identification of different file-related activities, such as the copying of images or the opening of documents. Hence, it is evident that USB forensics is an emerging field of study for digital forensic analysts, offering valuable assistance in examining and identifying relevant digital evidence.

Digital evidence is commonly preserved on various media devices, typically removable or internal memory storage devices. These storage devices house digital artifacts that are usually encountered and recovered at the location of a crime. These gadgets frequently encompass cellular phones, computers, portable media players, and digital cameras that utilize magnetic, electrical, or optical storage media. USB flash drives have emerged as the most widely adopted option [22]. Using USB flash drives for storing metadata might assist digital forensic experts in identifying comprehensive details of digital material. As mentioned, the data encompasses copyright information, geolocation data, and timestamps crucial for analyzing digital forensic evidence. Moreover, it is indisputable that USB storage devices are widely recognized as the prevailing method for transferring and safeguarding data files. Consequently, malicious actors exploit USB devices for data breaches [29]. Therefore, via a comprehensive understanding of the multifaceted nature of analyzing USB devices, digital forensic operations can derive significant advantages in tracing evidence that may lead to probable perpetrators for forensic analysts.

Furthermore, concerning the field of forensics, USB devices possess substantial digital traces inside diverse digital environments that are crucial for forensic analysis [30]. Furthermore, inside the USB specification, the Mass Storage Class (MSC) is widely recognized as the standard protocol for facilitating the establishment of a connection between portable drives. "MSC" is a protocol suite that facilitates communication between operating systems and USB devices [29]. The MSC protocol facilitates direct access to file systems, clusters, and sectors for digital forensic officers, as observed from a digital forensic perspective. Digital forensic professionals possess complete control over file systems, enabling them to discover, retrieve, and meticulously analyze digital evidence. Consequently, USB forensics can simplify the intricacies of digital forensic investigations and verify the authenticity of the obtained evidence.

16.4.2 Intrusion Detection

The subject of digital forensics has seen a significant rise in interest in intrusion detection systems (IDSs) due to advancements in information systems and the escalating frequency of network attacks. Based on the reference findings [31], IDS can identify and thwart unauthorized entry attempts that may result in system instability, inoperability, unauthorized access to crucial digital evidence, or the manipulation of information. These solutions are highly advantageous for digital forensic investigators since they effectively expose potentially illicit activities within the network. Similarly, using practical Intrusion Detection Systems (IDS) enables forensic analysts to readily ascertain whether the integrity of the computer system has been compromised or unauthorized access to the data is occurring [32]. As mentioned earlier, the information holds significant importance within forensic investigations, as it enables forensic experts to extract valuable material that can subsequently be offered as prospective evidence in a legal setting. Moreover, if a malevolent actor endeavors to undermine the integrity of a public or private network, an IDS promptly detects and initiates incident response (IR) protocols. Integrating digital forensic inquiry with incident response methods enables investigators to retain, collect, and ascertain real-time data [33]. Moreover, integrating digital forensic approaches IDS would ensure the preservation of the acquired content and evidence without any alterations. IDS can also aid in the identification of hostile and harmful network activity. This is accomplished by the analysis of collected packets, the prevention of attack connections, and the provision of alerts to system administrators to mitigate potential damages. These functionalities are of utmost importance in digital forensic inquiry, as the perpetrator would invariably try to eliminate any potential digital evidence.

Although digital forensics has facilitated the analysis and detection of cybercrimes, it is essential to acknowledge that it cannot offer absolute protection to networks or online storage. In this particular instance, the implementation of IDS has presented numerous prospects for the field of digital forensics. IDS not only possesses the capability to identify and flag hostile activities, but it also facilitates monitoring traffic data to ascertain the attack's characteristics [34]. Furthermore, IDS also can alert the system administrator if the system has been compromised. Upon identifying the occurrence, a subsequent digital forensic procedure can be initiated to ascertain the nature and scope of the breach. The primary goal of IDS is to detect potential hostile activities and trigger appropriate defensive actions. However, IDS can also be used with digital forensics to extract valuable digital evidence used in civil, legal, and criminal processes [35]. The primary objective of IDS is to effectively identify instances of misuse or unauthorized access to computer networks and systems, encompassing both external intrusions and internal threats posed by insiders. Digital forensics enables investigators to trace criminal, intrusive, or illegal activities to their perpetrators while concurrently acquiring substantial evidentiary support. Therefore, it can be inferred that IDS offers a range of prospects and possesses the capacity to aid in digital forensic inquiry. IDS can also safeguard acquired evidence and proficiently identify and address cybersecurity vulnerabilities.

16.4.3 Artificial Intelligence

The field of digital forensics faces challenges in effectively analyzing vast quantities of digital data, which have experienced significant growth. This necessitates the application of intelligence analysis and computational techniques. Artificial intelligence (AI) has emerged as a prominent and indispensable field within contemporary computer science that addresses intricate and computationally intensive challenges in real-time [36].

The challenges posed by the increasing intricacies and prevalence of cyber-crime, coupled with the constraints of limited resources and time, whether in terms of human expertise or computational power, severely impede the ability of digital forensic investigators to employ digital forensic techniques and achieve timely outcomes effectively. This issue can be resolved by integrating digital forensic methodologies, tools, and procedures with AI. Integrating these dynamic areas leads to intelligent forensics, an interdisciplinary method that optimizes resource utilization and leverages technical advancements to address digital forensic investigations [37]. Intelligent forensics encompasses various techniques and instruments derived from social network analysis, computer modelling, and artificial intelligence. Its objective is to enhance digital investigations' efficacy and overall reliability while reducing the time needed to retrieve digital evidence. The distinguishing characteristic of intelligent forensics is its capacity to do comprehensive digital forensic investigations, encompassing pre- and post-incident stages. Moreover, integrating AI technologies, such as machine learning in intelligent forensics, can aid digital forensic investigators in addressing challenges related to specificity and generality. This is achieved through the analysis of cyber-crime patterns.

Furthermore, integrating AI with digital forensics enables forensic professionals to proficiently employ digital forensic procedures in both a reactive manner, following the occurrence of cyber crime, and a proactive manner, before the commission of cyber crime. Including intelligent forensics in digital forensic investigations is a means of enhancing the reactive capability. This enhancement enables digital forensic officers to comprehensively understand the incident, hence facilitating the examination of data sources for potential evidence [37]. To achieve this objective, intelligent forensic methodologies employ various approaches, such as AI and social network analysis. Similarly, proactive utilization of intelligent forensics involves the application of advanced methods such as machine learning and deep learning to anticipate future risks. This is achieved by analyzing historical patterns and trends. This capability holds significant value for digital forensic investigators, enabling them to predict the specific digital resources that must be saved as potential digital evidence. Furthermore, utilizing computational intelligence and artificial intelligence might enhance the efficiency of digital forensic methodologies for forensic investigators while upholding the credibility and trustworthiness of the obtained results [38]. AI also significantly manages extensive datasets and gathers digital evidence for forensic investigations. Hence, it is evident that artificial intelligence possesses the potential to revolutionize the field of digital forensics by enhancing result accuracy and reducing the time required for extracting valuable digital evidence.

16.5 Conclusion

The field of digital forensics has garnered significant attention due to the rise in cybercrimes. Although the proliferation of digital technology has proven advantageous in some domains, it is undeniable that it has also introduced novel avenues for perpetrating cyber crimes. In addition, malicious software, methodology, and tools are continuously developed and deployed to compromise public and private networks. These threats aim to compromise data storage systems to extract and utilize valuable information. The occurrence of security vulnerabilities and breaches has catalyzed advancements in digital forensics. This has enabled the extraction of digital evidence from various digital devices, facilitating its utilization in criminal and civil legal procedures. This paper comprehensively examines the contemporary trends, prospective risks, and opportunities associated with digital forensics in cybersecurity to elucidate its significance.

References

1. Cyber Crime and Forensic Computing, in: *Cyber Crime and Forensic Computing*, Aug. 2021, doi: 10.1515/9783110677478.
2. Shrivastava, G., Kumar, P., Gupta, B.B., Bala, S., Dey, N., Handbook of research on network forensics and analysis techniques, in: *Handbook of Research on Network Forensics and Analysis Techniques*, pp. 1–509, Apr. 2018, doi: 10.4018/978-1-5225-4100-4.
3. Sharma, H., Kumar, P., Sharma, K., Identification of Device Type Using Transformers in Heterogeneous Internet of Things Traffic, in: *Lecture Notes in Networks and Systems*, vol. 537 LNNS, pp. 471–481, 2023, doi: 10.1007/978-981-99-3010-4_40.
4. Shrivastava, G., Sharma, K., Khari, M., Zohora, S.E., Role of Cyber Security and Cyber Forensics in India, in: *Cyber Law, Privacy, and Security*, pp. 1349–1368, May 2019, doi: 10.4018/978-1-5225-8897-9.CH067.
5. Gollub, T., Potthast, M., Beyer, A., Busse, M., Rangel, F., Rosso, P. *et al.*, Recent trends in digital text forensics and its evaluation: Plagiarism detection, author identification, and author profiling, in: *Lecture Notes in Computer Science (including subseries Lecture Notes in Artificial Intelligence and Lecture Notes in Bioinformatics)*.

6. Aminnezhad, A., Dehghantanha, A., Abdullah, M.T., A survey on privacy issues in digital forensics. *Int. J. Cyber-Security Digital Forensics* [Internet], 1, 4, 311–24, 2012 Oct 1 [cited 2023 Nov 15].
7. Norouzizadeh Dezfoli, F., Dehghantanha, A., Mahmoud, R., Fazlida Binti Mohd Sani, N., Daryabar, F., Digital forensics trends and future. *Int. J. Cyber-Security Digital Forensics (IJCSDF)*, 2, 2, 48–76, 2013 [Internet].
8. Sharma, B.K., Joseph, M.A., Jacob, B., Miranda, B., Emerging trends in Digital Forensic and Cyber security-An Overview. *ITT 2019 - Information Technology Trends: Emerging Technologies Blockchain and IoT*, pp. 309–13, 2019 Nov 1.
9. Wazid, M., Katal, A., Goudar, R.H., Rao, S., Hacktivism trends, digital forensic tools and challenges: A survey. *2013 IEEE Conference on Information and Communication Technologies, ICT*, pp. 138–44, 2013.
10. Pichan, A., Lazarescu, M., Soh, S.T., Cloud forensics: Technical challenges, solutions and comparative analysis. *Digit. Investig.* [Internet], 13, 38–57, 2015 Jun 1 [cited 2023 Nov 15].
11. Zawoad, S. and Hasan, R., Cloud Forensics: A Meta-Study of Challenges, Approaches, and Open Problems, 2013 Feb 25.
12. Aminnezhad, A., Dehghantanha, A., Abdullah, M.T., Damshenas, M., Cloud forensics issues and opportunities. *Int. J. Inf. Process. Manage.* [Internet], 4, 4, 76–85, 2013.
13. Ruan, K., Carthy, J., Kechadi, T., Baggili, I., Cloud forensics definitions and critical criteria for cloud forensic capability: An overview of survey results. *Digit. Investig.*, 1, 10, 1, 34–43, 2012.
14. Ruan, K., Carthy, J., Kechadi, T., Crosbie, M., Cloud forensics. *IFIP Adv. Inf. Commun. Technol.* [Internet], 361, 35–46, 2011.
14. Rocha, A., Scheirer, W.J., Forstall, C.W., Cavalcante, T., Theophilo, A., Shen, B. *et al.*, Authorship Attribution for Social Media Forensics. *IEEE Trans. Inf. Forensics Secur.*, 1, 12, 1, 5–33, 2017.
15. Baggili, I. and Breitinger, F., Data Sources for Advancing Cyber Forensics: What the Social World has to Offer. Electrical & Computer Engineering and Computer Science Faculty Publications [Internet], 2015 Jan 1 [cited 2023 Nov 15].
16. Al Mutawa, N., Baggili, I., Marrington, A., Forensic analysis of social networking applications on mobile devices. *Digit. Investig.*, 9, S24–33, 2012 Aug 1.
17. View of Web and Social Media Image Forensics for News Professionals [Internet], [cited 2023 Nov 15].
18. Zanella, A., Bui, N., Castellani, A., Vangelista, L., Zorzi, M., Internet of things for smart cities. *IEEE Internet Things J.*, 1, 1, 22–32, 2014 Feb 1.
19. Hegarty, R., Lamb, D., Attwood, A., Digital Evidence Challenges in the Internet of Things. *International Network Conference*, 2014.

20. Al Fahdi, M., Clarke, N.L., Furnell, S.M., Challenges to digital forensics: A survey of researchers & practitioners attitudes and opinions. *2013 Information Security for South Africa - Proceedings of the ISSA 2013 Conference*, 2013.
21. Karie, N.M. and Venter, H.S., Taxonomy of Challenges for Digital Forensics. *J. Forensic Sci.* [Internet], 60, 4, 885–93, 2015.
22. Balogun, A.M. and Zhu, S.Y., Privacy Impacts of Data Encryption on the Efficiency of Digital Forensics Technology. *Int. J. Adv. Comput. Sci. Appl.* [Internet], 4, 5, 36–40, 2013.
23. Vincze, E.A., Challenges in digital forensics. *Police Pract. Res.* [Internet], 17, 2, 183–94, 2016.
24. Raghavan, S., Digital forensic research: current state of the art. *CSI Trans. ICT*, 2012 1, 11, 1, 91–114, 2012.
25. Baig, Z.A., Szewczyk, P., Valli, C., Rabadia, P., Hannay, P., Chernyshev, M. *et al.*, Future challenges for smart cities: Cyber-security and digital forensics. *Digit. Investig.*, 22, 3–13, 2017 Sep 1.
26. Hong, I., Yu, H., Lee, S., Lee, K., A new triage model conforming to the needs of selective search and seizure of electronic evidence. *Digit. Investig.*, 1, 10, 2, 175–92, 2013.
27. Collie, J., The Windows IconCache.DB: A resource for forensic artifacts from USB-connectable devices. *Digit. Investig.*, 9, 3–4, 200–10, 2013 Feb 1.
28. Windows Registry Forensics: An Imperative Step in Tracking Data Theft via USB Devices
29. Deb, S.B. and Chetry, A., USB Device Forensics: Insertion and removal timestamps of USB devices in Windows 8. *2015 International Symposium on Advanced Computing and Communication, ISACC 2015*, pp. 364–71, 2016 Jan 8.
30. Verma, S., Singh, A., Singh, D., Laxmi, V., Computer forensics in IT audit and credit card fraud investigation - For USB devices. *2014 International Conference on Computing for Sustainable Global Development, INDIACom 2014*, pp. 730–3, 2014.
31. Agrawal, S. and Agrawal, J., Survey on Anomaly Detection using Data Mining Techniques. *Procedia Comput. Sci.*, 1, 60, 1, 708–13, 2015.
32. Ahmed, M., Naser Mahmood, A., Hu, J., A survey of network anomaly detection techniques. *J. Netw. Comput. Appl.*, 60, 19–31, 2016 Jan 1.
33. Grobler, C.P., Louwrens, C.P., Von Solms, S.H., A multi-component view of digital forensics. *ARES 2010 - 5th International Conference on Availability, Reliability, and Security*, pp. 647–52, 2010.
34. Khobragade, P.K. and Malik, L.G., Data generation and analysis for digital forensic application using data mining. *Proceedings - 2014 4th International Conference on Communication Systems and Network Technologies, CSNT 2014*, pp. 458–62, 2014.
35. Mitchell, F., The use of Artificial Intelligence in digital forensics: An introduction, in: *Digital Evidence and Electronic Signature Law Review*, 2023.

36. Irons, A. and Lallie, H., Digital Forensics to Intelligent Forensics. *Future Internet*, 6, 3, 584–96, 2014 Sep 12.
37. Muda, A.K., Choo, Y.H., Abraham, A., Srihari, S.N. (Eds.), *Computational Intelligence in Digital Forensics: Forensic Investigation and Applications*, Springer, Cham, Heidelberg, New York, Dordrecht, London, 2014.
38. Adedayo, O.M., Big data and digital forensics. *2016 IEEE International Conference on Cybercrime and Computer Forensic, ICCCF 2016*.

Index

Also of Interest

Other books in the series, "Advances in Cyber Security"

Artificial Intelligence and Cybersecurity in Healthcare, Edited by Rashmi Agrawal, Pramod Singh Rathore, Ganesh Gopal Devarajan, and Rajiva Ranjan Divivedi, ISBN: 9781394229796. *Artificial Intelligence and Cybersecurity in Healthcare* offers a vital exploration of the intersection of artificial intelligence and cybersecurity within healthcare Cyber Physical Systems, equipping readers with knowledge on how to navigate the transformative yet complex technological landscape shaping modern patient care and data protection.

CYBER SECURITY AND DIGITAL FORENSICS: Challenges and Future Trends, Edited by Mangesh M. Ghonge, Sabyasachi Pramanik, Ramchandra Mangrulkar, and Dac-Nhuong Le, ISBN: 9781119795636. Written and edited by a team of world renowned experts in the field, this groundbreaking new volume covers key technical topics and gives readers a comprehensive understanding of the latest research findings in cyber security and digital forensics.

CYBER SECURITY AND NETWORK SECURITY, Edited by Sabyasachi Pramanik, Debabrata Samanta, M. Vinay, and Abhijit Guha, ISBN: 9781119812494. Written and edited by a team of experts in the field, this is the most comprehensive and up to date study of the practical applications of cybersecurity and network security for engineers, scientists, students, and other professionals.

DEEP LEARNING APPROACHES TO CLOUD SECURITY, Edited by Pramod Singh Rathore, Vishal Dutt, Rashmi Agrawal, Satya Murthy Sasubilli, and Srinivasa Rao Swarna, ISBN: 9781119760528. Covering one of the most important subjects to our society today, this editorial team delves into solutions taken from evolving deep learning approaches, solutions allow computers to learn from experience and understand the world in terms of a hierarchy of concepts.

Other related titles

Cybersecurity in the Transportation Industry, Edited by Imdad Ali Shah and Noor Zaman Jhanjhi, ISBN: 9781394204267. This book offers crucial solutions and insights on how transportation companies can enhance their cybersecurity management and protect their corporate reputation and revenue from the increasing risk of cyberattacks.

SECURITY ISSUES AND PRIVACY CONCERNS IN INDUSTRY 4.0 APPLICATIONS, Edited by Shibin David, R. S. Anand, V. Jeyakrishnan, and M. Niranjanamurthy, ISBN: 9781119775621. Written and edited by a team of international experts, this is the most comprehensive and up-to-date coverage of the security and privacy issues surrounding Industry 4.0 applications, a must-have for any library.

MACHINE LEARNING TECHNIQUES AND ANALYTICS FOR CLOUD SECURITY, Edited by Rajdeep Chakraborty, Anupam Ghosh and Jyotsna Kumar Mandal, ISBN: 9781119762256. This book covers new methods, surveys, case studies, and policy with almost all machine learning techniques and analytics for cloud security solutions.

ARTIFICIAL INTELLIGENCE AND DATA MINING IN SECURITY FRAMEWORKS, Edited by Neeraj Bhargava, Ritu Bhargava, Pramod Singh Rathore, and Rashmi Agrawal, ISBN: 9781119760405. Written and edited by a team of experts in the field, this outstanding new volume offers solutions to the problems of security, outlining the concepts behind allowing computers to learn from experience and understand the world in terms of a hierarchy of concepts.

SECURITY DESIGNS FOR THE CLOUD, IOT AND SOCIAL NETWORKING, Edited by Dac-Nhuong Le, Chintin Bhatt and Mani Madhukar, ISBN: 9781119592266. The book provides cutting-edge research that delivers insights into the tools, opportunities, novel strategies, techniques, and challenges for handling security issues in cloud computing, Internet of Things and social networking.

DESIGN AND ANALYSIS OF SECURITY PROTOCOLS FOR COMMUNICATION, Edited by Dinesh Goyal, S. Balamurugan, Sheng-Lung Peng and O.P. Verma, ISBN: 9781119555643. The book combines analysis and comparison of various security protocols such as HTTP, SMTP, RTP, RTCP, FTP, UDP for mobile or multimedia streaming security protocol.

Printed in the USA/Agawam, MA
September 16, 2026

910661.127